MOGHUL
MICROWAVE

Also by Julie Sahni

Classic Indian Cooking (1980)

*Classic Indian Vegetarian and Grain
Cooking (1985)*

MOGHUL
MICROWAVE
COOKING INDIAN FOOD THE MODERN WAY
JULIE SAHNI

Line illustrations by Jonathan Combs

WILLIAM MORROW AND COMPANY, INC.
NEW YORK

Library of Congress Cataloging-in-Publication Data

Sahni, Julie.
    Moghul microwave : cooking Indian food the modern way / Julie Sahni.
        p.   cm.
    ISBN 0-688-08334-X
    1. Cookery, India.   2. Microwave cookery.   I. Title.
TX724.5.I4S242   1990
641.5'882—dc20   *90-5956*
                                                              CIP

Printed in the United States of America

First Edition

1 2 3 4 5 6 7 8 9 10

BOOK DESIGN BY JAYE ZIMET

To
Craig Claiborne
Pierre and Betty Franey
Maria Guarnaschelli

For their unyielding support, friendship, and love

PREFACE

The Moghuls were rulers of India from the sixteenth to the nineteenth century. Originally from Turkish Persia, they defined elegant food and presentation. They brought many cooking techniques and dishes from their native land, but combined these with Indian ingredients and codified this cuisine. Moghul food, like classic French cuisine, was the food of the aristocrats. Most people of India, then as now, ate what we have come to call "regional" cuisine.

Although there are many recipes in *Moghul Microwave* from various regions of India, the majority of the dishes are Moghul in origin. This is not because I consider Moghul cuisine to be "better" than Indian regional cooking, but because—due to the large percentage of braised dishes—the cooking style is extremely successful when adapted to the microwave.

The Moghuls strived for excellence not only in food but in art, music, literature, and the way they lived. Moghul cooking, not surprisingly, represents splendor, beauty, and a certain elegance in every dish. Interestingly, in today's India, *Moghul* means a refined art form and life-style and signifies a keen appreciation of art, including cooking. Great cooks as well as people with great palates and those with beautifully decorated homes are all known as "real Moghuls."

ACKNOWLEDGMENTS

Over the years, with my cookbooks, newspaper and magazine articles, and cooking classes, most people have come to know me as a classical cook—a guardian of Old World traditions. Therefore, my venturing into the field of microwave cooking and tackling it with confidence, obviously couldn't have been done without the support and foresightedness of some key individuals who played significant roles, some in molding my future, others in enriching my spirit and nourishing my morale.

I am indebted to my sister and brother-in-law Roopa and Subhash Gir and my friends Pat Adam Shakin, a computer consultant, and Bob Tieger and Rodney Madden, for their efforts in transforming me from a fountain-pen and note-pad writer with hired typing services into a space age persona outfitted with computer, modem, fax—the whole works. They paved the way for the possibilities of new wave cooking.

For her enthusiastic support, wise guidance, invaluable suggestions, and superb editing of this book, I express my utmost gratitude to Maria Guarnaschelli, editor par excellence. Even though a purist at heart like me, she entertained my idea of Indian microwave cooking without reservation, thus showing the extent of her faith in me and my work.

I also wish to thank the following people:

Barbara Kafka—a comrade and cooking's microwave priestess—for always finding time to discuss the finer points of microwave cooking and for her works, which enabled me to "come out of the closet."

My former husband, Viraht Sahni, for his advice. "Julie," he said, "you can fill the book with technical information and details, but remember what ultimately will matter to a cook is if the recipes work and produce delicious results." Those words of wisdom uttered while I was writing my first cookbook, *Classic Indian Cooking,* have remained implanted in my psyche as a guiding light and resound each time I test recipes, including those found here.

Denise Tillar Landis—a skilled recipe tester with a gifted palate—for her unrelenting research in analyzing techniques for simplicity and ingredients for consistency, often working into the early-morning hours to make sure there were no "loopholes" in these recipes.

Richard and Claudia Franey Jensen, for reminding me to concentrate on the important issue, which was not how fast a microwave oven cooked a dish but how much better the result was using this mode of cooking.

Dr. Chitra and Kumar Rajagopalan (my sister and brother-in-law), John Guarnaschelli, Milton and Doris Kaplan, Margaret Marrello, Brad Smith, and Jack Miller, for being a tasting panel with a discriminating palate.

Mark Bittman, for his friendship, for his eloquent help with the text, and for his many commentaries on microwaved foods. Patricia Baird, for her discussions on the merits of different microwave ovens and for bringing to my attention the idiosyncrasies of microwave features. Jody Eglston, director of the test kitchen at Corning Glass Works, for her discussions on safety in microwave cooking and the proper use and care of microwave cookware.

For their consultation on microwave ovens, I am grateful to Jeff Vogel, Home Appliances Group for Panasonic; Andrea Boren at Dorf Stanton Communications for Sharp; Nancy Longacre of Sanyo Electronics; Charles Witfield for Magic Chef; Charles Williamson for Toastmasters; Hugh Bennett for Litton; Denise Coco at Burson Marsteller for General Electric; Whyne Smith for Sunbean; Rachel Litner for Conair; and the technical staff at Whirlpool. For discussions on microwave cookware, I thank Al Donnelly and Cornelius O'Donnell at Corning Glass Works.

In addition, many individuals played important roles in the production of this book. I express my deepest gratitude for their dedication and commitment to excellence:

Bruce Hattendorf, for his advice and assistance and for remaining calm as a monk through chaotic and nerve-racking deadlines.
Dean Boranstein, for his illuminating illustrations.
Randee Marullo, for exquisite copyediting.
Paul Gamarello, for the stunning book jacket.
Jaye Zimet, for an elegant book design.
Harvey Hoffman, for keeping the production deadlines and schedules.
And, finally, Deborah Weiss Geline, for her patience and support through crises and for an impeccable manuscript.

CONTENTS

INTRODUCTION

I saw my first microwave in 1974. A friend who was working for Amana, the company that pioneered the "Radarange," was demonstrating this miraculous new machine in Washington, D.C. I was instantly fascinated by its ability to cook a hot dog "invisibly," and saw no end to its virtues. So I bought one. But I was embarrassed to use it, especially in front of other food professionals. The myth that microwave cooking was overly scientific and nonsensuous was too powerful, and I became intimidated.

That myth afflicted microwave cooking for nearly fifteen years, delaying the time that the appliance would be appreciated for what it is, rather than disparaged for what it is not. In 1982, my sister predicted that the microwave would be the appliance of the 1990s. "If you just concentrate on Indian food," she said, "you will do wonderful things with it." I tried again and got good results, but again shied off. Although millions of Americans were buying microwaves, nobody believed that the microwave would ever play a role in making really good food. It was for TV dinners, bacon, and reheating coffee.

It took Barbara Kafka's ground-breaking work, *Microwave Gourmet,* published in 1987, to turn things around. Kafka courageously demonstrated the real potential of the microwave—even convincing food snobs—and, finally, the machine began to gain respectability.

Still, there is resistance. Friends of mine, chefs and food writers, refuse to keep a microwave in their kitchen. Foodies who were quick to embrace the food processor deny the role of the space age microwave. "Food was not meant to be cooked this way," remarked one well-known author. He and other friends are still stunned with disbelief when I present them with perfectly cooked classic Indian dishes that I have prepared in the microwave.

Now I no longer distinguish between food that has been cooked in the microwave, on top of the stove, or under the broiler any more than I consider whether an onion was diced by hand or in the food processor. The microwave is neither savior nor devil, neither miracle nor monster; it is a tool for cooking food. It does not "threaten" the existence of conventional cooking any more than the food processor threatens the knife. Like the open flame of a stove top or the ambient heat of an oven, it is an imperfect tool. I would no sooner make Indian fried breads in the microwave than I would on a grill. The microwave excels at certain tasks; one reason it was originally treated with scorn is that manufacturers insisted it could do everything. Obviously, it cannot. Once you have accepted the limitations of the microwave and use it only for what it does best, you can truly appreciate it. I no more "love" my microwave ovens (while testing hundreds of recipes for this book, I accumulated six) than I love my stove. I simply know what each is good for.

With that knowledge has come comfort. As with any appliance, I had to become familiar with its idiosyncrasies in order to avoid its pitfalls. Now I have a natural feel for it; I am more comfortable with a microwave than I am with an outdoor grill. When you reach that point, not only will you become a more relaxed and successful cook, you will find your time spent in the kitchen more joyful. There are few cooking experiences more rewarding than that of cooking a good meal in the microwave quickly on a hot day, without raising the kitchen temperature one degree; previously the mere thought of turning on the oven would have driven you to a restaurant.

Today, the microwave is increasingly put to good use by fine home cooks. The food revolution—which brought the cuisines and ingredients of the entire world not only to specialty stores but to supermarkets—has taken a new turn. Our sharpened and discriminating palates demand convenient, quick cooking. Furthermore, our food must be healthy. For decades, good-tasting, healthy food took hours; quickly cooked food was bland or unhealthy; healthy food was uninteresting. That is yet another set of myths that has been laid to rest. And the practicality of putting together meals that are fast, tasty, and healthy is in large part thanks to the creative use of the microwave. Finally, the machine is being used to its full potential.

Nowhere is that potential more evident than in Indian cooking, in which trapped moist heat is used to create succulent foods with complex flavors. The techniques that form the basis for Indian cooking are braising, stewing, steaming, and poaching. The microwave produces many Indian dishes in half the traditional time and, because there is little danger of food sticking in a covered utensil in the microwave, the fat used in cooking has been virtually eliminated, except for its use as a flavoring.

Even more surprising to me when I began serious experimentation with the microwave was that the oven can produce many traditional Indian foods better than conventional cooking methods can. The Parsi dish called *dhanshak* (p. 124), for example, was one of my first great revelations. This is a stew in which chicken, lentils, squash, onions, herbs, and eggplant are combined in a covered pot and cooked. Using traditional methods, there is much agitation within the pot, caused by the boiling liquid and the stirring needed to keep the lentils from sticking to the bottom and burning. This causes much of the chicken to fall off the bone (and, despite stirring, the lentils usually burn anyway). The solution in restaurants was to broil the chicken and cook the lentils and vegetables separately; but that is not authentic *dhanshak*. Using the microwave, the dish is cooked for just thirty-five minutes—about a third of the traditional time—and the result is perfectly cooked, succulent whole chicken pieces. These are lifted out of the stew, and the remaining vegetables can be easily pureed to make a glistening sauce. Incidentally, all of this is done without a drop of oil. If you are skeptical about using the microwave, try making a pot of *dhanshak* in it—it improves with age and can be reheated for days, getting better all the time.

I began to see that my sister had been right: Microwave cooking works equally well with dozens of Moghul classics. Many Indian recipes began with a roux of onion, coconut, and spices, which inevitably sticks to the bottom of the pan unless you add lots of oil. Turn-fried dishes, such as the cherished *masala vangi*—eggplant slices smothered with a coconut spice paste—often become messy when cooked on top of the stove. When you are turning and coating the eggplant with the spice paste, it always falls apart. Until I made this dish in the microwave, I never dreamed it could look pretty; no matter who cooked it before—my mother, friends, or brilliant restaurant chefs—it came out a mess. Cooked in the microwave, the dish has the same flavor with the identical authentic fragrance, but now the food looks like eggplant.

Nor was I disappointed when I turned the microwave to the staples of Indian cuisine. Lentils cook in half the time without soaking. *Basmati* rice—used exclusively in this book—takes one quarter of the conventional time, and requires fewer steps. Roasted nuts, seeds, and spices, all of which are critical in genuine Indian dishes, gain a fragrant, toasty smokiness in the microwave in seconds; the nuts and seeds become satisfyingly crunchy but remain moist.

Both the stewing and steaming methods of cooking vegetables work marvelously well in the microwave. Braised dishes cook in less time, with less hassle, and without any compromise in flavor. And there is simply no better way to cook fish to perfection.

The machine even makes fast work of some of the more esoteric Indian preparations, and should encourage many Americans to make them for the first time. For example, *paneer*—Indian fresh cheese—required elaborate draining, compressing, and deep-frying before it could be included in recipes. Using the microwave, you go straight from making the cheese and draining it (for two minutes, rather than an hour and a half) to putting it in the oven for one minute. Not only that, the cheese is more tender than it ever was and holds its shape just as well.

After finally mastering the microwave, and cooking in it every day for more than two years, I eliminated those recipes that merely duplicated conventional cooking. For this book, I searched for those dishes in which using the microwave actually improved the food's flavor, appearance, or healthiness, such as *dhanshak* or *paneer;* those in which it saved significant amounts of time, such as lentils or *basmati* rice; and those that were simply much easier made in the microwave than they are using traditional methods, such as *masala vangi.* I was not interested in proving that the microwave can do what conventional cooking can.

Let me hasten to repeat that the microwave does not perform miracles. It has its limitations even when used by skilled cooks. For example, things happen very fast in the microwave. This is certainly not a disadvantage, but even when making the slow-cooked dishes of India, one must begin to think in seconds and minutes rather than minutes and hours. There is no doubt that you can do this: After all, humans made the same adjustment when we moved from the open hearth to the gas- or electric-powered stove top.

There is another issue I want to address about using the microwave, and that is safety. In my opinion, all kitchen appliances should be intrinsically safe, as should the cooking methods used with them. Many people look at the microwave with fear, suspicion, and trepidation. Not only is this undesirable, it is unnecessary.

With few exceptions, I have eliminated the need to stick your hands in the microwave, uncover a hot pot, stir the dish, and replace the cover. I have also done away with complicated food arrangements that supposedly take advantage of the patterns followed by microwaves. Since most of Moghul cooking is a technique that requires foods to be cooked gracefully by braising or stewing, the arrangement of food is not an issue here.

Contrary to the claims of manufacturers, cookware does indeed heat up in the microwave, especially when there is food in it (which is usually the case), and, inevitably, when you try to handle hot cookware in a tiny space without pot holders or mitts, you are going to get burned. This is especially true if you use plastic wrap to cover your cooking utensils, a procedure I cannot discourage strongly enough, and one that is, finally, beginning to fall into disfavor. In addition to the health questions surrounding warm plastic coming into contact with food as it cooks, I have what I believe to be a rational fear of that plastic bubble rising up in the microwave, one that must be pricked carefully and popped to release scalding hot steam before exposing the food.

Instead, I strongly recommend that you work with glass-topped cookware. Corning recently announced that they are producing glass tops for every piece of cookware they make, and other manufacturers have followed suit. Since this cookware is reasonably attractive, inexpensive, and easy to use, I don't see any reason to use plastic wrap. And glass-topped cookware works at least as well as plastic wrap. For me, the deciding factor was rice: I knew that if I could cook rice using a regular glass lid, then I could cook anything, because no food requires a tighter seal than rice. And it cooks perfectly in glass-topped cookware. When you open a pot with a lid, say a pot of boiling water for spaghetti, you must open the lid carefully, on the side away from you, because there will be steam in there.

I believe that every gadget is designed to perform one task best. The microwave oven is designed to cook food specifically by microwaves. When it is turned into a combo oven—to also bake, broil, toast, and grill, with expensive attachments such as probes, computers, and dozens of bells and whistles—I become wary. Conventional cooking adds grease, which in turn diminishes microwave efficiency. And those fancy features do not save you much time or make your cooking more accurate.

That accuracy, the skill that it takes to cook in a microwave, cannot be measured by devices. People continue to think of microwave cooking as scientific, precise, even inhumane. But that is erroneous. The microwave oven, which was given a bad name because of its invisible rays, offers just one more method of generating heat. Regardless of the method, there are many variables at work in cooking, variables that produce masterpieces and disasters, light meals and feasts—variables that evoke joy, pleasure, anxiety, success, and failure.

The microwave is not a robot into which you put food, guaranteed of the results;

you are still the cook. You must judge the difference between cooking room-temperature grated zucchini with a sauce in a 10-inch skillet in a 1-cubic-foot microwave with 500 watts of power and cooking cold whole zucchini in a covered saucepan in a 1.5-cubic-foot oven with 700 watts of power. These variables are not much different from those we deal with when cooking conventionally, and to become successful microwave cooks, we must understand them. In microwave cooking, as in conventional cooking, you cannot simply cook by time. You must compare texture, appearance, and taste. Ultimately, it is your judgment that will determine the success or failure of a given recipe.

The basic point is that food, no matter how it is cooked, should taste good. The microwave is a machine that can help us make good-tasting food. And in the case of the Moghul foods found here, it cooks better than any other method I know.

Julie Sahni
Brooklyn Heights, N.Y.

MOGHUL MICROWAVE
KITCHEN

lthough the microwave oven may be a high-tech marvel, learning to cook in it takes the same kind of dedication as learning to sauté. Like other methods of cooking, using the microwave is an art, not a science. The secret of success lies in knowing and understanding the variables that affect your microwave's performance. Mastering the skills needed to microwave will lead to your understanding that microwave Indian cooking is much the same as stove-top Indian cooking, only faster, neater, and healthier.

MICROWAVE VARIABLES

The recipes in this and other microwave cookbooks are based on a certain set of factors, including oven size and power, the temperature and amount of the food, and so on. Varying any one of these factors will vary the cooking time and results. But if you are conscious of these changes and their effects on cooking, you can easily make the necessary adjustments.

TEMPERATURE

The speed with which microwaves cook is such that a deviation of just a few seconds can mean the difference between success and failure. But no recipe can give perfect times. As the oven becomes warm, food is cooked more efficiently and quickly. For example, in making lentil wafers (*puppadum,* p. 10), the first wafer may take as long as fifty seconds, but each subsequent wafer will take five seconds less, until wafers are cooking in just thirty seconds. In addition, the difference between ingredients at room temperature and those taken straight from the refrigerator can affect cooking times by as much as 50 percent. Unless otherwise noted, the recipes in this book were tested with room temperature ingredients and a cool oven.

MOISTURE CONTENT AND FOOD SIZE

Since microwaves are more readily absorbed by water than by most other materials, foods with a high moisture content cook faster than drier foods. This explains why new potatoes cook more quickly than those that have been stored for several months, and why a recently purchased batch of *basmati* rice cooks faster than that which has sat on your shelf for a while (see Pilafs and Steamed Cakes, p. 298). It also explains why foods with skin (such as eggplant, potatoes, and squash), shells (such as coconut and chestnuts), membranes (such as egg yolk and liver), and casing (such as sausage) should be lightly pierced in a few places to prevent moisture buildup and subsequent bursting. Fats and sugars also absorb microwaves, explaining why rich and sweet foods cook at a faster rate.

Since microwaves penetrate to a depth of only about one and a half inches, the interior of large pieces of food cooks by conduction, the physical transfer of heat from that portion of the food that has already cooked. This not only is an inefficient use of microwave energy but can result in the drying out of the exterior of foods. The best solution to this is to cut food into uniform small portions, and increase the cooking area by using wide, shallow cooking dishes.

HEAT

Covering dishes during cooking speeds the process by causing a building up of heat within the cooking utensil. Most microwave cookware made today comes with glass covers; I recommend that those are the only covers you use in microwave cooking. The use of dinner plates, pie plates, or other makeshift covers may cause accidents resulting in burns. And, as I stressed in the introduction, I strongly discourage the use of stretched plastic wrap under any circumstances; it not only raises grave concerns of health hazards due to exposure to plasticized polyvinyl chloride, but it is also the most likely cover to cause steam burns.

Many of the recipes in this book include a standing time, during which the food remains covered and undisturbed after it has been removed from the oven. This is partly to enhance the taste of the dish, allowing complex and subtle flavors to continue to evolve, but also to provide time for food molecules to settle, enabling the dish to develop the proper texture and character.

THE MICROWAVE OVEN

Microwaves are high-frequency electromagnetic waves, similar to radio waves. They are generated by a magnetron and carried into the oven by a wave guide. Once inside the oven cavity, the waves are reflected off certain surfaces (such as metal), pass unaffected through others (such as glass and paper), and are absorbed by fats, sugars, and moisture, all of which are common in food. Microwaves cause no structural or chemical changes in those substances, but cause their molecules to rotate at a frequency of more than 2 billion times per second. The friction caused by this rapid rotation produces heat.

Microwaves travel in random patterns, bouncing around the oven cavity until they are absorbed by food. This makes the heat distribution in an oven rather uneven, and as a result some areas receive more microwaves, and therefore more heat, than do others. This is the explanation for the existence of so-called "hot spots" (areas in ovens where food may actually burn), and "cold spots" (areas in which food may cook more slowly).

These problems can be remedied by moving the food constantly. But stirring or rearranging the food is a time-consuming nuisance. The best solution is the use of a carousel or turntable that rotates the food through much of the oven without any effort on your part. Most microwave ovens now come equipped with turntables, but in the event that yours does not, consider purchasing one of the inexpensive portable models now on the market.

There are literally hundreds of models of microwave ovens available today, many with fancy attachments and dozens of features. But only a few factors determine a microwave oven's value in the kitchen.

SIZE: There are compact (under 0.8 cubic foot), mid-size (0.1 to 1.4 cubic feet), and full-size (1.5 or more cubic feet) microwaves; this measurement tells you the interior capacity of the oven. I have found the mid-size models to be the most versatile. Compact ovens are not powerful enough, do not come equipped with carousels, and do not accommodate the 10-inch skillet needed for many recipes. Full-size ovens, on the other hand, are bulky, relatively expensive, and distribute microwaves unevenly, making them more prone to hot and cold spots.

POWER: Expressed in terms of wattage, the power level of a microwave oven tells you the amount of microwave energy it can produce. The higher the wattage, the faster food will cook in the oven. For most microwave recipes, a power rating of 650 to 700 watts will give you a good combination of speed and fine results.

CONTROLS: Remote-controlled computer control panels may be flashy, but they do nothing for the cook. All you need are settings for full, half, and defrost power and an automatic timer. The rest is pure show.

I recommend that you steer clear of microconvection ovens and some of the fancy microwaves that double the price. The appeal of microconvection, which combines microwave power with electric heat in one unit, is obvious. A chicken can be baked to a golden crispness in half the time it takes using conventional means. But broiling or roasting chicken in a microconvection oven is a messy process, one that leaves behind a great deal of grease. And most ovens are not as easy to clean as the manufacturers claim. If, despite your best efforts, that grease begins to clog the outlet used by the microwaves to enter the oven, power will be reduced. And service costs are higher for microconvection ovens than for regular microwaves. Temperature probes, auto-sensor cooking devices, and other gadgets are usually imprecise at best, and unreliable at worst; they also add enormously to the cost of the oven.

Therefore, for everyday home cooking for a household of two to eight people, I recommend a mid-size oven of 1-cubic-foot capacity, full power (650 to 700 watts), and with a carousel and controls as mentioned above. It will perform admirably and should cost you around $200.

MICROWAVE COOKWARE

More than 80 million microwaves have been sold in this country, making the cookware market a big one. The pioneer in this field, and the manufacturer offering the largest selection, is Corning. Their Microwave Plus, Corning Ware, and Visions lines are all of unparalleled excellence.

Microwave cookware, made of glass, ceramic, china, or pottery, is "transparent" to microwaves, allowing them to pass through, unchanged, to the food. The two pieces of cookware most commonly used in recipes in this book are a 2½-quart covered casserole and a 10-inch covered skillet. It never hurts, however, to have a wider variety or additional stock in the event you are cooking and serving several dishes at one meal.

Contrary to the information provided by microwave cookbooks and manufacturers, even microwave cookware heats up. This includes the part in contact with the food—which gains additional heat by conduction—as well as the exposed part that is not. Therefore, cookware will become hot; perhaps not hot enough to cause burns, but certainly hot enough to cause discomfort and even pain. So use pot holders, mitts, or a towel to handle anything coming out of the oven and always place it on a heat-proof surface after you remove it from the oven.

BROWNING SKILLETS

Browning skillets look like other covered skillets, with one important exception: They come with a special coating on their undersides. This coating absorbs mi-

crowave energy, allowing the bottom of the skillet to reach and retain high temperatures. This special feature was originally created to brown meat, but it represents a useful, although not essential, development for Indian cooking in the microwave since it shortens cooking time by a few minutes.

Many Indian recipes call for the preparation of a spice-infused oil. The oil must become very hot—not smoking—but hot enough so that, for example, mustard seeds will pop and sputter and cumin seeds will puff and brown. This is important because undercooked mustard seeds remain bitter and chewy—lacking fragrance—and can be unpleasant. Spice-infused oils can be made successfully in a regular skillet in six minutes (for an average serving of eight). A browning skillet gives equally good results and is two minutes faster. The same is true for preparing caramelized fried onions—one of the basic preparations of Moghul cooking—as well as the fried onion-ginger-garlic mixture needed for many sauces, the crisp onions used to garnish pilaf, and many other pan-sautéed dishes.

The underside of the browning skillet retains heat for a considerable length of time, so when taking it out of the microwave, handle it carefully and make sure you place it on a heat-resistant surface. Follow the manufacturer's instructions for cleaning and maintenance. The most versatile browning skillets are the 8- and 10-inch sizes, though others are available.

UNSUITABLE DISHES FOR MICROWAVE OVENS

Metal is unsuitable for microwave cookware, since it is impervious to microwaves. In addition, unglazed pottery, thin plastic storage containers, and dinnerware made of melamine polystyrene and bone china are unsuitable. Except for an egg poacher/muffin tray, a piece of cookware that is available only in plastic although specifically recommended for microwave cooking, I personally do not like to use plastic in any form for microwave cooking.

APPETIZERS
AND FIRST COURSES

Appetizers and first courses should be titillating, visually appealing morsels with intriguing aromas and complex flavors that excite the eye and prime the palate. They should always be served in moderation; you want to stimulate rather than satisfy the appetite.

One of my favorite nibbles is *papad* (also called *puppadum*), crisp-toasted lentil wafers that are aromatic and spicy. Traditionally *puppadum* are deep-fried, an elaborate production that involves a good deal of time, cooking oil, mess, and a certain loss of flavor as the intensity of the spices leaches into the oil. But in the microwave they are roasted without fat, with no mess, in about thirty seconds. Even better, all the flavors are retained in the *puppadum* themselves; the pungency of pepper or aroma of cumin—in fact, the essence of any spice—is explosive. The dry roasting seems to intensify flavor rather than reduce it.

Indian spiced nuts, another classic nibble that is always a crowd pleaser, are especially wonderful made in the microwave. The nuts become crunchy without drying out, and their flavor is concentrated; this alone is reason enough to own a microwave oven.

Indian salads and first courses, such as the Warm Crayfish, Fennel, and Pine Nuts Salad with Dill or the tiny succulent shrimps swathed in creamy cumin-mustard dressing and arranged on endive boats, are visually stunning creatures. Either one would make an elegant and delectable beginning to a formal meal, and they are easily prepared in the microwave.

All of the appetizers and first courses here can be made in advance and briefly reheated to be served at a moment's notice to provide an elegant beginning to any meal, formal or informal. In addition to the first courses in this chapter, you can also start a meal with small portions of many of the dishes found in other sections of this book. Especially good are Steamed Fish in Ginger-Thyme Essence (p. 81), Malabar Salmon in Delicate Coconut Sauce (p. 89), Ginger Chicken Kabob (p. 109) or Creamed Chicken Kabob (p. 111), Savory Keema Cake (p. 147), Stuffed Cabbage Rolls with Fragrant Tomato Sauce (p. 161), Cauliflower and Fennel in Aromatic Oil (p. 209), and Broccoli in Spicy-Garlic Oil (p. 205).

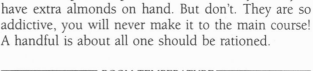

SPICY CANDIED ALMONDS

MASALA BADAAM

MICROWAVE

Yield
—3 cups
Preparation time
—5 minutes
Cooking time
—6 minutes
Heat
—100 percent power
MW oven size
—650 to 700 watts
MW cookware
—One 1½-quart cas-
serole or soufflé dish

These almonds are such a breeze to make that you will be tempted to produce a batch every time you have extra almonds on hand. But don't. They are so addictive, you will never make it to the main course! A handful is about all one should be rationed.

=========== ROOM TEMPERATURE ===========

½ cup sugar	2 teaspoons ground
¼ cup water	cumin
1 tablespoon unsalted	2 teaspoons cayenne
butter	pepper
3 cups (16 ounces)	1 teaspoon ground fennel
shelled raw whole un-	¼ teaspoon baking soda
blanched almonds	

1. Place sugar, water, and butter in a 1½-quart microwave-safe dish. Cook, uncovered, at 100 percent power in a 650- to 700-watt carousel oven for 4 minutes (or until syrup thickens and foams), stirring once.

2. Remove from oven and stir in almonds, cumin, cayenne, and fennel. Return to oven and cook, uncovered, at 100 percent power for 2 minutes (or until most of syrup is absorbed into almonds). Remove from oven.

3. Add baking soda and mix rapidly. The syrup will turn white and frothy. Immediately transfer the nuts to a lightly greased cookie sheet, spreading them into a single layer, and cool. If almonds cling together, gently press to separate. Serve immediately or store in an airtight container in a cool place.

NOTE Spicy candied almonds stay fresh, covered airtight, several weeks in a cool place and several months in the refrigerator.

SPICY CANDIED WALNUTS

MASALA AKHROT

Even though flavored exactly like Spicy Candied Almonds (p. 3), these nuts taste sweeter, probably due to the inherent sweetness in walnuts, and crunchier because roasted, not raw, nuts are used in this recipe. For a more intense and exotic flavor use jaggery, Indian raw sugar, in place of white sugar.

Yield
   —*3 cups*
Preparation time
   —*3 minutes*
Cooking time
   —*11 minutes*
Heat
   —*100 percent power*
MW oven size
   —*650 to 700 watts*
MW cookware
   —*One pie or dinner plate and one 1½-quart casserole or soufflé dish*

================= ROOM TEMPERATURE =================

3 cups (12 ounces) shelled raw whole walnuts	1 tablespoon unsalted butter
½ cup sugar	2 teaspoons ground cumin
¼ cup water	2 teaspoons cayenne pepper
	1 teaspoon ground fennel

1. Spread walnuts in a single layer on a microwave-safe pie or dinner plate. Roast, uncovered, at 100 percent power in a 650- to 700-watt carousel oven for 4 minutes 45 seconds (or until walnuts look slightly puffed and crack and exude a nutty fragrance). Remove from oven, transfer onto another plate, and cool.

2. Put sugar, water, and butter in a 1½ quart microwave-safe dish. Cook, uncovered, at 100 percent power for 4 minutes (or until syrup thickens and foams). Stir in cumin, pepper, and fennel and continue cooking, uncovered, at 100 percent power for an additional 2 minutes.

3. Remove from oven. Add walnuts, mix rapidly to coat them evenly with the spicy syrup, transfer quickly to a greased cookie sheet, spreading them into a single layer, and cool. If walnuts cling together, gently press to separate. Serve nuts immediately or store.

NOTE   The spicy candied walnuts remain fresh, stored in an airtight container, for 6 weeks in a cool place, 6 months in the refrigerator, and up to a year in the freezer.

PEPPERY CANDIED PISTACHIOS

MASALA PISTA

MICROWAVE

Yield
—3 cups
Preparation time
—5 minutes
Cooking time
—6 minutes
Heat
—100 percent power
MW oven size
—650 to 700 watts
MW cookware
—One 1½-quart cas-
serole or soufflé dish

NOTE Peppery candied pis-
tachio nuts stay fresh, stored in
an airtight container, for 6
weeks in a cool place, 6 months
in the refrigerator, and up to a
year in the freezer.

Another great addition to the cocktail-hour nibbles,
these also make an exquisite garnish, sliced and
sprinkled on puddings, pilafs, and special-occasion
salads.

=========== ROOM TEMPERATURE ===========

½ cup sugar
¼ cup water
1 tablespoon unsalted
butter
3 cups (16 ounces)
shelled raw whole un-
salted pistachios

1 teaspoon freshly
ground black pepper
1 teaspoon cayenne
pepper
1 teaspoon ground fennel
¼ teaspoon baking soda

1. Place sugar, water, and butter in a 1½-quart microwave-safe dish. Cook, uncovered, at 100 percent
power in a 650- to 700-watt carousel oven for 4 minutes (or until syrup thickens and foams), stirring twice.

2. Remove from oven. Add pistachio nuts, black pepper, cayenne pepper, fennel, and soda. Cook, uncovered, at 100 percent power for 2 minutes (or until
syrup froths and foams up over nuts), stirring once.
(The syrup eventually gets absorbed into the pistachios.)

3. Remove from oven, mix rapidly, transfer nuts using a slotted spoon to a greased cookie sheet, spreading them into a single layer, and cool. If nuts cling
together gently press to separate. Serve pistachio nuts
or store.

SPICED MIXED NUTS

MASALA KHAJA

MICROWAVE

Yield
  —2 cups
Preparation time
  —3 minutes
Cooking time
  —6 minutes
Heat
  —100 percent power
MW oven size
  —650 to 700 watts
MW cookware
  —One pie or dinner
   plate and one 1½-
   quart casserole or
   soufflé dish

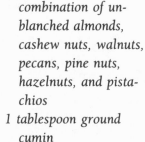

A classic from north India, this nibble is simply magical on the palate—crunchy and aromatic because the nuts are preroasted and the spices undercooked.

=========== ROOM TEMPERATURE ===========

2 cups (10 ounces)
  shelled raw whole un-
  salted mixed nuts (a
  combination of un-
  blanched almonds,
  cashew nuts, walnuts,
  pecans, pine nuts,
  hazelnuts, and pista-
  chios
1 tablespoon ground
  cumin
½ teaspoon ground
  fennel

1 tablespoon cayenne
  pepper
1 teaspoon dry mango
  powder (p. 483) or 2
  teaspoons lemon juice
¼ teaspoon ground black
  salt (p. 482)
  (optional)
½ cup sugar
2 teaspoons kosher salt
⅓ cup water

1. Spread nuts in a single layer on a microwave-safe pie or dinner plate. Roast, uncovered, at 100 percent power in a 650- to 700-watt carousel oven for 3 minutes 30 seconds (or until nuts are lightly browned and puffed), stirring once. Remove from oven, transfer onto another plate, and cool.

2. Mix cumin, fennel, cayenne, mango powder (if you are using lemon juice, do not add it here), and black salt in a small bowl and reserve.

3. Combine sugar, salt, lemon juice (if you are using it), and water in a 1½-quart microwave-safe dish. Cook, uncovered, at 100 percent power for 2 minutes

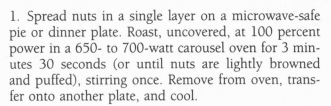

45 seconds (or until sugar melts and syrup thickens), stirring twice. Stir in nuts and continue cooking, uncovered, at 100 percent power for an additional 45 seconds (or until syrup is absorbed into nuts).

4. Remove from oven. Transfer nuts to a sieve held over the kitchen sink and drain off the excess syrup. Spread nuts on a cookie sheet or plate. Sprinkle spice mixture, a little at a time, on nuts and mix, turning and tossing, until nuts are evenly coated with spices. Cool and serve.

VARIATION

For spicier nuts increase cayenne to 2 tablespoons and reduce sugar to ⅓ cup in the syrup. For milder nuts decrease cayenne to 1 teaspoon.

NOTE The spiced nuts remain fresh, stored in an airtight container, for 6 weeks in a cool place, 6 months in the refrigerator, and up to a year in the freezer.

CAYENNE ALMONDS

MIRCH BADAAM

MICROWAVE

Yield
— 2 cups
Preparation time
— 3 minutes
Cooking time
— 6 minutes
Heat
— 100 percent power
MW oven size
— 650 to 700 watts
MW cookware
— One pie or dinner
plate and one 1½-
quart casserole or
soufflé dish

For those with an insatiable appetite for fire, here is a version of almonds laced with pure heat that is guaranteed to glow in your mouth.

==================== ROOM TEMPERATURE ====================

2 cups (12 ounces)
    shelled raw whole un-
    blanched almonds
½ cup sugar
1 tablespoon lemon juice
⅓ cup water

3 tablespoons cayenne
    pepper
4 teaspoons ground
    roasted cumin seeds
    (p. 465)
2 teaspoons kosher salt
2 tablespoons paprika

1. Spread nuts in a single layer on a microwave-safe pie plate or dinner plate. Roast, uncovered, at 100 percent power in a 650- to 700-watt carousel oven for 3 minutes 30 seconds (or until nuts are puffed and exude aroma), stirring once. Remove from oven, transfer onto another plate, and cool.

2. Combine sugar, lemon juice, and water in a 1½-quart microwave-safe dish. Cook, uncovered, at 100 percent power for 2 minutes 45 seconds (or until sugar melts and syrup thickens), stirring twice. Stir in cayenne, cumin, salt, and nuts and continue cooking, uncovered, at 100 percent power for an additional 45 seconds (or until syrup is absorbed into nuts).

3. Remove from oven. Transfer nuts to a sieve held over the kitchen sink and drain off the excess syrup. Spread nuts on a cookie sheet or plate. Sprinkle pa-

prika, a little at a time, on nuts and mix, turning and tossing, until nuts are evenly coated with the spice. Cool and serve.

VARIATION

For milder nuts decrease cayenne to 1 tablespoon.

NOTE   The spiced nuts remain fresh, stored in an airtight container, for 6 weeks in a cool place, 6 months in the refrigerator, and up to a year in the freezer.

TOASTED LENTIL WAFERS

PAPAD/PUPPADUM

MICROWAVE

Yield
—*4 wafers*
Cooking time
—*3 minutes*
Heat
—*100 percent power*
MW oven size
—*650 to 700 watts*
MW cookware
—*One pie or dinner*
plate

NOTE   The exact toasting time for a wafer depends upon two factors. One is its thickness—the thinner the wafer, the faster it cooks. For example, garlic-laced lentil wafers, which are thinner than plain, black pepper, or red pepper wafers take about 10 seconds less than all others. Second, the fresher (meaning more moist) the wafer, the quicker it will toast.

Until the microwave came along, toasting lentil wafers was always a chore, either deep-fried, which added all those unnecessary calories and numbed and diluted the delicate flavors of the spices, or flame-roasted, which, unless carefully monitored, created burnt spots. The microwave oven not only toasts wafers evenly and perfectly with no added calories or fat but also heightens the flavors of the spices. It is a clean, efficient, and healthy method of cooking that produces delicious results.

=============== *ROOM TEMPERATURE* ===============

4 lentil wafers, plain or flavored (p. 462)

Place a microwave-safe pie or dinner plate in a 650- to 700-watt carousel oven. Place one lentil wafer on the plate and toast at 100 percent power for 40 to 50 seconds (or until entire wafer changes to cream color and is fully cooked), moving it if necessary to ensure even cooking. Remove from oven, repeat with the remaining wafers, and serve. Toasted lentil wafers keep fresh and crisp for several hours at room temperature as long as the humidity is low. If it is high, within minutes they will get limp. No need for alarm here. Either quickly store the toasted wafers in a tightly covered container, or retoast all 4 wafers, stacked together, at 100 percent power for 10 to 20 seconds (or until warmed through and dried) before serving. There will be no loss of flavor.

BOMBAY COCONUT SHRIMP

NARIAL JHEENGA

MICROWAVE

Servings
—4 as an appetizer;
2 as a main course
Preparation time
—7 minutes
Cooking time
—4minutes 30
seconds
Heat
—100 percent power
MW oven size
—650 to 700 watts
MW cookware
—One 10-inch covered
skillet

In all my twenty-two years of bringing Indian food to the American public, I have never mentioned this preparation—coconut-coated shrimps, a classic from Bombay combining two of its most precious gifts of nature, succulent seafood and the divine coconut. This is because the traditional recipe calls for cooking shrimps by deep-frying—a technique I am known to shy away from when given a choice. But more important, in this particular case the coconut, because of its porous texture, soaks up a large quantity of oil, making it overly rich and altering the flavor of coconut from sweet and fragrant to greasy, coconut-oily tasting.

Now here is the good news. In the following microwave technique the shrimps are coated with pre-toasted coconut shreds and cooked in their own moisture. Due to the fact that in the microwave shrimps take hardly a minute or two to cook, the coconut coating remains crisp and, in addition, keeps the shrimps from drying out. Just a touch of cornstarch in the marinade secures the coconut from falling off the shrimps. The result is a clean, heightened taste of coconut and no added oil.

=== ROOM TEMPERATURE ===

½ cup dried unsweetened coconut flakes (p. 449)
½ pound medium-large shrimps (28–32 per pound)
½ teaspoon minced garlic
½ teaspoon crushed or grated fresh ginger

½ teaspoon lemon juice
½ teaspoon black peppercorns, crushed
½ teaspoon ground cumin
¼ teaspoon kosher salt
1 teaspoon cornstarch
Juice of half a small lemon

1. Spread coconut in a 10-inch microwave-safe skillet. Toast, uncovered, at 100 percent power in a 650- to 700-watt carousel oven for 3 minutes (or until lightly golden), stirring once. (The coconut will color unevenly, which is fine as it will add another dimension in flavor and appearance.) Remove from oven, and transfer coconut into a shallow bowl. Cool, and reserve.

MENU SUGGESTION

For a complete meal, serve a substantial rice pilaf such as Split Pea and Basmati Pilaf (p. 314) and a yogurt raita. A nice choice is Spinach and Yogurt Raita (p. 258).

2. Shell and devein shrimps, leaving the tails on, and wash thoroughly. Pat dry on kitchen towels and put them in a bowl. Add garlic, ginger, lemon juice, black pepper, cumin, salt, and cornstarch and mix well to coat shrimps with spices. Lift shrimps one at a time by their tails and dip in toasted coconut, coating evenly but lightly. Arrange shrimps in the skillet in petal fashion, with tails toward the center, and cover with the lid.

3. Cook at 100 percent power in a 650- to 700-watt carousel oven for 1 minute 30 seconds (or until shrimps are just done). Remove from oven and uncover. Serve shrimps hot, at room temperature, or cold, sprinkled with lemon juice and preferably accompanied with Sweet and Spicy Tomato Sauce (p. 370) or Fragrant Mint Sauce (p. 366).

SESAME SHRIMP

TIL JHEENGA

MICROWAVE

Servings
  —4 as an appetizer; 2
    as a main course
Preparation time
  —7 minutes
Cooking time
  —1 minute
Heat
  —100 percent power
MW oven size
  —650 to 700 watts
MW cookware
  —One 10-inch cov-
    ered skillet

Similar to Bombay Coconut Shrimp (p. 11), these are spectacular with cocktails. Both sea scallops and jumbo shrimps can be substituted using the same technique. For a spicy version, add one fresh hot green chili, stemmed, seeded, and minced, and ⅓ teaspoon ground cumin to the marinade.

ROOM TEMPERATURE

½ pound medium-large shrimps (28–32 per pound)
½ teaspoon minced garlic
½ teaspoon crushed or grated fresh ginger
½ teaspoon cayenne pepper
¼ teaspoon kosher salt

½ teaspoon cornstarch
⅓ cup toasted sesame seeds, homemade (p. 464) or store-bought
¾ teaspoons nigella seeds (p. 483) (optional)
Juice of half a small lemon

1. Shell and devein shrimps, leaving the tails on, and wash thoroughly. Pat dry on kitchen towels and put them in a bowl. Add garlic, ginger, cayenne, salt, and cornstarch and mix well to coat shrimps with spices.

2. Combine sesame seeds and nigella seeds in a shallow dish. Lift shrimps one at a time by their tails and dip in seeds, coating evenly but lightly. Arrange shrimps on a 10-inch microwave-safe skillet in petal fashion, with tails toward the center, and cover with the lid.

3. Cook at 100 percent power in a 650- to 700-watt carousel oven for 1 minute (or until shrimps are just done). Remove from oven and uncover. Serve shrimps hot, at room temperature, or cold, sprinkled with lemon juice and accompanied by Sweet and Spicy Fruit Sauce (p. 376) or Instant Prune Dip (p. 369).

MENU SUGGESTION

For a complete meal, serve an earthy rice pilaf such as Whole Mung Bean and Basmati Pilaf (p. 316) and a light yogurt raita. A nice choice is Sweet Pepper and Yogurt Raita (p. 256).

WARM MUSTARD
SHRIMPS ON ENDIVE

ROI JHEENGA

MICROWAVE

Yield
—2 cups
Servings
—6 to 8 as a first
course; 3 to 4 as a
main course
Cooking time
—14 minutes
Heat
—100 percent power
MW oven size
—650 to 700 watts
MW cookware
—One 10-inch cov-
ered skillet

Bengal in east India is world famous for two of its natural resources, mustard greens and fish. This preparation represents the sublime union of these two ingredients. In Bengal, a variety of slightly sharp-bitter mustard greens are used, for which Belgian endive works very well. Both bay scallops and white non-oily fish can be substituted very effectively in this recipe. This is a fairly hot and spicy preparation. For a milder version eliminate green chilies from the recipe.

=== *ROOM TEMPERATURE* ===

3 tablespoons light
vegetable oil
½ teaspoon cumin seeds
½ teaspoon mustard
seeds
¼ teaspoon fennel seeds
5 medium-size (4
ounces) shallots,
peeled and chopped
⅓ cup heavy cream
2 teaspoons tomato paste
3 tablespoons Dijon
mustard
½ teaspoon dry mustard

1–2 fresh hot green
chilies, stemmed,
seeded, and thinly
sliced
1 pound frozen peeled
small shrimps, de-
frosted, or 1⅓ pounds
small shrimps, peeled,
deveined, and halved
¼ cup minced sweet
green pepper
¼ cup chopped fresh
coriander
2 medium-size endives,
leaves separated

1. Heat the oil in a 10-inch microwave-safe covered skillet in a 650- to 700-watt carousel oven at 100 percent power for 3 minutes. Uncover, add cumin seeds, mustard seeds, and fennel seeds, and replace the lid. Cook at 100 percent power for 2 minutes (or

until mustard seeds begin to pop). Uncover, add shallots, and mix well. Cook, uncovered, at 100 percent power for 4 minutes (or until shallots begin to color).

2. Remove from oven, stir in cream, tomato paste, Dijon mustard, dry mustard, and chilies. Cook, uncovered, at 100 percent power for 2 minutes (or until sauce is bubbling). Add shrimps and mix. Cook, covered, at 100 percent power for 2 minutes 30 seconds (or until shrimps turn pink). Remove from oven.

3. Fold in peppers and coriander. Arrange endive leaves, petal fashion, on a serving platter. Spoon about 2 teaspoons shrimps on each and serve.

MENU SUGGESTION

To complete the meal, follow this delightful appetizer with Moghul Cornish Hen in Apricot Glaze (p. 128) and a rice pilaf such as Moghul-scented Basmati Pilaf (p. 302).

FRESH CHEESE TUNA DIP

KHADA CHENNA MAACH

MICROWAVE

Yield
—1½ cups
Servings
—6
Preparation time
—5 minutes
Cooking time
—2 minutes
Heat
—100 percent power
MW oven size
—650 to 700 watts
MW cookware
—One 8-inch skillet

This is a delightful, delicious way to use freshly made homemade Indian cheese that also happens to be low in calories. Thinned with a little low-fat milk or water to a sauce consistency, use it over cooked fish or vegetables.

5 ounces Indian chenna cheese made with 4 cups milk (p. 456)
⅔ cup low-fat milk
½ can (6½ ounces) chunk tuna in water, drained and flaked
1 small clove garlic, peeled and minced
2 tablespoons lemon juice
3 tablespoons finely chopped onion
3 tablespoons finely chopped celery with leaves
1 tablespoon chopped fresh coriander
1 teaspoon curry powder, homemade (p. 479) or store-bought
Freshly ground black pepper, if desired
Kosher salt, if desired

1. Place *chenna* cheese, milk, tuna, garlic, and lemon juice in the container of food processor. Process until the contents are smooth and blended. (Or, alternatively, rub cheese through a fine sieve, using a wooden spoon, into a bowl. Blend in milk, tuna, garlic, lemon juice, beating vigorously.) Transfer cheese mixture into a serving bowl. Stir in onion, celery, and coriander.

2. Toast the curry powder in an 8-inch microwave-safe skillet in a 650- to 700-watt carousel oven at 100 percent power for 2 minutes. Remove from oven, then

immediately scrape the spice onto the cheese dip. Add pepper and salt, if desired. Mix well and serve.

NOTE   The dip may be stored in the refrigerator in a tightly covered container for up to 2 days.

MENU SUGGESTION

To complete the meal, follow this lovely dip with Stuffed Cabbage Rolls with Fragrant Tomato Sauce (p. 161) and Plain Basmati Rice (p. 299).

INDIAN CHEESE SPREAD

KHADA CHENNA

Here is a true dieter's delight. Made with low-fat milk cheese and herbs, it is very low in calories and cholesterol. The wonderful flavor of the spread comes from the cheese itself—freshly made and used while still warm, moist, and fragrant of citrus whey. Although the cheese can also be cooked on top of the stove, the microwave technique yields softer, more velvety curd. You can use any combination of herbs in this recipe.

=============== ROOM TEMPERATURE ===============

4 cups whole or low-fat milk

3 tablespoons lemon juice

2 tablespoons minced scallions

2 tablespoons finely chopped fresh coriander

1 tablespoon finely chopped fresh, or 1 teaspoon dried, basil

1 tablespoon canned green peppercorns (p. 483), drained, rinsed, and chopped, or 2 fresh hot green chilies, stemmed, seeded, and thinly sliced

Kosher salt to taste, if desired

1–2 curly purple-tinted lettuce leaves

1. Place a medium-size strainer or colander lined with a layer of cheesecloth over a large bowl.

2. Pour milk into an 8-cup glass measure or a 3-quart microwave-safe casserole. Cook, uncovered, at 100 percent power in a 650- to 700-watt carousel oven for 10 minutes (or until milk comes to a boil).

3. Add 2 tablespoons lemon juice and stir lightly. Almost immediately the milk will curdle—milky-white

---

curd will float to the surface and liquid whey will turn greenish-yellow. If the curd does not form, add remaining lemon juice and cook milk, uncovered, at 100 percent power for an additional 30 to 45 seconds. Remove from oven.

4. Turn mixture into the strainer or colander and drain. When whey has drained, press cheese lightly with the back of a spoon for 30 seconds (or until most of the excess whey has drained). Do not squeeze or apply too much pressure to drain cheese completely as the cheese will taste dry, tough, and flavorless. Remove cheese from cheesecloth and transfer into a bowl.

5. Add all other ingredients and mix, pressing and crushing large curds, until smooth and blended. If you do not intend to serve the spread within an hour, transfer cheese into a covered container and refrigerate for up to a day

6. To serve, mound cheese spread on a lettuce leaf arranged on a serving plate and surround with crackers and crudités.

MENU SUGGESTION

To complete the meal, follow this light and soothing appetizer with a fiery curry such as Duck Vendaloo (p. 130) or Zesty Lemon Coriander Chicken (p. 116) and Plain Basmati Rice (p. 299). The cheese also makes a fine luncheon entrée accompanied by a salad, such as Fragrant Cabbage Salad with Ginger Slivers and Tomatoes (p. 245).

SPICY WARM SHREDDED BEEF SPREAD

KEEMA GOSHT

This is a unique process in which meat is cooked for a long period without much liquid, thus producing a classic pan-dried, slightly chewy texture. This beef is fragrantly spicy but not hot and is very addictive. I have seen an entire batch of spread consumed within five minutes by just one person! For variation, use lean boneless pork or lamb cut into 1-inch cubes.

MICROWAVE

Yield
  —1½ cups
Servings
  —4
Cooking time
  —37 minutes
Standing time
  —5 minutes
Heat
  —100 percent power
MW oven size
  —650 to 700 watts
MW cookware
  *—One 10-inch cov-
    ered skillet*

============ *ROOM TEMPERATURE* ============

2 teaspoons ground coriander	1 tablespoon finely chopped garlic
1 teaspoon ground cumin	1 tablespoon finely chopped fresh ginger
½ teaspoon turmeric	¾ pound stewing beef, trimmed of excess fat
¼ teaspoon cayenne pepper	
3 tablespoons light vegetable oil	1 cup finely chopped tomatoes (fresh or canned, drained)
¾ cup finely chopped onion	1 cup water
	1 teaspoon kosher salt

1. Combine coriander, cumin, turmeric, and cayenne in a small bowl and reserve.

2. Place the oil in a 10-inch microwave-safe skillet, uncovered, in a 650- to 700-watt carousel oven. Heat at 100 percent power for 3 minutes. Add onion, garlic, and ginger, lightly mix, and cook at 100 percent power for 9 minutes (or until onions are lightly browned), stirring once. Blend in the spice mixture and continue cooking, uncovered, at 100 percent power for an additional 1 minute (or until spices exude a fried aroma). Remove from oven.

3. Add beef, tomatoes, water, and salt, mix well, and cover with the lid. Cook at 100 percent power for 24 minutes (or until the beef is cooked dry and the sauce is thick), stirring once.

4. Remove from oven, uncover, stir the beef, and re-place cover. Let the dish stand, covered, for 5 minutes. Transfer beef, together with its sauce, into the container of a food processor and process until coarsely ground, making sure not to overgrind and turn it into a paste. The spread should have little bits of chewy beef. Serve immediately accompanied with corn chips, toasted pita triangles, Toasted Lentil Wafers (p. 10), or Melba toast, or transfer to a microwave-safe dish and refrigerate.

NOTE   The beef spread may be made ahead and set aside, in a microwave-safe covered container, in the refrigerator for up to 4 days. Take out from the refrigerator and heat, partially covered, at 100 percent power for 2 minutes (or until heated through).

For a salt-free and low-calorie dish, omit oil and salt from the recipe. Combine all other ingredients and cook in a 1½-quart covered casserole at 100 percent power for 18 minutes. Remove from oven and proceed as suggested in the recipe.

MENU SUGGESTION

To complete the meal, follow this spicy and hearty beef spread with a fragrant stew such as Parsi Chicken Braised in Spiced Pumpkin-Lentil Puree (p. 124) and Parsi Caramelized Onion Pilaf (p. 301).

WARM CABBAGE SALAD WITH CRABMEAT AND MANGOES

MANGA PORIYAL

A classic from the western coast of India, this salad traditionally does not contain any seafood, but I like to add it because it tempers and binds the sweetness of mango with the spices and cabbage. You can use cooked lobster or crayfish in place of crab.

MICROWAVE

Yield
 —*6 cups*
Servings
 —*8 as a first course;*
 4 as a light main
 course
Cooking time
 —*14 minutes*
Heat
 —*100 percent power*
MW oven size
 —*650 to 700 watts*
MW cookware
 —*One 5-quart covered*
 casserole and one
 10-inch covered
 skillet

=============== *ROOM TEMPERATURE* ===============

1¼ *pounds (one medium head) green cabbage, cored and cut into ½-inch pieces*

2 *tablespoons light sesame oil or light vegetable oil*

1 *teaspoon mustard seeds*

½ *teaspoon minced garlic*

1 *fresh hot green chili, stemmed, seeded, and thinly sliced*

½ *teaspoon turmeric*

Kosher salt to taste

½ *pound (1 cup) flaked cooked crabmeat*

1 *medium-size, underripe mango, peeled, pitted, and meat cut into ½-inch pieces*

Juice of ½ small lemon

FOR THE GARNISH:

¼ *cup coconut flakes (sweetened or un-sweetened) (p. 449)*

3 *tablespoons chopped fresh coriander*

1. Place cabbage in 5-quart microwave-safe casserole and cover with the lid. Cook at 100 percent power in a 650- to 700-watt carousel oven for 7 minutes (or

until cabbage looks wilted and just cooked). Remove from oven. Set aside, covered, for cabbage to steam for 10 minutes. Uncover and drain cabbage.

2. Place the oil in a 10-inch microwave-safe covered skillet in a 650- to 700-watt carousel oven. Heat at 100 percent power for 3 minutes. Uncover, add mustard seeds, and replace the lid. Cook at 100 percent power for 3 minutes (or until seeds pop). Uncover and add garlic, green chilies, and turmeric. Cook at 100 percent power for 1 minute (or until garlic is cooked). Remove from oven. Add cabbage and salt to taste. Carefully mix, tossing and turning, to coat cabbage with the spice-infused oil.

3. Transfer cabbage to a serving platter. Arrange crab and mango on top and sprinkle with lemon juice. Garnish with coconut and coriander and serve, preferably accompanied with Toasted Lentil Wafers (p. 10).

MENU SUGGESTION

To complete the meal follow the salad with Goanese Spicy Braised Pork Chops (p. 159) and Plain Basmati Rice (p. 299). The salad also makes a light luncheon entrée accompanied with Bombay Spicy Lentil Cakes (p. 327).

GLAZED CUCUMBER AND SCALLOP SALAD WITH CORIANDER

MACHI CHAT

Fish salads are the specialty of Calcutta, Bombay, and Goa. This recipe from Calcutta is traditionally made with white nonoily fish and served with rice. I find the salad quite delicate and complete in itself. Both shrimp and gray sole cut into 1½-inch pieces work very well here.

2 tablespoons mustard oil
  or light vegetable oil
1 teaspoon finely
  chopped fresh ginger
1 fresh hot green chili,
  stemmed, seeded, and
  minced, or ⅛ teaspoon
  cayenne pepper
1½ teaspoons fragrant
  spice powder (p. 481)
2 medium-size (¾
  pound) cucumbers,
  peeled, seeded, and cut
  into ⅛-inch thick
  rounds

½ pound sea scallops,
  cut into ⅛-thick slices
2 teaspoons lemon juice
2 cups mung bean or soy
  bean sprouts or shred-
  ded iceberg lettuce
½ cup lightly packed
  coriander leaves with
  tender stems

1. Place the oil, ginger, chilies or cayenne, and spice powder in a 10-inch microwave-safe covered skillet in a 650- to 700-watt carousel oven. Cook at 100 percent power for 4 minutes (or until spices lose raw

aroma.) Remove from oven, uncover and add cucumber slices, and mix well.

2. Cook, uncovered, at 100 percent power for 2 minutes (or until cucumber slices turn slightly soft). Remove from oven. Fold in scallop slices and cover with the lid. Cook at 100 percent power for 1 minute (or until scallops turn white and are barely cooked). Remove from oven and let the dish rest, covered, for 3 minutes. Uncover and stir in lemon juice. Spread bean sprouts or shredded iceberg lettuce and coriander attractively on a platter. Mound salad on top and serve.

MENU SUGGESTION

To complete the meal, follow this subtle salad with Tandoori Cornish Hen (p. 113) and a rice pilaf such as Mango and Basmati Pilaf (p. 310).

WARM CRAYFISH, FENNEL, AND PINE NUT SALAD WITH DILL

MACHI BAGHARA

MICROWAVE

Yield
—4 cups
Servings
—6 as a first course;
3 as a light main
course
Cooking time
—14 minutes
Standing time
—3 minutes
Heat
—100 percent power
MW oven size
—650 to 700 watts
MW cookware
—One 2½-quart cov-
ered casserole and
one 10-inch covered
skillet

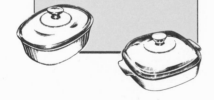

This dish was inspired by a local fishermen's specialty from the region along the western coast of India. When combined with sweet fennel and pine nuts in a mustard-infused oil dressing, the crayfish take on a subtle and sensuous dimension. If crayfish are unavailable, small- to medium-size shrimps make a fine substitute.

=== ROOM TEMPERATURE ===

3 (1¼ pounds) fennel
   bulbs, trimmed, rinsed,
   and cut into fine slices
2 tablespoons light vege-
   table oil
1 teaspoon mustard seeds
1 teaspoon minced garlic
2 fresh hot green chilies,
   stemmed, seeded, and
   shredded
⅓ teaspoon turmeric
¾ pound uncooked
   crayfish or small- to
   medium-size shrimps,
   peeled

2 tablespoons chopped
   fresh, or 2 teaspoons
   dried, dill
¼ cup sliced scallions
   (white and green
   parts)
Juice of ½ small lemon
Kosher salt to taste, if
   desired

FOR THE GARNISH:
¼ cup toasted pine nuts (p. 464)
Dill

1. Place fennel slices in a 2½-quart microwave-safe casserole and cover with the lid. Cook at 100 percent power in a 650- to 700-watt carousel oven for 5 minutes 30 seconds (or until fennel begins to steam and wilt). Do not overcook fennel or the licorice fragrance will be numbed. Remove from oven, uncover, mix, and replace cover. Set aside, covered, until needed.

2. Heat the oil in a 10-inch microwave-safe covered skillet in a 650- to 700-watt carousel oven at 100 percent power for 3 minutes. Remove from oven. Uncover, add mustard seeds, and replace lid. Cook at 100 percent power for 3 minutes (or until seeds pop). Uncover and add garlic, green chilies, and turmeric. Cook, uncovered, at 100 percent power for 30 seconds. Remove from oven. Add crayfish or shrimps. Mix well and cover with the lid.

3. Cook at 100 percent power for 2 minutes (or until seafood is just cooked). Remove from oven and uncover. Drain fennel and add it to the seafood along with dill and scallions and toss well. Season with lemon juice and salt, if desired, and transfer salad to a warm serving platter. Garnish with pine nuts and dill and serve.

MENU SUGGESTION

To complete the meal, serve Moghul Cornish Hen in Apricot Glaze (p. 128) and a rice such as Moghul-scented Basmati Pilaf (p. 302).

LENTIL SALAD IN CUMIN-CITRUS DRESSING

CHANE KI CHAT

MICROWAVE

Yield
—3 cups
Servings
—6
Preparation time
—5 minutes
Cooking time
—2 minutes
Standing time
—60 minutes
Heat
—100 percent power
MW oven size
—650 to 700 watts
MW cookware
—One 2½-quart cov-
    ered casserole

Composed of lentils with just a hint of orange, this salad is a smart addition to a buffet table, and perfect for cookouts, as it keeps well for several hours at room temperature. It also makes a fine side dish with chicken or duck as well as a stuffing for vegetables such as tomatoes and peppers.

===== *ROOM TEMPERATURE* =====

FOR THE DRESSING:
1 tablespoon minced
    garlic
1 cup finely chopped red
    onion
2 teaspoons fresh, or 1
    teaspoon dried, ore-
    gano or dill
1 teaspoon ground cumin

½ teaspoon dried ginger
    powder
2 tablespoons mustard
    oil or olive oil
2 tablespoons wine vine-
    gar
⅓ cup tomato puree
    (canned or fresh)
½ cup orange juice,
    fresh squeezed or
    canned

3 cups Cooked Brown
    Lentils (p. 279)
¼ cup minced scallions
1 tablespoon minced
    fresh coriander
Freshly ground black
    pepper to taste

2 endives, leaves sepa-
    rated, or 4 to 6 attrac-
    tive lettuce leaves
2 tablespoons toasted
    pine nuts (p. 464) or
    sliced almonds

1. Combine all the ingredients for the dressing in a 2½-quart microwave-safe casserole and beat with a whisk until thoroughly blended. Add cooked lentils

and toss well. Let salad rest, covered, for an hour, so that lentils absorb flavor, or refrigerate overnight. After removing from refrigerator, leave out for 30 minutes, or reheat, covered, in the same casserole, at 100 percent power in a 650- to 700-watt carousel oven for 2 minutes (or until salad loses its chill), stirring once.

2. Uncover, and toss in scallions and coriander. Season with black pepper. Arrange endive leaves in petal fashion, or place lettuce leaves, on a platter. Mound lentil salad in the center and spread nuts on top. Serve immediately.

VARIATIONS

CRAB AND LENTIL SALAD   Fold ½ pound cooked crabmeat into the salad before serving.

LENTIL AND MINCED CARROT SALAD   Add ½ cup minced tender carrots, 1 teaspoon minced green chilies, and 2 teaspoons lemon juice to the dressing for the lentils and marinate. Fold ⅓ cup sweetened coconut flakes into the salad before serving.

MENU SUGGESTION

To complete the meal, follow this hearty lentil salad with a chicken kabob such as Creamed Chicken Kabob (p. 111) and Cream of Wheat Pilaf with Tomatoes and Green Peas (p. 320).

BLACK-EYED PEA AND DICED RED PEPPER SALAD

LOBHIA CHAT

MICROWAVE

Yield
—3 cups
Servings
—8
Preparation time
—5 minutes
Heat
—100 percent power
MW oven size
—650 to 700 watts
MW cookware
—One 2-cup glass
measure

Black-eyed peas or, more correctly, beans are very popular with Indians, probably because of their unique character, which falls somewhere between legume and vegetable, giving them a less mealy yet meaty flavor. This salad is great for cookouts or buffets because of its exceptional keeping quality. Thinned with tomato or vegetable juice and coarsely pureed it makes a comforting soup.

=============== ROOM TEMPERATURE ===============

3 cups Cooked Black-
eyed Peas made with 1
cup dried black-eyed
peas (p. 292)
2 large (¾ pound) sweet
red peppers, cored,
seeded, and diced into
¼-inch pieces

1 medium-size cucumber,
peeled, seeded, and
diced into ¼-inch
cubes
½ cup thinly sliced scal-
lions (white and green
parts)
½ cup loosely packed
chopped fresh
coriander

FOR THE DRESSING:
3 tablespoons lemon juice
4 tablespoons light vege-
table oil
1 teaspoon minced garlic
1 tablespoon finely
chopped fresh ginger

2 teaspoons ground
roasted cumin seeds
(p. 465)
2 or more fresh hot
green chilies, stemmed,
seeded, and thinly
sliced

1 tablespoon minced
   fresh, or 1 teaspoon
   crushed dried, mint
Kosher salt to taste

5–6 attractive grape
   leaves or lettuce leaves

1. Place peas, peppers, cucumbers, and scallions in a medium-size mixing bowl.

2. Combine all the ingredients for the dressing in a 2-cup glass measure, whisk until thoroughly blended, and pour over the peas; toss well. Arrange grape or lettuce leaves on a serving platter, mound salad on top, and serve. The salad keeps well for several hours at room temperature. Refrigeration is not advised as it hardens the peas.

VARIATION

BLACK-EYED PEA AND CRACKED WHEAT SALAD   Substitute 2 large red ripe tomatoes, diced into ½-inch cubes, in place of sweet red peppers and double the recommended quantity of mint. Fold ½ cup bulgur, soaked for 4 hours in enough water to cover by at least an inch, drained through double layers of cheesecloth and squeezed dry, into the salad.

MENU SUGGESTION

To complete the meal, follow this robust salad with a light entrée such as Steamed Fish in Ginger-Thyme Essence (p. 81) and a fruity chutney such as Pineapple Apricot Chutney (p. 351).

SOUPS

$\mathcal{S}$oup is the most versatile course of a meal. When light and dominated by broth, it is an invigorating and palate-stimulating starter. Thick and hearty, it is substantial, the centerpiece of a light meal. Warm and steamy, it is comforting fare on a winter's night. Chilled, it refreshes the taste buds and the soul on a hot day.

Making soup conjures up images of day-long stirring, simmering, and watching. Yet the process of making soup in the microwave is neither tiresome nor labor-intensive. In most cases, you merely combine all the ingredients and cook. Soups that normally take two hours or more—such as Grandmother's Tomato Lentil Soup—can be made in less than an hour because the lentils cook so quickly. The result is a fresh, flavorful soup that requires little or no advance planning. And the soups here keep well for several days in the refrigerator. To reheat, cook, uncovered, at 100 percent power; one cup of soup takes two minutes, four cups take four minutes, and eight cups take nine minutes, stirring once.

These soups can be made with almost any cooking liquid: meat or chicken stock, vegetarian broth, or water. But I have created and tested them using only water, and the results are extraordinarily delicious. Although meat broth makes the soups more substantial and vibrant, it is far from essential. This will come as no surprise to anyone familiar with Indian cooking, who knows that the perfumed flavors come from highly aromatic herbs and spices.

In addition, the vegetables in microwave-cooked soup remain whole and colorful, rather than disintegrating into mush. Fragrant Cauliflower and Fennel Soup, for example, contains whole pieces of tasty cauliflower and licorice-scented fennel. No matter which soup you cook, the microwave gives you more control over texture; the soup's thickness is determined by the amount of stock and vegetables you puree. And vegetable flavors remain bold and pure.

Many dal and legume dishes (pp. 265 to 296), fragrant sauces (pp. 365 to 376), and yogurt raitas (pp. 251 to 264), thinned with a little liquid, also make lovely soups.

ASSAM AROMATIC LENTIL BROTH WITH SPINACH

PALAK DAL SHORVA

There is something very honest and soul-soothing about "down-home" cooking such as this refined lentil and spinach-leaf soup from the Darjeeling tea region. Both red lentils and mung beans have a natural affinity for spinach. So do cumin, coriander, and mustard and therefore, can be used interchangeably. The only problem is figuring out the right etiquette for handling the whole spinach leaves. Some even use a fork. Personally, I like drama at the table, which makes for a scintillating dining experience, but to make matters simpler you could chop the spinach.

MICROWAVE

Yield
—6½ cups
Servings
—6 to 8
Preparation time
—4 minutes
Cooking time
—18 minutes
Heat
—100 percent power
MW oven size
—650 to 700 watts
MW cookware
—One 5-quart covered
  casserole and one 8-
  inch covered skillet

========= ROOM TEMPERATURE =========

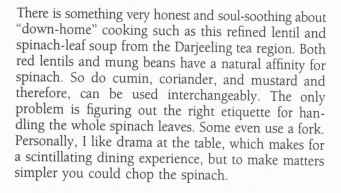

4 medium-size (1 pound)
  red ripe tomatoes
1-inch piece fresh ginger,
  peeled
2 or more fresh hot
  green chilies, stemmed
  and cut into 1-inch
  pieces

4 cups Red (Pink) Lentil
  Broth (p. 268) or
  Mung Broth (p. 490)
  or Instant Mung Broth
  (p. 491)
2 teaspoons ground
  cumin
2 teaspoons ground
  coriander
1 teaspoon minced fresh,
  or ½ teaspoon dried,
  thyme

FOR THE SPICE-INFUSED
OIL:
2 tablespoons light vege-
table oil

1 teaspoon mustard
seeds, crushed
1 teaspoon minced garlic
or ⅓ teaspoon ground
asafetida (p. 481)

FOR THE GARNISH:
2 tablespoons minced
fresh coriander
6–8 lemon wedges

1 pound fresh tender
small spinach leaves,
rinsed and left whole
or chopped
1 tablespoon lemon juice
2 teaspoons kosher salt,
or to taste

MENU SUGGESTION

Follow the soup with Butter
Cornish Hen (p. 126) or Indian Paneer Cheese and Peas
in Fragrant Tomato Sauce
(p. 179) accompanied with
Split Pea and Basmati Pilaf
(p. 314) and a cool raita
such as Spicy Potato and Yogurt Raita (p. 260).

1. Place tomatoes, ginger, and chilies into the container of a food processor and process until finely
pureed. Transfer tomato mixture into a 5-quart microwave-safe casserole. Add bean or lentil broth, cumin,
coriander, and thyme. Stir to mix.

2. Cook, uncovered, at 100 percent power in a 650-
to 700-watt carousel oven for 10 minutes (or until
soup is boiling and tomato loses its uncooked aroma).
Add spinach and cover with the lid. Continue cooking at 100 percent power for an additional 1 minute
(or until spinach just wilts). Remove from oven.

3. Uncover, stir in lemon juice and salt, and replace
cover.

4. Heat the oil in an 8-inch microwave-safe covered
skillet at 100 percent power for 3 minutes. Uncover,
add mustard seeds, and replace the lid. Cook at 100
percent power for 3 minutes (or until seeds pop). Uncover and add the garlic or asafetida. Cook, uncovered, for 30 seconds (or until garlic turns light golden).

5. Uncover soup. Pour the spice-infused oil on soup,
scraping the skillet with a rubber spatula to get all
the seasoning, and mix well. Ladle soup into soup
bowls and serve garnished with coriander and lemon
wedges.

CLASSIC PEPPERED TAMARIND SOUP

MULGATAWNI

MICROWAVE

Yield
  —6½ cups
Servings
  —6 to 8
Preparation time
  —3 minutes
Cooking time
  —13 to 15 minutes
Heat
  —100 percent power
MW oven size
  —650 to 700 watts
MW cookware
  —One 8-cup glass
    measure and one
    10-inch covered
    skillet

This mustard-fragrant tamarind soup, with its sweetish-sour flavor and hint of pepper, is very refreshing in any season. Since its consistency is more like a broth, the soup is best served in a deep bowl or in a generous-sized teacup.

════════════ *ROOM TEMPERATURE* ════════════

⅔ cup, or 5 frozen cubes, tamarind juice (p. 492)

5 cups water

4 teaspoons sambaar powder, homemade (p. 480) or store-bought

1½ tablespoons sugar

2 teaspoons kosher salt

1 teaspoon mustard seeds

½ teaspoon ground asafetida (p. 481) or 1 teaspoon minced garlic

3 medium-size (¾ pound) red ripe tomatoes, cut into ½-inch-thick wedges

3 tablespoons chopped fresh coriander

FOR THE SPICE-INFUSED OIL:

2 tablespoons light sesame oil or light vegetable oil

1. Place tamarind juice or cubes and 1 cup water in an 8-cup glass measure. Cook at 100 percent power in a 650- to 700-watt carousel oven for 1 to 3 minutes (or until tamarind cubes, if used, melt and the liquid is warm.) Add *sambaar* powder, sugar, and salt and continue cooking at 100 percent power for an additional 4 minutes (or until spices and tamarind lose their uncooked aroma). Add the remaining 4 cups water. Cook at 100 percent power for 9 minutes (or until soup boils). Remove from oven and set aside.

2. Heat the oil in a 10-inch microwave-safe covered skillet at 100 percent power for 3 minutes. Uncover, add mustard seeds, and replace the lid. Cook at 100 percent power for 3 minutes (or until seeds pop). Remove from oven, uncover, and stir in asafetida or garlic. Add tomatoes and mix, turning and tossing, to coat with oil.

3. Cook, uncovered, at 100 percent power for 2 minutes (or until tomatoes are barely cooked). Remove from oven.

4. Uncover soup. Add the tomato mixture to the soup. Mix well and ladle into cups or soup bowls. Serve sprinkled with coriander.

MENU SUGGESTION

The soup is extremely light, therefore, for a substantial meal, serve Lamb in Creamy Tomato Sauce (p. 151) or Spinach Dumplings in Yogurt Sauce (p. 198) accompanied with any of the rice pilafs (pp. 301–321), chutneys (pp. 337–358), and yogurt raitas (pp. 251–264).

GRANDMOTHER'S TOMATO LENTIL SOUP

TAMATO RASAM

MICROWAVE

Yield
  —*6 cups*
Servings
  —*6 to 8*
Preparation time
  —*2 minutes*
Cooking time
  —*21 minutes*
Heat
  —*100 percent power*
MW oven size
  —*650 to 700 watts*
MW cookware
  —*One 3-quart covered
    casserole and one 8-
    inch covered skillet*

Traditionally this soup is made with lentil broth, but I add chicken or meat stock because they mellow and enhance the starchy flavor of lentils. A plush blend of lentils, tomato, and curry spices, this soup is a classic from Tanjore in southern India, the home of my paternal grandmother, who nourished me with this soup during her many visits to our home in the north.

━━━━━━ *ROOM TEMPERATURE* ━━━━━━

2½ cups Pureed Yellow Lentils or American Yellow Split Peas (p. 272) or Cooked Red (Pink) Lentil Puree (p. 267)

1 cup cooked rice (optional)

1 tablespoon lemon juice, or to taste

Kosher salt to taste

1½ cups peeled crushed tomatoes (fresh or canned)

2 cups chicken or meat stock, homemade (p. 488) or store-bought, or water

¼ cup minced onion

1½ tablespoons curry powder, homemade (p. 479) or store-bought

---

FOR THE SPICE-INFUSED OIL:

1½ tablespoons light vegetable oil

¾ teaspoon mustard seeds

1 teaspoon minced garlic

3 tablespoons chopped fresh coriander

1. Combine lentil or pea puree, tomatoes, stock, onion, and curry powder in a 3-quart microwave-safe dish and cover with the lid.

2. Cook at 100 percent power in a 650- to 700-watt carousel oven for 14 minutes (or until soup is gently boiling). Add rice during the last minute of cooking. Remove from oven and stir in lemon juice and salt to taste.

3. Heat the oil in an 8-inch microwave-safe covered skillet at 100 percent power for 3 minutes. Uncover, add mustard seeds, and replace the lid. Cook at 100 percent power for 3 minutes (or until seeds pop). Uncover and stir in garlic. Cook, uncovered, at 100 percent power for 1 minute. Remove from oven. Pour the spice-infused oil on the soup, scraping the skillet with a rubber spatula to get every bit of the seasoning. Mix thoroughly and ladle soup into soup bowls, and serve sprinkled with coriander.

MENU SUGGESTION

To complete the meal, follow the soup with any dish that does not contain legumes or tomatoes, such as Moghul-braised Veal in Garlic Sauce (p. 149) or Moghul Vegetables in Cream Sauce (p. 173), Saffron Pilaf (p. 304), yogurt raita, *and chutney.*

WINTER WARM TOMATO-LENTIL BROTH

DAL SHORVA

This is a spicy and fragrant palate-warming soup. It is also very quick and easy to make because I substitute cooked canned chick-peas in place of lentils. It will take even less time if you use hot water in the recipe.

MICROWAVE

Yield
  —9 cups
Servings
  —8 to 12
Cooking time
  —26 minutes
Heat
  —100 percent power
MW oven size
  —650 to 700 watts
MW cookware
  —One 5-quart covered casserole and one 8-inch covered skillet

=============== *ROOM TEMPERATURE* ===============

1½ cups chopped tomatoes (fresh or canned, drained)	2 teaspoons ground cumin
1 19-ounce can chick-peas with its liquid	½ teaspoon cayenne pepper
¼ cup minced onion	¼ teaspoon freshly ground black pepper
1 teaspoon minced garlic	5 cups water
1-inch cube fresh ginger, peeled	2 tablespoons lemon juice
1 tablespoon ground coriander	1 tablespoon sugar
	1 tablespoon kosher salt, or to taste

FOR THE SPICE-INFUSED OIL:	¾ teaspoon mustard seeds
1½ tablespoons light vegetable oil	
	3 tablespoons chopped fresh coriander

1. Place tomatoes, chick-peas and liquid, onion, garlic, and ginger in the container of a blender or food processor and process until liquefied or finely puréed. Transfer puree into a 5-quart microwave-safe dish. Add ground coriander, cumin, cayenne, black pepper, water, lemon juice, sugar, and salt and cover with the lid.

2. Cook at 100 percent power in a 650- to 700-watt carousel oven for 20 minutes (or until soup is gently boiling). Remove from oven and uncover.

3. Heat the oil in an 8-inch microwave-safe covered skillet at 100 percent power for 3 minutes. Uncover, add mustard seeds, and replace the lid. Cook at 100 percent power for 3 minutes (or until seeds pop). Remove from oven. Uncover and pour the spice-infused oil on the soup. Add fresh coriander and mix thoroughly. Ladle soup into cups or mugs and serve immediately.

MENU SUGGESTION

This soup is marvelous to sip by a fire, followed by Chicken Frazer (p. 120) or Shrimp in Fiery Goanese Vendaloo Sauce (p. 99), Steamed Rice Cakes with Herbs (p. 332), and Sweet Cranberry Pistachio Chutney with California Black Figs (p. 344).

AUTUMN TOMATO SOUP WITH SPICY CROUTONS

TAMATAR KA SHORVA

MICROWAVE

Yield
  —6 cups
Servings
  —8
Preparation time
  —5 minutes
Cooking time
  —13 minutes
Heat
  —100 percent power
MW oven size
  —650 to 700 watts
MW cookware
  *—One 2½-quart cov-
    ered casserole or
    soufflé dish*

Even if you don't like tomatoes, you will still love this creamy soup—a true palate-awakener on a cool autumn evening. Besides, the soup couldn't be easier to make. All you need to do is puree the ingredients and "zap" in the microwave!

=========== ROOM TEMPERATURE ===========

1 28-ounce can peeled Italian tomatoes, or 2½ cups (4 medium-size) peeled, chopped fresh tomatoes	1 teaspoon dry mustard
	¼ teaspoon ground clove
	1 teaspoon sugar
	2 tablespoons prune butter (p. 462)
2 large cloves garlic, peeled	1½ cups whole or low-fat milk
1 tablespoon fragrant spice powder (p. 481)	1 cup heavy cream

FOR THE GARNISH:
1 cup spicy croutons (p. 487)

1. Place all the ingredients except heavy cream and croutons in the container of a blender or food processor and process until liquified or smoothly pureed. Pour the tomato mixture into a 2½-quart microwave-safe dish and cover with the lid.

2. Cook at 100 percent power in a 650- to 700-watt carousel oven for 12 minutes (or until soup is boiling). Uncover, add cream, and replace cover. Continue cooking at 100 percent power for 1 minute (or until soup is heated through). Remove from oven.

Uncover, and ladle piping-hot soup into soup bowls. Distribute spicy croutons on top and serve.

NOTE   The soup may be set aside before adding cream and stored in a microwave-safe container for 4 hours at room temperature or up to 3 days in the refrigerator or frozen. Reheat in the same container, partially covered, add cream, and serve.

MENU SUGGESTION

To complete the meal, follow this soup with a substantial stew such as Parsi Chicken Braised in Spiced Pumpkin-Lentil Puree (p. 124) or Malabar Vegetable Stew with Coconut (p. 187) and some rice. A nice choice would be Crisp Okra and Spiced Basmati Pilaf (p. 306) or Parsi Caramelized Onion Pilaf (p. 301).

CREAM OF EGGPLANT SOUP WITH CORIANDER
BAIGAN KA SHORVA

Subtle and velvety, this soup bursts with the fragrance of coriander, for it is added in three forms and at three different stages. First ground coriander is cooked into the broth to lend a piquant-woodsy flavor, then the herb is infused into the hot soup, and last smoky ground roasted coriander seed is sprinkled on the soup to mellow and bind the fragrance of eggplant with the other ingredients. For best results use only fresh, tender young eggplants that feel firm to the touch and use a blender to liquify soup—to ensure satiny smoothness. The soup stays grainy pureed in a food processor, although its flavor is just as good.

MICROWAVE

Yield
 —5 cups
Servings
 —6
Preparation time
 —5 minutes
Cooking time
 —12 minutes
Heat
 —100 percent power
MW oven size
 —650 to 700 watts
MW cookware
 —One 2½-quart covered casserole or soufflé dish

=============== ROOM TEMPERATURE ===============

2 small or 1 medium-size eggplant (about 1½ pounds), cut into 1-inch cubes
1 cup 1-inch-cube potatoes
½ cup sliced shallots
2 cups chopped peeled tomatoes with juices (fresh or canned)
2 teaspoons finely chopped garlic
¼ cup lightly packed coriander leaves and tender stems

2 teaspoons chopped fresh, or 1 teaspoon dried, thyme
2–4 fresh hot green chilies, stemmed and seeded
1 tablespoon ground coriander
½ teaspoon turmeric
3 cups chicken or meat broth, homemade (p. 488) or store-bought, or water
½–¾ cup heavy cream
Kosher salt to taste

2 tablespoons minced
    fresh coriander

1 teaspoon ground
    roasted coriander
    seeds (p. 466)

FOR THE GARNISH:

6 coriander sprigs   6 lemon slices

MENU SUGGESTION

To complete the meal, serve Fragrant Beef with Peas I (p. 143) or II (p. 145) or Potatoes and Peas Vendaloo (p. 177) and a rice dish such as Coconut Rice (p. 300), Toasted Lentil Wafers (p. 10), and a fruity chutney.

1. Combine eggplant, potatoes, shallots, tomatoes, garlic, chopped coriander, thyme, chilies, ground coriander, turmeric, and half the broth in a 2½-quart microwave dish and cover with the lid. Cook at 100 percent power in a 650- to 700-watt carousel oven for 12 minutes (or until vegetables are soft). Remove from oven.

2. Process soup in batches in a blender or food processor until the contents are liquefied, using additional broth as necessary. Return soup to the dish. Add the remaining broth and ½ cup heavy cream. Stir to mix. Check and add water or milk to thin soup to desired consistency. Stir in salt to taste and fresh coriander. Serve soup hot or chilled, ladled into soup bowls, sprinkled with roasted coriander, and garnished with coriander sprigs and lemon slices.

NOTE   The soup may be made ahead and stored in a microwave-safe covered container in the refrigerator for up to 3 days. Reheat, partially covered, at 100 percent power for 5 minutes (or until soup is heated through). Remove from oven. Serve garnished as suggested above.

CREAMY SCALLOP SOUP

MACHI KA SHORVA

MICROWAVE

Yield
   —3 cups
Servings
   —4
Preparation time
   —3 minutes
Cooking time
   —10 minutes
Heat
   —100 percent power
MW oven size
   —650 to 700 watts
MW cookware
   —One 2½-quart cov-
   ered casserole or
   soufflé dish

The sweetness in this soup is lent by two ingredients—coconut and onions. It is the fennel, however, that heightens the sweet flavor of the scallops. For variation, use shrimp, crab, or lobster in place of scallops or use them in combination.

========= ROOM TEMPERATURE =========

1½ tablespoons corn-
   starch
2 cups coconut milk
   (p. 450), or use 1 cup
   coconut milk and 1 cup
   light cream or milk
3 tablespoons light
   vegetable oil
1 medium-size onion,
   minced
1 tablespoon minced
   garlic
1 tablespoon ground
   coriander
¼ teaspoon ground
   fennel

¼ teaspoon turmeric
¼ teaspoon cayenne
   pepper
1 pound bay scallops,
   trimmed of tough
   muscle
Kosher salt to taste
2 teaspoons lemon juice
1 fresh hot or mild green
   chili, stemmed, seeded,
   and minced
1 tablespoon finely
   minced fresh coriander
   leaves

1. Dissolve cornstarch in coconut milk in a small bowl and set aside.

2. Combine oil, onion, garlic, coriander, fennel, turmeric, and cayenne in a 2½-quart microwave-safe dish. Cook, uncovered, at 100 percent power for 5 minutes

(or until onions and spices are cooked). Stir in scallops and coconut mixture and cover with a lid.

3. Cook at 100 percent power for an additional 5 minutes (or until scallops are barely cooked and liquid is piping hot.) Take out the dish from oven and add salt to taste. Stir in lemon juice and chilies. Ladle soup into soup bowls and serve sprinkled with coriander.

MENU SUGGESTION

This scallop soup is rich and filling. All you need is a pilaf and a vegetable dish or a salad and some bread to complete the meal.

MOGHUL PISTACHIO SOUP

PISHTE KA SHORVA

MICROWAVE

Yield
—*7 cups*
Servings
—*6 to 8*
Preparation time
—*3 minutes*
Cooking time
—*20 minutes*
Heat
—*100 percent power*
MW oven size
—*650 to 700 watts*
MW cookware
—*One 5-quart covered casserole*

This exquisitely flavored cream of pistachio soup is served at the royal feasts and official presidential banquets in India. The Moghul *garam masala*, a spice blend aromatic with cardamom, cinnamon, and clove, lends the soup its spicy-rich flavor. The soup's sweetness and emerald color come not from the pistachio nuts, as one might guess, but from the tender, sweet green peas. But it is the pistachio nuts that, finally, velvetize and temper the soup to such a sublime level.

=== ROOM TEMPERATURE ===

FOR THE SOUP:
1 cup chopped cauli-
flower
½ cup chopped carrots
½ cup chopped green
pepper
½ cup chopped shallots
or onions
1 10-ounce package fro-
zen green peas
¼-inch piece fresh gin-
ger, peeled and
roughly chopped
1 fresh hot green chili,
stemmed and chopped
½ cup blanched, sliced
almonds
2 tablespoons shelled raw
unsalted pistachio nuts

¾ teaspoon Moghul
garam masala
(p. 477)
1 cup whole milk

3 cups chicken stock,
homemade (p. 488) or
store-bought, or milk
1½ teaspoons kosher
salt, or to taste
¼ teaspoon or more
freshly ground white
pepper
1½ tablespoons lemon
juice, or to taste
½ cup heavy cream

FOR THE GARNISH:

¼ cup sliced unsalted pistachio nuts

1. Combine all the ingredients for cooking the soup in a 5-quart microwave-safe dish and cover with a lid. Cook at 100 percent power in a 650- to 700-watt carousel oven for 12 minutes (or until vegetables are cooked soft). Remove from oven.

2. In a blender or food processor, process the vegetable mixture in two batches until completely liquefied or pureed, using ⅔ cup stock.

3. Return soup to the dish. Add the remaining broth, and salt and pepper to taste. If the soup looks thick, stir in a few tablespoons of milk or water and thin to desired consistency, and cover with the lid. Serve soup hot or chilled. To heat, cook at 100 percent power for 8 minutes (or until piping hot). Remove from oven.

4. Uncover and stir in lemon juice and cream. Serve soup ladled into soup bowls, garnished with the pistachio nuts.

NOTE The soup may be kept stored in a microwave-safe covered container in the refrigerator for up to 3 days. Reheat, partially covered, at 100 percent power for 5 minutes (or until heated through).

MENU SUGGESTION

For an elegant meal, follow the soup with Goanese Roast Pork with Cinnamon-Ginger Gravy (p. 157), Coconut Rice (p. 300), Broccoli in Spicy-Garlic Oil (p. 205), and Moghul Saffron and Mango Yogurt Raita (p. 254).

CREAM OF VEGETABLE SOUP

SABZI SHORVA

MICROWAVE

Yield
—*7 cups*
Servings
—*6 to 8*
Preparation time
—*3 minutes*
Cooking time
—*20 minutes*
Heat
—*100 percent power*
MW oven size
—*650 to 700 watts*
MW cookware
—*One 5-quart covered casserole*

A delightful soup to bring out the essence of vegetables. Make it when you have farm-fresh vegetables.

=================== *ROOM TEMPERATURE* ===================

FOR THE SOUP:

1 cup chopped cauli-flower
½ cup chopped carrots
2 cups chopped tomatoes (fresh or canned) with juices
½ cup chopped shallots or onions
1 10-ounce package frozen green peas
¼-inch piece fresh ginger, peeled and roughly chopped
1 fresh hot green chili, stemmed and chopped
½ cup peeled, blanched, sliced almonds

2 tablespoons shelled, raw, unsalted pistachio nuts
1 teaspoon fragrant spice powder (p. 481)
1 cup whole milk

3 cups chicken stock, homemade (p. 488) or store-bought, or milk
1½ teaspoons kosher salt, or to taste
¼ teaspoon or more freshly ground white pepper
1½ tablespoons lemon juice, or to taste
½ cup heavy cream

FOR THE GARNISH:
1 cup spicy croutons (p. 487)

1. Combine all the ingredients for cooking the soup in a 5-quart microwave-safe dish and cover with a lid. Cook at 100 percent power in a 650 to 700-watt carousel oven for 12 minutes (or until vegetables are cooked soft). Remove from the oven.

2. In a blender or food processor, process the vegetable mixture in two batches until completely liquefied or pureed, using ⅔ cup stock.

3. Return soup to the dish. Add the remaining broth, and salt and pepper to taste. If the soup looks thick, stir in a few tablespoons of milk or water and thin to desired consistency, and cover with the lid. Serve soup hot or chilled. To heat, cook at 100 percent power for 8 minutes (or until piping hot). Remove from oven.

4. Uncover and stir in lemon juice and cream. Serve soup ladled into soup bowls, garnished with the spicy croutons.

NOTE   The soup may be kept stored in a microwave-safe covered container in the refrigerator for up to 3 days. Reheat, partially covered, at 100 percent power for 5 minutes (or until heated through).

MENU SUGGESTION

Follow the soup with Tandoori Cornish Hen (p. 113), Saffron Pilaf (p. 304), and Broccoli in Spicy-Garlic Oil (p. 205).

CHILLED SUMMER YOGURT SOUP

DAHI SHORVA

MICROWAVE

Yield
  —6 cups
Servings
  —6
Preparation time
  —5 minutes

For centuries Indians have enjoyed yogurt soup fla- vored with every imaginable spice and herb to beat the heat and humidity. Its consistency, seasonings, and presentation vary from region to region. In north In- dia it is served in unglazed terra-cotta cups, while in southern India it is eaten in freshly made banana-leaf bowls or hollowed-out coconut shells. But one rule never changes: The Brahmins do not use garlic (con- sidered a warm seasoning and an aphrodisiac by Hindu dietary laws) for fear of evoking the forbidden "sen- suous pleasures."

2 cups water
⅓ cup packed sweetened
  coconut flakes (p. 449)
1-inch cube fresh ginger,
  peeled
1 medium-size clove
  garlic, peeled
1 small green pepper,
  cored and seeded
1 medium-size cucumber,
  peeled, seeded, and
  coarsely chopped
¼ cup loosely packed
  fresh, or 2 tablespoons
  crushed dried, mint

¼ cup loosely packed
  fresh, or 1 tablespoon
  dried, dill
1 teaspoon roasted
  ground cumin seeds
  (p. 465) or fragrant
  spice powder (p. 481)
3 cups plain low-fat or
  nonfat yogurt
Freshly ground black
  pepper to taste
Kosher salt to taste

FOR THE GARNISH:

½ *pint red raspberries,*
or 1 large tomato,
halved, seeded, and
finely diced

3 *tablespoons chopped*
roasted pistachio nuts
or walnuts (p. 463)
Mint sprigs

MENU SUGGESTION

To complete the meal, follow the soup with Ooty-style Sole in Fragrant Tomato Sauce (p. 83) or Braised Okra with Spices and Tomatoes (p. 167), a rice pilaf such as Whole Mung Bean and Basmati Pilaf (p. 314), a cool salad, and a fruity chutney.

1. Place all the ingredients for the soup except yogurt, black pepper, and salt into the container of a blender or food processor and process until finely pureed. Transfer the mixture into a deep bowl. Add yogurt and beat the mixture with a whisk until it is smoothly blended. Add pepper and salt to taste.

2. To serve, stir soup thoroughly and ladle into soup bowls. Distribute raspberries and pistachios on top and garnish with mint sprigs.

NOTE   The soup may be made ahead and kept, covered, in the refrigerator for up to 3 days.

CHILLED INDIAN-SUMMER TOMATO SOUP

TAMATAR SHORVA

MICROWAVE

Yield
  —6 cups
Servings
  —6
Preparation time
  —5 minutes

Nothing could be simpler than this recipe. All you do is put the ingredients in the food processor or blender and puree to a velvety cream. The soup is flavored with one of two spice blends. The fragrant spice powder, as the name suggests, is mild and aromatic, while the spicy curry powder is hot and spicy.

1 28-ounce can peeled Italian tomatoes, with the juices
2 large cloves garlic, peeled
2 tablespoons prune butter (p. 462) or 1 tablespoon tamarind concentrate (p. 491)

1 tablespoon fragrant spice powder (p. 481) or curry powder, homemade (p. 479) or store-bought
1 teaspoon dry mustard
1/4 teaspoon ground allspice
1/4 teaspoon freshly ground white pepper
1 1/2 cups milk
1/2 cup heavy cream

FOR THE GARNISH:
1/4 cup loosely packed coriander sprigs

1/4 cup loosely packed basil leaves

Combine all the ingredients except heavy cream and herbs and process in a blender or food processor until completely liquefied, in batches if necessary. Pour soup into 6 soup bowls. Distribute cream on top, lightly swirling it in, and serve garnished with coriander and basil.

MENU SUGGESTION

For a light summer meal, follow the soup with Steamed Fish in Ginger-Thyme Essence (p. 81), Peach Chutney with Raisins and Walnuts (p. 349), and a rice pilaf such as Split Pea and Basmati Pilaf (p. 314).

CHILLED ESSENCE OF SHALLOT SOUP

PIAZ SHORVA

MICROWAVE

Yield
—*7 cups*

Servings
—*6 to 8*

Preparation time
—*5 minutes plus
additional time for
chilling*

Cooking time
—*6 minutes*

Heat
—*100 percent power*

MW oven size
—*650 to 700 watts*

MW cookware
—*One 2½-quart cov-
ered casserole or
soufflé dish*

When fully cooked, shallots exude a spicy fragrance but taste sweet, even sweeter than garlic or onion. In this soup, their sweetness is accentuated by coconut milk while the citrus tempers their fragrance. Accompanied by a salad and some wafers or bread, this makes a fabulous light meal.

═════════════ *ROOM TEMPERATURE* ═════════════

6 medium-size (⅓ pound) shallots, peeled and quartered

1 large (½ pound) baking potato, peeled and cut into ½-inch cubes

½ tablespoon chopped fresh ginger

1 fresh hot green chili, stemmed and cut into ½-inch pieces

2 teaspoons curry powder, homemade (p. 479) or store-bought

2 teaspoons sugar

2 cups coconut milk (p. 450) or whole milk or their combination

1 cup orange juice (fresh squeezed or frozen)

2 teaspoons lemon juice, or to taste

Freshly ground black pepper to taste

1 teaspoon kosher salt, or to taste

½ cup heavy cream

FOR THE GARNISH:
1 cup spicy croutons (p. 487) (optional)

1. Place shallots, potatoes, ginger, green chili, curry powder, sugar, and ½ cup coconut milk in a 2½-quart microwave-safe dish and cover with the lid. Cook at 100 percent power in a 650- to 700-watt carousel oven for 6 minutes (or until potatoes are cooked soft). Remove from oven.

2. Transfer the potato mixture into the container of a food processor and process until pureed but not liquified, using remaining coconut milk. Return soup to the dish and stir in orange juice. Check consistency and add a little milk or water to thin soup as desired. Stir in lemon juice, pepper, and salt to taste. Cover and chill. Just before serving add cream and mix thoroughly. Ladle soup into soup bowls and serve, if desired, garnished with spicy croutons.

NOTE   The soup keeps well stored in a covered container in the refrigerator for up to 5 days.

MENU SUGGESTION

The soup is quite substantial by itself; therefore serve a light main course such as Moghul Shrimp in Fragrant Tomato Sauce (p. 95) or Sweet and Sour Stewed Okra, Mountain-style (p. 169) and Moghul-scented Basmati Pilaf (p. 302).

COLD BUTTERNUT SQUASH SOUP

LAUKI SHORVA

MICROWAVE

Yield
  —7 cups
Servings
  —8
Preparation time
  *—3 minutes plus addi-
    tional time for chill-
    ing*
Cooking time
  —20 minutes
Heat
  —100 percent power
MW oven size
  —650 to 700 watts
MW cookware
  *—One pie or dinner
    plate and one 8-inch
    skillet*

A classic of the Anglo-Indians of Kanpur in northern India, this recipe traditionally uses tropical pumpkin, but butternut squash, which is widely available, makes an excellent substitute. The soup is extremely subtle, with only a hint of curry, so as not to mask the delicate flavor of squash.

*1 large or two small
  (about 1¾ pounds)
  butternut squash*
*2 tablespoons unsalted
  butter*
*1½ tablespoons ground
  coriander*
*1½ teaspoons fragrant
  spice powder (p. 481)*
*1½ cups (2 medium-
  size) chopped onions*
*1 fresh hot green chili,
  stemmed, seeded, and
  chopped, or ¼ tea-
  spoon cayenne pepper*

2 tablespoons sugar
2½ teaspoons kosher salt
*¼ cup lightly packed
  fresh basil or corian-
  der leaves*
1½ cups water
3 cups whole milk
1 tablespoon lemon juice
*Freshly grated nutmeg to
  taste*
*Freshly ground black
  pepper to taste*

FOR THE GARNISH:

*1 cup spicy croutons
  (p. 487)*

*8 basil or coriander
  sprigs*

1. Slash butternut squash in 6 to 8 places and place on a microwave-safe pie or dinner plate.

2. Cook, uncovered, at 100 percent power in a 650- to 700-watt carousel oven for 10 minutes (or until squash feels soft when pressed). Remove from oven. When cool enough to handle, cut squash in half and scoop out seeds and fibrous core and discard. Peel squash and chop meat coarsely or, alternatively, scoop out the meat in large chunks and reserve.

3. Place butter in an 8-inch microwave-safe skillet. Cook, uncovered, at 100 percent power for 1 minute 30 seconds (or until melted). Add coriander, spice powder, onion, chili, sugar, and salt. Stir to mix. Cook, uncovered, at 100 percent power for 6 minutes (or until onions look limp and glazed and spices exude fried aroma). Remove from oven.

4. Transfer onion-and-spice mixture into the container of a blender or food processor. Add squash, basil, and 1 cup water. Process until the contents are smoothly pureed. Transfer soup into a large bowl. Stir in the remaining water, milk, lemon juice, and freshly grated nutmeg and pepper to taste. Cover and chill. Ladle into soup bowls and distribute spicy croutons on top. Garnish with basil sprigs and serve immediately.

NOTE The soup keeps well, covered, in the refrigerator for up to 5 days.

COOL CREAM OF MINT SOUP

SHAHI PODINA SHORVA

MICROWAVE

Yield
  —6 cups
Servings
  —6
Preparation time
  —5 minutes plus addi-
    tional time for soak-
    ing lentils and for
    chilling soup
Cooking time
  —15 minutes
Heat
  —100 percent power
MW oven size
  —650 to 700 watts
MW cookware
  —One 5-quart covered
    casserole

If you are as fond of minty, creamy soups on a hot summer day at the beach as I am, this is the one for you. The split peas are added to provide a creamier body and a sweeter taste. For a thinner and lighter-tasting soup, substitute red (pink) lentils in place of the yellow split peas.

FOR THE SOUP:
½ cup American yellow split peas (p. 461)
3 cups water or whole or low-fat milk
1½ cups packed watercress
1½ cups chopped peeled, seeded pumpkin or butternut-squash meat or eggplant
1½ cups peeled, chopped baking potato
1 cup chopped onion
1 tablespoon chopped fresh ginger
2 teaspoons minced garlic

¾ teaspoon ground coriander
¾ teaspoon ground cumin
¾ teaspoon ground fennel
¾ teaspoon cayenne pepper

4 tablespoons packed chopped fresh, or 2 tablespoons crushed dried, mint
2 tablespoons chopped fresh coriander
2¼ cups whole milk
2½ teaspoons kosher salt, or to taste

FOR THE GARNISH:
1 cup heavy cream, lightly whipped

1 cup chopped roasted walnuts (p. 463)
8 mint sprigs

1. Pick clean peas, rinse, and place in a medium-size bowl. Add enough water to cover the peas by at least an inch and a half and soak for 8 hours or overnight (maximum 18 hours). Drain, rinse, and drain again.

2. Place peas in a 5-quart microwave-safe dish. Add 1½ cups water and all other ingredients for cooking soup and cover with the lid. Cook at 100 percent power in a 650- to 700-watt carousel oven for 15 minutes (or until split peas are soft). Remove from oven.

3. Uncover, and add mint and coriander. Transfer the soup in batches into the container of a blender or food processor and process until liquified or as finely pureed as possible, using additional water as needed. Return soup to the casserole. Add the remaining water, milk, and salt to taste. Cover and chill. Ladle soup into soup bowls and serve garnished with cream, walnuts, and mint sprigs.

NOTE   The soup keeps well stored in a covered container in the refrigerator for up to 2 days.

MENU SUGGESTION

Tandoori Cornish Hen (p. 113) or Warm Mung Bean Salad in Cumin-Tomato Dressing (p. 286) with Crushed Cucumber Salsa (p. 239) and Plain Basmati Rice (p. 299) go well after this soup.

CUMIN-SCENTED GREEN BEAN AND POTATO SOUP

PHALION KA SHORVA

MICROWAVE

Yield
 —5 cups
Servings
 —4 to 6
Cooking time
 —14 minutes
Standing time
 —3 minutes
Heat
 —100 percent power
MW oven size
 —650 to 700 watts
MW cookware
 *—One 2½-quart cov-
  ered casserole or
  soufflé dish*

This is a mild yet filling soup that tastes best when made with garden-fresh tender string or yard beans and tiny newly harvested whole potatoes. One wonderful aspect of cooking this soup in the microwave is that the beans remain vibrantly green against the pearl-white potatoes, which, even after prolonged cooking, retain their shape and do not become mushy. For a variation use slightly sweet yellow turnips in place of potatoes.

=================== *ROOM TEMPERATURE* ===================

4 tablespoons light vege-
 table oil
2 teaspoons ground
 cumin
¼ teaspoon ajowan seeds
 (p. 481), or 2 tea-
 spoons chopped fresh,
 or 1 teaspoon dried,
 thyme
¾ teaspoon turmeric
½–1 teaspoon red
 pepper flakes
1 tablespoon fresh ginger
 cut into julienne strips
¾ pound fresh green
 beans, cut into 1-inch
 pieces

¾ pound potatoes, peeled
 and cut into ¾-inch
 cubes
2 tablespoons tomato
 paste
3 cups chicken or meat
 stock, homemade
 (p. 488) or store-
 bought, or water
2 teaspoons kosher salt,
 or to taste
1 teaspoon ground
 roasted cumin seeds
 (p. 465)
2–3 teaspoons lemon
 juice
4 tablespoons chopped
 fresh coriander

1. Pour oil into a 2½-quart microwave-safe dish. Heat, uncovered, at 100 percent power in a 650 to 700-watt carousel oven for 2 minutes. Add cumin, ajowan (if you are using thyme do not add it yet), turmeric, and red pepper. Stir to mix. Cook, uncovered, at 100 percent power for 1 minute (or until spices exude a fried aroma). Remove from oven.

2. Add ginger, green beans, potatoes, tomato paste, and chicken or meat stock or water. Add salt to taste and thyme (if you are using it). Mix well and cover with the lid. Cook at 100 percent power for 11 minutes (or until vegetables are cooked). Remove from oven.

3. Uncover, stir in cumin, lemon juice, and half the coriander, and replace cover. Let soup stand, covered, for 3 minutes. Uncover, stir soup, crushing some of the potatoes to give it a rustic appeal, and ladle into soup bowls. Serve sprinkled with the remaining coriander.

NOTE   The soup may be made ahead, set aside in a microwave-safe covered container in the refrigerator for a day, and served reheated. The green beans, however, lose that appealing color, but not the flavor.

MENU SUGGESTION

This scrumptious soup is a meal in itself accompanied with Bombay Spicy Lentil Cakes (p. 327). For a more substantial meal, follow the soup with Kafta Kabob in Creamed Tomato Sauce (p. 140), Fiery Mangalorean Eggplant (p. 213), and a cool Avocado and Cucumber Yogurt Raita (p. 251).

FRAGRANT CAULIFLOWER AND FENNEL SOUP

TARI GOBHI

MICROWAVE

Yield
  —5 cups
Servings
  —6
Preparation time
  —3 minutes
Cooking time
  —16 minutes
Heat
  —100 percent power
MW oven size
  —650 to 700 watts
MW cookware
  —One 2½-quart covered casserole or soufflé dish

Cauliflower is considered a royal vegetable in India not because of any aristocratic origin but for its versatility and its unique ability to hold its own delicate flavor against spices. In this soup, the sweetness of cauliflower and fennel comes through the mildly spicy coriander-scented tomato broth. For a variation, substitute equal portions of kohlrabi, celery, or mushrooms in place of fennel.

=== ROOM TEMPERATURE ===

4 tablespoons light vegetable oil

2 teaspoons ground cumin

1 tablespoon ground coriander

1 teaspoon turmeric

½ teaspoon cayenne pepper

1 cup 1-inch-cube boiling potatoes

1½ cups cauliflower florets

1½ cups sliced fennel bulb

2 cups chopped peeled tomatoes (fresh or canned)

½ cup canned tomato puree, or 2 tablespoons tomato paste dissolved in ⅓ cup water

3 cups water

2 teaspoons kosher salt, or to taste

½ cup green peas (fresh or frozen)

Freshly ground black pepper to taste

3 tablespoons chopped fresh coriander

1. Place oil in a 2½-quart microwave-safe dish. Heat, uncovered, at 100 percent power in a 650- to 700-watt carousel oven for 2 minutes. Add cumin, coriander, turmeric, and cayenne. Stir to mix. Cook, uncovered, at 100 percent power for an additional minute (or until spices exude a fried aroma). Remove from oven.

2. Fold in potatoes and cover with the lid. Cook at 100 percent power for 3 minutes (or until potatoes are barely cooked). Uncover, add cauliflower, fennel, chopped tomatoes, tomato puree, water, and salt, and replace cover. Cook at 100 percent power for 10 minutes (or until vegetables are cooked). Add peas during the last 2 minutes of cooking. Remove from oven.

3. Uncover, and add pepper to taste. Stir well and ladle soup into soup bowls. Sprinkle with coriander and serve.

NOTE   The soup may be made ahead, set aside in a microwave-safe covered container in the refrigerator for 2 days, and served reheated

MENU SUGGESTIONS

This cauliflower soup makes a lovely meal served with salad and wafers or bread. For a more substantial meal follow the soup with Duck Vendaloo (p. 130) or Indian Paneer Cheese and Sweet Peppers in Fragrant Spinach Sauce (p. 181) and Plain Basmati Rice (p. 299).

BOMBAY CHICKEN CORN SOUP

MURGH SHORVA

MICROWAVE

Yield
  —8 cups
Servings
  —6 to 8
Preparation time
  —5 minutes
Cooking time
  —18 minutes
Heat
  —100 percent power
MW oven size
  —650 to 700 watts
MW cookware
  —One 5-quart covered
    casserole

Corn soups are very popular in India, particularly in the central, western, and northern regions, which raise the crop. Although Indian corn is extremely fragrant, far more so than American corn, it is not very sweet. Therefore, corn soups traditionally contain coconut milk as compensation. Corn soup, as a rule, does not contain any spices so that the subtle flavor of the corn can be relished on the palate.

=============== ROOM TEMPERATURE ===============

1 (¾ pound) skinless, boneless chicken breast, trimmed of fat

5½ cups chicken stock, homemade (p. 488) or store-bought

2 cups corn kernels (about 6 medium-size fresh corn on the cob or 1 10-ounce package frozen cut corn)

1 cup (2 medium-size) thinly sliced carrots

3 tablespoons cornstarch dissolved in ¼ cup water

1 cup coconut milk (p. 450)

1 fresh hot green chili, stemmed, seeded, and minced

1 tablespoon lemon juice

¼ cup chopped fresh coriander

1 teaspoon kosher salt, or to taste

1. Cut chicken-breast meat into thin 2-inch-long julienne strips and reserve.

2. Combine chicken stock, corn, and carrots in a 5-quart microwave-safe casserole and cover with the lid. Cook at 100 percent power in a 650- to 700-watt carousel oven for 14 minutes (or until liquid is boil-

ing and carrots are cooked but not mushy). Remove from oven.

3. Uncover and stir in chicken and cornstarch solution. Cook, uncovered, at 100 percent power for 2 minutes (or until soup thickens). Add coconut milk and continue to cook at 100 percent power for an additional 2 minutes (or until soup is piping hot). Remove from oven.

4. Stir in chilies, lemon juice, and half the coriander. Check seasonings and add salt to taste. Ladle soup into soup bowls and serve sprinkled with the remaining coriander.

MENU SUGGESTION

Although not essential, Toasted Lentil Wafers (p. 10) or Steamed Rice Cakes with Herbs (p. 332) are nice accompaniments to the soup. If desired, precede soup with Sesame Shrimp (p. 13), or Creamed Chicken Kabob (p. 111), Broccoli in Spicy-Garlic Oil (p. 205), and with a chutney sauce such as Sweet and Spicy Tomato Sauce (p. 370).

CURRIED SUMMER VEGETABLE SOUP

SABZI SHORVA

MICROWAVE

Yield
 —*5 cups*
Servings
 —*6*
Preparation time
 —*3 minutes*
Cooking time
 —*18 minutes*
Heat
 —*100 percent power*
MW oven size
 —*650 to 700 watts*
MW cookware
 —*One 2½-quart cov-
  ered casserole or
  soufflé dish*

Garden-fresh zucchini, tomatoes, carrots, peas, and potatoes are combined with onion, fragrant spices, and crystal-clear mountain-spring water to create this specialty of the rustic Pahadi (the people settled along the foothills of the Himalayas). The soup is light, spicy, and refreshing.

=================== *ROOM TEMPERATURE* ===================

¼ cup minced onion
*2 teaspoons ground
 cumin*
*1 tablespoon fragrant
 spice powder (p. 481)*
*2 fresh hot green chilies,
 stemmed, seeded, and
 sliced*
*½ teaspoon cayenne
 pepper*
*4 tablespoons light vege-
 table oil*
1½ cups sliced zucchini
1½ cups sliced carrots

*1 cup 1-inch-cube boiling
 potatoes*
*2½ cups peeled tomatoes
 pureed with juices
 (fresh or canned)*
*3 cups bottled spring
 water, not carbonated*
*2 teaspoons kosher salt,
 or to taste*
*½ cup green peas (fresh
 or frozen)*
*Freshly ground black
 pepper to taste*
*3 tablespoons chopped
 fresh coriander*

1. Combine onion, cumin, spice powder, chilies, cayenne, and oil in a 2½-quart microwave-safe dish. Cook at 100 percent power in a 650- to 700-watt carousel oven for 5 minutes (or until onions are cooked and begin to brown). Remove from oven.

2. Add zucchini, carrots, potatoes, tomatoes, water, and salt, stir to mix, and cover with the lid. Cook at 100 percent power for 13 minutes (or until vegetables are cooked but not mushy). Add peas during the last minute of cooking. Remove from oven.

3. Ladle soup into soup bowls and serve sprinkled with black pepper to taste and coriander.

NOTE   The soup may be made ahead, set aside in a microwave-safe covered container in the refrigerator for a day, and served reheated.

MENU SUGGESTION

The soup makes a nice meal accompanied with Bombay Spicy Lentil Cakes (p. 327) or Cream of Wheat Pilaf with Shallots and Chilies (p. 318), Toasted Lentil Wafers (p. 10), and a cool Moghul Shake (p. 438).

PEASANT SPLIT PEA AND EGGPLANT SOUP/STEW WITH DILL

DAL BAIGAN

MICROWAVE

Yield
 —8 cups
Servings
 —6 as a main course;
 12 as a side dish
Preparation time
 —3 minutes plus 8
 hours for soaking
Cooking time
 —48 minutes
Heat
 —100 percent power
MW oven size
 —650 to 700 watts
MW cookware
 —One 5-quart covered
 casserole and one 8-
 inch skillet

In this soup you can distinctly taste and smell each of its main ingredients while simultaneously enjoying its harmonious heartwarming whole. Microwave cooking is ideal for this recipe because the peas can cook to utmost tenderness without becoming mushy.

=========== ROOM TEMPERATURE ===========

¾ cup dried American green or yellow split peas or a combination (p. 461)

2 medium-size (8 ounces) onions, peeled and chopped

2 medium-size (8 ounces) new red wax potatoes, peeled and cut into ¾-inch cubes

1 tablespoon fragrant spice powder (p. 481) or curry powder, homemade (p. 479) or store-bought

½ teaspoon turmeric

2½ teaspoons kosher salt, or to taste

3 cups water

1 pound eggplant, cut with the skin into ¾-inch cubes

2 medium-size (12 ounces) red ripe tomatoes, chopped

2 tablespoons chopped fresh coriander

FOR THE SPICE-INFUSED
OIL:
2 tablespoons usli ghee
(p. 492)or light vege-
table oil
1 teaspoon minced garlic
1 teaspoon ground cumin

⅛ teaspoon crushed
ajowan seeds (p. 481),
or ¼ teaspoon dried
thyme
1 tablespoon minced
fresh, or 1 teaspoon
dried, dill

MENU SUGGESTION

This is a very hearty and filling soup which I serve as a complete meal in deep bowls, on occasion with Toasted Lentil Wafers (p. 10). If you wish, you could also add one of the salads (pp. 239–250), a rice pilaf (pp. 301–321), and a fruity chutney (pp. 339–358).

1. Pick clean split peas, rinse, and put in a medium-size bowl. Add enough water to cover peas by at least an inch and a half and soak for 4 hours or overnight (maximum 18 hours). Drain, rinse, and drain again.

2. Place peas, onion, potatoes, spice or curry powder, turmeric, salt, and 2 cups water in a 5-quart microwave-safe casserole and cover with the lid. Cook at 100 percent power in a 650- to 700-watt carousel oven for 25 minutes (or until peas are cooked and soft). Remove from oven.

3. Add the remaining 1 cup water, eggplant, and tomatoes and replace cover. Cook at 100 percent power for 18 minutes (or until vegetables are very soft). Remove from oven.

4. Uncover and stir, mashing some of the peas and vegetables with the back of the spoon to thicken the soup.

5. Heat the *usli ghee* or oil in an 8-inch microwave-safe skillet at 100 percent power for 2 minutes 30 seconds. Add garlic, cumin, and ajowan (or thyme). Cook at 100 percent power for 2 minutes (or until spices turn several shades darker and garlic is light golden). Remove from oven. Pour the spice-infused *ghee* or oil in the soup, scraping the skillet with a rubber spatula to get every bit of seasoning. Add dill and mix thoroughly. Ladle soup into soup bowls and serve sprinkled with coriander.

NOTE   The soup may be made ahead, set aside in a microwave-safe covered container in the refrigerator for 3 days, and served reheated.

KOHLRABI, TOMATO, AND CHICK-PEA SOUP

GANTHGOBHI SHORVA

MICROWAVE

Yield
  —5 cups
Servings
  —6
Preparation time
  —2 minutes
Cooking time
  —13 minutes
Heat
  —100 percent power
MW oven size
  —650 to 700 watts
MW cookware
  —One 2½-quart covered casserole or soufflé dish

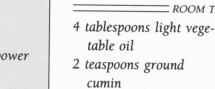

Kohlrabi, a turniplike knob vegetable, is a delicacy in southern India, where it was introduced by the British Raj during the last century. It is prized for its delicate flavor reminiscent of the tastes of cauliflower stem, white radish, and mustard greens. This soup, which combines kohlrabi with chick-peas, and tomatoes in a cumin-rich broth, is one of my favorites during late spring, when the new crop of kohlrabi, tender and fiberless, appears in the market.

═══════ *ROOM TEMPERATURE* ═══════

4 tablespoons light vegetable oil

2 teaspoons ground cumin

1 tablespoon ground coriander

1 teaspoon turmeric

½ teaspoon cayenne pepper

3 cups peeled and thinly sliced kohlrabi (about 1½ pounds)

1 cup cooked chick-peas (canned or homemade), lightly crushed

2 cups chopped tomatoes (fresh or canned with juices)

3 tablespoons tomato paste

3 cups chicken stock, homemade (p. 488) or store-bought, or water

Kosher salt to taste

1 teaspoon ground roasted cumin seeds (p. 465)

3 tablespoons chopped fresh coriander

1. Place oil in a 2½-quart microwave-safe dish. Heat, uncovered, at 100 percent power in a 650- to 700-watt carousel oven for 1 minute. Stir in cumin, coriander, turmeric, and cayenne. Continue cooking, un-

covered, at 100 percent power for 3 minutes (or until spices begin to brown). Remove from oven.

2. Add kohlrabi, chick-peas, tomatoes, tomato paste, and stock or water. Mix well and cover with the lid. Cook at 100 percent power for 9 minutes (or until kholrabi is cooked and soup is rapidly boiling). Remove from oven. Uncover and stir in salt to taste and cumin. Ladle soup into soup bowls and serve sprinkled with coriander.

NOTE   The soup may be made ahead, set aside in a microwave-safe covered container in the refrigerator for 3 days, and served reheated.

MENU SUGGESTION

This is a lovely soup that is a complete meal in itself. For a more substantial meal, serve Bombay Coconut Shrimp (p. 11), Indian Beef Sausage Kabob (p. 138), Mango and Basmati Pilaf (p. 314), and Cool Yogurt Sauce (p. 365).

HEARTY WHOLE MUNG BEAN AND GREEN PEPPER SOUP/STEW

MIRCH AUR SABAT MOONG

MICROWAVE

Yield
—2½ cups

Servings
—2 as a main course;
4 as a side dish dal

Preparation time
—3 minutes plus 8
hours for soaking

Cooking time
—21 minutes

Heat
—100 percent power

MW oven size
—650 to 700 watts

MW cookware
—One 2½-quart cov-
ered casserole or
soufflé dish and one
8-inch skillet

This is a delicious, very filling soup that I often enjoy serving as a main course. The microwave does wonders to these beans, turning them into plump little nuggets that are moist and meaty rather than starchy-tasting. The soup is best enjoyed the day it is made.

===== *ROOM TEMPERATURE* =====

½ cup dried whole mung beans (p. 462)

1 medium-size (6 ounces) new red wax potato, peeled and cut into ¾-inch cubes

1 medium-size (4 ounces) onion, peeled and chopped

2 cups water

1 teaspoon ground cumin

½ teaspoon turmeric

1 teaspoon kosher salt

1 medium-size (4 ounces) green pepper, diced into ¼-inch cubes

1 medium-size (4 ounces) red ripe tomato, diced into ¼-inch cubes

1 tablespoon chopped fresh coriander

FOR THE SPICE-INFUSED OIL:

2 tablespoons mustard oil or olive oil

¼ teaspoon cumin seeds

¾ teaspoon minced garlic

⅛ teaspoon crushed ajowan seeds (p. 481) or ⅓ teaspoon dried thyme

1. Pick clean beans, rinse, and place in a medium-size bowl. Add enough water to cover the peas by at least an inch and a half. Soak beans for 8 hours or overnight (maximum 18 hours). Drain, rinse, and drain again.

2. Place beans in a 2½-quart microwave-safe dish. Add potatoes, onion, water, cumin, turmeric, and salt and cover with the lid. Cook at 100 percent power in a 650- to 700-watt carousel oven for 13 minutes (or until beans are soft and potatoes are cooked). Uncover, add peppers and tomatoes, and replace cover. Cook at 100 percent power for an additional 4 minutes (or until vegetables are very soft). Remove from oven.

3. Uncover and mash some of the potatoes and beans, stirring and crushing with the back of the spoon, to lend the soup body. Replace cover and set aside while you make the spice infusion.

4. Heat the oil in an 8-inch microwave-safe skillet at 100 percent power for 3 minutes. Add cumin, garlic, and ajowan. Cook at 100 percent power for 1 minute (or until spices exude aroma). Remove from oven. Uncover soup and pour the oil-spice mixture onto it, scraping the skillet with a rubber spatula. Mix well. The consistency of the soup should be that of American split-pea soup. If it is not, add enough hot water to thin it. Ladle soup into deep soup bowls and serve sprinkled with coriander.

MENU SUGGESTIONS

For an elaborate meal, follow the soup with Yogurt Chicken (p. 118) or Eggplant Slices Smothered with Coconut-Spice Paste (p. 215), Zucchini and Walnut Yogurt Raita (p. 262), Tomato Basmati Pilaf (p. 308), and Sweet Persimmon and Plum Chutney with Cinnamon (p. 353).

BASMATI RICE AND LENTIL SOUP WITH GLAZED PEPPERS

KHITCHREE

MICROWAVE

Yield
—*4 cups*

Servings
—*4*

Preparation time
—*3 minutes*

Cooking time
—*26 minutes*

Heat
—*100 percent power*

MW oven size
—*650 to 700 watts*

MW cookware
—*One 8-cup glass
measure and one
10-inch covered
skillet*

Khitchree literally means hodgepodge, and this soup represents just that—a combination of rice, lentils, and vegetables with spices and seasoning. The resulting soup, however, ends up so delicious and satisfying that in India it is often served as a special treat at weekend brunch. Microwave cooking is ideal for this soup. In addition to cutting short the cooking time, microwaving prevents the soup from lumping, sticking to the bottom of the pan, and burning during the last ten minutes of cooking, a common problem with the conventional method.

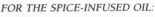

=== *ROOM TEMPERATURE* ===

*½ cup dried red (pink)
    lentils (p. 460)*

*½ cup basmati rice,
    picked clean and
    rinsed*

½ teaspoon turmeric

2½ cups water

Kosher salt to taste

*1 teaspoon cumin seeds,
    crushed*

*½ teaspoon freshly
    ground black pepper*

*3 medium-size (1 pound)
    sweet green peppers,
    stemmed, cored, and
    cut into 1-inch pieces*

FOR THE SPICE-INFUSED OIL:

*3 tablespoons usli ghee (p. 492) or light vegetable
    oil*

FOR THE GARNISH:

*2 tablespoons chopped
    fresh coriander*

*¼ cup fried onion shreds
    (p. 475) (optional)*

4 lemon wedges

1. Pick clean and rinse lentils and place in an 8-cup glass measure. Add rice, turmeric, and 1½ cups water. Stir to mix. Cook at 100 percent power in a 650- to 700-watt carousel oven for 10 minutes (or until most of the water has evaporated and contents are half-cooked). Stir in the remaining 1 cup water and continue cooking at 100 percent power for 8 minutes (or until both rice and lentils are cooked). Remove from oven.

2. There should be 4 cups of soup. If not, add enough hot water to bring it to that amount. Cook at 100 percent power for 2 minutes (or until soup comes to a boil). Remove from oven and stir in salt to taste. Keep warm, loosely covered with foil, while you make the spice-infused *ghee* and peppers.

3. Heat the *ghee* or oil in a 10-inch microwave-safe skillet, uncovered, at 100 percent power for 3 minutes. Remove from oven. Add cumin, black pepper, and sweet green peppers and mix rapidly, turning and tossing to coat the peppers with the spices, and cover with the lid. Cook at 100 percent power for 3 minutes (or until peppers are cooked but still crisp). Remove from oven. Ladle soup into soup bowls, distribute peppers on top, and serve garnished with coriander and, if desired, fried onion shreds. Place a lemon wedge on each dish.

MENU SUGGESTION

Accompany the soup with a fruity chutney (pp. 339–358), a refreshing salad (pp. 239–250), and a cool shake (pp. 437–438) to sip alongside. For a more substantial meal, include a kabob dish such as Ginger Chicken Kabob (p. 109).

FISH AND
SEAFOOD

India, which is surrounded by water on three sides, has a rich and time-honored tradition of cooking fish. The coastal waters are bountiful, and four distinct cultures—the Bengali, Goanese, Madrasi, and Malabari—have developed unique techniques for flavoring fish and seafood. Bengali cooking explores the use of mustard in all of its forms, and gives us Spicy Mustard-rubbed Tuna, in which the fish is coated with a spice mixture of cayenne and mustard before being cooked in a cream sauce and laced with lemon juice, which tempers and mellows the complex heat of the rub. The Goanese often prepare shrimps in a fiery paste of tamarind, cayenne, and cumin, offset by lightly cooked diced onions. In the microwave the onions retain their crispness and their sweetness is heightened—so much so that one of my guests recently mistook them for water chestnuts.

The Madrasis turn their fish red hot, ladening it with hot red chili pods, but then quickly temper it with sweet coconut and sweetish-sour tamarind fruit. Curry leaves, cubeb berries, and mustard all create intrigue for a delicious experience.

The Malabaris are known for their *molee,* gently braised salmon in delicate green chili and cumin-laced coconut sauce. Garlic, turmeric, and coriander all become part of the flavoring. The overall effect is sublime, with spices creating the surge.

In all of these recipes I have covered the fish with a sauce before cooking—a traditional Indian technique—and, in some recipes, prescribed a brief standing time, eliminating uncooked cold spots and reducing the risk of overcooked fish. Again, the microwave shows its usefulness in producing braised fish quickly; many of these dishes can be prepared, start to finish, in less than fifteen minutes. And microwaved fish retains its shape as well as its flavor; this is even true of the most delicate species, such as sole and salmon.

I have also found that as long as you do not overcook shrimps the first time around, they can actually be reheated in the microwave without becoming dry and hard. Nor need you worry about their spoiling; thanks to the spices and herbs, all will keep from losing flavor for at least a day and often more. But since fish and seafood take hardly any time to cook, the best game plan is to do all preparation beforehand and have the dish micro-ready to cook just before serving.

STEAMED FISH IN GINGER-THYME ESSENCE

BHAPPA MACH

MICROWAVE

Servings

   —3 as a main course;
   6 as a first course

Preparation time

   —5 minutes

Cooking time

   —4 minutes

Heat

   —100 percent power

MW oven size

   —650 to 700 watts

MW cookware

   —One 10-inch cov-
    ered skillet

This is one of those sublime fish preparations that seems to have been created with the microwave in mind. The fish fillets are first rubbed with a mixture of ginger, garlic, and thyme, and then rolled into pinwheels and cooked in enclosed heat, where they become infused with delicate herbal fragrances. Make sure to cook the fish fully or else the flavors of the herbs will not penetrate all the way through the flesh of the fish. A *fully* cooked fish is *not* an *over*cooked fish and therefore should be moist.

While cooking in the microwave, fish fillets exude juices that can be either served over them or stirred into soups, stocks, or sauces.

This fish preparation is particularly good accompanied with fragrant tomato sauce (p. 467) or *vendaloo* sauce (p. 470) or Crushed Cucumber Salsa (p. 239).

1¼ pounds skinless, boneless nonoily fish fillets such as sole, flounder, haddock, etc. (about 6 thin or 3 thick fillets)

1 teaspoon grated or crushed fresh ginger

½ teaspoon minced garlic

½ teaspoon kosher salt

2 teaspoons lemon juice

½ teaspoon ajowan seeds (p. 481), crushed, or 1 teaspoon dried thyme

½ teaspoon white pepper

6 6-inch-long coriander sprigs

½ cup lightly packed grated carrots

1. Cut each thick fish fillet into 2 thin ones. Lay fillets on a plate. Combine all seasonings except coriander sprigs and rub over fish. Roll each fillet into a pinwheel, securing with a toothpick and wrapping a coriander sprig around it. Arrange fish petal fashion in a 10-inch microwave-safe skillet and cover with the lid.

2. Cook at 100 percent power in a 650- to 700-watt carousel oven for 2 minutes. Uncover, turn fish with tongs, and replace cover. Continue cooking for an additional 2 minutes (or until fish turns opaque and is just cooked). Remove from oven. Uncover and serve fish fillets sprinkled with grated carrots, and, if desired, spoon over accumulated juices. Serve hot or cold.

MENU SUGGESTION

A nice soup to precede this fish preparation is Autumn Tomato Soup with Spicy Croutons (p. 43). To complete the meal serve Moghul Glazed Peach Pilaf (p. 312), Mustard-braised Endive (p. 218), and Zucchini and Walnut Yogurt Raita (p. 262).

OOTY-STYLE SOLE IN FRAGRANT TOMATO SAUCE

PULICHA MEEN

MICROWAVE

Servings
   —2 to 4 as a main
    course; 4 to 6 as a
    first course
Cooking time
   —22 minutes
Standing time
   —3 minutes
Heat
   —100 percent power
MW ovensize
   —650 to 700 watts
MW cookware
   —One 10-inch cov-
    ered skillet

This is one of the mildest, most delicate fish preparations from southern India (a region notorious for its fondness for cayenne). It was popular with the English during the time of the British Raj in Ooty (a resort in the Nilgiri Hills in south India similar to Kashmir in the northern Himalayan mountains), where they escaped the summer's heat. You can make the dish using any white nonoily fish. The fish can also be cooked and refrigerated and served chilled as a salad on a bed of shredded endive and aromatic greens.

1 teaspoon ground cumin
¾ teaspoon ground fenugreek seeds (p. 483) or fennel seeds
1 teaspoon ground coriander
½ teaspoon dry mustard
¼ teaspoon turmeric
¼ teaspoon cayenne pepper
3 tablespoons usli ghee (p. 492) or olive oil
1 cup finely chopped onions
1 tablespoon finely chopped fresh ginger

½ teaspoon minced garlic
3 medium-size (¾ pound) red ripe tomatoes, chopped
1 cup water
1 tablespoon cornstarch dissolved in 2 tablespoons water
2 skinless, boneless sole fillets (12 ounces)
1 tablespoon finely chopped fresh coriander, dill, or parsley

1. Combine cumin, fenugreek or fennel, coriander, mustard, turmeric, and cayenne in a small bowl and reserve.

2. Heat *usli ghee* or oil in a 10-inch skillet, uncovered, at 100 percent power in a 650- to 700-watt carousel oven for 1 minute. Add onion, ginger, and garlic and stir to mix. Cook, uncovered, at 100 percent power for 5 minutes (or until onions begin to color), stirring once. Mix in spices and continue cooking, uncovered, for 2 minutes (or until spices lose their raw aroma). Remove from oven.

3. Add tomatoes and water and cover with the lid. Cook at 100 percent power for 10 minutes (or until tomatoes are very soft and sauce has slightly thickened). Uncover and stir in cornstarch mixture. Cook, uncovered, at 100 percent power for an additional 1 minute (or until sauce thickens). Slip fish fillets into the sauce and cover with the lid. Cook at 100 percent power for 3 minutes 30 seconds (or until fish is cooked through).

4. Remove from oven and let the dish stand, covered, for 3 minutes. Uncover and sprinkle with coriander, dill, or parsley. Serve fish with the sauce, hot or chilled.

MENU SUGGESTION

A nice soup to precede this delicate fish preparation is Cool Cream of Mint Soup (p. 61). To complete the meal serve Whole Mung Bean and Basmati Pilaf (p. 316), Glazed Peppered Cucumber (p. 211), Spinach and Yogurt Raita (p. 258), and Instant Coconut Chutney (p. 339).

BENGAL-STYLE SPICY MUSTARD-RUBBED TUNA

MACHI SHARSHA

MICROWAVE

Servings
  —2 to 4
Preparation time
  —3 minutes
Cooking time
  —7 minutes
Heat
  —100 percent power
MW oven size
  —650 to 700 watts
MW cookware
  —One 10-inch cov-
    ered skillet

Here is a divine preparation for tuna with sweet peppers from Bengal, with just enough creamy-hot mustard sauce to bind and glaze the fish and vegetables. The initial searing step is not to brown or crisp the tuna but to fry its spice coating—a technique similar to the Cajun pan-blackening method popularized by Paul Prudhomme of New Orleans. As a result, the tuna has a complex smoky-spicy flavor. For variation you can substitute salmon, haddock, or flounder.

1 teaspoon cayenne
  pepper
1 teaspoon dry mustard
1 teaspoon ground cumin
1 teaspoon minced garlic
3 tablespoons mustard oil
  or olive oil
1 pound tuna steak or
  red snapper fillets, cut
  into 2–4 serving por-
  tions
2 tablespoons julienne of
  fresh ginger

1 small sweet green
  pepper, cored and cut
  into julienne strips
1 small sweet red pepper,
  cored and cut into
  julienne strips
Kosher salt to taste, if
  desired
3 tablespoons heavy
  cream, milk, or water
1 tablespoon Dijon
  mustard
1 teaspoon lemon juice

1. Combine cayenne, dry mustard, cumin, and garlic with 2 teaspoons oil into a paste in a small bowl and rub over tuna. Cover and marinate for 15 minutes.

2. Heat remainder of oil in a 10-inch microwave-safe skillet, uncovered, at 100 percent power in a 650- to 700-watt carousel oven for 3 minutes. Remove from

oven, add tuna, and turn to coat with oil. Scatter ginger and pepper strips around tuna and sprinkle with salt. Combine cream and mustard paste and pour over vegetables and tuna. Turn and roll tuna and peppers lightly to coat with cream mixture and cover with the lid.

3. Cook at 100 percent power for 3 minutes 30 seconds (or until tuna is just cooked). Remove from oven, uncover, and arrange tuna and vegetables on a heated platter. Stir lemon juice into the sauce, pour over tuna, and serve.

MENU SUGGESTION

For a more substantial meal, accompany tuna with Tomato Basmati Pilaf (p. 308) and any of the fruity chutneys. A cold soup such as Chilled Essence of Shallot Soup (p. 57) is a good beginning to this meal.

BRAISED COD IN AROMATIC MOGHUL SAUCE

SHAHI MACHI PATIALA

MICROWAVE

Servings
—4 to 6
Preparation time
—1 minute
Cooking time
—20 minutes
Standing time
—3 minutes
Heat
—100 percent power
MW oven size
—650 to 700 watts
MW cookware
—One 10-inch cov-
ered skillet

I love cod, particularly when it is ocean-fresh. Its subtle flesh possesses the unique ability to stand up to the most assertive of sauces. Here cod is braised in tomato sauce flavored with fragrant but not chili-hot spices. Ajowan or carom seeds, the spice from the thyme plant—a common flavoring for fish in the Moghul tradition—lends the fish its characteristic herbal undertone. Be careful not to stir the finished dish because cod flakes easily once it is cooked.

2 teaspoons cumin seeds
1 teaspoon mustard seeds
¼ teaspoon ajowan seeds (p.481) or ½ teaspoon dried thyme
¼ teaspoon turmeric
4 tablespoons light vegetable oil
¾ cup finely chopped shallots (6 medium-size) or red onions
1 teaspoon minced garlic
2 or more fresh hot green chilies, stemmed, seeded, and minced

3 medium-size (¾ pound) red ripe tomatoes, finely chopped
1 teaspoon paprika
¾ cup water
Kosher salt to taste, if desired
2 teaspoons cornstarch dissolved in 1½ tablespoons water
1½ pounds cod steaks, skin removed and cut into 2 × 2 × 2½-inch pieces

Freshly ground black
pepper to taste

2 tablespoons finely
chopped fresh
coriander

1. Combine cumin, mustard, and ajowan seeds in a spice mill or coffee grinder and process until coarsely ground. Remove to a bowl, stir in turmeric, and set aside.

2. Heat the oil in a 10-inch microwave-safe skillet, uncovered, at 100 percent power in a 650- to 700-watt carousel oven for 2 minutes. Add spice mixture, shallots, garlic, and chilies, mixing well. Cook, uncovered, at 100 percent power for 5 minutes (or until shallots look lightly fried), stirring once. Add tomatoes, paprika, water, and salt and cover with the lid. Cook at 100 percent power for 8 minutes (or until contents are reduced to a thick sauce). Remove from oven.

3. Uncover, add cornstarch solution, and mix, stirring with a whisk, to smoothen sauce. Slip cod pieces into the sauce and replace cover. Cook at 100 percent power for 5 minutes (or until fish is cooked through). Remove from oven and let the dish stand, covered, for 3 minutes. Uncover and serve sprinkled with pepper and coriander.

MENU SUGGESTION

To complete the meal, accompany the cod with Moghul-scented Basmati Pilaf (p. 302), Spicy Fried Okra (p. 223), and if you like, Green Mango Chutney (p. 348), and precede with Lentil Salad in Cumin-Citrus Dressing (p. 29).

MOGHUL MICROWAVE

MALABAR SALMON IN DELICATE COCONUT SAUCE

SALMON MOLEE

MICROWAVE

Servings
— 4 as a main course;
8 as a first course
Preparation time
— 2 minutes plus 15
minutes for mari-
nating
Cooking time
— 12 minutes
Heat
— 100 percent power
MW oven size
— 650 to 700 watts
MW cookware
— One 10-inch cov-
ered skillet

Malabar, along the western coast of India, is famous for its fish and seafood preparations. One of my personal favorites from that region is fish poached in sweet coconut milk. Salmon, shark, and sea bass are traditional in this recipe because their subtle flavor blends more harmoniously with the delicate coconut-green chili sauce.

---

1 pound fresh salmon,
shark, or sea bass
fillets
2½ tablespoons light
vegetable oil
1½ teaspoons ground
cumin
1½ teaspoons ground
coriander
1 teaspoon cayenne
pepper
⅛ teaspoon turmeric
1 teaspoon kosher salt

¾ cup sliced onion
1–4 fresh hot green
chilies, stemmed,
seeded, and thinly
sliced (optional)
3 large cloves garlic,
peeled and thinly
sliced
1 tablespoon julienne of
fresh ginger
1 cup coconut milk
(p. 450)

1. Using tweezers, pull out the fine bones of fish fillets and cut fish into 4 pieces (8 if you want to serve it as a first course), leaving the skin on the underside attached. Place fish fillets on a plate and coat them with 1½ teaspoons oil. Combine cumin, coriander, cayenne, turmeric, and salt and rub on fillets. Set aside to marinate for 15 minutes.

---

2. Heat 1½ tablespoons oil in a 10-inch microwave-safe skillet, uncovered, at 100 percent power in a 650- to 700-watt carousel oven for 3 minutes. Remove from oven and add fish fillets, skin side up. Cook, uncovered, at 100 percent power for 1 minute. Remove from oven. Turn fillets in oil until they lose their uncooked color and turn light pink on all sides (1 minute). Remove fillets to a plate.

3. Add the remaining 1½ teaspoons oil, onion, chilies, garlic, and ginger to the skillet and mix well. Cook, uncovered, at 100 percent power for 4 minutes (or until onions are barely cooked). Add coconut milk and continue cooking, uncovered, for an additional 2 minutes (or until sauce is boiling). Slip fish fillets skin side down into the sauce, along with the accumulated liquid. Cook, covered, at 100 percent power for 1 minute 30 seconds (or until salmon is just cooked). Remove from oven. Uncover and arrange salmon fillets on heated plates. Spoon onions and sauce over and serve immediately.

MENU SUGGESTION

An elegant way to begin this meal is with Moghul Pistachio Soup (p. 49). To ensure that nothing interferes with the delicate flavor of salmon, serve Ceylonese Steamed Rice Cakes (p. 330) or Coconut Rice (p. 300), Fiery Mangalorean Eggplant (p. 213), and Pear and Green Peppercorn Yogurt Raita (p. 253).

MADRAS FISH IN RED GRAVY

MEEN KARI

MICROWAVE

Servings
—*4 to 6*
Preparation time
—*4 minutes*
Cooking time
—*14 minutes 30 seconds*
Standing time
—*5 minutes*
Heat
—*100 percent power*
MW oven size
—*650 to 700 watts*
MW cookware
—*One 10-inch covered skillet*

This slightly piquant, tempered-hot fish in red gravy is just one of many ingenious flavoring techniques used by southern cooks. In this preparation the heat of the chilies is first infused into the oil, then, before adding the fish, it is mellowed with sweet coconut. Don't be put off by the long list of ingredients in the recipe. The process itself is very simple. All you need to do is cook the spices, add the sauce mixture, and then slip in the fish to braise.

FOR THE SPICE MIXTURE:
2 tablespoons American yellow split peas (p. 461)
1 teaspoon mustard seeds
2 tablespoons coriander seeds
2 teaspoons cumin seeds
6 cubeb berries (p. 482) or 1 long pepper (p. 483) or 4 allspice berries

8 dried whole hot red chili pods, broken into halves, or 1½ teaspoons cayenne pepper
½ teaspoon turmeric
2 teaspoons paprika
2 teaspoons kosher salt, or to taste

FOR THE SAUCE MIXTURE:
½ cup unsweetened flaked coconut (p. 449)
16 fresh, or 2 tablespoons crushed dried, curry leaves (p. 482), (optional)

¼ cup, or 2 frozen cubes, tamarind juice, defrosted, or 2 teaspoons tamarind concentrate (p. 491)
1½ cups water

---

3 tablespoons light
  sesame oil or peanut
  oil
½ cup minced onion
1½ teaspoons finely
  chopped garlic

1½ pounds thick cod, sea
  bass, or salmon fillets,
  preferably with skin
  still attached to one
  side, cut into 6–8
  serving pieces

MENU SUGGESTION

Cold Butternut Squash Soup
(p. 59) is lovely before this
spicy fish preparation. Mango
and Basmati Pilaf (p. 310),
Sweet Pepper and Yogurt
Raita (p. 256), and Smothered Cabbage with Mustard
Oil (p. 207) are excellent
accompaniments. A perfect
finish would be a platter of
fruits or vanilla ice cream
with Warm Five-Nectar
Sauce (p. 407).

FOR THE GARNISH:
Coconut slivers, sliced fresh green chilies, and
  chopped fresh coriander

1. Combine yellow split peas, mustard, coriander, cumin, cubeb berries, and chili pods and grind into a fine powder in batches using a spice mill or coffee grinder. Remove to a bowl, stir in turmeric, paprika, and salt, and set aside.

2. Place coconut, optional curry leaves, tamarind, and ¾ cup water into the container of a blender or food processor and process until smoothly pureed. Blend in the remaining water and reserve.

3. Heat the oil in a 10-inch microwave-safe skillet, uncovered, at 100 percent power in a 650- to 700-watt carousel oven for 2 minutes. Add onion, garlic, and spice mixture, and stir to mix. Cook, uncovered, at 100 percent power for 4 minutes (or until onions are soft), stirring once. Remove from oven.

4. Stir in coconut mixture and cover with the lid. Cook at 100 percent power for 6 minutes (or until coconut and tamarind lose their raw fragrance and the sauce thickens). Uncover, carefully slip in fish fillets, and replace cover. Cook at 100 percent power for 2 minutes 30 seconds (or until fish is just cooked). Remove from oven and let the dish stand, covered, for 5 minutes. Uncover and serve garnished with coconut slivers, green chili slices, and chopped coriander.

FIERY GOANESE SHRIMP

GOAN JHEENGA

MICROWAVE

Servings
—4
Preparation time
—3 minutes
Cooking time
—8 minutes
Heat
—100 percent power
MW oven size
—650 to 700 watts
MW cookware
—One 10-inch cov-
ered skillet

A popular preparation of the Christian community in Goa, these shrimps, although coated with red chilies, do not taste as hot as one might expect because of the addition of tamarind and onions. The shrimps, as a result, taste sweet yet leave a glow in your mouth. For an even hotter version, use the greater amount of cayenne suggested in the recipe.

2 tablespoons, or 1 frozen cube, tamarind juice, defrosted, or 1 teaspoon tamarind concentrate (p. 491) dissolved in 1 teaspoon water
1–2 teaspoons cayenne pepper
¼ teaspoon freshly ground black pepper
1 teaspoon paprika
1 teaspoon ground cumin
⅛ teaspoon turmeric
1 teaspoon kosher salt
1 pound medium-size shrimps, peeled and deveined, tails left on
3 tablespoons mustard oil or light vegetable oil
2 medium-size (½ pound) onions, peeled and sliced into ½-inch-thick rings
1 teaspoon lemon juice

1. Combine tamarind, cayenne, black pepper, paprika, cumin, turmeric, and salt in a bowl and mix thoroughly. Add shrimps, toss well to coat, and reserve.

2. Place oil and onion in a 10-inch microwave-safe skillet. Cook, uncovered, at 100 percent power in a 650- to 700-watt carousel oven for 6 minutes (or un-

til onions are cooked and glazed), stirring once. Remove from oven.

3. Add shrimps, mix well, and cover with the lid. Cook at 100 percent power for 2 minutes (or until shrimps are barely cooked), stirring once. Remove from oven, uncover, and serve sprinkled with lemon juice.

MENU SUGGESTION

Precede these Goanese shrimp with the delicately fragrant Cream of Eggplant Soup with Coriander (p. 45). To complete the meal serve Coconut Rice (p. 300), Fragrant Cabbage Salad with Ginger Slivers and Tomatoes (p. 245), and Pineapple Apricot Chutney (p. 351). Almond Rice Pudding (p. 383) can be a soothing finale.

MOGHUL SHRIMP IN FRAGRANT TOMATO SAUCE

MASALA JHEENGA

MICROWAVE

Servings
  —4 to 6
Cooking time
  —10 minutes
Heat
  —100 percent power
MW oven size
  —650 to 700 watts
MW cookware
  *—One 10-inch cov-
  ered skillet*

This classic shrimp preparation from the royal courts of the Moghul emperor Akbar the Great is a breeze to make in the microwave. The shrimps are cooked with onions in a lovely fennel- and cumin-laced tomato sauce. The only tricky part is the frying of spices. Your complete, undivided attention is needed because the spices brown in just a few seconds.

*2 tablespoons light vege-
  table oil*
1 teaspoon cumin seeds
½ teaspoon fennel seeds
1 cup chopped onion
*¼ teaspoon cayenne
  pepper*
*¼ teaspoon freshly
  ground black pepper*
1 cup chopped tomatoes
1 teaspoon paprika
*1 pound medium-large
  shrimps (28 to 32 per
  pound), peeled and
  deveined, tails left on*
1 teaspoon lemon juice
*½ teaspoon garam mas-
  ala (p. 478) or ground
  roasted cumin seeds
  (p. 465)*
*Kosher salt to taste, if
  desired*

FOR THE GARNISH:
2 tablespoons chopped fresh coriander, mint, or basil

1. Heat the oil in a 10-inch microwave-safe skillet, uncovered, at 100 percent power in a 650- to 700-watt carousel oven for 3 minutes. Add cumin and fennel seeds. Cook, uncovered, at 100 percent power

for 1 minute (or until spices turn a few shades darker). Remove from oven; then add onions, cayenne, and black pepper, stirring well.

2. Cook, uncovered, at 100 percent power for 2 minutes (or until onions just begin to wilt). Blend in tomatoes and paprika and continue cooking, uncovered, at 100 percent power for an additional 2 minutes (or until tomatoes begin to soften).

3. Remove from oven, fold in shrimps, and cover with the lid. Cook at 100 percent power for 2 minutes 30 seconds (or until shrimps turn pink and are cooked), stirring once. Remove from oven. Uncover, stir in lemon juice, *garam masala,* and salt, and serve garnished with chopped coriander, mint, or basil.

MENU SUGGESTION

Precede this shrimp dish with Cold Butternut Squash Soup (p. 59). To complete the meal serve Moghul-scented Basmati Pilaf (p. 302), Broccoli in Spicy-Garlic Oil (p. 205), and Peach Chutney with Raisins and Walnuts (p. 349).

MANGALORE CAYENNE SHRIMP

MEEN VADAKAL

MICROWAVE

Servings
  —4 as a main course;
  6 as a first course
Preparation time
  —5 minutes
Cooking time
  —10 minutes
Standing time
  —3 minutes
Heat
  —100 percent power
MW oven size
  —650 to 700 watts
MW cookware
  —One 10-inch covered skillet

These shrimps are spicy and fiery and unbelievably addictive once the palate begins to recognize the flavors, which come later. In the microwave the shrimps cook evenly and quickly, thus retaining their moistness. They are also lovely served over a bed of greens as a first course.

1 pound medium-large shrimps (28–32 per pound)	½ teaspoon dry mustard
	½ teaspoon kosher salt
	1 teaspoon wine vinegar
½ teaspoon turmeric	2 medium-size baking potatoes
2 teaspoons cayenne pepper	

1. Shell and devein shrimps, leaving the tails on, and wash thoroughly. Pat dry on kitchen towels and put in a 10-inch microwave-safe skillet. Add turmeric, cayenne, mustard, salt, and vinegar and toss to coat shrimps. Cover with the lid and let the shrimps marinate while you bake the potatoes.

2. Prick potatoes in 2 to 3 places. Bake, uncovered, at 100 percent power in a 650- to 700-watt carousel oven for 7 minutes (or until potatoes give when pressed). Remove from oven, peel and slice potatoes, and set aside, covered, until needed.

3. Cook shrimps, covered, at 100 percent power for 2 minutes 30 seconds (or until they are barely cooked), stirring once. Remove from oven. Let shrimps stand, covered, for 3 minutes. Spread sliced potatoes on a heated plate. Uncover and arrange shrimps on top.

Pour any sauce accumulated in the dish over the shrimps and serve.

SHRIMP IN FIERY GOANESE VENDALOO SAUCE

PRAWN VENDALOO

MICROWAVE

Servings
—6 as a main course;
12 as a first course
Cooking time
—9 minutes
Standing time
—5 minutes
Heat
—100 percent power
MW oven size
—650 to 700 watts
MW cookware
—One 2½-quart cov-
ered casserole or
soufflé dish

This is perhaps one of the quickest and easiest dishes to put together if you happen to have *vendaloo* sauce on hand. Otherwise, consider adding an extra thirteen minutes to the cooking time for preparing the *vendaloo* sauce first. Eight and a half minutes may seem like a long time for shrimps to cook, but it is not. Most of that time is for the sauce to come to a boil before the shrimps begin cooking.

═══════════ ROOM TEMPERATURE ═══════════

2 pounds medium-large
shrimps (28–32 per
pound), peeled and
deveined, tails left on
1 medium-size green
pepper, stemmed,
seeded, and cut into
½-inch-wide julienne
strips

½ cup chopped fresh
coriander
2½ cups (1 recipe) ven-
daloo sauce (p. 470)
1 medium-size (⅓
pound) tomato, cut
into ½-inch-thick
wedges

1. Combine shrimps, green peppers, half the coriander, and 1 cup *vendaloo* sauce in a 2½-quart microwave-safe casserole and cover with the lid. Cook at 100 percent power in a 650- to 700-watt carousel oven for 5 minutes (or until shrimps are partially cooked and green peppers begin to sweat and soften), stirring twice. Remove from oven.

2. Add the remaining sauce and tomatoes, mix well, and cover with the lid. Cook at 100 percent power

for 3 minutes 30 seconds (or until sauce is boiling and shrimps are fully cooked), stirring twice. Remove from oven and let *vendaloo* stand, covered, for 5 minutes. Uncover and serve sprinkled with coriander.

MENU SUGGESTION

Shrimp vendaloo is great-tasting served hot and at room temperature over a bed of greens. For a complete meal include sweet Coconut Rice (p. 300), Tamil Potato Salad with Shallots (p. 243), Raita of Crisp Fried Okra and Cool Yogurt (p. 263), and Pineapple Apricot Chutney (p. 351).

SCALLOPS IN GARLICKY MUSTARD OIL

ROI MACH

MICROWAVE

Servings
— 4 as a main course;
  6 as a first course
Cooking time
— 7 minutes
Heat
— 100 percent power
MW oven size
— 650 to 700 watts
MW cookware
— One 10-inch cov-
  ered skillet

Scallops, because they cook so quickly and because the wave distribution is so uneven, are a little tricky to do in a microwave, especially without a sauce and uncovered. I have found that if scallops are cooked in a covered browning skillet, the enclosed heat provides an ideal cooking medium: The scallops cook evenly and fully and remain plump and juicy. This dish is delicious served hot or cold.

3 tablespoons mustard oil or olive oil
1 teaspoon mustard seeds, crushed
¼ teaspoon ajowan seeds (p. 481), crushed, or ½ teaspoon dried thyme
3 large cloves garlic, peeled and thinly sliced

2 fresh hot green chilies, stemmed, seeded, and thinly sliced
⅛ teaspoon turmeric
1½ pounds bay scallops, trimmed of tough muscle
Juice of ½ small lime
1 tablespoon minced fresh coriander, basil, or dill

1. Heat the oil in a 10-inch microwave-safe covered skillet at 100 percent power in a 650- to 700-watt carousel oven for 3 minutes. Uncover, add mustard and ajowan seeds, garlic, chilies, and turmeric, stirring well, and replace the lid. Cook at 100 percent power for 1 minute (or until spices exude aroma). Remove from oven. Uncover, fold in scallops, and replace the lid.

2. Cook at 100 percent power for 2 minutes 30 sec-

onds (or until scallops are just cooked and turn white), stirring twice. Remove from oven. Uncover, sprinkle scallops with lime juice and herbs, and serve with their juices.

MENU SUGGESTIONS

Cream of Vegetable Soup (p. 51) is lovely before this light and fragrant scallop dish. To complete the meal, serve Tomato Basmati Pilaf (p. 308), Avocado and Cucumber Yogurt Raita (p. 251), and Cauliflower and Fennel in Aromatic Oil (p. 209).

SCALLOPS WITH CUCUMBER IN COCONUT SAUCE

LAU MACH MALAI

MICROWAVE

Servings
—4
Cooking time
—12 minutes
Standing time
—5 minutes
Heat
—100 percent power
MW oven size
—650 to 700 watts
MW cookware
—One 10-inch covered skillet

In this preparation scallops are braised in a coconut sauce. The cucumber is added to lend a distinct herbal fragrance to the seafood. Zucchini, pattypan, and snake squash are excellent substitutes for the cucumber. I love to eat this dish hot as well as at room temperature, over a bed of bean sprouts, topped with crispy noodles.

3 tablespoons light vegetable oil

¾ cup minced onion

1 tablespoon curry powder, homemade (p. 479) or store-bought

1 tablespoon grated or crushed fresh ginger

1 cup coconut milk (p. 450)

1 pound sea scallops, cut into ⅛-inch-thick slices

2 small tender cucumbers (½ pound), peeled, seeded, and cut into ⅛-inch-thick slices

Kosher salt to taste, if desired

1 tablespoon lemon juice

2 fresh hot green chilies, stemmed, seeded, and minced (optional)

2 tablespoons chopped fresh basil

1. Heat the oil in a 10-inch microwave-safe skillet, uncovered, at 100 percent power in a 650- to 700-watt carousel oven for 2 minutes. Stir in onion and curry powder and continue cooking, uncovered, at 100 percent power for 5 minutes (or until onions are

soft and glazed but not brown), stirring once. Remove from oven.

2. Add ginger, coconut milk, scallops, cucumber, and salt, mix well, and cover with the lid. Cook at 100 percent power for 4 minutes 30 seconds (or until scallops turn opaque and cucumber translucent), stirring once. Remove from oven. Uncover, stir in lemon juice and chilies, if you are using them, and replace cover. Let scallops stand, covered, for 5 minutes. Uncover and serve sprinkled with basil.

MENU SUGGESTION

This scallop preparation is a meal in itself served with a green salad, but you can, if desired, include Crisp Okra and Spiced Basmati Pilaf (p. 306) and Spicy-Sweet Cranberry Walnut Chutney (p. 346).

SCALLOPS IN GARLIC-COCONUT SAUCE WITH TOMATOES

MACHI MALAI

MICROWAVE

Servings
  *—3 to 4 as a main
    course; 6 as a first
    course*
Preparation time
  —2 minutes
Cooking time
  —11 minutes
Standing time
  —5 minutes
Heat
  —100 percent power
MW oven size
  —650 to 700 watts
MW cookware
  *—One 10-inch cov-
    ered skillet*

Orissa, along the eastern coast of India, is famous for its coconut-poached fish preparation, which is flavored with a generous amount of garlic—a distinctive feature of Orissan cooking. Traditionally, this dish is prepared using a fish similar to sea bass, but I find scallops more appealing in both flavor and texture. The acidic accent of tomato is great with the sweet scallops. You can turn this dish into a delicious soup by adding low-fat milk and adjusting the seasonings.

3 tablespoons light vege-
  table oil
1 tablespoon ground
  coriander
¼ teaspoon cayenne
  pepper
¼ teaspoon turmeric
¾ cup minced onion
1 tablespoon minced
  garlic
1 cup coconut milk
  (p. 450)
1 pound bay scallops,
  trimmed of tough
  muscle

2 medium-size (½
  pound) tomatoes,
  peeled, seeded, and cut
  into ¼-inch pieces
Kosher salt to taste, if
  desired
1 tablespoon lemon juice
1–4 fresh hot green
  chilies, stemmed and
  sliced into rings, seeds
  discarded
2 tablespoons chopped
  fresh coriander

1. Heat oil in a 10-inch microwave safe skillet, uncovered, at 100 percent power in a 650- to 700-watt

carousel oven for 2 minutes. Add coriander, cayenne, turmeric, onion, and garlic, stirring lightly. Cook, uncovered, at 100 percent power for 5 minutes (or until onions are soft and glazed but not brown), stirring once. Remove from oven.

2. Stir in coconut milk and scallops and cover with the lid. Cook at 100 percent power for 3 minutes (or until scallops turn opaque), stirring once. Uncover, add tomatoes, and replace cover. Continue cooking, covered, for an additional minute (or until tomatoes are heated through). Remove from oven. Uncover, stir in salt, lemon juice, and chilies, and replace cover. Let scallops stand, covered, for 5 minutes. Uncover and serve sprinkled with coriander.

MENU SUGGESTION

This is a delicate and delicious preparation of scallops that I prefer to serve with Cream of Wheat Pilaf with Shallots and Chilies (p. 318), Minted Red Onion Salad (p. 241), and Spicy Tomato Ginger Chutney (p. 357). For a substantial meal, include a hearty soup such as Cumin-scented Green Bean and Potato Soup (p. 63).

CHICKEN
AND OTHER FOWL

O f all the protein sources available, chicken is the most adaptable to microwave cooking. There is almost no danger of overcooking, especially in these recipes, most of which contain sauces and take a relatively long time to cook (in microwave terms). Even Creamed Chicken Kabob does not get tough if it is cooked an extra minute or so.

Because the chicken skin is usually discarded in Indian cooking—Indians consider it as inedible as feathers—and because there is so little oil needed to braise chicken in the microwave, most of these dishes eliminate unnecessary calories. Yet they are intensely favorful, because chicken absorbs the character of spices and herbs so brilliantly. The microwave also allows you to enjoy fat-free duck; I cannot think of a preparation that preserves the bird's deep, gamy flavor more than Duck Vendaloo, yet the skin and fat are discarded.

Finally, many of these dishes require very little work; the ingredients are combined and cooked for about thirty minutes, less than half the time they require using traditional methods. You can even cook chicken *tandoori*-style in the microwave in six minutes. And the results are excellent, because the secret lies in the marinade rather than in the cooking method.

GINGER CHICKEN KABOB

MURGH TIKKA KABAB

MICROWAVE

Servings
—*2 to 4*
Preparation time
—*9 minutes plus 15
minutes for
marinating*
Cooking time
—*2 minutes*
Standing time
—*2 minutes*
Heat
—*100 percent power*
MW oven size
—*650 to 700 watts*
MW cookware
—*One 10-inch cov-
ered browning skil-
let or regular skillet*

Ginger Chicken Kabob is a famous preparation be-
longing to the *tandoori* family. To make these kabobs,
boneless morsels of chicken, marinated in a highly
aromatic ginger-herb mixture, are threaded on skewers and grilled in the *tandoor*.

This recipe is particularly suited for microwaving
because although kabobs in general are expected to
have that grilled appeal, these are an exception. One
problem that arises when this dish is grilled in the
traditional way has been the *tandoor*'s extremely high
and dry heat, which causes the kabobs to dry out
during cooking. This problem is resolved with the
microwave. The moist microwave heat not only cooks
them to perfection, keeping them tender and succulent, but, in addition, makes them more aromatic and
buttery-tasting.

While cooking in the microwave the kabobs exude
juices that can either be served over them or stirred
into stocks or sauces such as fragrant tomato sauce
(p. 467), butter sauce (p. 469), or fiery *vendaloo* sauce
(p. 470).

---

*1¼ pounds skinless,
boneless, lean chicken-
breast meat*
1 teaspoon ground cumin
*2 teaspoons crushed or
grated fresh ginger*
½ teaspoon dry mustard
1 teaspoon minced garlic

½ teaspoon kosher salt
*2 fresh hot green chilies,
stemmed, seeded, and
minced*
*1½ tablespoons mustard
oil or olive oil*
*⅓ cup finely chopped
fresh coriander*

---

1. Place chicken breasts between two layers of plastic wrap and pound lightly to an even thickness. Cut chicken along the grain into 2-inch wide strips. Place chicken meat in a small bowl. Add all other ingredients except coriander and mix well. Let chicken marinate for 15 minutes at room temperature or refrigerate for up to 2 days. Roll chicken pieces into pinwheels.

2. Heat a 10-inch browning skillet, uncovered, at 100 percent power in a 650- to 700-watt carousel oven for 4 minutes. Remove from oven. Add chicken kabobs and cover with the lid. Brown kabobs, shaking and tilting the skillet to roll them on all their sides, for 1 minute. If you are using a regular microwave-safe covered skillet, then skip this step and simply arrange chicken pinwheels in it.

3. Cook at 100 percent power for 2 to 3 minutes (or until chicken is just cooked through and clear juices run when pierced with a skewer), uncovering and turning them with tongs once. Remove from oven and let kabobs rest for 2 minutes, then lift, one at a time, and generously coat with chopped coriander and arrange on a heated serving platter. Accompany with the accumulated juices, heated at 100 percent power for 30 seconds (or until piping hot), in a small bowl.

MENU SUGGESTION

These kabobs are wonderful as a first course or cut into bite-size pieces as appetizers with cocktails accompanied with Fragrant Mint Sauce (p. 366), Cool Yogurt Sauce (p. 365), or Sweet and Spicy Tamarind Sauce (pp. 372, 374). To serve as a main course, accompany with Garlic-braised Tomatoes (p. 232), Fragrant Spiced Lentils with Herbs (p. 273), and Plain Basmati Rice (p. 299).

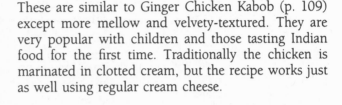

CREAMED CHICKEN KABOB

MURGH MALAI KABAB

These are similar to Ginger Chicken Kabob (p. 109) except more mellow and velvety-textured. They are very popular with children and those tasting Indian food for the first time. Traditionally the chicken is marinated in clotted cream, but the recipe works just as well using regular cream cheese.

1¼ pounds skinless, boneless, lean chicken-breast meat	½ teaspoon kosher salt
1 teaspoon minced garlic	3 tablespoons plain or chive-flavored whipped cream cheese
2 teaspoon crushed or grated fresh ginger	Paprika
⅓ teaspoon ground fennel	3 tablespoons fresh, or 1½ tablespoons crushed dried, chives
⅛ teaspoon freshly grated nutmeg	

1. Cut chicken along the grain into 1-inch-wide strips. Cut each strip into 2-inch-long pieces. Place chicken meat in a small bowl. Add all other ingredients except paprika and chives and mix well. Let chicken marinate for 15 minutes at room temperature or refrigerate up to 2 days. Roll chicken pieces into pinwheels.

2. Heat a 10-inch browning skillet, uncovered, at 100 percent power in a 650- to 700-watt carousel oven for 4 minutes. Remove from oven. Add chicken kabobs and cover with the lid. Brown kabobs, shaking and tilting the skillet to roll them on all their sides,

for 1 minute. If you are using a regular microwave-safe covered skillet, then skip this step and simply arrange chicken pinwheels in it.

3. Cook at 100 percent power for 2 to 3 minutes (or until the chicken is just cooked through and juices run clear when pierced with a skewer), uncovering and turning them with tongs once. Remove from oven and let kabobs rest for 2 minutes, then sprinkle lightly with paprika. Lift kabobs, one at a time, and lightly coat with chives and arrange on a heated serving platter. There will be a reasonable amount of accumulated juices in the plate. *Do not discard them.* Accompany the kabobs with the juices, heated at 100 percent power for 30 seconds (or until piping hot) in a small bowl. The juices may also be reserved and used in place of cooking liquid and stocks or stirred into one of the sauces such as fragrant tomato sauce (p. 467), butter sauce (p. 469), or fiery *vendaloo* sauce (p. 470) as an added enricher.

MENU SUGGESTION

These kabobs are a great first course or cut up into bite-size pieces as appetizers with cocktails accompanied with Fragrant Mint Sauce (p. 366), Sweet and Spicy Tomato Sauce (p. 370), or Sweet and Spicy Fruit Sauce (p. 376). To serve as a main course, accompany with Cauliflower and Fennel in Aromatic Oil (p. 209) and Moghul Glazed Peach Pilaf (p. 312).

TANDOORI CORNISH HEN
TANDOORI MURGHI

MICROWAVE

Servings
—*2 to 4*
Preparation time
—*12 minutes plus
overnight
marinating*
Cooking time
—*10 minutes*
Standing time
—*2 minutes*
Heat
—*100 percent power*
MW oven size
—*650 to 700 watts*
MW cookware
—*One bacon/meat
rack and one 10-
inch browning
skillet*

Tandoori Cornish hen or chicken gets its name from the clay oven *tandoor,* into which marinated poultry threaded on long skewers is lowered and roasted. To my delight, the most popular dish in Indian cuisine can also be made successfully in the microwave! The flavor is as good as it can be in the absence of smoke cooking and the hens are moister and more tender than when cooked in a *tandoor.*

The secret flavor of *tandoori* food comes not so much from the clay oven or the smoke but from the highly aromatic yogurt-and-herb marinade. The following *tandoori* marinade recipe is one I developed as an executive chef for restaurant use. Since the traditional recipe calls for very small, young chickens weighing around one pound, I recommend using Cornish game hens.

This technique of cooking *tandoori* hens will also please the weight and cholesterol watchers as the yogurt-and-herb marinade is extremely low in calories and fat.

Although *tandoori* Cornish hen cooks gloriously in the microwave, it does not develop its characteristic grilled appeal and taste, a known shortcoming of microwave cooking. But I have remedied this by searing the cooked hens in a browning skillet. This step, in fact, is not too different from the traditional technique where the hens, before serving, are grilled for the second time in the *tandoor* to get that "*tandoori* look."

The deep reddish-orange color of *tandoori* Cornish hen—a trademark of all *tandoori* foods—however, is purely for aesthetics; therefore, if desired, it can be eliminated.

The Tandoori Cornish Hen is scrumptious by itself or turned into Butter Cornish Hen (p. 126).

2 medium-size (1¼ pounds each) Cornish hens	2 teaspoons yellow food coloring (optional) 1 teaspoon red food coloring (optional)

FOR THE MARINADE:
1 tablespoon plain yogurt
1 tablespoon lemon juice
1 tablespoon minced garlic
1 tablespoon crushed or grated fresh ginger
1 teaspoon dry ginger powder
1 teaspoon ground roasted cumin seeds (p. 465)

2 teaspoons ground roasted coriander seeds (p. 466)
1 teaspoon ground cardamom
½–1 teaspoon cayenne pepper
1 teaspoon kosher salt

FOR THE GARNISH:
2 tablespoons melted usli ghee (p. 492), unsalted butter, or olive oil (optional)
1 medium-size onion (preferably red), peeled and sliced

1 medium-size green pepper, cored and sliced
1 lemon, cut into wedges

1. With poultry shears, split hens. Pull the skin off the hens, using paper towels to get a better grip. Prick hens all over with a fork or a thin skewer. Make diagonal slashes, ½ inch deep and 1 inch apart—2 on the breast, 2 on the thigh, and 1 on the drumstick. Place hens in a large shallow dish. Combine the food coloring in a small bowl and brush over the hens evenly.

MENU SUGGESTION

This dish is lovely accompanied with Cool Yogurt Sauce (p. 365), Crushed Cucumber Salsa (p. 239), and Saffron Pilaf (p. 304). For an elaborate meal, precede with Warm Mustard Shrimps on Endive (p. 15).

2. Mix all the ingredients for the marinade and rub it on the Cornish hen halves. Mix thoroughly, turning several times, pushing marinade into slits and coating pieces evenly. Cover and refrigerate overnight (maximum 2 days).

3. Remove hens from the refrigerator and arrange them, meaty side up, on a 10-inch microwave-safe bacon/meat rack. Cook at 100 percent power in a 650- to 700-watt carousel oven for 6 minutes (or until hens are fully cooked). Remove from oven.

4. If you are using fat, brush hens lightly with *usli ghee,* melted butter, or olive oil.

5. Heat a 10-inch browning skillet, uncovered, at 100 percent power for 4 minutes. Remove from oven and add hens, meaty side down, to the skillet. Let hens sear until sizzling stops (about 1½ minutes), pressing the hens down. Cook hens at 100 percent power for 2 minutes (or until hens turn crimson red and glazed). Remove from oven.

6. While hens are cooking, add accumulated juices from the bacon rack to the onions and peppers in a bowl and mix well. Spread vegetables on bacon rack. Cook vegetables at 100 percent power for 2 minutes. Remove from oven. Arrange *tandoori* hens on a heated platter and serve surrounded with onions, peppers, and lemon wedges.

NOTE Tandoori Cornish Hen used for making Butter Cornish Hen may be prepared ahead and set aside, covered, for a couple of hours at room temperature or overnight in the refrigerator.

ZESTY LEMON CORIANDER CHICKEN

MURGHI HARI CHATNI

MICROWAVE

Servings
—4
Preparation time
—5
Cooking time
—7 minutes
Standing time
—2 minutes
Heat
—100 percent power
MW oven size
—650 to 700 watts
MW cookware
—One 10-inch covered skillet

Very fragrant, very delicious, and very easy to make. I am a big fan of coriander, therefore I use a large portion of the herb with just a touch of mint, basil, and thyme. This recipe works just as well with fish, shrimps, and scallops, and they take the same length of time to cook.

=== ROOM TEMPERATURE ===

1½ pounds (1½) boneless and skinless chicken breasts	1–4 fresh hot green chilies, stemmed, seeded, and minced
2 tablespoons light vegetable oil	4 tablespoons thinly sliced scallions (green and white parts)
1 teaspoon minced garlic	½ cup packed chopped herbs (a combination
1 teaspoon ground cumin	of fresh coriander
2 teaspoons sugar	leaves and tender
1 teaspoon kosher salt	stems, mint leaves,
2 tablespoons lemon juice	basil, and thyme)
2 tablespoons julienne of fresh ginger	1 teaspoon lemon zest

1. Place chicken breasts flat on a work board and slice horizontally into halves, making thin scallopini. Cut each scallopini in half lengthwise and put in a bowl. Add oil, garlic, cumin, sugar, and salt, toss well, and reserve.

2. Heat the oil in a 10-inch microwave-safe skillet, uncovered, at 100 percent power in a 650- to 700-watt carousel oven for 3 minutes. Remove from oven. Add chicken and turn to coat with oil (about 1 minute).

3. Add lemon juice, ginger, chilies, scallions, and herbs. Toss chicken to coat with the herb mixture and cover with the lid. Cook at 100 percent power for 4 minutes (or until chicken is cooked and tender). Remove from oven. Uncover, sprinkle on lemon zest, and replace cover. Let chicken stand, covered, for 2 minutes before serving.

MENU SUGGESTION

To complete the meal, serve Minted Red Onion Salad (p. 241), Fiery Mangalorean Eggplant (p. 213), and Plain Basmati Rice (p. 299).

YOGURT CHICKEN

DAHI MURGHI

MICROWAVE

Servings
—*2 to 4*
Preparation time
—*5 minutes*
Cooking time
—*11 minutes*
Standing time
—*3 minutes*
Heat
—*100 percent power*
MW oven size
—*650 to 700 watts*
MW cookware
—*One 10-inch cov-
ered skillet*

In Indian cooking, yogurt is commonly used in sauces, partly for its healthful, digestive qualities but mainly because it blends and tempers the spices very gracefully. Yogurt chicken with walnuts, a common preparation from Kashmir in north India, is easy and quick to make in the microwave. I prefer using breast meat in this recipe because it tastes more flavorful, in addition to looking beautiful against the walnuts and coriander.

═══════════ *ROOM TEMPERATURE* ═══════════

1½ pounds skinless, boneless, lean chicken breasts

1 tablespoon light vegetable oil

2 tablespoons minced shallots

½ cup finely chopped walnuts

1 tablespoon grated or crushed fresh ginger

½ teaspoon minced fresh hot green chilies

½ cup plain yogurt or a combination of sour cream and plain yogurt

1 tablespoon minced fresh, or 1½ teaspoon crushed dried, mint leaves or dill

1 teaspoon kosher salt, or to taste

2 tablespoons heavy cream, sour cream, or plain yogurt

¾ teaspoon ground roasted cumin seeds (p. 465)

3 tablespoons finely chopped fresh coriander

1. Place chicken breasts between two layers of plastic wrap and pound lightly to an even thickness. Cut chicken along the grain into 2-inch-wide strips. Cut each strip into 2-inch-long pieces. Place chicken meat

in a bowl. Add oil, shallots, walnuts, ginger, and chilies, toss well, and set aside.

2. Combine yogurt, mint, coriander, and salt in a cup and reserve.

3. Heat the oil in a 10-inch microwave safe skillet, uncovered, at 100 percent power in a 650- to 700-watt carousel oven for 3 minutes. Remove from oven. Add chicken meat and turn to coat with oil (about 1 minute). Stir in yogurt mixture and cover with the lid.

4. Cook at 100 percent power for 8 minutes (or until chicken is cooked through and tender), stirring once. Remove from oven. Uncover, stir in cream and cumin, and replace cover. Let chicken stand for 3 minutes, then uncover and sprinkle with coriander. Serve hot or cold.

MENU SUGGESTION

To complete the meal, accompany with a rice pilaf such as Moghul-scented Basmati Pilaf (p. 302), a green vegetable such as Eggplant Slices Smothered with Coconut-Spice Paste (p. 215), and, if desired, Bombay Sweetish-Sour Garlic Lentils (p. 275).

CHICKEN FRAZER

MURGH JHAL FRAZI

An Anglo-Indian specialty, this dish is named after Colonel Frazer of the Royal British Army, stationed in India during the time of the British Raj. It is made by combining chicken, tomatoes, and peppers in a mild curry-flavored sauce. Chicken Frazer is particularly easy to make in the microwave because the chicken-breast meat cooks flawlessly in no time at all. You can also make the dish using sliced roast chicken, beef, pork, or even shrimps in place of chicken breasts.

MICROWAVE

Servings
  —4
Preparation time
  —3 minutes
Cooking time
  —4 minutes
Standing time
  —3 minutes
Heat
  —100 percent power
MW oven size
  —650 to 700 watts
MW cookware
  —One 10-inch covered skillet

=== ROOM TEMPERATURE ===

4 tablespoons usli ghee (p. 492), unsalted butter, or light vegetable oil

1½ pounds (2 to 3 whole) boneless, skinless chicken breasts, split

1 teaspoon minced garlic

1 medium-size onion, peeled and sliced

2 medium-size sweet green peppers, cored and cut into julienne strips

2–3 teaspoons curry powder, homemade (p. 479) or store-bought

½ cup fragrant tomato sauce (p. 467) or butter sauce (p. 469) or canned stewed tomatoes, pureed

3 tablespoons heavy cream or milk

1 teaspoon kosher salt

Freshly ground black pepper to taste

Juice of ½ lemon

FOR THE GARNISH:

2 tablespoons chopped fresh coriander

8 lemon slices

1. Heat 2 tablespoons *usli ghee* or oil in a 10-inch microwave-safe covered skillet at 100 percent power in a 650- to 700-watt carousel oven for 3 minutes. Remove from oven, uncover, add chicken breasts, and turn to coat with *ghee* (about 1 minute); then replace lid.

2. Cook at 100 percent power for 3 minutes (or until chicken breasts are half-cooked). Remove from oven and uncover. Cut chicken into ½-inch-thick slices. Put chicken and the accumulated juices into a re-served bowl.

3. Add the remaining 2 tablespoons oil to the skillet along with the garlic, onion, peppers, and curry powder. Mix well. Cook, uncovered, at 100 percent power for 6 minutes (or until vegetables are cooked crisp and spices lose their raw aroma). Remove from oven.

4. Add tomato sauce, heavy cream, reserved juices of chicken, salt, and black pepper, stir to mix, then carefully fold in chicken. Cook, uncovered, at 100 percent power for 2 minutes (or until chicken is fully cooked and sauce is steaming hot). Remove from oven. Uncover and sprinkle with lemon juice. Serve chicken with the sauce spooned over and garnished with black pepper, chopped coriander, and lemon slices.

MENU SUGGESTION

This Anglo-Indian specialty is good accompanied with the fragrant Coconut Rice (p. 300). To complete the meal serve Pineapple Apricot Chutney (p. 351) and Toasted Lentil Wafers (p. 10). Precede this light curry with an equally light first course such as Sesame Shrimp (p. 13).

CHICKEN AND ENDIVE BRAISED IN COCONUT

NARIAL MURGH

Endive is one of those few vegetables as yet undiscovered in India, although its delicate, slightly bitter flavor is most adaptable and complementary to Indian spices, particularly in conjunction with coconut. Although this fennel-scented, coconut-braised classic from eastern India calls for cabbage, I prefer endive because it imparts a far more complex flavor. This dish can be turned fairly mild by eliminating the hot green chilies and substituting sweet peppers in place of the mild chilies.

=========== ROOM TEMPERATURE ===========

*¼ teaspoon ground
  cinnamon*
*¼ teaspoon ground
  cloves*
*½ teaspoon ground
  cumin*
*1 teaspoon ground
  cardamom*
⅛ teaspoon turmeric
*¼–½ teaspoon cayenne
  pepper*
*5 tablespoons light
  vegetable oil*
*½ cup finely chopped
  onion*
*2 teaspoons minced
  garlic*

*2 endives, shredded as
  for coleslaw*
*1½ pounds (2 small)
  skinless, boneless
  chicken breasts, split*
*1½-inch piece fresh
  ginger, peeled and cut
  into fine julienne
  shreds*
*¼ cup sliced mildly hot
  fresh green chilies or
  sweet red pepper*
*2 teaspoons kosher salt,
  if desired*
*¾ cup coconut milk
  (p. 450)*
*½ cup heavy cream,
  milk, or more coconut
  milk*

1. Combine cinnamon, clove, cumin, cardamom, turmeric, and cayenne pepper in a small bowl and reserve.

2. Heat oil in a 10-inch microwave safe skillet, uncovered, at 100 percent power in a 650- to 700-watt carousel oven for 2 minutes. Add onions and cook, uncovered, at 100 percent power for 4 minutes (or until onions begin to brown). Stir in garlic and spice mixture and cook for 45 seconds (or until garlic turns light golden and spices exude a fried aroma). Remove from oven.

3. Add endive and toss to coat with the spice-infused oil. Place chicken breast halves on top petal fashion, thin side facing inward. Sprinkle ginger, chilies or peppers, and salt on top, pour the coconut milk and heavy cream over all, and cover with the lid.

4. Cook at 100 percent power for 7 minutes (or until chicken is just cooked). Remove from oven and let the dish stand, covered, for 3 minutes. Uncover and carefully transfer chicken to a heated platter. Stir the sauce and pour over chicken. Serve immediately.

MENU SUGGESTION

Precede this fragrant, slightly hot chicken preparation with Autumn Tomato Soup with Spicy Croutons (p. 43). To complete the meal, serve Split Pea and Basmati Pilaf (p. 314), Garlic-braised Tomatoes (p. 232), and Green Mango Chutney (p. 348).

PARSI CHICKEN BRAISED IN SPICED PUMPKIN-LENTIL PUREE

DHANSHAK

MICROWAVE

Servings
  —6
Preparation time
  —6 minutes
Cooking time
  —35 minutes
Heat
  —100 percent power
MW oven size
  —650 to 700 watts
MW cookware
  —One 5-quart covered
   casserole

Dhanshak is the most famous dish of the Parsi (Persian descent) community in India. In this preparation chicken is combined with eggplant, pumpkin, lentils, and fragrant herbs and spices and cooked until meltingly tender. The vegetables and lentils fall apart in the prolonged cooking and turn into a velvety-smooth sauce. The following microwave recipe for *dhanshak* is one of my very favorites because not only is it wonderfully flavored and amazingly easy to prepare—all one needs to do is combine all ingredients and cook until done—but it is completely fat-free. For variation, you can substitute one small four-pound duck or two or three Cornish game hens, skinned and trimmed of excess fat, in place of the chicken.

The pureed vegetables and lentils that form the sauce in this dish are really an elaborate *dal* (see more on page 266), and therefore are best served accompanied with cooked rice, with the sauce generously spooned over it.

=== *ROOM TEMPERATURE* ===

¾ cup dried red (pink)
  lentils (p. 460), picked
  clean and rinsed
2½ cups water
1 teaspoon ground
  coriander
1 teaspoon ground cumin
1 teaspoon ground fennel

1 teaspoon cayenne
  pepper
1½ teaspoons turmeric
2 teaspoons kosher salt
¼ cup loosely packed
  fresh mint leaves
¼ cup loosely packed
  fresh coriander leaves
  and stems

1-inch cube fresh ginger, peeled and coarsely chopped
4 large cloves garlic, peeled and coarsely chopped
1 3½-pound chicken, skinned, trimmed of all visible fat, and cut into 8–10 pieces

1½ cups chopped eggplant with skin
1½ cups chopped, peeled, and seeded pumpkin or butternut squash meat
1 cup chopped onion

MENU SUGGESTION

This richly flavored, very satisfying chicken preparation is very filling. All one needs to complete the meal is Parsi Caramelized Onion Pilaf (p. 301) or Tomato Basmati Pilaf (p. 308) and a salad such as Crushed Cucumber Salsa (p. 239). Although not essential, Lemons in Peppered Syrup (p. 361) is a nice addition.

FOR THE GARNISH:
3 tablespoons chopped fresh coriander

1. Arrange all the ingredients, in the order listed above, in a 5-quart microwave-safe casserole and cover with the lid. Cook at 100 percent power in a 650- to 700-watt carousel oven for 35 minutes (or until chicken is cooked tender and lentils are soft). Remove from oven.

2. Uncover, carefully take out chicken pieces, and arrange them in a heated deep serving dish. Cover with foil to keep them warm. Transfer half the contents of the casserole into a blender or food processor and process until pureed but not liquefied. A little texture adds to the character of the sauce. Pour the sauce over the chicken. Repeat with the remaining sauce the same way and add to the chicken. Garnish with coriander and serve.

NOTE   The *dhanshak* may be made ahead, set aside, covered, in the same container in the refrigerator for 3 days, and served reheated.

BUTTER CORNISH HEN

MAKHANI MURGHI

MICROWAVE

Servings
—4

Preparation time
—4 minutes

Cooking time
—10 minutes

Standing time
—2 minutes

Heat
—100 percent power

MW oven size
—650 to 700 watts

MW cookware
—One 2½-quart
covered casserole or
soufflé dish

Butter Cornish Hen is the ingenious creation of *tandoori* chefs for using up leftover *tandoori* Cornish hens. In this dish, *tandoori* hen pieces, or kabobs, are simmered in a wonderful cumin-and-herb-flavored creamy tomato sauce until they soak up the juices and turn butter-tender. Since sauce is the main ingredient of this dish, you can use any leftover cooked chicken or duck in this recipe.

=================== ROOM TEMPERATURE ===================

4 cooked Tandoori Cornish Hen halves (p. 113)	2½ cups butter sauce (p. 469) ⅓ cup heavy cream

FOR THE GARNISH:
⅓ teaspoon freshly ground black pepper
⅓ cup finely chopped fresh coriander

4–8 fresh hot green chilies, stemmed and thinly sliced
2 tablespoons julienne of fresh ginger

1. Cut *tandoori* hens in half to make 8 pieces all together. Combine butter sauce, *tandoori* hen pieces, cream, and half the ingredients for the garnish in a 2½-quart microwave-safe dish and cover with the lid.

2. Cook at 100 percent power in a 650- to 700-watt carousel oven for 10 minutes (or until sauce is boiling). Remove from oven. Let dish stand, covered, for 2 minutes. Uncover and serve sprinkled with the remaining black pepper, coriander, green chilies, and fresh ginger.

NOTE   The Butter Cornish Hen may be made ahead, set aside, covered, in the same container in the refrigerator for 2 days, and served reheated.

<hr>

MENU SUGGESTION

To complete the meal, accompany with a rice pilaf such as Crisp Okra and Spiced Basmati Pilaf (p. 306), a green vegetable such as Garlic Potatoes Smothered with Greens (p. 228), and cool Zucchini and Walnut Yogurt Raita (p. 262)

MOGHUL CORNISH HEN IN APRICOT GLAZE

MURGH KHOOBANI

MICROWAVE

Servings
  —4
Preparation time
  —3 minutes
Cooking time
  —29 minutes
Standing time
  —2 minutes
Heat
  —100 percent power
MW oven size
  —650 to 700 watts
MW cookware
  *—One 10-inch cov-
    ered skillet and one
    2½-quart covered
    casserole or soufflé
    dish*

In this classic Moghul recipe, Cornish hens (game hens are my choice over chicken as they are more flavorful and succulent) are braised in a mildly spiced, fennel-fragrant apricot sauce. The natural sweetish-tart flavor of the apricot against the mellow hens is a wondrous experience on the palate.

Microwaving is particularly suited for this dish with dried apricots because while apricots normally require several hours of soaking to soften, in this technique, they miraculously turn meltingly soft in just a few minutes without soaking.

ROOM TEMPERATURE

3 tablespoons usli ghee (p. 492), unsalted butter, or light vegetable oil
¾ cup finely chopped onion
1 teaspoon ground cumin
¾ teaspoon ground fennel
⅛ teaspoon freshly grated nutmeg
¼ teaspoon cayenne pepper
¼ teaspoon freshly ground black pepper
1 cup (4 ounces) chopped dried apricots

1 cup chopped tomatoes (fresh or canned), drained
1 tablespoon chopped fresh ginger
⅓ cup chicken stock (p. 488) or water
2 small Cornish game hens (2½–3 pounds), split, skinned, and trimmed of excess fat
2 teaspoons cornstarch dissolved in 2 tablespoons stock or water

FOR THE GARNISH:

Parsley or coriander sprigs

MENU SUGGESTION

To complete the meal, accompany with a rice pilaf such as Moghul-scented Basmati Pilaf (p. 302), a green vegetable such as Broccoli in Spicy-Garlic Oil (p. 205), and, if desired, Bombay Sweetish-Sour Garlic Lentils (p. 275).

1. Place *usli ghee,* butter, or oil in a 10-inch microwave-safe skillet. Heat, uncovered, at 100 percent power in a 650- to 700-watt carousel oven for 1 minute. Add onion, stir to mix, and cook, uncovered, at 100 percent power for 7 minutes (or until onions just begin to brown), stirring twice during the last 2 minutes of cooking when onions fry rapidly. Remove from oven.

2. Stir in first cumin, fennel, nutmeg, cayenne, and black pepper, then apricots, tomatoes, ginger, and stock, and cover with the lid. Cook at 100 percent power for 7 minutes 30 seconds (or until contents reduce to a thick sauce). Remove from oven.

3. Uncover, and stir sauce to crush the apricots and smoothen the texture. Slip in Cornish hen halves in a layer, making sure they are covered with the sauce, and cover with the lid. Cook at 100 percent power for 8 minutes. Uncover, turn hens, and replace cover. Cook at 100 percent power for an additional 4 minutes (or until hens are cooked through—clear juices run when pierced with a skewer at the thigh joint). Remove from oven.

4. Uncover and transfer hens to a heated serving platter. Stir cornstarch mixture into the sauce. Cook, uncovered, at 100 percent power for 1 minute (or until sauce thickens). Remove from oven. Distribute sauce over hens and serve garnished with parsley or coriander sprigs.

NOTE   This dish may be made ahead, set aside, covered, in the same container in the refrigerator for 2 days, and served reheated.

DUCK VENDALOO
VATHO VENDALOO

MICROWAVE

Servings
—4
Preparation time
—3 minutes
Cooking time
—18 minutes
Standing time
—5 minutes
Heat
—100 percent power
MW oven size
—650 to 700 watts
MW oven size
—One 2½-quart
    covered casserole or
    soufflé dish

A peppery and soul-soothing dish from the Goanese Christians (of Portuguese descent), *vendaloo* is particularly welcome on days when one's body and palate crave a chili fix. Although considered one of the hottest dishes in the world, *vendaloo* is, in fact, quite palatable because the Goanese cooks temper and tame chilies by cooking them with sweet seasonings and spices such as tamarind, sugar, cinnamon, and cloves. As a result, all one feels is a gentle glow at the back of one's mouth.

If you already have a batch of *vendaloo* sauce on hand, as I usually do, this dish is a snap to put together. You need only combine the duck with the sauce and cook until it is done! *Vendaloo* is also delicious made with equal amounts of chicken, game hen, squab, or turkey in place of the duck.

=============== ROOM TEMPERATURE ===============

1 4–5-pound Long Island duck, skinned, trimmed of all visible fat, and cut into 8–10 pieces (2 pounds meat with bones after trimming)

2½ cups (1 recipe) vendaloo sauce (p. 470)

3 tablespoons chopped fresh coriander

FOR THE GARNISH:

Coriander sprigs

Sliced green chilies

Precede this hot-and-spicy Goanese curry with the delicate and subtle Creamy Scallop Soup (p. 47). To complete the meal, serve Steamed Rice Cakes with Herbs (p. 332), Hyderabad Coconut-braised Potato Curry (p. 230), and Peach Chutney with Raisins and Walnuts (p. 349). Bombay Cheese Pudding (p. 387) is a soothing finale.

1. Arrange duck pieces in a 2½-quart oval or round microwave-safe casserole. Distribute *vendaloo* sauce over duck, making sure to cover all the pieces, and cover with the lid. Cook at 100 percent power in a 650- to 700-watt carousel oven for 18 minutes (or until duck is fully cooked). Remove from oven.

2. Let the *vendaloo* stand, covered, for 5 minutes. Uncover and carefully spoon out excess oil accumulated at the surface. (Reserve the oil for use over lentil purees [*dals*] or in cooking vegetables.) Transfer duck to a heated serving plate. Stir chopped coriander into the sauce and pour over duck. Serve immediately garnished with coriander sprigs and green chilies.

NOTE   The *vendaloo* may be made ahead, set aside, covered, in the same container in the refrigerator for 4 days, and served reheated.

DUCK BRAISED IN CURRIED VEGETABLE-LENTIL PUREE

BATAKH DAL

MICROWAVE

Servings
—6
Preparation time
—6 minutes
Cooking time
—28 minutes
Heat
—100 percent power
MW oven size
—650 to 700 watts
MW cookware
—One 5-quart covered
casserole

I love sauces made with creamy pureed lentils. Not only do they take the sharp edge off the spices, they lend a rich body and flavor to the sauce. In this classic Moghul preparation, freshly killed wild fowl is combined with fragrant seasoning, spices, and lentils and slowly steamed until the bird absorbs the delicate flavor of lentils and, in turn, enriches the sauce with its essence.

Once again, the microwave is magical for this recipe. First, the dish is a simple process—combine all the ingredients and cook. Second, the moist microwave heat keeps the duck succulent and intact, without falling apart in the sauce. For variation, substitute a combination of dill and parsley in place of mint and coriander, and, if desired, chicken or turkey in place of the duck.

The pureed vegetables and lentils that form the sauce in this dish are really an elaborate *dal* (see more on page 266), and therefore are best served accompanied with cooked rice, with the sauce generously spooned over it.

―――――― ROOM TEMPERATURE ――――――

¾ cup dried red (pink)
  lentils (p. 460), picked
  clean and rinsed
2½ cups chicken stock
  (p. 488), vegetarian
  stock (p. 489), or
  water

1 tablespoon chopped
  fresh ginger
2 teaspoons finely
  chopped garlic
1 tablespoon curry
  powder, homemade
  (p. 479) or store-
  bought

1 teaspoon turmeric
2½ teaspoons kosher salt
4 tablespoons packed
   chopped fresh, or 2
   tablespoons crushed
   dried, mint
2 tablespoons chopped
   fresh coriander
2–4 fresh hot green
   chilies, stemmed,
   seeded, and minced

1 4–5-pound Long Island
   duck, skinned,
   trimmed of all visible
   fat, and cut into 8–10
   pieces (2 pounds meat
   with bones after
   trimming)
1 cup chopped zucchini
1 cup thinly sliced
   carrots
1½ cups chopped onion
¼ cup heavy cream

MENU SUGGESTION

This fragrant duck curry is nice preceded by Sesame Shrimp (p. 13). To complete the meal, serve Moghul-scented Basmati Pilaf (p. 302), Eggplant Slices Smothered with Coconut-Spice Paste (p. 215), and, if desired, Sweet Persimmon and Plum Chutney with Cinnamon (p. 353).

FOR THE GARNISH:
Mint sprigs

1. Arrange all the ingredients except cream, in the order listed above, in a 5-quart microwave-safe casserole and cover with the lid. Cook at 100 percent power in a 650- to 700-watt carousel oven for 26 minutes (or until duck is cooked tender and lentils are soft). Remove from oven.

2. Uncover, carefully take out duck pieces and arrange them in a heated deep serving dish, and cover loosely to keep them warm. Mix sauce, beating with a whisk, to crush some of the lentils and vegetables. Stir in cream. Cook, uncovered, at 100 percent power for 2 minutes (or until sauce is boiling hot). Pour sauce over duck and serve immediately garnished with mint.

NOTE   This dish may be made ahead, set aside, covered, in the same container in the refrigerator for 3 days, and served reheated.

MEAT

The microwave is ideal for cooking Indian meat dishes because most of the preparations are stewed, braised, steamed, or pot roasted. The meat cooks tender and more succulent in the moist trapped heat. The stewed dishes such as Lamb in Creamy Tomato Sauce (p. 151) or Fragrant Beef with Peas I or II (pp. 143 and 145) cook splendidly in sauce. The lamb pieces do not fall apart or become tough even when overcooked, and the ground beef is tender but still retains a springy texture without getting pasty. Similarly, the microwave oven provides the perfect environment for braised dishes as, for example, in Kafta Kabob in Hot Vendaloo Sauce (p. 142). Kaftas, in the moist heat, absorb more juices and become puffier than when they are cooked by any other technique.

An important thing to remember when cooking meat in the microwave is that the smaller and more uniform in size the pieces are the better and faster the dish will cook. This is because of the limited penetrating power of microwaves—about one and a half inches into the interior from the surface of the food. The larger pieces thus cook through dispersion of heat from the more quickly cooked portion of meat. Naturally, ground beef will cook faster than cubed meat or a roast. For additional details see Microwave Variables: Moisture Content and Food Size (p. xx).

Meat loaf was one of the first American dishes found to respond beautifully to the microwave, and the Savory Keema Cake (p. 147), which is an Indian meat loaf–like dish, is also ideal. Since ground beef releases moisture during cooking, I like to add chopped nuts and bulgur to the dish; they cook in this excess moisture and give the cake a wonderfully chewy texture. One other reason I love keema cake: It cooks in seven minutes.

Because of the rapid speed at which microwaves cook and tenderize meat—most of the dishes here take less than half the time it takes to cook them by conventional means—the flavors of spices and herbs are fresher and more intense, with better color and fragrance. The meat itself is also more flavorful because it is cooked with almost no added fat.

Using meat with some marbling but no surface fat will also speed cooking—microwaves are readily absorbed by fat—and the result is food with a glazed, velvety appearance and a soft, luxurious texture. Generally speaking, ground chuck with higher fat content is better than ground round or sirloin; similarly, cuts from the shoulder are better than those from the loin or leg. They are also less expensive. But keep in mind that with added fat comes additional calories and cholesterol. The trick, therefore, is to try to balance the two factors. You may want to substitute ingredients. I have made specific recommendations in each recipe to help get you started.

A lean roast is normally a disaster when roasted in the microwave: Lack of marbling coupled with long cooking often dries out the exterior meat. Goanese Roast Pork with Cinnamon-Ginger Gravy (p. 157) however, is an exception. The pork loin is coated with an herb and spice mixture that, during cooking, sets and forms a seal to trap the moisture within and keep the roast from drying out. (This dish is a special favorite of mine, one that keeps well in the refrigerator for a week or more and lovely when served cold in slices.)

INDIAN BEEF SAUSAGE KABOB

SEEKH KABAB

MICROWAVE

Yield
—12 3-inch kabobs
Servings
—4
Preparation time
—9 minutes
Cooking time
—2 minutes
Heat
—100 percent power
MW oven size
—650 to 700 watts
MW cookware
—One 10-inch
browning skillet or
regular skillet

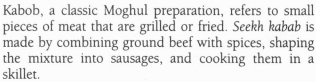

Kabob, a classic Moghul preparation, refers to small pieces of meat that are grilled or fried. *Seekh kabab* is made by combining ground beef with spices, shaping the mixture into sausages, and cooking them in a skillet.

Making this dish in the microwave would not be feasible had manufacturers of microwave cookware not come up with the browning skillet (see more on p. xxvii). Searing the kabob is essential in order to get that browned meat flavor. And a browning skillet does just that. The microwave cooks kabobs not only fast but also all the way through (as is traditionally done in Moghul cooking) without drying them out. But the moist heat also dulls the "seared" appearance. Therefore, I coat the kabobs with chopped fragrant herbs before serving them, which adds not only visual appeal but fragrance as well.

While cooking in the microwave, the kabobs exude juices that can be either served over kabobs or stirred into sauces such as fragrant tomato sauce (p. 467), butter sauce (p. 469), or fiery *vendaloo* sauce (p. 470).

===================== ROOM TEMPERATURE =====================

1-inch cube fresh ginger, peeled	1 pound lean ground beef chuck
2 large cloves garlic, peeled	2 teaspoons ground roasted cumin seeds (p. 465)
1–4 fresh hot green chilies, stemmed and cut into 1-inch pieces	¾ teaspoon ground cardamom
1 medium-size onion, peeled and quartered	½ teaspoon cayenne pepper

1¼ teaspoons kosher salt   ½ cup finely chopped fresh coriander

1. Put ginger, garlic, and chilies into the container of a food processor and process until the ingredients are finely chopped. Add onion and run the machine with the pulse motion until the onions are finely chopped. Add beef, cumin, cardamom, cayenne, and salt. Continue processing until the spices are evenly blended and the beef looks pasty. Remove beef mixture into a bowl and divide into 12 equal portions. Roll each portion into either a thin sausage or a round ball.

2. Heat a 10-inch browning skillet at 100 percent power in a 650- to 700-watt carousel oven for 4 minutes. Remove from oven. Add kabobs in one layer. Let kabobs sizzle, undisturbed, for 1 minute, then carefully turn kabobs using tongs, rolling the kabobs to sear all sides. If you are using a regular microwave-safe covered skillet, then skip this step and simply arrange kabobs in it.

3. Cook, uncovered, at 100 percent power for 2 minutes (or until meat is fully cooked—kabob springs back when touched). Remove from oven. Baste kabobs with the juices accumulated at the bottom of the dish. Remove kabobs, generously coat with chopped coriander, and serve accompanied with the juices, heated at 100 percent power for 30 seconds (or until piping hot), in a small bowl.

MENU SUGGESTION

To complete the meal, serve Crisp Okra and Spiced Basmati Rice (p. 306) and Cauliflower and Fennel in Aromatic Oil (p. 209). These kabobs are lovely cut into bite-size pieces and served as appetizers with cocktails with any of the yogurt or fruity dipping sauces (pp. 365–376).

KAFTA KABOB IN CREAMED TOMATO SAUCE

MALAI KOFTA

Kafta kabob, an Italian meatball-like dish, is another Moghul classic. Kafta kabobs are very similar to sausage kabobs (p. 138) except they are simmered in a sweet, creamy tomato sauce until puffed and juicy after being grilled or fried. Traditionally served at banquets and special feasts, *malai kofta* is meant to have a rich, creamy sauce. For a lighter version, however, some of the cream may be replaced with milk or water, but *not yogurt* as it will increase the acidity level in the dish.

While cooking in the microwave, the kafta balls exude juices that must not be discarded but are stirred back into the creamy tomato sauce.

=== ROOM TEMPERATURE ===

FOR THE KAFTA:
1 pound extra-lean
    ground beef round
1 tablespoon crushed or
    grated fresh ginger
2 teaspoons minced
    garlic
1–4 fresh hot green
    chilies, stemmed,
    seeded, and minced

1 teaspoon garam masala
    (p. 478) or curry
    powder, homemade
    (p. 479) or store-
    bought
⅓ cup fresh bread
    crumbs
1 large egg
1¼ teaspoons kosher salt

2½ cups fragrant tomato
    sauce (p. 467)

¼ cup heavy cream,
    light cream, half-and-
    half, or milk

¼ cup finely chopped fresh coriander

1. Combine all the ingredients for the kafta in a bowl and mix, kneading the mixture until thoroughly blended. Divide the mixture into 12 equal portions and roll each into a round ball.

2. Heat a 10-inch browning skillet at 100 percent power in a 650- to 700-watt carousel oven for 4 minutes. Remove from oven. Add kaftas in one layer. Let kabobs sizzle undisturbed for 1 minute, then carefully turn kaftas using tongs, rolling the kaftas to sear on all sides, and cover with the lid. If you are using a regular microwave-safe covered skillet, then skip this step and simply arrange kabobs in it.

3. Cook at 100 percent power for 2 minutes (or until meat is fully cooked—kafta springs back when touched). Remove from oven. Set aside, covered, until needed.

4. Pour the sauce and cream in a 2½-quart microwave-safe casserole and cover with the lid. Cook at 100 percent power for 4 minutes (or until sauce is gently boiling). Uncover and add kaftas together with the accumulated juices. Mix lightly and replace cover. Cook at 100 percent power for 4 minutes (or until contents are heated through and kaftas are puffed). Remove from oven. Let the dish stand, covered, for 5 minutes. Uncover and serve kaftas, spooning the sauce over them and sprinkling with coriander.

NOTE The kafta kabob may be made ahead and set aside, covered, in the same container in the refrigerator for 2 days, and served reheated.

MENU SUGGESTION

These delicate kafta kabobs in a mildly fragrant cream sauce are lovely served with Saffron Pilaf (p. 304). You may also wish to include Mustard-braised Endive (p. 218) and a fruity chutney such as Pineapple Apricot Chutney (p. 351).

KAFTA KABOB IN HOT VENDALOO SAUCE
KOFTA VENDALOO

MENU SUGGESTION

These kaftas, spicy-hot due to the fiery vendaloo *sauce, are best enjoyed with Plain Basmati Rice (p. 299). You may also, if desired, include Garlic Potatoes Smothered with Greens (p. 228) and a cool* raita *such as Zucchini and Walnut Yogurt Raita (p. 262).*

Follow all the directions for making Kafta Kabob in Creamed Tomato Sauce (p. 140), except substitute fiery *vendaloo* sauce (p. 470) in place of fragrant tomato sauce and use coconut milk (p. 450) in place of heavy cream.

FRAGRANT BEEF WITH PEAS I

KEEMA MATAR

MICROWAVE

Servings
  —4
Cooking time
  —19 minutes
Standing time
  —5 minutes
Heat
  —100 percent power
MW oven size
  —650 to 700 watts
MW cookware
  *—One 10-inch cov-
    ered skillet*

Keema can best be described as an Indian version of Tex-Mex chili, except that it is a lighter and more intricately flavored dish. A classic Moghul preparation, *keema* can range from very mild to spicy-hot, soupy like chili to thick as a taco filling. The following recipe produces a *keema* that is spicy, fragrant, and moderately thick. For an even spicier version, fold 1 teaspoon minced green chilies into the finished *keema.*

===== *ROOM TEMPERATURE* =====

1 teaspoon ground cumin

*2 teaspoons ground
  coriander*

½ teaspoon turmeric

*1 teaspoon cayenne
  pepper*

*3 tablespoons light
  vegetable oil*

*¾ cup finely chopped
  onion*

*1 teaspoon finely
  chopped garlic*

*1 tablespoon grated or
  crushed fresh ginger*

*1 pound lean ground beef
  chuck*

*2 tablespoons tomato
  paste*

*⅓ cup plain yogurt,
  coconut milk (p. 450),
  or water*

*¾ cup green peas (fresh
  or frozen)*

*2 tablespoons heavy
  cream, half-and-half,
  or milk*

*1 teaspoon garam masala
  (p. 478) or ground
  roasted cumin seeds
  (p. 465)*

Kosher salt to taste

*4 tablespoons chopped
  fresh coriander*

1. Combine cumin, coriander, turmeric, and cayenne in a small bowl and reserve.

2. Place oil, onion, garlic, and ginger in a 10-inch microwave-safe skillet. Cook, uncovered, at 100 percent power in a 650- to 700-watt carousel oven for 8 minutes (or until onions are lightly colored). Stir in the spice mixture and continue cooking, uncovered, for an additional 1 minute. Remove from oven.

3. Add beef, tomato paste, and yogurt and mix thoroughly. Cook, covered, at 100 percent power for 8 minutes (or until beef is fully cooked), stirring once. Uncover, add peas and cream, and replace cover. Cook, covered, for an additional 2 minutes (or until sauce comes to a boil). Remove from oven. Uncover, stir in *garam masala,* salt to taste, and 2 tablespoons coriander, and replace cover. Let the dish stand for 5 minutes, then uncover and serve sprinkled with the remaining coriander.

NOTE   The *keema* may be made ahead and set aside, covered, in the same container in the refrigerator for 4 days, and served reheated.

MENU SUGGESTION

Although not essential, Toasted Lentil Wafers (p. 10) provide a nice textural contrast to this beef dish. To complete the meal, serve Moghul-scented Basmati Pilaf (p. 302), Green Beans in Peppered-Mustard Dressing (p. 220), and Crushed Cucumber Salsa (p. 239) or a cool Zucchini and Walnut Yogurt Raita (p. 262).

FRAGRANT BEEF WITH PEAS II

KEEMA MATAR

This is a milder, more creamy-tasting *keema* as compared to the previous version, although it contains no cream or milk. The peanut butter in the recipe makes a smoother-finished sauce as well as enriching the flavor. For an even milder version, eliminate cayenne and increase the peanut butter to 4 tablespoons.

MICROWAVE

Servings
  —2
Preparation time
  —3 minutes
Cooking time
  —18 minutes
Standing time
  —3 minutes
Heat
  —100 percent power
MW oven size
  —650 to 700 watts
MW cookware
  —One 10-inch covered skillet

=== ROOM TEMPERATURE ===

2 teaspoons ground coriander

1 teaspoon ground cumin

½ teaspoon turmeric

¼ teaspoon cayenne pepper

3 tablespoons light vegetable oil

¾ cup finely chopped onion

1 tablespoon finely chopped garlic

1 tablespoon finely chopped fresh ginger

¾ pound lean ground beef chuck

1 cup finely chopped tomatoes (fresh or canned), drained

2 tablespoons peanut butter

1 teaspoon kosher salt

½ cup green peas (fresh or frozen)

2 tablespoons chopped fresh coriander

1. Combine coriander, cumin, turmeric, and cayenne in a small bowl and reserve.

2. Heat oil in a 10-inch microwave-safe browning skillet, uncovered, in a 650- to 700-watt carousel oven at 100 percent power for 2 minutes. Add onion, garlic, and ginger and mix lightly. Cook, uncovered, at 100 percent power for 9 minutes (or until onions are lightly browned), stirring once. Blend in the spice mixture

and continue cooking, uncovered, for an additional 1 minute (or until spices exude a fried aroma). Remove from oven.

3. Add beef, tomatoes, peanut butter, and salt, mix well, and cover with the lid. Cook at 100 percent power for 6 minutes (or until beef is cooked). Remove from oven, uncover, stir in peas, and replace cover. Let the dish stand, covered, for 3 minutes. Uncover, add coriander and lightly fold in, and serve.

NOTE   The *keema* may be made ahead and set aside, covered, in the same container in the refrigerator for 2 days, and served reheated.

MENU SUGGESTION

Follow the menu suggestions given for Fragrant Beef with Peas I (p. 143). To complete the meal you could instead serve Split Pea and Basmati Pilaf (p. 314), Garlic-fried Okra with Tamarind (p. 224), and the very fragrant Minted Red Onion Salad (p. 241).

SAVORY KEEMA CAKE

KEEMA KABAB

MICROWAVE

Servings
—*6*
Preparation time
—*3 minutes*
Cooking time
—*7 minutes*
Standing time
—*5 minutes*
Heat
—*100 percent power*
MW oven size
—*650 to 700 watts*
MW cookware
—*One 10-inch tart or
quiche plate or
skillet*

You must make this wonderful *keema* cake to experience what *flavor* means, particularly since it takes hardly any time and effort. All you do is combine the ingredients, pat them down into a pie plate, and cook. In a matter of minutes the cake emerges, lightly puffed and full of fragrance, to be sliced into wedges and served. For a spicier version, fold two to four fresh hot green chilies, stemmed, seeded, and sliced, into the meat mixture.

While cooking in the microwave the cake will release about a tablespoon of juice, which can be served over the cake. In any event, the juice will be absorbed into the cake as it cools.

=== ROOM TEMPERATURE ===

*1½ pounds lean ground
  beef round*
*3 tablespoons bulgur
  (p. 449)*
*4 tablespoons finely
  chopped walnuts*
1 cup fresh bread crumbs
*1 tablespoon tomato
  paste*
1 large egg
*½ cup finely chopped
  onion*
1 teaspoon minced garlic
*1 tablespoon crushed or
  grated fresh ginger*

*2 teaspoons ground
  cumin*
*⅓ teaspoon freshly
  ground black pepper*
*⅓ teaspoon cayenne
  pepper*
1½ teaspoons kosher salt
*2 tablespoons finely
  chopped fresh, or
  1 tablespoon crushed
  dried, mint*
*2 tablespoons finely
  chopped fresh
  coriander*

1. Combine all the ingredients in a mixing bowl and pack into a 10-inch microwave-safe pie or quiche plate or 10-inch microwave-safe skillet.

2. Cook, uncovered, at 100 percent power in a 650- to 700-watt carousel oven for 7 minutes (or until meat is cooked and a toothpick inserted in the middle of cake comes out clean). Remove from oven. Let cake rest for 5 minutes before serving. Serve sliced into wedges and accompanied with Spicy Indian Tomato Sauce (p. 368) or Cool Yogurt Sauce (p. 365).

NOTE   This *keema* cake may be made ahead and set aside, covered, in the same container in the refrigerator for 2 days, and served reheated.

MOGHUL BRAISED VEAL IN GARLIC SAUCE

ROGAN JOSH

MICROWAVE

Servings
  —4 to 6
Preparation time
  —5 minutes
Cooking time
  —29 minutes
Heat
  —100 percent power
MW oven size
  —650 to 700 watts
MW cookware
  —One 2½-quart covered casserole or soufflé dish and one 8-inch skillet

A classic of Moghul cooking, this dish from the valley of Kashmir combines two of the most popular ingredients of their cuisine—garlic and cream. Both veal and lamb work well in the recipe, creating the authentic flavor. The beauty of the microwave is that it not only cooks the meat three times as fast and to a wonderful succulence but also diffuses its flavor into the sauce, thus lending *rogan josh* more character. In the Moghul tradition, *rogan josh* is meant to be rich and creamy. You can, if you wish, reduce or eliminate the cream in the recipe, but the results will not be as good.

=============== ROOM TEMPERATURE ===============

3-inch piece fresh ginger, peeled and roughly chopped

4 medium-size (1 pound) onions, peeled and quartered

1½ pounds stewing veal

2 cups sour cream, plain yogurt, or their combination

1 teaspoon ground cardamom

1 teaspoon cayenne pepper

2 tablespoons ground coriander

2 teaspoons kosher salt, or to taste

FOR SEASONING THE STEW:

3 tablespoons usli ghee (p. 492), unsalted butter, or light vegetable oil

2 teaspoons minced garlic

1 teaspoon ground cumin

1 teaspoon Moghul
  garam masala (p.
  477) or garam masala
  (p. 478)

2 teaspoons cornstarch
½ cup heavy cream
4 tablespoons chopped
  fresh coriander

MENU SUGGESTION

This delicate Moghul veal curry is best served with Saffron Pilaf (p. 304), Broccoli in Spicy-Garlic Oil (p. 205), and Moghul Saffron and Mango Yogurt Raita (p. 254). Bombay Coconut Shrimp (p. 11) is particularly nice before this dish.

1. With the steel blade attached, turn on the food processor. While the machine is running, drop ginger through the feed tube into the container and process until finely minced. Add onions and continue processing until they are finely minced.

2. Transfer the mixture into a 2½-quart microwave-safe casserole and add all other ingredients for cooking the stew. Mix well and cover with the lid. Cook at 100 percent power in a 650- to 700-watt carousel oven for 23 minutes (or until veal is fork-tender). Remove from oven and set aside while you make the seasonings.

3. Heat the *usli ghee,* butter, or oil in an 8-inch microwave-safe skillet at 100 percent power for 2 minutes 30 seconds. Add garlic, cumin, and Moghul *garam masala* and mix well. Cook at 100 percent power for 1 minute. Remove from oven. Uncover stew and pour the entire contents of the skillet on it, scraping with a rubber spatula to capture all the spices. Blend the cornstarch into the cream and add to the stew. Mix well and cover with lid. Cook at 100 percent power for 3 minutes (or until heated through). Remove from oven, uncover, sprinkle with coriander, and serve.

NOTE This *rogan josh* may be made ahead and set aside, covered, in the same dish in the refrigerator for 3 days, and served reheated.

LAMB IN CREAMY TOMATO SAUCE

MALAI GOSHT

I love this fragrant, creamy lamb with tomatoes. It is delicate and mild like most Moghul dishes. Thinned with water or low-fat milk it makes a filling soup. This is one of those recipes that works gloriously in the microwave. Not only are the steps simple and quick, but the lamb cooks to an uncommonly moist tenderness. The sauce becomes rather thick and gelatinous with keeping, therefore check consistency and add water to thin accordingly before serving.

MICROWAVE

Servings
　—4 to 6
Preparation time
　—3 minutes
Cooking time
　—32 minutes
Standing time
　—10 minutes
Heat
　—100 percent power
MW oven size
　—650 to 700 watts
MW cookware
　—One 5-quart covered casserole

ROOM TEMPERATURE

1 medium-size (¼ pound) onion, peeled and quartered

1½ cups peeled, chopped, and drained tomatoes (fresh or canned)

2-inch piece fresh ginger, peeled and roughly chopped

3 large cloves garlic, peeled

½ cup lightly packed coriander leaves

1½ cups whole or low-fat plain yogurt

1½ pounds lean, boneless lamb shoulder or leg or beef chuck, cut into 1-inch cubes

½ pound (2 medium-size) new red wax potatoes, peeled and cut into 1-inch cubes

2 tablespoons ground coriander

½ teaspoon turmeric

1 teaspoon cayenne pepper

2 teaspoons kosher salt

2 teaspoons cornstarch

½ cup heavy cream, light cream, or whole milk

2 teaspoons garam masala (p. 478) or ground roasted cumin seeds (p. 465)

2 tablespoons finely chopped fresh coriander

1. Puree onion, tomatoes, ginger, garlic, and fresh coriander in a food processor, using yogurt as necessary, in 2 batches. Transfer contents into a 5-quart microwave-safe casserole. Add the remaining yogurt, lamb, potatoes, ground coriander, turmeric, cayenne, and salt. Mix well and cover with the lid.

2. Dissolve cornstarch in cream and set aside.

3. Cook at 100 percent power in a 650- to 700-watt carousel oven for 30 minutes (or until lamb is fork-tender). Uncover, stir in cornstarch-cream mixture and *garam masala* or cumin, and replace cover. Continue cooking at 100 percent power for 2 minutes (or until cream is heated through). Remove from oven.

4. Uncover, stir well to mix, and replace cover. Let lamb rest, covered, for 10 minutes. Uncover and serve sprinkled with coriander.

NOTE   This creamy lamb dish may be made ahead and set aside, covered, in the same dish in the refrigerator for 3 days, and served reheated.

NOTE   For a salt-free and low-calorie dish, omit salt and use fat-free yogurt and low-fat milk or water in place of whole-milk yogurt and cream.

MENU SUGGESTION

This lovely braised dish of lamb with creamy tomato sauce is perfect served with Saffron Pilaf (p. 304). You may also wish to include Broccoli in Spicy-Garlic Oil (p. 205) and a fruity chutney such as Peach Chutney with Raisins and Walnuts (p. 349).

LAMB
IN MINT-FLAVORED
LENTIL SAUCE

DAL GOSHT

MICROWAVE

Servings
—6
Preparation time
—3 minutes
Cooking time
—32 minutes
Standing time
—5 minutes
Heat
—100 percent power
MW oven size
—650 to 700 watts
MW cookware
—One 5-quart covered
casserole

This is a popular, everyday dish from Pakistan in which lamb, lentils, and fragrant herbs and spices are packed into a pot and slowly simmered until the meat turns meltingly tender and the lentils reduce to a smooth, velvety puree. Don't be alarmed by the long list of ingredients; the process itself couldn't be simpler. All you do is combine and cook. And in the microwave the dish is done in one-third the usual time taken by conventional cooking. Cornstarch is added to the sauce primarily for aesthetic reasons—to bind the sauce as both coconut and regular milk curdle during cooking. Any leftovers, thinned with milk, coconut milk, or water, make a deliciously filling soup.

========= ROOM TEMPERATURE =========

2 medium-size (½ pound) onions, peeled and quartered

1-inch cube fresh ginger, peeled and roughly chopped

4 medium-size cloves garlic, peeled

2 or more, to taste, fresh hot green chilies, stemmed

⅓ cup lightly packed mint leaves

2½ cups coconut milk (p. 450), light cream, or whole or low-fat milk

1½ pounds lean, boneless lamb shoulder, cut into 1-inch cubes

¾ cup dried red (pink) lentils (p. 460), picked clean and rinsed

1 tablespoon ground coriander

1 teaspoon ground
cardamom
2 teaspoons kosher salt

2 tablespoons cornstarch
dissolved in ½ cup
heavy cream, light
cream, milk, or water
2 tablespoons finely
chopped fresh mint

FOR THE GARNISH:

Mint sprigs

MENU SUGGESTION

This is a hearty, filling casserole of lamb. All you need is some bread such as store-bought or homemade pita or chapati with this dish. The casserole is also good with rice and salad, such as Tomato Basmati Pilaf (p. 308) and Fragrant Cabbage Salad with Ginger Slivers and Tomatoes (p. 245). Sesame Shrimp (p. 13) is a particularly nice way to start this meal.

1. Combine onion, ginger, garlic, chilies, and mint leaves in the container of a food processor and process until pureed, using coconut milk as needed.

2. Transfer the mixture into a 5-quart microwave-safe casserole. Add the remaining coconut milk, lamb, lentils, coriander, cardamom, and salt. Stir to mix and cover with the lid. Cook at 100 percent power in a 650- to 700-watt carousel oven for 30 minutes (or until lamb is fork-tender and lentils are soft), stirring once. Uncover, stir in cornstarch-cream solution, and replace cover. Continue cooking at 100 percent power for 2 minutes (or until heated through). Remove from oven.

3. Let lamb rest, covered, for 5 minutes before serving. Uncover, stir in chopped mint, and serve garnished with mint sprigs.

NOTE   This minted lamb curry may be made ahead and set aside, covered, in the same container in the refrigerator for a day, and served reheated. The mint, however, loses its appealing color but not its flavor.

NOTE   For a salt-free and low-calorie dish, omit salt and use low-fat milk or water in place of coconut milk and heavy cream.

MOGHUL LAMB IN CREAMED SPINACH SAUCE

SAAG GOSHT

MICROWAVE

Servings
—6 to 8
Preparation time
—3 minutes
Cooking time
—34 minutes
Standing time
—10 minutes
Heat
—100 percent power
MW oven size
—650 to 700 watts
MW cookware
—One 5-quart covered
casserole

This is another famous braised preparation of Moghul cooking, in which pieces of lamb cooked in a subtly spiced onion-tomato sauce are served folded into a spinach puree fragrant with coriander. Whether it is the rich, complex flavor of the lamb, or the appeal of glistening spinach, or its nutritive values, no one knows for certain, but certainly this is one of the two most popular Indian dishes (*tandoori* chicken being the other) in America. The microwave wilts spinach so that it remains bright and green.

=== ROOM TEMPERATURE ===

1 medium-size onion, peeled and quartered

1½ cups peeled, crushed tomatoes (fresh or canned)

2-inch piece fresh ginger, peeled and roughly chopped

3 large cloves garlic, peeled

4 or more fresh hot green chilies, stemmed

½ cup lightly packed coriander leaves

1 cup chicken or beef stock (p. 488) or water

1½ pounds lean, boneless lamb shoulder or butt, cut into 1-inch cubes

1 tablespoon ground coriander

2 teaspoons ground cumin

1 teaspoon turmeric

1 tablespoon paprika

2 teaspoons kosher salt

4 tablespoons tomato paste

1 pound fresh leaf spinach, rinsed and finely chopped

2 teaspoons garam mas-
   ala *(p. 478) or ground
   roasted cumin seeds
   (p. 465)*

4 tablespoons finely
   chopped fresh
   coriander
¼ cup heavy cream,
   light cream, or whole
   milk

1. Finely puree onion, tomatoes, ginger, garlic, chilies, and fresh coriander in a food processor, using stock or water as necessary, in two batches.

2. Transfer contents into a 5-quart microwave-safe casserole. Add the remaining stock or water, lamb, ground coriander, cumin, turmeric, paprika, and salt. Mix well and cover with the lid. Cook at 100 percent power in a 650- to 700-watt carousel oven for 30 minutes (or until beef is fork-tender). Remove from oven.

3. Uncover and stir in tomato paste. Pack spinach on top and cover with the lid. Cook at 100 percent power for 4 minutes (or until spinach is wilted). Remove from oven. Uncover, quickly stir in *garam masala*, coriander, and cream, and replace cover. Let the dish stand, covered, for 10 minutes before serving.

NOTE   The lamb with spinach may be made ahead, set aside, covered, in the same container in the refrigerator for a day, and served reheated. The spinach, however, loses its appealing color but not its flavor.

NOTE   For a salt-free and low-calorie dish, omit salt and cream.

MENU SUGGESTION

Serve this hearty lamb in spinach sauce with a simple yet fragrant rice such as Moghul-scented Basmati Pilaf (p. 302). Zucchini Braised in Tomato Cumin Sauce (p. 234) and cool Spicy Potato and Yogurt Raita (p. 260) are nice additions.

GOANESE ROAST PORK WITH CINNAMON-GINGER GRAVY

LAI THAO

MICROWAVE

Servings
  —8
Preparation time
  *—5 minutes plus 2
    hours for
    marinating*
Cooking time
  —31 minutes
Standing time
  —15 minutes
Heat
  —100 percent power
MW oven size
  —650 to 700 watts
MW cookware
  *—One 2½-quart
    covered oval casse-
    role or bacon/meat
    rack*

In India, it is the Christians, from Goa in particular, who cook and enjoy pork, as religious taboos forbid most others from eating it. In this recipe the pork is coated with garlic, cayenne, and wine vinegar, as in the Portuguese tradition. But Goans add sweet, fragrant cinnamon, clove, jaggery, mustard, and ginger to temper the heat and round off the flavors. The roast becomes exceptionally succulent in the microwave, requiring no basting of any sort. In addition, molasses is substituted for jaggery in the recipe, which, without deviating from classic flavor, lends a richer color to the roast. The leftover meat and sauce are lovely served cold or at room temperature in salads and sandwiches.

=== ROOM TEMPERATURE ===

FOR THE SPICE MIXTURE:
2 tablespoons minced
  garlic
1 tablespoon crushed or
  grated fresh ginger
2 tablespoons red wine
  vinegar
2 teaspoons mustard
  seeds, crushed

2 teaspoons ground
  cinnamon
½ teaspoon ground
  cloves
1 teaspoon turmeric
1½ teaspoons cayenne
  pepper
½ teaspoon freshly
  ground black pepper

FOR THE PORK:
1 3½-pound boneless
  pork loin roast, tied at
  1-inch intervals

2 tablespoons unsulfured
  molasses
¾ cup water

1½ teaspoons cornstarch,   ¾ teaspoon lemon juice
   dissolved in 1 table-
   spoon water

1. Combine all the spices in a bowl.

2. Place the pork roast in a shallow dish and prick all over with a fork. Spread the spice mixture evenly over the pork. Cover and marinate for 2 hours (it may be refrigerated for up to 2 days but should be taken out at least 30 minutes before cooking, or allow additional time during cooking).

3. Place the pork in a 2½-quart microwave-safe oval casserole and cover with the lid. Or place the pork on a microwave-safe bacon rack and cover the ends of the roast to a width of 1 inch with aluminum foil to prevent them from overcooking and drying out. Cook at 100 percent power in a 650- to 700-watt carousel oven for 24 minutes (27 minutes if refrigerated), removing the foil after 16 minutes of cooking.

4. Uncover or remove aluminum foil and dribble molasses on top of the roast. Continue cooking, uncovered, at 100 percent power until the pork is cooked and a meat thermometer inserted in the center registers 160 degrees (about 5 minutes). Remove from oven. Transfer roast to a platter. Let roast rest, loosely covered to keep warm, for 15 minutes for the juices to settle. Meanwhile, make the gravy.

5. Pour ¾ cup water into the dish, scraping the bottom of the pan to loosen drippings. If you are using the roasting rack, pour the juices into a 2-cup glass measure. Stir in cornstarch solution and cook, uncovered at 100 percent power for 1 minute 15 seconds (or until gravy thickens). Remove from oven and stir in lemon juice.

6. To serve, remove and discard the trussing strings, cut the meat into thin slices, and arrange on a heated serving platter. Accompany with gravy on the side.

MENU SUGGESTION

This elegant roast is lovely preceded with a delicate Creamy Scallop Soup (p. 47). To complete the meal, serve Split Pea and Basmati Pilaf (p. 314), Garlic-fried Okra with Tamarind (p. 224), and a cool Avocado and Cucumber Yogurt Raita (p. 251). Rich, creamy ice cream topped with Warm Mango Sauce with Almonds (p. 406) is a grand finale to this meal.

NOTE The pork roast may be made ahead and set aside, covered, in the refrigerator for 5 days. For best results, serve the roast cold, as reheating alters the meat's delicate flavor.

GOANESE SPICY BRAISED PORK CHOPS

BAFFAT

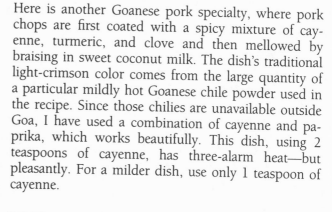

MICROWAVE

Servings
  — 4
Preparation time
  — 4 minutes
Cooking time
  —18 minutes
Standing time
  —2 minutes
Heat
  —100 percent power
MW oven size
  —650 to 700 watts
MW cookware
  *—One 10-inch cov-
  ered browning skil-
  let or regular skillet*

Here is another Goanese pork specialty, where pork chops are first coated with a spicy mixture of cayenne, turmeric, and clove and then mellowed by braising in sweet coconut milk. The dish's traditional light-crimson color comes from the large quantity of a particular mildly hot Goanese chile powder used in the recipe. Since those chilies are unavailable outside Goa, I have used a combination of cayenne and paprika, which works beautifully. This dish, using 2 teaspoons of cayenne, has three-alarm heat—but pleasantly. For a milder dish, use only 1 teaspoon of cayenne.

ROOM TEMPERATURE

4 1-inch-thick loin pork
  chops, trimmed of
  bone and excess fat
2 tablespoons usli ghee
  (p. 492), unsalted but-
  ter, or light vegetable
  oil
1 teaspoon minced garlic
2 teaspoons cayenne
  pepper, or to taste
2 teaspoons paprika
1 teaspoon ground
  cinnamon
½ teaspoon turmeric
½ teaspoon ground
  cloves

1 teaspoon kosher salt
2 small red onions,
  peeled and cut into ½-
  inch-thick slices
2 tablespoons julienne of
  fresh hot green chilies
  or sweet green peppers
  or a combination
1 tablespoon Dijon
  mustard
1 teaspoon cornstarch
⅓ cup coconut milk
  (p. 450) or half-and-
  half

1. Heat a 10-inch browning skillet at 100 percent power in a 650- to 700-watt carousel oven for 4 minutes. Remove from oven. Add pork chops and brown, turning, until the chops stop searing (about 2 minutes). Remove chops and reserve. If you are using a regular microwave-safe covered skillet, then skip this step.

2. Add *usli ghee* to the skillet and stir in garlic, cayenne, paprika, cinnamon, turmeric, cloves, and salt. Cook, uncovered, at 100 percent power for 1 minute 30 seconds (or until spices exude an aroma). Remove from oven.

3. Add pork chops and turn them in the spice-laced oil to coat thoroughly. Scatter onion and chilies around chops.

4. Blend mustard and cornstarch into the coconut milk, pour over chops and vegetables, and cover with the lid. Cook at 100 percent power for 9 minutes. Uncover, turn chops, and replace cover. Continue cooking at 100 percent power for 7 minutes (or until pork chops are cooked through). Remove from oven. Let the dish stand, covered, for 2 minutes. Uncover and serve chops immediately with vegetables and sauce.

MENU SUGGESTION

To complete the meal, serve Coconut Rice (p. 300), Fiery Mangalorean Eggplant (p. 213), and a cool raita *such as Papaya and Green Peppercorn Yogurt Raita (p. 253). Caramelized Rice Pudding (p. 381) would be a nice, soothing ending.*

STUFFED CABBAGE ROLLS WITH FRAGRANT TOMATO SAUCE

BANDHGOBHI DUM

MICROWAVE

Yield
—12 cabbage rolls
Servings
—6
Preparation time
—13 minutes
Cooking time
—25 minutes
Standing time
—5 minutes
Heat
—100 percent power
MW oven size
—650 to 700 watts
MW cookware
—One 5-quart covered
casserole

In Indian cooking, vegetables are often combined with meat, partly for the enhancement of flavor but mainly to stretch the serving portions for meat, thus making the dish lighter and more nutritive. The microwave works particularly well in this recipe as blanching the cabbage and baking the stuffed rolls are achieved in two simple steps.

═══════════ ROOM TEMPERATURE ═══════════

1 large (⅔ pound) green cabbage
1½ pounds lean ground beef round
½ cup finely chopped onion
2 teaspoons minced garlic
1 tablespoon crushed or grated fresh ginger
2 teaspoons ground cumin
½ teaspoon ground allspice

½ teaspoon cayenne pepper
2 teaspoons garam masala (p. 478) or fragrant spice powder (p. 481)
2 teaspoons kosher salt, or to taste
2 large eggs
4 tablespoons chopped coriander leaves and tender stems

FOR THE SAUCE:
½ cup finely chopped walnuts
¼ cup dark raisins

1 pound red ripe tomatoes, pureed with the skins
2 tablespoons tomato paste

1 teaspoon kosher salt,
or to taste

1 fresh hot green chili,
stemmed and minced
with seeds

2 tablespoons grated or
crushed fresh ginger

FOR THE GARNISH:

⅓ cup lightly packed coriander sprigs and leaves

MENU SUGGESTION

Although not essential, Toasted Lentil Wafers (p. 10) are a nice accompaniment to these cabbage rolls. To complete the meal, serve Split Pea and Basmati Pilaf (p. 314) and New Delhi Spicy Potatoes (p. 226). A sweet chutney, such as Sweet Date and Plum Chutney (p. 355), is a good addition.

1. Core cabbage, cutting the stem all the way in so that the leaves can be separated easily.

2. Place cabbage in a 5-quart microwave-safe casserole and cover with the lid. Cook at 100 percent power in a 650- to 700-watt carousel oven for 10 minutes (or until cabbage looks limp). Remove from oven and uncover. When cool enough to handle, carefully separate cabbage leaves and drain on paper towels.

3. Combine all other ingredients for cabbage rolls in a bowl and divide into 12 portions. Place one large, or two small, cabbage leaf at a time on the work board. Place a portion of the meat mixture in the center of a leaf and fold, jelly-roll fashion, tucking in the ends as you roll. There should be 12 stuffed cabbage rolls in all.

4. Spread walnuts and raisins at the bottom of the casserole. Arrange rolls in a layer. Combine the remaining ingredients for the sauce, pour over the cabbage rolls, and cover with the lid. Cook at 100 percent power for 15 minutes (or until stuffing is fully cooked—the rolls spring back when touched). Remove from oven. Let the dish stand, covered, for 5 minutes. Uncover and serve cabbage rolls with the sauce spooned over them, garnished with coriander.

NOTE These cabbage rolls may be made ahead, set aside in the same covered dish in the refrigerator for 2 days, and served reheated. The cabbage, however, loses its appealing color but not its flavor.

VEGETARIAN
D I S H E S

Although health and diet trends have caused people to look to vegetarian protein more than ever before, there are important culinary reasons to consider vegetarian dishes. One is that they can add drama to your cooking repertoire, providing exotic flavors not available from animal protein sources. Second, vegetables, particularly in the microwave, take less time to cook than meat, giving a time-constrained cook a feasible, last-minute, yet attractive option. Third, to a prudent cook's delight, vegetarian ingredients cost far less than meat.

Finally, since vegetarian dishes are made with fiber-rich wholesome ingredients such as lentils, beans, and peas; garden-fresh vegetables; protein-rich chick-pea flour; and milk in all its forms—yogurt, cheese, and buttermilk—they are light and easy to digest, making them especially appropriate in summer, or for late luncheons or suppers.

Indian vegetarian dishes are among the world's most sophisticated, combining vegetables, fruits, legumes, herbs, and spices to produce fragrant, full-flavored dishes in which the absence of meat is never noticed. So do not think of these as only side dishes. (Vegetable side dishes can be found in the following chapter.) All are as wholesome and hearty as any other main course; with rice and bread, and possibly a green salad, they make a fine meal.

Many Indian vegetarian dishes require combining several vegetables. Using traditional cooking techniques, with frequent mixing and stirring, the vegetables could become mushy and soft, losing their color and shape. Not so in the microwave, where vegetables retain their integrity (even eggplant holds its shape), color (broccoli, okra, and carrots actually become brighter), and fragrance (fennel and cauliflower intensify) while becoming butter-tender. As in meat cooking, take care to cut vegetables to the sizes specified in the recipes so that they cook quickly and evenly.

GARLIC-BRAISED EGGPLANT, CHICK-PEAS, AND TOMATO CASSEROLE

KHATTI BHAJI

MICROWAVE

Servings
  —6 to 8
Preparation time
  —2 minutes
Cooking time
  —23 minutes
Heat
  —100 percent power
MW oven size
  —650 to 700 watts
MW cookware
  *—One 10-inch cov-
  ered skillet*

A delicious and very garlicky combination of eggplant, tomatoes, and meaty chick-peas, this thick stew is ideal made in the microwave as the vegetables cook to melting tenderness without falling apart. You have full control over the consistency of the sauce by adding pureed chick-peas, which give it the desired thickness. This dish keeps beautifully for several days in the refrigerator. In fact, I love it cold, with some salad or grilled fish. Try it also in place of ratatouille with grilled lamb or as a pizza topping.

=== ROOM TEMPERATURE ===

2 cups cooked chick-peas with liquid, or use 1 19-ounce can chick-peas with the liquid

6 tablespoons light vegetable oil

1½ teaspoons cumin seeds

½ teaspoon fennel seeds

12 large cloves garlic, peeled and thickly sliced

1 teaspoon whole peppercorns

1 teaspoon red pepper flakes

2 teaspoons dry mustard

2 medium-size (½ pound) onions, peeled and sliced into ¼-inch thick wedges

¾ pound eggplant (with skin), cut into ½ × 1 × 2-inch pieces

2 tablespoons tomato paste

1 teaspoon kosher salt, or to taste

6 tablespoons chopped
  fresh coriander or
  mint

5 (1½ pounds) red ripe
  tomatoes, cut into 1-
  inch-thick wedges

1. Process half the chick-peas with the liquid in a food processor or blender until coarsely pureed. Combine whole and pureed chick-peas and set aside until needed.

2. Heat the oil in a 10-inch microwave-safe skillet, uncovered, at 100 percent power in a 650- to 700-watt carousel oven for 3 minutes. Add cumin, fennel, garlic, and peppercorns. Cook, uncovered, at 100 percent power for 1 minute 30 seconds (or until spices are puffed and garlic is light golden). Remove from oven.

3. Stir in red pepper and mustard. Fold in onions and eggplant. Cook, uncovered, at 100 percent power for 5 minutes (or until eggplant is slightly soft). Remove from oven.

4. Add chick-peas, tomato paste, salt, and half the coriander and mix thoroughly. Spread the tomato wedges on top and cover with the lid. Cook for 13 minutes (or until vegetables are cooked and sauce is slightly thickened). Remove from oven. Uncover and serve garnished with the remaining coriander.

NOTE   The dish may be made ahead, set aside in the same covered container in the refrigerator for 4 days, and served reheated.

MENU SUGGESTION

This beautifully flavored and visually appealing casserole is a complete meal in itself accompanied with a simple pilaf such as Moghul-scented Basmati Pilaf (p. 302) and a cool Papaya and Green Peppercorn Yogurt Raita (p. 253). For a more substantial meal, include a fruity chutney such as Sweet Date and Plum Chutney (p. 355) and precede the dish, maintaining the vegetarian theme, with Indian Cheese Spread (p. 19).

BRAISED OKRA WITH SPICES AND TOMATOES

BHINDI PATIALA

MICROWAVE

Servings
  —4
Preparation time
  —1 minute
Cooking time
  —20 minutes
Heat
  —100 percent power
MW oven size
  —650 to 700 watts
MW cookware
  —One 10-inch skillet

Even though cauliflower is the most prestigious vegetable of India, most Indians, when asked their *favorite* vegetable, would most likely point to okra. They may even recite you their favorite okra recipe, generations old, handed down like an heirloom, and lovingly prepared by their mothers. This kinship with okra, the tropical-plentiful vegetable and soul food of India, dates back thousands of centuries.

This is my favorite okra recipe, and possibly my very favorite vegetable dish. The fennel-flavored garlicky tomato sauce and sweet okra taste in perfect harmony. Pomegranate lends a lovely piquant flavor to the okra while also retracting its viscous juices. And the microwave keeps the okra glistening green against the scarlet tomato slices. I love this stew warm and at room temperature as well as straight out of the refrigerator.

===== *ROOM TEMPERATURE* =====

2 teaspoons pomegranate
  seeds (p. 484), dry
  mango powder
  (p. 483), or lemon juice
1 teaspoon mustard seeds
2 teaspoons coriander
  seeds
1 teaspoon cumin seeds
1 teaspoon fennel seeds
½ teaspoon cayenne
  pepper
½ teaspoon freshly
  ground black pepper

4 tablespoons mustard oil
  or light vegetable oil
1 pound fresh okra,
  trimmed, slit, and left
  whole
1 medium-size onion,
  peeled, halved, and cut
  into ½-inch-thick
  slices
2 medium-size (½
  pound) tomatoes,
  sliced into ½-inch-
  thick wedges

1½ teaspoons kosher salt, or to taste

1. Combine pomegranate (if you are using mango powder or lemon juice do not add it yet), mustard, coriander, cumin, and fennel seeds and grind to a coarse powder using a spice mill or coffee grinder. Transfer into a bowl, blend in cayenne, black pepper, and mango powder (if you are using it), and reserve.

2. Heat the oil in a 10-inch microwave-safe skillet at 100 percent power in a 650- to 700-watt oven for 3 minutes. Add okra and spice mixture. Cook at 100 percent power for 4 minutes. Remove from oven and fold in onions.

3. Cook at 100 percent power for 10 minutes (or until okra is cooked and lightly browned). Stir in lemon juice (if you are using it) after 5 minutes of cooking. Distribute tomatoes on top and continue cooking at 100 percent power for an additional 3 minutes (or until tomatoes look soft), stirring once. Remove from oven. Add salt to taste and serve.

NOTE   The braised okra may be made ahead, set aside in a microwave-safe covered dish in the refrigerator for 2 days, and served reheated.

MENU SUGGESTION

This okra-tomato dish flavored with fennel makes a delightful light meal served with Malabar Shrimp and Rice Cakes (p. 334) or Moghul-scented Basmati Pilaf (p. 302) and a cool Papaya and Green Peppercorn Yogurt Raita (p. 253). To elaborate the meal include a dal such as Fragrant Spiced Lentils with Herbs (p. 273) and a fruity chutney such as Sweet Persimmon and Plum Chutney with Cinnamon (p. 353).

SWEET AND SOUR STEWED OKRA, MOUNTAIN-STYLE

PAHADI BHINDI

MICROWAVE

Servings
  —4 to 6
Preparation time
  —1 minute
Cooking time
  —13 minutes
Heat
  —100 percent power
MW oven size
  —650 to 700 watts
MW cookware
  —One 10-inch skillet

I love okra, cooked in every imaginable way, plain or fancy—sautéed, fried, stewed, or stuffed. But I am, like other Indians, fussy about it. It must be rendered totally nonviscous and crisp for me to relish it. To achieve this, Indians follow two rules of thumb. First, always cook the okra first, uncovered, before adding any liquid seasonings or sauce, so that the excess moisture completely evaporates. Second, add an acid (lemon juice, tamarind, vinegar, etc.) during cooking to draw and neutralize the viscous juice further.

Normally the microwave would be disastrous for okra as the moist heat is what one would want to avoid in cooking it, but the uncovered skillet keeps the okra sizzling and evaporation rapid. The okra not only cooks and crisps beautifully but also remains sweet and flavorful.

═══ ROOM TEMPERATURE ═══

1½ teaspoons ground
  coriander
½ teaspoon cayenne
  pepper
¼ teaspoon ground
  turmeric
3 tablespoons mustard oil
  or light vegetable oil

2 medium-size (⅓
  pound) red onions
  with sprouts, or 1
  bunch scallions,
  trimmed and cut into
  1-inch pieces
2 teaspoons grated or
  crushed fresh ginger
1 pound tender okra,
  trimmed and cut into
  1-inch pieces

½ cup peeled, chopped
tomatoes (fresh or
canned), drained

2 tablespoons tamarind
juice (p. 492) or 1
tablespoon balsamic
vinegar
1 teaspoon sugar
½ teaspoon kosher salt

MENU SUGGESTION

Precede this lovely piquant okra stew with a creamy mellow soup such as Cool Cream of Mint Soup (p. 61). To complete the meal, serve Moghul-scented Basmati Pilaf (p. 302) or Split Pea and Basmati Pilaf (p. 314), Crushed Cucumber Salsa (p. 239), and, if desired, Avocado and Cucumber Yogurt Raita (p. 251). Indian Spiced Peach Cake (p. 398) is a wonderful way to end the meal.

1. Combine coriander, cayenne, and turmeric in a small bowl and reserve.

2. Heat the oil in a 10-inch microwave-safe skillet at 100 percent power in a 650- to 700-watt carousel oven for 3 minutes. Remove from oven and add onion, ginger, and okra. Sprinkle spice mixture on top and mix rapidly, stirring and tossing, to coat vegetables with oil.

3. Cook at 100 percent power for 7 minutes (or until okra is quite tender), stirring twice. Remove from oven. Stir in tomatoes, tamarind, and sugar. Cook at 100 percent power for an additional 3 minutes (or until okra is fully cooked and tomatoes are soft). Remove from oven. Add salt and serve.

NOTE   The stew may be made ahead, set aside in a microwave-safe covered dish in the refrigerator for 2 days, and served reheated.

MUSHROOMS IN CURRY SAUCE

KHOMBI TARKARI

MICROWAVE

Servings
 —4
Cooking time
 —11 minutes
Heat
 —100 percent power
MW oven size
 —650 to 700 watts
MW cookware
 *—One 10-inch cov-
 ered skillet*

I love to make this creamy curry of mushrooms. It's effortless in the microwave. The mushrooms first release juices which combine with onions, garlic, and curry and transform into a sublime sauce. Then the mushrooms absorb some of the sauce and turn plump and juicy. These curried mushrooms are lovely with grilled meat, over toast, or as an omelet, quiche, or canapé filling.

Almost any variety of fresh mushrooms, wild and cultivated, can be used in this recipe. Chanterelles, morels, cèpes, creminis, oyster, shiitake, and common button mushrooms, in any combination, work wonderfully well.

=========== ROOM TEMPERATURE ===========

*3 tablespoons light vege-
 table oil*
¾ cup sliced onion
*4 cloves garlic, peeled
 and sliced*
*2 teaspoons curry pow-
 der, homemade
 (p. 479) or store-bought*
1 teaspoon ground cumin
*¼ teaspoon freshly
 ground black pepper*

*1¼ pounds mushrooms
 (a combination of
 oyster, shiitake, and
 creminis), sliced*
*1 teaspoon cornstarch
 dissolved in 1 table-
 spoon heavy cream or
 milk*
Kosher salt to taste
*2 tablespoons chopped
 fresh coriander*

1. Heat the oil in a 10-inch microwave-safe skillet, uncovered, at 100 percent power in a 650- to 700-watt carousel oven for 2 minutes. Add onion, garlic, curry powder, cumin, and pepper and continue cook-

ing for another 3 minutes (or until onions and spices begin to brown). Remove from oven.

2. Fold in mushrooms and cover with the lid. Cook at 100 percent power for 5 minutes (or until mushrooms are cooked). Remove from oven.

3. Uncover, stir in cornstarch solution, and replace cover. Cook at 100 percent power for an additional 1 minute (or until sauce is thickened). Remove from oven. Add salt to taste and serve sprinkled with coriander.

NOTE   The dish may be made ahead and set aside, covered, for a few hours at room temperature, and served reheated.

MENU SUGGESTION

These simple and light curried mushrooms should be served with Tomato Basmati Pilaf (p. 308) or Cream of Wheat Pilaf with Shallots and Chilies (p. 318). For a more elaborate meal include Green Beans in Peppered-Mustard Dressing (p. 220), Fragrant Spiced Lentils with Herbs (p. 273), and Spicy Potato and Yogurt Raita (p. 260).

MOGHUL VEGETABLES IN CREAM SAUCE

MAKHANI SABZI KORMA

MICROWAVE

Servings
—4
Preparation time
—10 minutes
Cooking time
—18 minutes
Standing time
—5 minutes
Heat
—100 percent power
MW oven size
—650 to 700 watts
MW cookware
—One 5-quart covered
casserole

Korma, an aristrocratic vegetarian masterpiece, is a Moghul classic. It is prepared by first cooking the vegetables in milk, then combining the cooked vegetables with a creamy, rich sauce containing tomatoes, nut butter, or fruit purees. Kormas are popular throughout India and there are many variations. In this recipe from north India, carrots, turnips, green beans, and cauliflower are combined with a sublime tomato sauce and flavored with cardamom, cinnamon, and clove. This korma is particularly easy to make in the microwave as all one needs to do is cook the vegetables and combine them with the sauce. Additionally, in the microwave the vegetables retain their shape and color and the sauce does not stick and burn.

=== ROOM TEMPERATURE ===

2 small (⅓ pound) carrots	2½ cups butter sauce (p. 469)
1 medium-size (⅓ pound) white turnip or red wax potato	½ cup heavy cream
	½ teaspoon Moghul garam masala (p. 477) or ground cardamom
⅓ pound green beans	
1 small head (1 pound) cauliflower	¼ teaspoon white pepper
½ cup whole milk	Kosher salt to taste

FOR THE GARNISH:
4 tablespoons roasted slivered almonds (p. 463)

1. Peel carrots and turnip (or potatoes) and cut them into ½ × ½ × 2-inch pieces. Cut green beans into 2-

inch pieces. Trim the stem and leaves off the cauliflower and separate or cut florets into 1½-inch pieces.

2. Pile vegetables in a 5-quart microwave-safe casserole. Add milk and cover with a lid. Cook at 100 percent power in a 650- to 700-watt carousel oven for 12 minutes (or until vegetables are cooked but not mushy). Remove from oven.

3. Uncover and add all other ingredients except almonds. Mix until vegetables are coated with the sauce and replace cover. Cook at 100 percent power for 6 minutes (or until sauce is boiling). Remove from oven and let the dish stand, covered, for 5 minutes. Uncover and stir well. Serve immediately garnished with almonds.

NOTE   The stew may be made ahead, set aside in the same covered container in the refrigerator for 3 days, and served reheated.

MENU SUGGESTION

Precede this royal vegetarian classic with the delicate Chilled Indian-Summer Tomato Soup (p. 55). To complete the meal, accompany this dish with Saffron Pilaf (p. 304) and Papaya and Green Peppercorn Yogurt Raita (p. 253), and serve Indian Spiced Mango Cake (p. 400) as a grand finale.

WHOLE CAULIFLOWER WITH VENDALOO SAUCE

GOBHI VENDALOO

MICROWAVE

Servings
  —6 to 8
Preparation time
  —3 minutes
Cooking time
  —19 minutes
Heat
  —100 percent power
MW oven size
  —650 to 700 watts
MW cookware
  *—One 2½-quart cov-
  ered casserole or
  soufflé dish and one
  1½-quart covered
  casserole or soufflé
  dish*

One of the most sought-after vegetables in Indian cooking is cauliflower, partly for its visual appeal but mainly because it takes on spices exquisitely. As a result there are innumerable cauliflower preparations in Indian cooking, each distinct and stunning. In this recipe the whole cauliflower is first steamed and then served in a blanket of spicy hot sauce. The pearl-white cauliflower against the crimson sauce looks very elegant. Before cooking, it is important to trim the cauliflower carefully so that it rests flat on the plate and thus can be cut for easy serving. The cooking time for cauliflower given below is approximate, as the vegetable varies widely in size and moisture content. Remember to cook cauliflower until its stem becomes soft but not limp. For a milder variation you can substitute fragrant tomato sauce (p. 467) in place of *vendaloo* sauce.

=========== *ROOM TEMPERATURE* ===========

1 medium-size (1¼ pounds) cauliflower	½ teaspoon kosher salt
2 tablespoons lemon juice	2½ cups (1 recipe) vendaloo *sauce* (p. 470)

FOR THE GARNISH:	4 tablespoons chopped fresh coriander
6–8 fresh mildly hot green chilies	

1. Cut off the entire stem from the cauliflower, coming in as close as possible to the florets. Trim the hard outer leaves. Leave a few tender inner leaves that are both attractive and edible attached. Rub lemon juice all over cauliflower and sprinkle with salt. Place cau-

---

VEGETARIAN DISHES

liflower, stem side down, in a 2½-quart microwave-safe dish and cover with the lid.

2. Cook at 100 percent power in a 650- to 700-watt carousel oven for 12 to 13 minutes (or until cauliflower is cooked through but still holding shape). Remove from oven. Let cauliflower stand, covered, for 5 minutes.

3. Pour *vendaloo* sauce in a 1½-quart microwave-safe dish and cover with the lid. Cook at 100 percent power for 1½ minutes (or until boiling hot). Remove from oven.

4. To serve, pour sauce on a heated deep serving platter. Cut cauliflower into 8 neat wedges and arrange in the center of the plate over the sauce. Garnish with chilies and coriander and serve immediately.

MENU SUGGESTION

This elegant whole cauliflower with a spicy cayenne sauce should be preceded with a delicate mellow first course such as Lentil Salad in Cumin-Citrus Dressing (p. 29) or Cold Butternut Squash Soup (p. 59). To complete the meal, serve Crisp Okra and Spiced Basmati Pilaf (p. 306) and Moghul Saffron and Mango Yogurt Raita (p. 254).

POTATOES AND PEAS VENDALOO

BATATA VENDALOO

MICROWAVE

Servings
—8
Preparation time
—5 minutes
Cooking time
—14 minutes
Heat
—100 percent power
MW oven size
—650 to 700 watts
MW cookware
—One 5-quart covered
casserole

Delicious, devilish, and downright satisfying is how I would describe the *vendaloo* curries of the Goanese Christians. They can make you an addict even if you don't like spicy foods. This is because Goan cooks (the descendants of the Portuguese sailors who introduced chili peppers to India in the sixteenth century) know the chemistry of chilies and how to temper and diffuse their heat so that they flirt with your palate and not burn it. I like to make this *vendaloo* with tiny new potatoes, the size of cranberries, as they are most aromatic and attractive.

========= ROOM TEMPERATURE =========

8 small (about 1½ pounds) new red wax potatoes

2 tablespoons mustard oil or olive oil

2 tablespoons water

2½ cups (1 recipe) vendaloo *sauce* (p. 470)

1 cup green peas (fresh or frozen)

12 fresh, or 1 tablespoon crushed dried, curry leaves (p. 482) (optional)

2 tablespoons chopped fresh coriander

1. Cut potatoes in half (large ones in quarters) and place in a 5-quart microwave-safe casserole. Add oil and water, toss to mix, and cover with the lid. Cook at 100 percent power in a 650- to 700-watt oven for 8½ minutes (or until potatoes are cooked and very soft). Remove from oven.

2. Uncover, add sauce, peas, and curry leaves, stir to mix, and replace cover. Cook at 100 percent power

for 5 minutes (or until sauce is bubbling). Remove from oven and serve sprinkled with coriander.

NOTE   The *vendaloo* may be made ahead, set aside in the same covered container in the refrigerator for 5 days, and served reheated.

MENU SUGGESTION

This cayenne-laced, rather filling curry should be preceded with a delicate soup such as Cold Butternut Squash Soup (p. 59) or Assam Aromatic Lentil Broth with Spinach (p. 35). To complete the meal, serve Coconut Rice (p. 300) or Ceylonese Steamed Rice Cakes (p. 330) and Avocado and Cucumber Yogurt Raita (p. 251).

INDIAN PANEER CHEESE AND PEAS IN FRAGRANT TOMATO SAUCE

MATAR PANEER

MICROWAVE

Servings
  —4 to 6
Preparation time
  —3 minutes
Cooking time
  —16 minutes
Heat
  —100 percent power
MW oven size
  —650 to 700 watts
MW cookware
  —One 10-inch cov-
    ered skillet

This is the most popular of all dishes in the vegetarian cuisine of India. Homemade cheese, freshly made and compressed into julienne slices, is simmered in a cumin-and-coriander-scented tomato sauce. It is gorgeous in both flavor and appeal. I particularly like to make this dish in the microwave because the cheese becomes softer and creamier and the sauce develops a lovely springlike flavor. You can also make this dish using firm tofu slices (p. 459). Visually it will be similar but the flavor and texture will be different.

══════════ *ROOM TEMPERATURE* ══════════

2 teaspoons ground
  coriander
1 teaspoon ground cumin
½ teaspoon turmeric
1 teaspoon minced garlic
½ teaspoon minced fresh
  hot green chilies, or
  more to taste
2 tablespoons finely
  chopped fresh ginger
2 tablespoons light
  vegetable oil
1 cup chopped onion
1½ cups pureed tomatoes
  (fresh or canned)

1½ teaspoons paprika
½ teaspoon kosher salt,
  or to taste
1 cup green peas (fresh
  or frozen)
1 recipe Indian paneer
  cheese (p. 458)
¾ teaspoon garam
  masala (p. 478), fra-
  grant spice powder
  (p. 481), or ground
  roasted cumin seeds
  (p. 465)
4 tablespoons chopped
  fresh coriander or
  basil

1. Combine coriander, cumin, turmeric, garlic, chilies, and ginger in a small bowl and reserve.

2. Heat the oil in a 10-inch microwave-safe skillet, uncovered, at 100 percent power in a 650- to 700-watt oven for 2 minutes 30 seconds. Add onion and continue cooking, uncovered, at 100 percent power for 5 minutes (or until onions are soft and glazed), stirring once. Add spice mixture and continue cooking, uncovered, at 100 percent power for an additional 1 minute (or until spices loose their raw aroma). Remove from oven.

3. Add tomato puree, paprika, and salt, mix well, and cover with the lid. Cook at 100 percent power for 5 minutes (or until tomato sauce is cooked). Uncover, add peas and cheese, and replace cover. Cook at 100 percent power for 2 minutes (or until contents are heated through). Remove from oven. Uncover, stir in the *garam masala* or the fragrant spice powder or cumin seeds and half the coriander, and serve sprinkled with the remaining coriander.

NOTE   The dish may be made ahead, set aside in a microwave-safe covered dish in the refrigerator for 2 days, and served reheated.

MENU SUGGESTION

Precede this tomato-cumin–flavored stew with the cool Chilled Essence of Shallot Soup (p. 57). To complete the meal, serve the dish with Whole Mung Bean and Basmati Pilaf (p. 316) and Zucchini and Walnut Yogurt Raita (p. 262), and serve Glazed Carrot Fudge (p. 396) as a soothing finale.

INDIAN PANEER CHEESE AND SWEET PEPPERS IN FRAGRANT SPINACH SAUCE

SAAG PANEER

MICROWAVE

Servings
  —6
Preparation time
  —3 minutes
Cooking time
  —8 minutes
Heat
  —100 percent power
MW oven size
  —650 to 700 watts
MW cookware
  —One 2½-quart covered casserole or soufflé dish

Indian cheese cubes known as *paneer* are a delicacy in North India. *Saag paneer* is one of the most popular preparations, where the cheese cubes and sweet green peppers are gently braised in an aromatic spinach puree. It is a very tasty and visually stunning dish.

One wonderful thing about making *saag paneer* in the microwave is that it cooks much lighter and fresher-tasting. First, the *paneer* is totally fat-free because it is not fried, as it is when conventionally done. Second, the microwave does wonders with spinach, blanching it to perfection so that the greens get greener! Finally, the tomato sauce made in the microwave has a clean, acid-free flavor. Together, the three elements create magic on the palate. *Saag paneer* is a traditional chili-hot dish, but you can cut down on the heat by reducing or eliminating the chilies. There will not be any loss in flavor. Swiss chard, collard, kale, and mustard greens all make fine substitutes for spinach.

=============== *ROOM TEMPERATURE* ===============

1 pound fresh spinach, trimmed, rinsed, and chopped
2 tablespoons light vegetable oil

2 tablespoons crushed dried fenugreek leaves (p. 482) or minced parsley

2 medium-size sweet red
or green peppers,
cored and cut length-
wise into thin ⅛-inch
strips
2½ cups fragrant tomato
sauce (p. 467) or
butter sauce (p. 469)
⅓ cup heavy cream
1 teaspoon minced fresh
hot green chilies, or to
taste

3 tablespoons minced
fresh coriander
1 teaspoon or more
ground roasted cumin
seeds (p. 465)
Kosher salt to taste
1 recipe Indian paneer
cheese (p. 458) or ½
recipe firm tofu slices
(p. 459)

MENU SUGGESTION

This north Indian specialty
is good accompanied with a
rich northern pilaf such as
Moghul-scented Basmati Pilaf (p. 302). To complete the
meal, serve Mustard- and
Garlic-flavored American
Yellow Split Peas (p. 277)
and a cool Spinach and Yogurt Raita (p. 258). Precede
this spicy stew with a mellow first course such as Sesame Shrimp (p. 13).

1. Place spinach in a 2½-quart microwave-safe dish.
Add oil and fenugreek, toss well, and cover with the
lid. Cook at 100 percent power in a 650- to 700-watt
carousel oven for 2 minutes 30 seconds (or until
spinach is wilted). Remove from oven.

2. Uncover, add peppers, tomato sauce, cream, chilies, coriander, cumin, and salt, and stir to blend.
Carefully fold in cheese or tofu slices and cover with
the lid. Cook at 100 percent power for 5 minutes 30
seconds (or until sauce is boiling). Remove from oven.
Uncover and serve.

NOTE   The dish may be made ahead, set aside in a microwave-safe covered dish in the refrigerator for a day, and
served reheated. The spinach, however, loses its appealing
color but not its flavor.

GREEN PEPPERS IN
SPICY YOGURT SAUCE

MORU KOYAMBOO

MICROWAVE

Servings
  —6
Preparation time
  —2 minutes
Cooking time
  —22 minutes
Heat
  —100 percent power
MW oven size
  —650 to 700 watts
MW cookware
  *—One 10-inch cov-
  ered skillet*

Soothing yogurt sauces enriched and thickened with coconut and chick-pea flour are very popular in south India. Often mustard-infused oils, called *talish*, along with ginger and chilies are added to seal in the flavors. If you can find tiny buds of sweet green peppers, the size of small limes, as I often can at greenmarkets, the dish will taste more herbal and flavorful. The microwave is a great tool for yogurt dishes as the sauce does not stick or separate. For a richer flavor and texture, substitute sour cream for some of the yogurt in the recipe.

=============== ROOM TEMPERATURE ===============

FOR THE SAUCE:
*2 cups plain yogurt
  mixed with 1 cup
  water, or 3 cups low-
  or full-fat buttermilk*
*½ cup unsweetened
  flaked coconut
  (p. 449)*
*1-inch piece fresh ginger,
  peeled*

1 teaspoon cumin seeds
*5 fresh hot green chilies,
  stemmed*
*¼ teaspoon cayenne
  pepper*
1 teaspoon kosher salt
*3 tablespoons chick-pea
  flour (p. 449)*

FOR THE VEGETABLES:
*1 tablespoon light sesame
  oil or vegetable oil*
1 teaspoon mustard seeds

*3 medium-size (1 pound)
  sweet green peppers,
  cored and cut into 1-
  inch pieces*

1. Put ½ cup yogurt mixture or buttermilk and the remaining ingredients for the sauce into the container

of a food processor and process until finely pureed and smoothly blended. Stir in the remaining yogurt mixture or buttermilk and reserve.

2. Heat the oil in a 10-inch microwave-safe covered skillet at 100 percent power in a 650- to 700-watt carousel oven for 3 minutes. Uncover, add mustard seeds, and replace the lid. Cook at 100 percent power for 3 minutes (or until seeds pop). Remove from oven, uncover, stir in peppers, and replace the lid.

3. Cook at 100 percent power for 3 minutes (or until peppers are cooked but still crisp). Uncover and add yogurt mixture. Mix lightly. Cook, uncovered, at 100 percent power for 13 minutes (or until yogurt loses its uncooked flavor, sauce thickens, and peppers look very soft). Remove from oven and serve immediately.

NOTE   This dish may be made ahead and set aside, covered, for a few hours at room temperature, and served reheated.

MENU SUGGESTION

Yogurt dishes from south India as a general rule contain plenty of sauce. This delicate and fragrant yogurt curry is best enjoyed with a simple rice dish such as Plain Basmati Rice (p. 299) or Madras Steamed Rice Cakes (p. 325). To complete the meal, serve Fiery Mangalorean Eggplant (p. 213) and Tamil Potato Salad with Shallots (p. 243). Precede the dish with fragrant Lentil Salad in Cumin-Citrus Dressing (p. 29).

TOMATOES AND GREENS IN FRAGRANT BUTTERMILK SAUCE

TAMATAR KI KADHI

MICROWAVE

Servings
—4 to 6
Preparation time
—2 minutes
Cooking time
—20 minutes
Heat
—100 percent power
MW oven size
—650 to 700 watts
MW cookware
—One 2½-quart cov-
ered casserole or
soufflé dish and one
10-inch covered
skillet

Kadhi is one of the most popular yogurt-based preparations in Indian cooking. *Kadhi* is made by cooking chick-pea flour, yogurt (or buttermilk) with spices, and adding additional ingredients such as steamed or fried vegetables, lentil wafers, dumplings, nuts, and fruits. It is both nourishing and substantial. This version of *kadhi* is from Bengal, in eastern India.

Indian cooks generally like their vegetables in this *kadhi* very soft and their greens limp and buttery. Such prolonged cooking I find dulls vegetables, therefore in this recipe I cook them for a shorter period, just long enough for them to get fully cooked but still retain their individual flavors and characters. If you prefer them very soft, then cook for an additional three minutes.

=========== ROOM TEMPERATURE ===========

FOR THE SAUCE:

3 cups low-fat or full-fat
  buttermilk or 2 cups
  plain yogurt mixed
  with 1 cup water
3 tablespoons chick-pea
  flour (p. 449)
½-inch piece fresh gin-
  ger, thinly sliced

¼ teaspoon cayenne
  pepper
2 teaspoons sugar
1 teaspoon kosher salt

FOR THE VEGETABLES:
3 tablespoons light vegetable oil
¾ teaspoon cumin seeds
½ teaspoon fenugreek seeds (p. 483) or mustard seeds, crushed
¼ teaspoon ground asafetida (p. 481) or ½ teaspoon minced garlic

½ pound fresh mustard, fenugreek, Swiss chard, or amaranth greens, trimmed, rinsed, drained, and coarsely shredded
½ pound red ripe tomatoes, preferably Italian plum, cut into ½-inch-thick wedges

FOR THE GARNISH:
2 tablespoons chopped fresh coriander

¼ cup fried onion shreds (p. 475) (optional)

MENU SUGGESTION

This spicy-tart yogurt curry with delicate greens makes a perfect vegetarian luncheon entrée accompanied with a rich pilaf such as Mango and Basmati Pilaf (p. 310) or Moghul-scented Basmati Pilaf (p. 302), Minted Red Onion Salad (p. 241) or Crushed Cucumber Salsa (p. 239), and, if desired, Toasted Lentil Wafers (p. 10).

1. Place all the ingredients for the sauce in a 2½-quart microwave-safe casserole, mix, beating with a whisk until smoothly blended, and cover with the lid. Cook at 100 percent power in a 650- to 700-watt carousel for 12 minutes (or until sauce boils for a few minutes), stirring twice. Remove from oven and set aside, covered.

2. Heat the oil in a 10-inch microwave-safe skillet, uncovered, at 100 percent power for 3 minutes. Add cumin and fenugreek seeds or mustard seeds, and cover with the lid. Cook at 100 percent power for 1 minute 30 seconds (or until spices turn a few shades darker). Remove from oven. Uncover, stir in asafetida or garlic, and immediately toss in shredded greens. Place tomato wedges on top, and replace the lid.

3. Cook at 100 percent power for an additional 3 minutes 30 seconds (or until greens are wilted and tomatoes are just barely cooked). Remove from oven and transfer the vegetables, mixed together with the spice-infused oil, onto the yogurt sauce. Stir carefully to mix and sprinkle with coriander and, if desired, fried onion shreds. Serve immediately.

NOTE   The dish may be made ahead and set aside, covered, at room temperature for a few hours, and served reheated.

MALABAR VEGETABLE STEW WITH COCONUT

AVIAL

MICROWAVE

Servings
—6 to 8
Preparation time
—4 minutes
Cooking time
—23 minutes
Heat
—100 percent power
MW oven size
—650 to 700 watts
MW cookware
—One 10-inch cov-
ered skillet

In *avial*, one of the most subtly spiced stews from Malabar, a state along the Western coast of India, steamed garden vegetables are combined with a fragrant cumin-scented coconut sauce. It is as delicious as it is visually stunning. The microwave is particularly suited for cooking this stew as the vegetables come out perfectly without losing their luster and turning mushy. In addition, the coconut sauce intensifies in flavor without burning or releasing its oil.

=========== *ROOM TEMPERATURE* ===========

FOR THE VEGETABLES:
8 small or 2 medium-size
   (½ pound) new red
   wax potatoes
1 medium-size (¼
   pound) onion
1 medium-size (¼
   pound) carrot
1 stalk (¼ pound)
   broccoli
1 medium-size (¼
   pound) sweet green
   pepper

1 small (¼ pound)
   zucchini
1 small (½ pound) un-
   ripe, tart, or medium-
   ripe green mango
½ cup corn kernels
   (fresh or frozen)
½ cup green peas (fresh
   or frozen)
1 teaspoon kosher salt

FOR THE SAUCE:
4 fresh hot green chilies,
   stemmed and coarsely
   chopped
1½ teaspoons cumin
   seeds

¾ cup water
1¼ cups packed grated
   coconut (p. 449)
1 cup sour cream or
   plain yogurt, lightly
   beaten (optional)

---

3 tablespoons light ses-
   ame oil or light vege-
   table oil

MENU SUGGESTION

*Precede this yogurt-and-co-
conut-rich vegetable stew
with a spicy soup such as
Grandmother's Tomato Len-
til Soup (p. 39). To complete
the meal, serve Ceylonese
Steamed Rice Cakes (p. 330)
or Steamed Rice Cakes with
Herbs (p. 332), Fiery Mangalorean Eggplant (p. 213),
and, if desired, Toasted Lentil Wafers (p. 10).*

---

1. If you are using tiny potatoes, prick them in a couple of places and leave them whole; otherwise, peel and cut potatoes into 1-inch cubes. Peel and halve onion and cut into ¼-inch slices. Peel carrot and cut, at bias, into ½-inch pieces. Put the vegetables in a bowl and reserve.

2. Separate broccoli florets into 1-inch pieces and cut stem into ⅛-inch slices. Core green pepper and slice into 1-inch pieces. Cut zucchini into ⅛-inch rounds. Peel and pit mango and cut flesh into 1-inch pieces. Put these four in another bowl.

3. Put chilies, cumin, water, and coconut into the container of a blender or food processor, process until the contents are finely pureed, and reserve.

4. Heat the oil in a 10-inch microwave-safe covered skillet at 100 percent power in a 650- to 700-watt carousel oven for 3 minutes. Uncover, add mustard seeds, and replace the lid. Cook at 100 percent power for 3 minutes (or until seeds pop). Remove from oven, uncover, and add potato mixture. Mix thoroughly and replace the lid. Cook at 100 percent power for 6 minutes (or until potatoes are soft).

5. Uncover, fold in broccoli mixture, and replace cover. Cook at 100 percent power for 5 minutes 30 seconds (or until vegetables are soft). Remove from oven.

6. Add coconut mixture, corn and peas, and salt. Mix until vegetables are coated with sauce. Cook, uncovered, at 100 percent power for 5 minutes (or until sauce is bubbling). Add sour cream or yogurt and continue cooking at 100 percent power for 30 seconds (or until sauce is heated through). Remove from oven, stir well, and serve immediately.

NOTE The *avial* may be made ahead and set aside, covered, for a few hours at room temperature, and served reheated.

LENTIL STEW WITH BROCCOLI, CARROTS, AND PEARL ONIONS

TANDOO SAMBAAR

MICROWAVE

Yield
  —6 cups
Servings
  —4 to 6
Preparation time
  —3 minutes
Cooking time
  —24 minutes
Heat
  —100 percent power
MW oven size
  —650 to 700 watts
MW cookware
  —One 5-quart covered
    casserole and one 8-
    inch covered skillet

This is a classic vegetarian dish of southern Indians made by combining varieties of green and root vegetables with curry-flavored lentils. Normally a stew like this takes a considerable amount of time to prepare, but in a microwave the task is reduced to minutes. In addition, I have found, and so have many chefs at Indian restaurants that serve such southern specialties, that pureed canned chick-peas work just as well in the recipe as does cooked lentil puree. The assertive flavors of curry spices and the tempering of mustard-infused oil smooth out the flavors. This stew is also fabulous served, thinned out, as a hearty soup accompanied with salad.

=== ROOM TEMPERATURE ===

3 cups Cooked Red
  (Pink) Lentil Puree
  (p. 267) or Cooked
  Yellow Lentils or
  American Yellow Split
  Peas (p. 269)
    or
1 19-ounce can chick-
  peas with the liquid
4 cups broccoli, trimmed,
  peeled, and cut into 1-
  inch pieces
1¼ cups sliced carrots

16 small (1½ pounds)
  pearl onions, peeled
1½ cups peeled, crushed
  tomatoes (fresh or
  canned)
2 tablespoons sambaar
  powder or curry
  powder, homemade
  (p. 480 or p. 479) or
  store-bought
1½ teaspoons paprika
⅔ cup water
2 teaspoons kosher salt,
  or to taste

FOR THE SPICE-INFUSED
   GHEE OR OIL:
2 tablespoons usli ghee
   (p. 492) or light vegetable oil
1½ teaspoons mustard
   seeds

1 teaspoon minced garlic
   or ⅓ teaspoon ground
   asafetida (p. 481)

2 teaspoons lemon juice
4 tablespoons chopped
   fresh coriander

MENU SUGGESTION

This simple yet very satisfying vegetable-lentil stew is
good accompanied with Plain
Basmati Rice (p. 299) or Coconut Rice (p. 300), Raita of
Crisp Fried Okra and Cool
Yogurt (p. 263), and some
Toasted Lentil Wafers (p. 10).
Precede with another southern specialty—Classic Peppered Tamarind Soup (p. 37).

1. If you are using canned chick-peas, puree them
along with their liquid in a food processor or blender.
Transfer puree into a 4-cup glass measure and add
enough water to make 3 cups.

2. Pour split-pea or chick-pea puree into a 5-quart
microwave-safe casserole. Add all other ingredients for
cooking the stew, mix well, and cover with the lid.
Cook at 100 percent power in a 650- to 700-watt
carousel oven for 18 minutes (or until vegetables are
cooked), stirring once. Remove from oven and set aside
while you make the spice-infused oil.

3. Heat the oil in an 8-inch microwave-safe covered
skillet at 100 percent power for 3 minutes. Uncover,
add mustard seeds, and replace the lid. Cook at 100
percent power for 3 minutes (or until seeds pop). Remove from oven, add garlic or asafetida, and stir for
20 seconds (or until seasonings look lightly fried).
Immediately pour the entire contents of the skillet on
the stew. Add lemon juice and some of the coriander
and mix well. Serve the stew in deep plates sprinkled
with the remaining coriander.

NOTE   The stew may be made ahead, set aside in the same
covered container in the refrigerator for 3 days, and served
reheated.

EGGPLANT-LENTIL STEW WITH TAMARIND AND GARLIC

KATRIKA SAMBAAR

MICROWAVE

Yield
— *5 cups*
Servings
— *4 to 6*
Preparation time
— *6 minutes*
Cooking time
— *27 minutes*
Standing time
— *5 minutes*
Heat
— *100 percent power*
MW oven size
— *650 to 700 watts*
MW cookware
— *One 10-inch covered skillet*

This is another version of the popular southern specialty *sambaar*, combining eggplant with curry-flavored lentils. The steeped, cooked flavor of curry spices—cumin, coriander, and fenugreek—comes through the creamy, sweet lentils. Traditionally the dish is made with tiny two-inch-long eggplants, but the thin, long Japanese variety makes a good substitute. Tamarind is the favorite seasoning of southern India and lends the stew a distinct sweetish-sour taste and a pronounced yet delicate herbal aroma.

=================== ROOM TEMPERATURE ===================

1¼–1½ pounds tiny Italian, long Japanese, or regular oval eggplant

1 medium-size onion

3 cups Cooked Red (Pink) Lentil Puree (p. 267) or Cooked Yellow Lentils or American Yellow Split Peas (p. 269)

or

1 19-ounce can chickpeas with the liquid

4 teaspoons sambaar powder or curry powder, homemade (p. 480 or p. 479) or store-bought

1 teaspoon turmeric

12 fresh, or 1 tablespoon crushed dried, curry leaves (p. 482), or 1 teaspoon dried thyme

2 teaspoons kosher salt, or to taste

*2 tablespoons, or 1 fro-
zen cube, tamarind
juice or 1 teaspoon ta-
marind concentrate
(p. 491), or 2 tea-
spoons lemon juice*

---

*FOR THE SPICE-INFUSED
OIL:*

*2 tablespoons light
sesame oil or light
vegetable oil*

*1½ teaspoons mustard
seeds*

*2 tablespoons thickly
sliced garlic cloves*

*1–4 fresh hot green
chilies, stemmed,
seeded, and thinly
sliced*

*4 tablespoons chopped
fresh coriander*

MENU SUGGESTION

*Precede this spicy-rich
southern stew with a delicate
soup such as Cold Butternut
Squash Soup (p. 59). To
complete the meal, serve
Cream of Wheat Pilaf with
Tomatoes and Green Peas
(p. 320) or Tomato Basmati
Pilaf (p. 308), Spinach and
Yogurt Raita (p. 258), and,
if desired, Toasted Lentil
Wafers (p. 10). Madras
Bridal Pudding with Cashew
Nuts (p. 390) is a perfect
grand finale.*

1. Cut the stems off the eggplant and quarter length-wise. Cut each segment into ¼-inch-thick slices. Peel and slice onion into ¼-inch-thick-wedges. Set aside.

2. If you are using canned chick-peas, place them in the container of a food processor or blender along with their liquid and process until pureed. Be careful not to liquefy the peas or the sauce will have a starchy appeal. Transfer chick-pea or split-pea puree into a 4-cup glass measure and add enough water to make 3½ cups puree. Stir in *sambaar* powder, turmeric, curry leaves, and salt and reserve.

3. Heat the oil in a 10-inch microwave-safe covered skillet at 100 percent power in a 650- to 700-watt carousel oven for 3 minutes. Uncover, add mustard seeds, and replace the lid. Cook at 100 percent power for 3 minutes (or until seeds pop). Uncover, and stir in garlic and chilies. Cook, uncovered, for 45 seconds (or until garlic is lightly colored). Remove from oven.

4. Add vegetables and mix to coat with the spiced oil. Pour the lentil mixture over the vegetables, lightly toss, and cover with the lid. Cook at 100 percent power for 17 minutes (or until vegetables are cooked), stir-ring twice. Uncover, add tamarind or lemon juice, and

replace cover. Continue cooking, covered, for an additional 3 minutes (or until tamarind loses its raw aroma). Remove from oven.

5. Uncover, stir in some of the coriander, and replace cover. Let stew stand for 5 minutes. Uncover and serve garnished with the remaining coriander.

NOTE The stew may be made ahead, set aside in a microwave-safe covered dish in the refrigerator for 3 days, and served reheated.

VISHAL'S CAULIFLOWER SAMBAR STEW

GOBHI SAMBAAR

MICROWAVE

Yield
—5 cups

Servings
—4 to 6

Preparation time
—3 minutes

Cooking time
—18 minutes

Heat
—100 percent power

MW oven size
—650 to 700 watts

MW cookware
—One 5-quart covered
casserole and one 8-
inch covered skillet

Sambaar is the most commonly prepared dish—the staple—of southern India. It is made by combining vegetables with cooked lentil puree, fresh herbs, and aromatic spices. The exchange of flavors of the vegetables and lentils provides the complex taste of *sambaar*. *Sambaar* can be served both as a stew and a soup.

I created this fragrant stew for my son, combining four of his favorite ingredients: cauliflower, tomatoes, garlic, and lentils. The aromatic coriander, mustard, and cumin balance the sweetness of lentils against the tart tomatoes. The stew is spicy but not hot, as no chilies, peppers, or hot seasonings are called for. In the microwave the stew takes a few minutes. In addition, the vegetables retain their shape without getting mushy, far better than when cooked any other way. My son enjoys this preparation both as a stew and as a soup. A little melted *usli ghee* poured over it is a festive touch.

═══════════ ROOM TEMPERATURE ═══════════

3 cups Cooked Red
(Pink) Lentil Puree
(p. 267) or Cooked
Yellow Lentils or
American Yellow Split
Peas (p. 269)
1 small (1¼ pounds)
cauliflower, trimmed
and cut into 1-inch
florets
1 cup chopped onions

1 cup pureed tomatoes
(fresh or canned)
1 tablespoon ground
coriander
1½ teaspoons ground
cumin
⅓ teaspoon turmeric
⅔ cup water
2 teaspoons kosher salt,
or to taste

1 large (⅓ pound) red
ripe tomato, cut into
¼-inch-thick wedges

3 tablespoons chopped
fresh coriander

FOR THE SPICE-INFUSED
GHEE OR OIL:
2 tablespoons usli ghee
(p. 492) or light vege-
table oil

1½ teaspoons mustard
seeds, crushed
1 teaspoon minced garlic

MENU SUGGESTION

Serve this simple stew with
Plain Basmati Rice (p. 299).
If desired, accompany with
New Delhi Spicy Potatoes
(p. 226) and Toasted Lentil
Wafers (p. 10).

1. Combine all the ingredients for cooking the stew, except tomato wedges and fresh coriander, in a 5-quart microwave-safe casserole and cover with the lid. Cook at 100 percent power in a 650- to 700-watt carousel oven for 14 minutes (or until cauliflower is cooked soft), stirring twice.

2. Uncover, add tomatoes, and replace cover. Continue cooking at 100 percent power for 3 minutes (or until tomatoes are soft). Remove from oven, uncover, and stir in coriander. Set aside while you make the spice-infused oil.

3. Heat the oil in an 8-inch microwave-safe covered skillet at 100 percent power for 3 minutes. Uncover, add *ghee*, mustard, and garlic, and replace the lid. Cook at 100 percent power for 1 minute (or until garlic is fried). Remove from oven. Pour the contents of the skillet on the stew. Mix well and serve.

NOTE   The dish may be made ahead, set aside in the same covered container in the refrigerator for 3 days, and served reheated.

MUSTARD GREEN DUMPLINGS IN FRAGRANT TOMATO SAUCE

PAKODE KI BHAJI

MICROWAVE

Servings
—4 to 6
Preparation time
—11 minutes
Cooking time
—17 minutes
Heat
—100 percent power
MW oven size
—650 to 700 watts
MW cookware
—One 10-inch cov-
ered skillet

I have cheated a little with this recipe. This dish is traditionally made by first deep-frying the dumplings in oil. Then they are added to the sauce and simmered, where they puff up. But you cannot deep-fry in the microwave; besides, you probably know by now that I avoid deep-frying in general if possible. Here is, therefore, the modified recipe, where dumplings are instead steamed before being added to the sauce. The result, I think, is very good as the microwave cooks and puffs the dumplings to a light fluffiness in just a few minutes. The eliminated calories from frying in oil should please everyone.

NOTE While making the dumplings, take care not to pack them into tight rounds before steaming as they will become dense and hard. Besides, loose-textured, rustic-looking dumplings have more character.

—————————— ROOM TEMPERATURE ——————————

½ pound fresh mustard
　　leaves
3 fresh hot green chilies,
　　stemmed, seeded, and
　　minced
2 tablespoons chopped
　　fresh coriander leaves

2 tablespoons buttermilk
　　or 4 teaspoons plain
　　yogurt mixed with 2
　　teaspoons water
½ teaspoon kosher salt
¾ cup chick-pea flour
　　(p. 449)
Pinch of baking soda
3 tablespoons mustard oil
　　or light vegetable oil

¾ teaspoon mustard
    seeds
¾ teaspoon cumin seeds
¼ teaspoon ground asa-
    fetida (p. 481) or ½
    teaspoon minced garlic

2½ cups butter sauce
    (p. 469) or fragrant
    tomato sauce
    (p. 467)
Kosher salt to taste

MENU SUGGESTION

These richly flavored and
rather filling dumplings in
butter or tomato sauce should
be preceded with a delicate
soup such as Moghul
Pistachio Soup (p. 49). To
complete the meal, serve Plain
Basmati Rice (p. 299),
Garlic-braised Tomatoes
(p. 232), and Crushed Cu-
cumber Salsa (p. 239).

1. Rinse mustard leaves in several changes of water and lightly drain. Chop greens and put in a medium-size bowl. Add chilies, coriander, buttermilk, and salt and mix thoroughly. Combine chick-pea flour and baking soda and sprinkle over the greens. Mix, tossing, until the mixture adheres together.

2. Heat the oil in a 10-inch microwave-safe covered skillet at 100 percent power in a 650- to 700-watt carousel oven for 3 minutes. Uncover, and add mustard seeds, and replace the lid. Cook at 100 percent power for 3 minutes (or until seeds pop). Remove from oven, uncover, and stir in cumin and asafetida. Scoop half the batter by the teaspoonful and place half an inch apart, in the skillet, making 16 dumplings, and cover with the lid.

3. Cook at 100 percent power for 2 minutes. Uncover, gently turn dumplings with tongs, and replace cover. Cook at 100 percent power for an additional 2 minutes (or until dumplings are cooked). Remove from oven. Remove dumplings to a plate and make the remaining 16 dumplings the same way. Combine all the dumplings in the skillet and set aside, covered, until needed.

4. Uncover, pour sauce over the dumplings, and replace cover. Cook at 100 percent power for 3 minutes (or until sauce is boiling). Remove from oven. Uncover, sprinkle salt to taste, and serve.

NOTE The dish may be made ahead, set aside in the same covered container at room temperature for a few hours, and served reheated.

SPINACH DUMPLINGS IN YOGURT SAUCE

KADHI

Dumplings in yogurt sauce, called *kadhi,* are one of the most popular dishes of India. They cook in the microwave with ease, speed, and many fewer calories, as the dumplings are steamed, not deep-fried. There are many lovely variations to this dish, which change from one region to another, one caste to another. The following *kadhi* recipe is from the western state of Gujarat, where the cooks infuse mustard, cumin, and an onion-garlic-flavored spice called asafetida into the sauce, and add a pinch of sugar to render it sweetish-sour.

MICROWAVE

Servings
　—4 to 6
Preparation time
　—10 minutes
Cooking time
　—33 minutes
Heat
　—100 percent power
MW oven size
　—650 to 700 watts
MW cookware
　*—One 10-inch cov-
　　ered skillet and one
　　5-quart covered cas-
　　serole*

===== ROOM TEMPERATURE =====

FOR THE DUMPLINGS:
½ *pound fresh spinach
　leaves*
1 *fresh hot green chili,
　stemmed, seeded, and
　minced*
2 *tablespoons chopped
　fresh coriander leaves*
2 *tablespoons plain
　yogurt*
1 *teaspoon kosher salt*

¾ *cup chick-pea flour
　(p. 449)*
Pinch of baking soda
3 *tablespoons light vege-
　table oil*
¾ *teaspoon mustard
　seeds*
¾ *teaspoon cumin seeds*
¼ *teaspoon ground
　asafetida (p. 481) or ½
　teaspoon minced garlic*

FOR THE SAUCE:
2 *cups plain yogurt
　mixed with 1 cup
　water*

3 *tablespoons chick-pea
　flour*
1 *teaspoon grated or
　crushed fresh ginger*

¼ teaspoon cayenne
  pepper
⅓ cup water

2 teaspoons sugar
1 teaspoon kosher salt,
  or to taste

FOR THE GARNISH:
2 tablespoons chopped
  fresh coriander

¼ cup fried onion shreds
  (p. 475) (optional)

MENU SUGGESTION

These richly flavored spinach dumplings in a delicate yogurt sauce make a perfect vegetarian luncheon entrée accompanied with a light pilaf such as Tomato Basmati Pilaf (p. 308) or Cream of Wheat Pilaf with Tomatoes and Green Peas (p. 320) and Minted Red Onion Salad (p. 241) or Crushed Cucumber Salsa (p. 239). A chilled yogurt shake (pp. 437–445) is a nice addition.

1. Trim spinach and rinse in several changes of water. Lightly drain, finely chop or mince, and put in a medium-size bowl. Add chilies, coriander, yogurt, and salt and mix thoroughly. Combine chick-pea flour with baking soda and sprinkle over the spinach. Mix, tossing, until the mixture adheres together.

2. Heat the oil in a 10-inch microwave-safe skillet at 100 percent power in a 650- to 700-watt carousel oven for 3 minutes. Uncover, and add mustard seeds, and replace the lid. Cook at 100 percent power for 3 minutes (or until seeds pop). Remove from oven, uncover, and stir in cumin and asafetida. Scoop half the batter by the teaspoonful and place, half an inch apart, in the skillet, making 16 dumplings, and cover with the lid.

3. Cook at 100 percent power for 2 minutes. Uncover, gently turn dumplings with tongs, and replace cover. Cook at 100 percent power for an additional 2 minutes (or until dumplings are cooked). Remove from oven. Remove dumplings to a plate and make the remaining 16 dumplings the same way. Combine all the dumplings in the skillet and set aside, covered, until needed.

4. Place all the ingredients for the sauce in a 5-quart microwave-safe casserole. Stir, beating with a whisk, until chick-pea flour is completely blended with the yogurt.

5. Cook, uncovered, at 100 percent power for 10 minutes (or until sauce comes to a boil), stirring once. Add dumplings, along with oil and spices, and cover with the lid. Cook at 100 percent power for 9 min-

utes (or until the dumplings are puffed and the sauce loses uncooked yogurt fragrance and thickens). Remove from oven. Uncover and serve garnished with coriander and, if desired, fried onion shreds.

NOTE   The dish may be made ahead, set aside in the same covered container at room temperature for a few hours, and served reheated.

FRESH BLACK-EYED PEAS IN SPICY YOGURT SAUCE

LOBHIA DAHI

MICROWAVE

Servings
  —6
Preparation time
  —3 minutes
Cooking time
  —24 minutes
Heat
  —100 percent power
MW oven size
  —650 to 700 watts
MW cookware
  —One 10-inch covered skillet

I remember picking these sweet, crunchy peas as a teenager at a farm near Kanpur, the town I grew up in in India, and my mother's watchful piercing eyes preventing me from quietly munching them raw when she wasn't looking!

I have seen plenty of fresh, tender black-eyed peas down South in the United States, where they grow abundantly, but elsewhere they are slightly hard to come by. Supermarkets specializing in tropical and Southern produce are the first places to begin looking. I wouldn't bother with the specialty grocers, who also carry them on and off, depending upon the availability, as they are almost always ridiculously overpriced.

The following recipe is from Gujarat in western India, where the peas are simmered in a chili-spiked ginger-yogurt sauce. The sweet, mellow peas against the spicy, tart sauce are wonderful. The advantage of cooking this dish in the microwave is that the yogurt sauce, without stirring, produces a lump-free, smooth, creamy sauce.

=========== ROOM TEMPERATURE ===========

½ cup grated coconut (p. 449)

1-inch piece fresh ginger, peeled

5 fresh hot green chilies, stemmed

1 cup water

3 tablespoons chick-pea flour (p. 449)

2 cups plain yogurt

2 teaspoons ground coriander

¼ teaspoon turmeric

1 tablespoon light sesame
  oil or light vegetable
  oil
1 teaspoon mustard seeds
12 fresh, or 2 table-
  spoons crushed dried,
  curry leaves (optional)

2 cups fresh, or 1 10-
  ounce package de-
  frosted, black-eyed
  peas
1 teaspoon kosher salt
1½ teaspoons sugar
2 teaspoons lemon juice
2 tablespoons chopped
  fresh coriander

MENU SUGGESTION

This spicy-sweet black-eyed
peas stew, rather rich and
filling, is nice preceded with
a light soup such as Classic
Peppered Tamarind Soup
(p. 37) or Indian Cheese
Spread (p. 19). To complete
the meal, serve Tomato Basmati Pilaf (p. 308) or Cream
of Wheat Pilaf with Shallots
and Chilies (p. 318), Pear
and Green Peppercorn Yo-
gurt Raita (p. 253), and, if
desired, Spicy-Sweet Cranberry Walnut Chutney (p.
346).

1. Put coconut, ginger, chilies, water, and chick-pea
flour into the container of a blender or food processor
and process until the contents are smoothly blended.
Add yogurt, coriander, and turmeric, continue processing until blended, and reserve.

2. Heat the oil in a 10-inch microwave-safe covered
skillet at 100 percent power in a 650- to 700-watt
carousel oven for 3 minutes. Uncover and add mustard seeds and replace the lid. Cook at 100 percent
power for 3 minutes (or until seeds pop). Remove
from oven, uncover, and stir in optional curry leaves,
black-eyed peas, and yogurt mixture; mix lightly, and
replace the lid.

3. Cook at 100 percent power for 18 minutes (or
until yogurt loses its raw flavor and thickens and peas
are cooked). Remove from oven. Uncover, add salt,
sugar, and lemon juice, and serve sprinkled with
chopped coriander.

NOTE   The stew may be made ahead, set aside in the same
covered container at room temperature for a few hours,
and served reheated.

VEGETABLES

Most Indian vegetables are cooked either by turn-frying, which is akin to sautéing, or by steaming, in which case they are then flavored by a dressing of spice-infused oil. The microwave handles both techniques wonderfully. In turn-frying, it reduces both the amount of oil and the need for stirring, resulting in less breakage of soft vegetables. The microwave allows vegetables to steam in a minimum of water, and gives them a light, saladlike appearance while making them perfectly tender in just a few minutes.

Don't restrict these vegetable dishes by serving them only with Indian meals; they are wonderful side dishes. Braised in spices or scented with aromatic oils of mustard or sesame, they make brilliant accompaniments to grilled lamb, barbecue, or the full-flavored main dishes of almost any culture. And, served in larger portions, they can become a fine meal in themselves, served with a yogurt *raita* and bread or rice. And the addition of spices and herbs not only gives the vegetables intriguing flavor and color, it makes leftovers exceptionally useful. Try any of these dishes folded into a green salad straight from the refrigerator or mixed with cooked rice to make a quick pilaf.

BROCCOLI IN SPICY-
GARLIC OIL

HARIGOBHI SABZI

MICROWAVE

Servings
—4
Preparation time
—5 minutes
Cooking time
—10 minutes
Heat
—100 percent power
MW oven size
—650 to 700 watts
MW cookware
—One 10-inch cov-
ered skillet

Indians think of broccoli as green cauliflower because of their resemblance. For that reason and its inexpensiveness and year-round availability, broccoli is used extensively in Indian cooking. I love its flavor and its ability to take on spicing without losing its character. Microwave cooking, I believe, is the best way to cook broccoli. Even when fully cooked, it retains its beautiful green color and crispness.

These crisp broccoli spears imbued with garlic and aromatic spices are great accompanied with any *tandoori* dish, kabobs, and roasts. They may be served hot, at room temperature, or cold as an appetizer, first course, or side-dish vegetable. For variation try pasta tossed in for a light meal.

===================== *ROOM TEMPERATURE* =====================

1 medium-size (about
1¼ pounds) bunch
broccoli
3 tablespoons light
vegetable oil
¼ cup thickly sliced
garlic

2 teaspoons fragrant
spice powder (p. 481)
or curry powder,
homemade (p. 479) or
store-bought
½ teaspoon sugar
2 teaspoons lemon juice,
or to taste
Kosher salt to taste

1. Trim broccoli. Cut and separate florets into long spears and peel the stems. Set aside.

2. Heat the oil and garlic in a 10-inch microwave-safe covered skillet at 100 percent power in a 650- to 700-watt carousel oven for 3 minutes. Remove from oven, uncover, add broccoli spears, and turn in oil to

coat (about 1 minute). Blend in spice powder and sugar, and cover with the lid.

3. Cook at 100 percent power for 7 minutes (or until broccoli is just cooked). Remove from oven. Uncover and turn broccoli to coat with garlic oil. Sprinkle on lemon juice and salt to taste and serve.

NOTE   The broccoli may be made ahead and set aside, covered, for a few hours at room temperature, or refrigerated for a day, and served reheated.

SMOTHERED CABBAGE WITH MUSTARD OIL

BANDHGOBHI SABZI

MICROWAVE

Servings
—4 to 6
Preparation time
—3 minutes
Cooking time
—19 minutes
Heat
—100 percent power
MW oven size
—650 to 700 watts
MW cookware
—One 3-quart covered
casserole and one 8-
inch covered skillet

Not until I experienced authentic Bengali food and the food along the northern border regions did I learn of and start appreciating mustard oil—the favorite seasoning there. Mustard oil, sweet and delicate, is magical for fish, legumes, and vegetables, but first it has to be "tempered," or else it is almost unpalatable. This is because mustard oil contains the pungent and highly irritating mustard gas. The oil, therefore, has to be heated, which volatilizes the gas, thus rendering the oil sweet, fragrant, and mellow.

This cabbage dish is extremely easy to prepare in the microwave. All you do is steam-cook cabbage and then dress it with spice-infused mustard oil. Remember to keep your face (especially your eyes) turned away while working with the oil as the fumes that are released are very irritating.

This cabbage preparation may be served hot or at room temperature, as either a first course or a side-dish vegetable. It is particularly good with dishes containing piquant sauces such as Duck Vendaloo (p. 130).

=============== *ROOM TEMPERATURE* ===============

1 small (1¾–2 pounds),
   green cabbage, cored
   and shredded as for
   coleslaw

1 cup peeled tomatoes
   (fresh or canned with
   juices), coarsely
   chopped
¾ cup thinly sliced
   onion
2 tablespoons julienned
   fresh ginger

2 tablespoons mustard oil
  or light vegetable oil
1 teaspoon mustard seeds
1 teaspoon cumin seeds
4 tablespoons chopped
  fresh coriander

1 teaspoon lemon juice,
  or to taste
1 teaspoon kosher salt,
  or to taste

1. Combine cabbage, tomatoes, onion, and ginger in a 3-quart microwave-safe casserole and cover with the lid. Cook at 100 percent power in a 650- to 700-watt carousel oven for 13 minutes (or until cabbage is cooked and tender). Remove from oven and set aside, covered, until needed.

2. Heat the oil in a 8-inch microwave-safe covered skillet at 100 percent power in a 650- to 700-watt carousel oven for 3 minutes. Uncover, add mustard seeds and cumin seeds, and replace the lid. Cook at 100 percent power for 3 minutes (or until mustard seeds pop). Remove from oven, uncover, and add chopped coriander. Mix rapidly, shaking the skillet, and pour the spice-infused oil on the cabbage, scraping the skillet with a rubber spatula to get all the seasoning. Add lemon juice and salt to taste, toss to blend in flavorings, and serve.

NOTE   The cabbage may be made ahead and set aside, covered, for a few hours at room temperature, or refrigerated for a day, and served reheated.

CAULIFLOWER AND FENNEL IN AROMATIC OIL

GOBHI-SAUNF SABZI

Fennel bulb, because of its fragrance, is generally used in combination with other vegetables and lentils as an enhancer, without searing, thus eliminating any fear of it developing brown spots. It remains plump, crisp, and glistening pale. The microwave works very well in this recipe as the vegetables remain bright and crisp.

This is an extremely versatile dish that goes well with any entrée, particularly chicken and fish in red piquant sauces. It may be served hot, at room temperature, or cold. For a quick pilaf, toss into cooked rice and garnish with toasted nuts.

=== *ROOM TEMPERATURE* ===

1 tablespoon finely
  chopped fresh ginger
2 teaspoons ground
  coriander
1½ teaspoons ground
  cumin
½ teaspoon cayenne
  pepper
½ teaspoon turmeric
4 tablespoons mustard oil
  or light vegetable oil

1 cup chopped scallions
  (both green and white
  parts)
1 small (1 pound) cauli-
  flower, trimmed and
  cut into 1-inch florets
1½ cups sliced fennel
  bulb
Kosher salt to taste

FOR THE GARNISH:
2 tablespoons chopped fresh coriander

1. Combine ginger, coriander, cumin, cayenne, and turmeric in a small bowl and reserve.

MICROWAVE

Servings
  —4 to 6
Preparation time
  —1 minute
Cooking time
  —10 minutes
Heat
  —100 percent power
MW oven size
  —650 to 700 watts
MW cookware
  —One 10-inch cov-
   ered skillet

2. Heat the oil in a 10-inch microwave-safe skillet, uncovered, at 100 percent power in a 650- to 700-watt carousel oven for 3 minutes. Remove from oven and add scallions and spice mixture. Stir rapidly for 30 seconds to 1 minute. Add cauliflower and fennel, toss to coat them with oil, and cover with the lid.

3. Cook at 100 percent power for 7 minutes (or until vegetables are soft but not mushy). Remove from oven. Uncover, add salt to taste, and serve garnished with coriander.

NOTE   The cauliflower may be made ahead and set aside, covered, for a few hours at room temperature, or refrigerated for a day, and served reheated.

GLAZED PEPPERED CUCUMBER

KHEERA SABZI

MICROWAVE

Servings
  —4

Preparation time
  —3 minutes

Cooking time
  —5 minutes

Heat
  —100 percent power

MW oven size
  —650 to 700 watts

MW cookware
  —One 10-inch skillet

Cooks in the southern regions of India treat cucumber as a squash vegetable. In order not to mask their delicate flavor, cucumber slices are minimally spiced (such as the pinch of cumin used in this recipe) and steamed in their own juices. Microwave cooking is ideal for preparing this dish as the cucumbers retain their crispness and their beautiful jade color.

This subtle and mild cucumber dish may be served hot, at room temperature, or straight out of the refrigerator. It pairs well with any lightly spiced fish or chicken preparation. For a light meal serve a fragrant pilaf and a sweet chutney, such as Tomato Basmati Pilaf (p. 308) and Sweet Cranberry Pistachio Chutney with California Black Figs (p. 344).

===== *ROOM TEMPERATURE* =====

2 medium-size (¾ pound) cucumbers	*1 teaspoon ground cumin*
1 tablespoon mustard oil or light vegetable oil	*¼ teaspoon freshly ground black pepper*
	1 teaspoon lemon juice
	Kosher salt to taste

1. Peel cucumbers, cut in half lengthwise, and scoop out the seeds. Cut cucumbers, at bias, into ⅛-inch-thick slices.

2. Heat the oil in a 10-inch microwave-safe skillet at 100 percent power in a 650- to 700-watt carousel oven for 3 minutes. Remove from oven. Add cumin, black pepper, and cucumber slices. Stir to coat vegetable with oil.

3. Cook at 100 percent power for 2 minutes (or until cucumber is cooked but not mushy). Remove from oven. Sprinkle on lemon juice and add salt to taste.

NOTE   The cucumber may be made ahead and set aside, covered, for a few hours at room temperature, or refrigerated for a day, and served reheated.

FIERY MANGALOREAN EGGPLANT

MASALA VANGI

MICROWAVE

Servings
—4

Preparation time
—9 minutes

Cooking time
—11 minutes

Heat
—100 percent power

MW oven size
—650 to 700 watts

MW cookware
—One 10-inch cov-
ered skillet

Another fabulous eggplant preparation that cooks perfectly in the microwave. If you use long, thin Japanese-variety eggplants (as recommended in the recipe), the dish will taste more flavorful.

These fiery-hot and fragrant eggplant slices are particularly good served with mild and herbal dishes. They may be served as either a side-dish vegetable or a light vegetarian main course, hot or at room temperature. A substantial pilaf and a salad, such as Whole Mung Bean and Basmati Pilaf (p. 316) and Warm Cabbage Salad with Crabmeat and Mangoes (p. 23), will make a fine, complete meal.

==================== ROOM TEMPERATURE ====================

1 medium-size (1 pound) eggplant, Japanese or oval American

4 tablespoons light sesame oil or light vegetable oil

1–2 teaspoons cayenne pepper

1 teaspoon paprika

¾ teaspoon ground cumin

⅛ teaspoon turmeric

Kosher salt to taste, if desired

2 small (⅓ pound) onions, peeled and thinly sliced into rings

2 tablespoons, or 1 frozen cube, defrosted, tamarind juice or 1 teaspoon tamarind concentrate (p. 491) dissolved in 1 tablespoon water

1. If you are using oval American eggplant, first quarter it lengthwise. Cut eggplant into ¼-inch-thick slices and place in a shallow dish. Pour 1 tablespoon oil over eggplant and mix until vegetable is evenly coated. Combine cayenne, paprika, cumin, turmeric, and salt

and sprinkle over the eggplant. Toss lightly and re-serve.

2. Heat the remaining oil in a 10-inch microwave-safe skillet, uncovered, at 100 percent power in a 650- to 700-watt carousel oven for 3 minutes. Remove from oven.

3. Add eggplant slices and stir rapidly until evenly coated with oil. Spread onion slices on top, pushing them between eggplant slices, and cover with the lid. Cook at 100 percent power for 4 minutes (or until eggplant is cooked). Uncover, dribble tamarind juice on top, and replace cover. Cook, uncovered, at 100 percent power for 4 more minutes (or until eggplant is soft). Remove from the oven and serve.

NOTE   The eggplant may be made ahead and set aside, covered, for a few hours at room temperature, or refrigerated for a day, and served reheated.

EGGPLANT SLICES SMOTHERED WITH COCONUT-SPICE PASTE

MASALA VANGI

MICROWAVE

Servings
—4 to 6
Preparation time
—5 minutes
Cooking time
—19 minutes
Standing time
—5 minutes
Heat
—100 percent power
MW oven size
—650 to 700 watts
MW cookware
—One 10-inch cov-
ered skillet

The first time my mother taught me how to make this gorgeous Bombay specialty, the spice mixture stubbornly got stuck to the pan as the eggplant cooked. Stirring only crushed the eggplant, turning them into a paste. This dish traditionally becomes a mess while cooking, even when cooked in a well-seasoned wok, which I had done. I mention this experience to you so that you will appreciate your microwave's virtues. The microwave cooks this dish to perfection. The eggplant slices become soft but remain intact and the spice paste develops a lovely roasted aroma and flavor. And by now you should know that nothing sticks in the microwave!

This eggplant preparation may be served hot or at room temperature as either a side-dish vegetable or a vegetarian main course. For a simple light meal, serve it with Bombay Sweetish-Sour Garlic Lentils (p. 275) and a cool Avocado and Cucumber Yogurt Raita (p. 251). You can also toss the eggplant into cooked rice and turn it into a pilaf.

=== ROOM TEMPERATURE ===

2 tablespoons American
yellow split peas
(p. 461)
2 tablespoons coriander
seeds

2 teaspoons cumin seeds
¼ teaspoon fenugreek
seeds (p. 483) or
ajowan seeds (p. 481)
or ¼ teaspoon dried
thyme
½ cup unsweetened
flaked coconut
(p.449)

¼ teaspoon cayenne
  pepper (optional)
⅔ cup water
3 tablespoons light ses-
  ame oil or peanut oil
1 teaspoon mustard seeds
4 medium-size cloves
  garlic, peeled and
  thinly sliced
½ cup chopped onion

¼ cup, or 2 frozen
  cubes, tamarind juice,
  or 2 teaspoons tamar-
  ind concentrate
  (p. 491) dissolved in 3
  tablespoons water
1 medium-size (about 1
  pound) eggplant,
  stemmed, halved, and
  cut into ½-inch-thick
  slices
2 teaspoons kosher salt,
  or to taste

FOR THE GARNISH:
Grated coconut and chopped fresh coriander
  (optional)

1. Combine split peas, coriander, cumin, and fenugreek or ajowan in a spice mill or coffee grinder and
grind to a fine powder. Transfer spice mixture to a
small bowl and reserve.

2. Place coconut, cayenne, and water in the container
of a food processor or blender, process until finely
pureed, remove into another bowl, and reserve.

3. Heat the oil in a 10-inch microwave safe covered
skillet at 100 percent power in a 650- to 700-watt
carousel oven for 3 minutes. Uncover, add mustard
seeds, and replace the lid. Cook at 100 percent power
for 3 minutes (or until seeds pop). Uncover, stir in
spice mixture, garlic, and onion, and replace cover.
Cook at 100 percent power for 4 minutes (or until
onions are soft). Remove from oven.

4. Uncover, add coconut mixture and tamarind and
mix thoroughly. Cook uncovered at 100 percent power
for 3 minutes (or until coconut and tamarind lose
their raw fragrance and spice paste begins to thicken).
Remove from oven.

5. Add eggplant and salt, mix until vegetables are evenly coated with the spice paste, and cover with the lid. Cook at 100 percent power for 6 minutes (or until eggplant is cooked soft but not mushy). Remove from oven and let the dish stand, covered, for 5 minutes. Uncover and serve, if desired, garnished with coconut and coriander.

NOTE The eggplant may be made ahead and set aside, covered, for a few hours at room temperature, or refrigerated for a day, and served reheated.

MUSTARD-BRAISED ENDIVE

SABZI SHARSHA

These buttery shreds of endive swathed in mustard cream are pure pleasure on the palate, all the more for knowing how effortlessly this dish can be made in the microwave. The endive cooks in the moist heat without searing (thus eliminating all fears of brown spots), yet retains its plump and juicy yet crisp texture, and a delicate ivory color. This Bengali specialty is generally made with a local green of the cabbage family, but endive, which I love, makes an exciting substitute.

This may be served as a side-dish vegetable with fish or chicken. For contrast, pair it with hot and spicy dishes containing cayenne and tomatoes.

═══════════ *ROOM TEMPERATURE* ═══════════

1 tablespoon dry mustard	2 teaspoons kosher salt,
½ teaspoon ground	or to taste
cumin	8 medium-size endive,
½ teaspoon ground fennel	cored and shredded
¼ teapoon turmeric	into ¼-inch strips
¼ teaspoon cayenne or	2 large (½ pound) Ana-
black pepper	heim chilies or 2 small
4 tablespoons mustard oil	sweet (Italian) green
or light vegetable oil	peppers, cored and cut
½ teaspoon mustard	into fine ⅛-inch strips
seeds	½ cup crushed spicy
1 small onion, peeled	croutons (p. 487) or
and thinly sliced	regular toasted
¼ cup heavy cream	croutons or roasted
2 tablespoons Dijon	slivered almonds
mustard	(p. 463)

1. Combine dry mustard, cumin, fennel, turmeric, and cayenne in a bowl and reserve.

2. Heat the oil in a 10-inch microwave-safe covered skillet at 100 percent power in a 650- to 700-watt carousel oven for 3 minutes. Uncover, add mustard seeds, and replace the lid. Cook at 100 percent power for 3 minutes (or until seeds pop). Uncover and add onion and spice mixture. Mix well to coat onions with the oil.

3. Cook, uncovered, at 100 percent power for 1 minute (or until spices exude a fried aroma). Remove from oven.

4. Stir in cream, Dijon mustard, and salt. Add vegetables, turn them with tongs to coat with the sauce, and cover with the lid. Cook at 100 percent power for 8 minutes (or until endive is wilted and soft). Remove from oven and serve sprinkled with crushed croutons or almonds.

NOTE The endive may be made ahead and set aside, covered, for a few hours at room temperature, or refrigerated for a day, and served reheated.

GREEN BEANS IN PEPPERED-MUSTARD DRESSING

SAME BHUJIA

MICROWAVE

Servings
—4

Preparation time
—2 minutes

Cooking time
—13 minutes

Heat
—100 percent power

MW oven size
—650 to 700 watts

MW cookware
—One 10-inch cov-
ered skillet

Green beans, like broccoli, are wonderful cooked in the microwave as they remain crisp and bright. In this recipe from Bengal in eastern India, green beans are steamed in the trapped vapor of cumin-and-garlic-laced chili oil. The sweet cinnamon, mustard, and sugar temper the chili's heat, thus the beans taste warm, not spicy. The beans may be served hot, at room temperature, or straight out of the refrigerator as an appetizer, first course, or side-dish vegetable. They are especially good with *tandoori* dishes, kabobs, and roasts.

=== ROOM TEMPERATURE ===

¼ teaspoon turmeric
1 teaspoon ground cumin
⅛ teaspoon ground
    cinnamon
1 teaspoon dry mustard
2 teaspoons sugar
1 teaspoon kosher salt,
    or to taste
2 tablespoons light vege-
    table oil

8 dried whole hot red
    chili pods
1 teaspoon cumin seeds
4 large cloves garlic,
    peeled and thinly
    sliced
1 pound green beans,
    trimmed and left
    whole or cut into 1-
    inch pieces
Juice of half a lemon

1. Combine turmeric, cumin, cinnamon, mustard, sugar, and salt in a small bowl and reserved.

2. Heat oil in a 10-inch microwave-safe skillet, uncovered, at 100 percent power in a 650- to 700-watt carousel oven for 3 minutes. Add red chilies, cumin,

and garlic. Cook at 100 percent power for 2 minutes (or until spices turn a few shades darker). Remove from oven. Add spice mix, stir for a second, and immediately add green beans. Mix thoroughly to coat vegetable with spiced oil and cover with the lid.

3. Cook at 100 percent power for 8 minutes (or until beans are cooked tender). Remove from oven. Uncover, stir in lemon juice, and serve.

NOTE   The green beans may be made ahead and set aside, covered, for a few hours at room temperature, or refrigerated for a day, and served reheated.

CRISP FRIED OKRA

VENDAKAI VADAKAL

To get the okra crisp, as the name suggests, you have to make this dish in a browning skillet, which has a hot base that keeps the okra sizzling, or else it will steam-cook and turn limp. This dish is a snap to cook in the microwave—just add okra to the hot skillet. Basic fried okra has many uses in Indian cooking, including its addition to *raitas* (pp. 251–264) and pilafs (pp. 301–321). Crisp okra is also good sprinkled over creamy *dals* and soups.

=============== *ROOM TEMPERATURE* ===============

*3 tablespoons sesame oil
  or light vegetable oil*
*1 pound tender okra,
  trimmed and cut into
  ⅜-inch-thick rings*

*2 fresh hot green chilies,
  stemmed, seeded, and
  chopped (optional)*
1 teaspoon lemon juice

1. Heat the oil in a 10-inch microwave-safe skillet at 100 percent power in a 650- to 700-watt carousel oven for 3 minutes. Remove from oven, add okra, and chilies, and stir rapidly to coat vegetables with oil.

2. Cook, uncovered, at 100 percent power for 13 minutes (or until okra is browned and glazed), stirring 4 times. Remove from oven and stir in lemon juice.

NOTE The okra may be made ahead and set aside, covered, for a few hours at room temperature, or refrigerated for a day, and served reheated.

SPICY FRIED OKRA

BHINDI SABZI

MICROWAVE

Servings
—4
Cooking time
—14 minutes
Heat
—100 percent power
MW oven size
—650 to 700 watts
MW cookware
—One 10-inch skillet

This dish is similar to Crisp Fried Okra (p. 222) except not as crackling crisp, hence it takes less time to make. It may be served warm or at room temperature, as either a side-dish vegetable or a light vegetarian main course. I particularly like this spicy okra with creamy tomato-based dishes such as Lamb in Creamy Tomato Sauce (p. 151) or Ooty-style Sole in Fragrant Tomato Sauce (p. 83). For a light meal, serve with Tomato Basmati Pilaf (p. 308) and Spinach and Yogurt Raita (p. 258).

========== ROOM TEMPERATURE ==========

2 tablespoons light vege-
    table oil
1 pound tender okra,
    trimmed and cut into
    ¼-inch-thick rings
1 medium-size onion,
    peeled, halved, and
    thinly sliced

2 fresh hot green chilies,
    stemmed, seeded, and
    thinly sliced
2 teaspoons curry pow-
    der, homemade
    (p. 479) or store-
    bought
2 teaspoons lemon juice
½ teaspoon kosher salt,
    or to taste

1. Heat the oil in a 10-inch microwave-safe skillet at 100 percent power in a 650- to 700-watt carousel oven for 3 minutes. Remove from oven, and add okra and onion. Sprinkle over chilies and curry powder and stir rapidly to coat vegetables with oil.

2. Cook, uncovered, at 100 percent power for 7 minutes (or until okra is lightly browned), stirring twice. Stir in lemon juice and continue cooking, uncovered, at 100 percent power for 4 minutes (or until okra is browned and glazed), stirring twice. Remove from oven. Add salt to taste and serve.

NOTE The okra may be made ahead and set aside, covered, for a few hours at room temperature, or refrigerated for a day, and served reheated.

GARLIC-FRIED OKRA WITH TAMARIND

VENDAKAI VADAKAL

MICROWAVE

Servings
— 4
Preparation time
— 4 minutes
Cooking time
— 11 minutes
Heat
— 100 percent power
MW oven size
— 650 to 700 watts
MW cookware
— One 10-inch skillet

Another delicious okra preparation, flavored with cayenne and mustard-infused oil and tempered with the sweetish-sour juices of tamarind. This spicy-piquant okra preparation is particularly good with delicately mellow main dishes containing cream, coconut, or lentil purees. It may be served hot or at room temperature as either a side dish or a light vegetarian main course accompanied with Moghul-scented Basmati Pilaf (p. 302), New Delhi Fragrant Creamy Mung Beans (p. 284), and cool Zucchini and Walnut Yogurt Raita (p. 262).

=== ROOM TEMPERATURE ===

3 tablespoons sesame oil
  or light vegetable oil
2 large cloves garlic,
  peeled and thinly
  sliced
1 teaspoon mustard
  seeds, crushed
1 teaspoon ground cumin
½ teaspoon cayenne
  pepper

⅛ teaspoon ajowan seeds
  (p. 481), crushed, or
  ⅓ teaspoon dried
  thyme
1 pound tender okra,
  trimmed and cut into
  ½-inch-thick slices
2 tablespoons, or 1
  frozen cube, de-
  frosted, tamarind juice
  (p. 492)
½ teaspoon salt

1. Heat oil in a 10-inch microwave-safe skillet at 100 percent power in a 650- to 700-watt carousel oven for 1 minute 30 seconds. Add garlic, mustard, cumin, cayenne, and ajowan. Continue cooking, uncovered, at 100 percent power for 2 minutes (or until garlic is cooked). Remove from oven.

2. Add okra and mix until well coated with spices. Cook, uncovered, at 100 percent power for 7 minutes (or until okra is lightly browned), stirring twice. Add tamarind and continue cooking, uncovered, at 100 percent power for 4 minutes (or until okra is browned and glazed), stirring twice. Remove from oven. Add salt to taste and serve.

NOTE The okra may be made ahead and set aside, covered, for a few hours at room temperature, or refrigerated for a day, and served reheated.

NEW DELHI SPICY POTATOES

SOOKHA ALOO

MICROWAVE

Servings
— *4*

Preparation time
— *4 minutes*

Cooking time
— *11 minutes*

Heat
— *100 percent power*

MW oven size
— *650 to 700 watts*

MW cookware
— *One 10-inch cov-
    ered skillet*

This very aromatic warm potato salad, exploding with the fragrance of cumin and fennel, is great made in the microwave as it makes the spices taste more pungent and intense. Whole tiny new potatoes are wonderful in this recipe. Remember to prick or lightly slash each potato before cooking so that the steam from within escapes, thus preventing them from cracking and bursting.

This is an ideal picnic food. It is good served with gravy dishes as well as *tandoori* dishes and kabobs. For a light meal, serve with Glazed Cucumber and Scallop Salad with Coriander (p. 25) and Tomato Basmati Pilaf (p. 308).

=== *ROOM TEMPERATURE* ===

1 teaspoon ground coriander	3 tablespoons light vegetable oil
¼ teaspoon turmeric	½ teaspoon cumin seeds
¼ teaspoon cayenne pepper	½ teaspoon fennel seeds
¼ teaspoon black pepper	3 medium-size (1 pound) new red wax potatoes, peeled and cut into ½-inch cubes
1 teaspoon kosher salt, or to taste	3 tablespoons water
½ teaspoon minced fresh hot green chilies	2 tablespoons chopped fresh coriander

1. Combine coriander, turmeric, cayenne pepper, black pepper, salt, and chilies in a bowl and reserve.

2. Heat the oil in a 10-inch microwave-safe skillet at 100 percent power in a 650- to 700-watt carousel

oven for 3 minutes. Add cumin and fennel. Cook at 100 percent power for 2 minutes (or until spices turn a few shades darker). Remove from oven, add ground-spice mixture, stir for a second, and immediately add potatoes. Stir rapidly to coat potatoes with the oil. Sprinkle water over and cover with the lid.

3. Cook at 100 percent power for 6 minutes (or until potatoes are soft). Remove from oven. Uncover and serve sprinkled with coriander.

NOTE The potatoes may be made ahead and set aside, covered, for a few hours at room temperature, or refrigerated for a day, and served reheated.

GARLIC POTATOES SMOTHERED WITH GREENS

SAAG ALOO

MICROWAVE

Servings
  —4
Preparation time
  —5 minutes
Cooking time
  —11 minutes
Heat
  —100 percent power
MW oven size
  —650 to 700 watts
MW cookware
  *—One 3-quart covered
    casserole and one
    10-inch covered
    skillet*

This is one of my favorite ways to cook greens in the microwave—very garlicky and studded with creamy-tasting potatoes. This recipe produces bright-green and crisp-tasting greens. If you prefer creamy-soft greens, then add them along with the potatoes.

These greens are nice served hot or at room temperature. They are good with fish and chicken. Accompanied with Plain Basmati Rice (p. 299), New Delhi Fragrant Creamy Mung Beans (p. 284), and Sweet Pepper and Yogurt Raita (p. 256), they make a complete meal. You can also make a quick *raita* by folding them into plain yogurt.

=============== *ROOM TEMPERATURE* ===============

*1 pound fresh greens
  (spinach, mustard,
  collard, kale, Swiss
  chard, beet, and radish
  greens)*
*1 tablespoon mustard oil,
  sesame oil, or olive oil*
*½ teaspoon mustard
  seeds*
*2 medium-size cloves
  garlic, peeled and
  thinly sliced*

⅛ teaspoon turmeric
*½ teaspoon kosher salt,
  or to taste*
*1 medium-size (⅓
  pound) new red wax
  potato, peeled and cut
  into ¼ × ¼ × 2-
  inch-long julienne
  strips*
*1½ teaspoons lemon
  juice*

1. Trim stems off the greens and wash thoroughly in several changes of water. Drain and place in a 3-quart microwave-safe casserole and cover with the lid.

2. Cook at 100 percent power in a 650- to 700-watt carousel oven for 4 minutes (or until greens wilt). Remove from oven. Transfer greens into a bowl of cold water. Drain, squeezing lightly to remove excess water. Place greens on work board, finely chop, and reserve.

3. Heat the oil in a 10-inch microwave-safe covered skillet at 100 percent power for 3 minutes. Uncover, add mustard seeds, and replace the lid. Cook at 100 percent power for 3 minutes (or until seeds pop). Uncover and add garlic cloves, turmeric, and salt. Cook uncovered for 1 minute. Remove from oven. Fold in potatoes and replace cover.

4. Cook at 100 percent power for 3 minutes (or until potatoes are just cooked). Uncover and stir in greens. Continue cooking, uncovered, at 100 percent power for 1 minute (or until contents are heated through). Remove from oven. Stir in lemon juice and serve.

NOTE The potatoes may be made ahead and set aside, covered, for a few hours at room temperature, or refrigerated for a day, and served reheated.

HYDERABAD COCONUT-BRAISED POTATO CURRY

ALOO KARI

MICROWAVE

Servings
  —4 to 6
Preparation time
  —1 minute
Cooking time
  —21 minutes
Heat
  —100 percent power
MW oven size
  —650 to 700 watts
MW cookware
  *—One 10-inch cov-
    ered skillet*

Although potatoes cook fabulously in the microwave, you can make a very disappointing dish by using the *wrong* potatoes. They vary in flavor and texture, and therefore cannot be used interchangeably, especially if a recipe calls for a specific variety. New red waxy potatoes, with their creamy yet tight texture, are what you need in this dish as they retain their shape and stay moist.

These coconut-fragrant potatoes can be served warm as well as at room temperature. Think of it as a warm potato salad and take it along on picnics and to cook-outs. You can serve these potatoes as a vegetarian main dish accompanied with a salad and a bread or muffin, such as Warm Crayfish, Fennel, and Pine Nut Salad with Dill (p. 27) and Bombay Spicy Lentil Cakes (p. 327).

=== ROOM TEMPERATURE ===

½ cup finely chopped onion

2 large cloves garlic, peeled and thinly sliced

4 fresh hot green chilies, stemmed, seeded, and thinly sliced

2 teaspoons curry powder or sambaar powder, homemade (p. 479 or p. 480) or store-bought

4 tablespoons light vegetable oil

¾ teaspoon cumin seeds

½ teaspoon fennel seeds

3 medium-size (1 pound) new red wax potatoes, peeled and cut into 1-inch cubes

½ cup coconut milk (p. 450)

2 teaspoons kosher salt, or to taste

2 medium-size (¾ pound) red or green peppers, cored and cut into 1-inch pieces

1 teaspoon lemon juice

FOR THE GARNISH:
Coriander leaves

1. Combine onion, garlic, chilies, and curry powder in a small bowl and reserve.

2. Heat the oil in a 10-inch microwave-safe skillet, uncovered, at 100 percent power in a 650- to 700-watt carousel oven for 3 minutes. Add cumin and fennel. Cook at 100 percent power for 1 minute 30 seconds (or until spices turn a few shades darker). Add onion mixture and mix. Cook, uncovered, at 100 percent power for 2 minutes (or until ground spices are browned). Remove from oven.

3. Add potatoes, coconut milk, and salt, mix well, and cover with the lid. Cook at 100 percent power for 10 minutes (or until potatoes are soft). Uncover, add green peppers, and replace cover. Continue cooking for an additional 4 minutes (or until peppers are cooked but still crisp). Remove from oven. Uncover, stir in lemon juice, and serve garnished with coriander.

GARLIC-BRAISED TOMATOES

TAMATAR KOOT

MICROWAVE

Servings
—4
Cooking time
—15 minutes
Standing time
—10 minutes
Heat
—100 percent power
MW oven size
—650 to 700 watts
MW cookware
—One 10-inch cov-
ered skillet

This dish of lightly stewed meaty wedges of tomatoes studded with garlic slivers and glistening in spice oil is one of my all-time favorites. In the microwave the dish cooks delicately and quickly and the tomatoes intensify in flavor. For best results use red vine-ripened tomatoes that have a high acid content; otherwise the dish will taste bland. While cooking in the microwave the tomatoes exude juices that should be served with the tomatoes and garlic slivers. For a milder flavor, remove chili pods from the stew and discard before serving. The dish is lovely served warm, at room temperature, or straight out of the refrigerator with mild fish and chicken dishes such as Steamed Fish in Ginger-Thyme Essence (p. 81) or Ginger Chicken Kabob (p. 109). It is also good over Indian cheese, omelets, toast, and fresh cheese. Try it with grilled lamb and as a pizza topping.

=== ROOM TEMPERATURE ===

3 tablespoons mustard oil
   or light vegetable oil
1 teaspoon mustard seeds
6 dried whole hot red
   chili pods
8 large cloves garlic,
   peeled and thickly
   sliced

1 teaspoon curry powder,
   homemade (p. 479) or
   store-bought, or
   ground cumin
4 medium-size (1 pound)
   red ripe tomatoes, cut
   into ½-inch-thick
   wedges
1 teaspoon lemon juice
Kosher salt to taste

1. Heat the oil in a 10-inch microwave-safe covered skillet at 100 percent power in a 650- to 700-watt carousel oven for 3 minutes. Uncover, add mustard seeds, and replace the lid. Cook at 100 percent power for 3 minutes (or until seeds pop). Uncover and add chilies and garlic.

2. Cook, uncovered, at 100 percent power for 1 minute (or until chili pods turn almost black and garlic is light brown). Remove from oven, stir in curry powder, then carefully fold in tomatoes. Cook, uncovered, at 100 percent power for 8 minutes (or until tomatoes are stewed). Remove from oven. Let the dish stand, uncovered, for 10 minutes. Add lemon juice and salt to taste and serve.

NOTE The dish may be made ahead and set aside, covered, for a few hours at room temperature, or refrigerated for a day, and served reheated.

ZUCCHINI BRAISED IN TOMATO CUMIN SAUCE

LAUKI BHAJI

You can make this very popular preparation from north India in just a few minutes using any variety of summer squash. I particularly like the firm, crisp texture of squash and the springlike flavor of the dish. It may be served as either a side-dish vegetable with a subtle chicken or seafood preparation such as Creamed Chicken Kabob (p. 111) or a light vegetarian main course. For a light meal, serve a *dal* and a simple pilaf such as Mustard- and Garlic-flavored American Yellow Split Peas (p. 277) and Moghul-scented Basmati Pilaf (p. 302).

MICROWAVE

Servings
— *4 to 6*
Cooking time
— *13 minutes*
Heat
— *100 percent power*
MW oven size
— *650 to 700 watts*
MW cookware
— *One 10-inch covered skillet*

===== ROOM TEMPERATURE =====

4 tablespoons light vegetable oil

1 tablespoon grated or crushed fresh ginger

1½ teaspoons finely chopped garlic

3 fresh hot green chilies

5 medium-size (2 pounds) zucchini, cut into ¼-inch slices

1 cup chopped tomatoes (fresh or canned)

2 teaspoons lemon juice

Kosher salt to taste, if desired

1 teaspoon ground roasted cumin seeds (p. 465)

FOR THE GARNISH:
2 tablespoons chopped fresh coriander

1. Heat the oil in a 10-inch microwave-safe skillet, uncovered, at 100 percent power in a 650- to 700 watt carousel oven for 1 minute. Add ginger, garlic,

and chilies. Cook, uncovered, at 100 percent power for 4 minutes (or until seasonings are lightly fried). Remove from oven.

2. Add zucchini and tomatoes. Mix well and cover with the lid. Cook at 100 percent power for 8 minutes (or until vegetables are soft). Remove from oven. Uncover, stir in lemon juice, salt, and cumin, and serve garnished with coriander.

NOTE The zucchini may be made ahead and set aside, covered, for a few hours at room temperature, or refrigerated for a day, and served reheated.

SALADS
AND YOGURT RAITAS

$\mathcal{S}$alads and yogurt *raitas*—yogurt mixed with vegetables, nuts, or fruits—are traditional accompaniments to any Indian meal, especially when a soothing, cool taste is needed to offset a fiery main dish. In addition, they provide the moisture that may be lacking in foods such as kabobs, meat cakes, roasts, and *tandoori* chicken.

Think of yogurt *raita* as a salad, and cucumber, onion, green pepper, and zucchini are popular vegetables used in it. Fruits used are usually juicy and fragrant: mango, papaya, banana, pear, and peaches, for example; and walnuts, pecans, cashews, and almonds are all added for flavor and crunch. Many *raitas,* thinned with buttermilk, water, or nonfat milk, can be served as refreshing, cool soups in summer. It is important that the yogurt used in *raita* is fresh and not excessively tart; check the dates when you purchase yogurt and buy the "youngest" available.

Salads differ from yogurt *raitas* in that the dressing is based on lemon juice, oil, or other flavorful liquids rather than yogurt. All of the recipes in this section are extremely easy to make in the microwave: All you need to do is cook the vegetable—a process that takes minutes or even seconds—and fold it into the dressing or seasoned yogurt. Many of the yogurt *raitas* are flavored with ground roasted spices, such as cumin and coriander, which too can be made effortlessly in the microwave in just a few minutes (see Roasted Spices in Moghul Microwave Pantry, p. 465). Besides, the spices develop a more intensely, smoky aroma.

CRUSHED CUCUMBER SALSA

TOHYAL

MICROWAVE

Yield
—1½ cups
Servings
—6 to 8
Preparation time
—5 minutes
Cooking time
—7 minutes
Heat
—100 percent power
MW oven size
—650 to 700 watts
MW cookware
—One 8-inch skillet

Tohyal is a classic south Indian salad. Made with salad greens, fruits, cooked or smoked vegetables, lemon juice or tamarind, and a highly aromatic spice-infused dressing, *tohyal* takes on many interesting forms and flavors. It can be subtly mellow or assertively fiery on the palate, depending on whether you prefer a light diplike sauce or a more substantial preparation.

This one resembles Mexican salsa. It is made with cucumbers, tomatoes, and coriander and flavored with lemon juice and green chilies. One distinctive feature of this *tohyal* is the mustard-infused oil, which, folded into the salsa, imparts a sweet-smoky flavor. Serve the salsa with *tandoori* dishes, kabobs, and roasts.

⅓ cup fresh coriander
  leaves
2 fresh hot green chilies,
  or more to taste,
  stemmed, seeded, and
  cut into 1-inch pieces
2 medium-size (¾
  pound) cucumbers,
  peeled, seeded, and cut
  into 1-inch pieces
1 medium-size tomato
  (⅓ pound), seeded and
  diced into ¼-inch
  pieces

2 tablespoons lemon juice
¼ teaspoon kosher salt,
  or to taste
1½ tablespoons mustard
  oil or olive oil
⅓ teaspoon mustard
  seeds
½ teaspoon minced
  garlic
½ teaspoon ground
  cumin

1. Place coriander and chilies in the container of a food processor and process until finely chopped. Add cucumber and continue processing, with a pulse motion, until the cucumber is finely chopped and lightly crushed. Transfer the mixture into a bowl and stir in tomatoes, lemon juice, and salt.

2. Heat the oil in an 8-inch microwave-safe covered skillet at 100 percent power in a 650- to 700-watt carousel oven for 3 minutes. Uncover, add mustard seeds, and replace the lid. Cook at 100 percent for 3 minutes (or until seeds pop). Uncover and stir in garlic and cumin. Cook, uncovered, at 100 percent power for 20 seconds (or until garlic is cooked). Remove from oven. Pour the spice-infused oil, scraping the skillet with a rubber spatula, onto the cucumber mixture. Mix thoroughly and serve at room temperature or chilled.

NOTE   The salsa may be made up to a day ahead and kept, covered, in the refrigerator.

MINTED RED ONION SALAD

PIAZ SALAT

This is a crowd-pleasing salad that traditionally accompanies *tandoori* Cornish hen, kabobs, and other dry (without sauce) dishes. It is made with dry-textured red onions, chilies, and lemon juice. The roasted cumin and mint lend a spicy-herbal hypnotic aroma. It is textural and very tasty. The onions are rendered sweet by blanching, a step often used by Indian cooks.

=== ROOM TEMPERATURE ===

2 medium-size (⅔ pound) red onions, peeled and thinly sliced

1 cup water

3 tablespoons Fragrant Mint Sauce (p. 366)
   or
¼ cup fresh mint leaves, minced

2 fresh hot green chilies, stemmed, seeded, and minced

1 teaspoon sugar

1 tablespoon lemon juice

¼ teaspoon ground roasted cumin seeds (p. 465)

¼ teaspoon kosher salt, or to taste

FOR THE GARNISH:
⅓ cup toasted pine nuts (p. 464)

1. Place onion slices in a medium-size bowl.

2. Heat 1 cup of water in a 1-cup measure, uncovered, at 100 percent power in a 650- to 700-watt carousel oven for 2 minutes (or until boiling). Remove from oven.

3. Pour water over onion slices and cover the bowl

with a plate and let them steam for 30 seconds. Drain, refresh onion in cold water, and drain again.

4. Return onion to the bowl. Add all other ingredients except salt. Toss well, cover, and marinate for 10 minutes. Just before serving, add salt to taste. Garnish with pine nuts and serve immediately.

TAMIL POTATO SALAD WITH SHALLOTS

PODIMAS

Shallots are a popular vegetable with the Brahmins of southern India, but not the shallots we know. They use shallots akin to an onion (which they call "little onions") in a wide variety of dishes but usually in combination with other vegetables or lentils. In this classic south Indian salad, potatoes and shallots are combined in a spicy dressing. The shallots here not only lend a sweet undertone but also mellow and bind the flavors of hot seasonings. Microwave cooking is particularly flattering to shallots as it accentuates their sweetness. This potato salad is great with southern specialties, seafood, and vegetarian main courses. It is also good on picnics and at cookouts.

MICROWAVE

Yield
  —3 cups
Servings
  —6
Preparation time
  —3 minutes
Cooking time
  —7 minutes
Heat
  —100 percent power
MW oven size
  —650 to 700 watts
MW cookware
  —One 10-inch covered skillet

ROOM TEMPERATURE

4 medium-size (1 pound) new red wax potatoes
2 tablespoons light vegetable oil
¾ teaspoon mustard seeds
½ teaspoon ground asafetida (p. 481) or 1 teaspoon minced garlic
½ teaspoon turmeric
12 medium-size (½ pound) shallots, peeled and quartered

1–4 fresh hot green chilies, stemmed, seeded, and thinly sliced
2 teaspoons finely chopped fresh ginger
1 teaspoon kosher salt, or to taste
2–4 tablespoons water, as needed
2 teaspoons lemon juice
¼ cup chopped fresh coriander
¼ cup roasted cashew nuts (p. 463)

1. Peel potatoes and dice into ¼-inch cubes. Place potatoes in a 10-inch microwave-safe skillet and cover with the lid. Cook at 100 percent power in a 650- to 700-watt carousel oven for 6 minutes (or until potatoes are fully cooked and soft). Remove from oven, uncover, and transfer potatoes into a shallow bowl and set aside.

2. Rinse and dry the skillet and heat the oil, covered, at 100 percent power in a 650- to 700-watt carousel oven for 3 minutes. Uncover, add mustard seeds, and replace the lid. Cook at 100 percent power for 3 minutes (or until seeds pop). Uncover and stir in asafetida or garlic, turmeric, shallots, and chilies. Cook, uncovered, at 100 percent power for 3 minutes (or until shallots look limp). Remove from oven.

3. Fold in potatoes, ginger, and salt. Add a few tablespoons of water if the potatoes look a little dry. Cook, covered, at 100 percent power for 2 minutes (or until potatoes are heated through). Remove from oven. Stir in lemon juice, coriander, and cashew nuts. Serve hot, at room temperature, or chilled.

NOTE   The potato salad may be made ahead up to 2 days and kept, covered, in the refrigerator.

FRAGRANT CABBAGE SALAD WITH GINGER SLIVERS AND TOMATOES

PORIYAL

MICROWAVE

Yield
—4 cups
Servings
—6
Cooking time
—15 minutes
Heat
—100 percent power
MW oven size
—650 to 700 watts
MW cookware
—One 5-quart covered
casserole and one
10-inch covered
skillet

In this light salad the cabbage remains crisp and bright and is mixed with tomatoes, ginger, and fresh coriander. The main flavor comes from the dressing, which is made by infusing the fragrances of fennel, turmeric, and coriander spice. *Poriyal* is lovely visually. Serve it with all fish and chicken preparations or as a first course.

=== ROOM TEMPERATURE ===

1¼ pounds green cab-
  bage, cored and cut
  into ½-inch pieces
3 tablespoons light vege-
  table oil
1 teaspoon cumin seeds
½ teaspoon fennel seeds
1½ teaspoons ground
  coriander
⅓ teaspoon turmeric
2 fresh hot green chilies,
  sliced and seeded

¼ cup julienne of fresh
  ginger
2 medium-size (½
  pound) fresh tomatoes,
  cored and cut into fine
  julienne strips
1 teaspoon kosher salt,
  or to taste
1 teaspoon lemon juice
4 tablespoons chopped
  fresh coriander

1. Place cabbage in a 5-quart microwave-safe casserole and cover with the lid. Cook at 100 percent power in a 650- to 700-watt carousel oven for 7 minutes (or until cabbage looks wilted and is just cooked). Remove from oven. Set aside, covered, for cabbage to steam, for 10 minutes. Uncover and drain cabbage.

2. Heat oil in a 10-inch microwave-safe skillet, uncovered, at 100 percent power in a 650- to 700-watt carousel oven for 3 minutes. Add cumin and fennel seeds. Cook at 100 percent for 1 minute 30 seconds (or until spices begin to turn darker). Remove from oven, add coriander, turmeric, chilies, and ginger, mix well, add tomatoes, and mix again.

3. Cook, uncovered, at 100 percent power for 3 minutes (or until tomatoes are slightly soft). Remove from oven. Add cabbage, salt, lemon juice, and coriander, toss well, and serve hot, at room temperature, or chilled.

NOTE   The cabbage salad may be made ahead up to a day and kept, covered, in the refrigerator.

WARM CABBAGE SALAD IN MUSTARD-INFUSED DRESSING

PORIYAL

Here is another version of cabbage salad from southern India, made with a lot of fresh coriander which is treated as a green. Mustard, asafetida, and red pepper are infused into the oil and poured over the salad. Curry leaves, although not essential, lend an exotic aura to the salad. The beautifully balanced flavor comes from adding lemon juice and sweet coconut. It is spicy-sweet, lovely with steamed fish, kabobs, and light vegetarian courses.

MICROWAVE

Yield
  —*4 cups*
Servings
  —*6*
Cooking time
  —*15 minutes*
Heat
  —*100 percent power*
MW oven size
  —*650 to 700 watts*
MW cookware
  —*One 5-quart covered casserole and one 10-inch covered skillet*

=== *ROOM TEMPERATURE* ===

1½ pounds green cabbage, cored and cut into ½-inch pieces
2 tablespoons light vegetable oil
1 teaspoon mustard seeds
½ teaspoon turmeric
¼ teaspoon ground asafetida (p. 481) or ½ teaspoon minced garlic
¼ teaspoon red pepper flakes

15 fresh, or 1 tablespoon crushed dried, curry leaves (p. 482) (optional)
1 teaspoon kosher salt, or to taste
1 teaspoon lemon juice
⅓ cup chopped fresh coriander
⅓ cup shredded coconut (p. 449)

1. Place cabbage in a 5-quart microwave-safe casserole and cover with the lid. Cook at 100 percent power in a 650- to 700-watt carousel oven for 7 minutes (or until cabbage looks wilted and is just cooked). Re-

move from oven. Set aside, covered, for cabbage to steam for 10 minutes. Uncover and drain cabbage.

2. Heat the oil in a 10-inch microwave-safe covered skillet at 100 percent power in a 650- to 700-watt carousel oven for 3 minutes. Uncover, add mustard seeds, and replace the lid. Cook at 100 percent power for 3 minutes (or until seeds pop). Remove from oven, uncover, and stir in turmeric, asafetida or garlic, pepper flakes, and curry leaves (if you are using it). Add cabbage, salt, and lemon juice, toss well, and cover with the lid.

3. Cook at 100 percent power for 2 minutes (or until salad has heated through and flavors have blended). Remove from oven. Uncover, and fold in coriander and coconut. Serve hot or at room temperature.

NOTE   The cabbage salad may be made ahead up to a day and kept, covered, in the refrigerator.

THYME-LACED ZUCCHINI AND BLACK-EYED PEA SALAD

MATAR MASALA

MICROWAVE

Yield
—3 cups
Servings
—4 to 6
Cooking time
—15 minutes
Heat
—100 percent power
MW oven size
—650 to 700 watts
MW cookware
—One 10-inch skillet

Bean salads are very popular in Indian cooking. Every state has its unique dressing, garnishes, and local vegetables, added raw and cooked. This one, popular in central India, consists of black-eyed peas, onions, zucchini, and tomatoes and flavored with garlic and thyme-flavored ajowan seeds. I love its garlicky-thyme and peppery flavor. Since it is filling, serve this salad with a light main entrée. Spoon over endive leaves for a dazzling appetizer.

═══════════════ ROOM TEMPERATURE ═══════════════

4 tablespoons light vegetable oil
½ cup finely chopped onion
1½ teaspoons minced garlic
⅛ teaspoon ajowan seeds (p. 481), crushed, or ½ teaspoon dried thyme
½ teaspoon red pepper flakes
½ teaspoon black pepper
3 medium-size (1 pound) zucchini, cut into 1-inch cubes

1½ cups cooked black-eyed peas—1 16-ounce can, drained, or ½ recipe homemade (p. 292)
2 teaspoons lemon juice
Kosher salt to taste, if desired
1 large (½ pound) tomato, peeled, seeded, and thinly sliced
2 tablespoons chopped fresh coriander

SALADS AND YOGURT RAITAS

1. Combine oil, onion, garlic, ajowan seeds, pepper flakes, and black pepper in a 10-inch microwave-safe skillet. Cook, uncovered, at 100 percent power in a 650- to 700-watt carousel oven for 7 minutes (or until onions are cooked and begin to color). Remove from oven.

2. Fold in zucchini and black-eyed peas. Cook, uncovered, at 100 percent power for 8 minutes (or until zucchini is cooked but still crisp). Remove from oven. Add lemon juice, salt, and tomatoes and gently fold until blended. Sprinkle with chopped coriander, and serve hot or at room temperature.

NOTE   The zucchini and black-eyed pea salad may be made ahead and set aside at room temperature for several hours.

AVOCADO AND CUCUMBER YOGURT RAITA

AVCADOO RAITA

MICROWAVE

Yield
—6 cups
Servings
—8
Preparation time
—3 minutes

You can make this smoky-spicy *raita* in less than a minute if you already have roasted cumin or coriander seeds; otherwise allow a few minutes for preparing them. Serve with northern curries such as Fragrant Beef with Peas I or II (p. 143 or p. 145) or Zesty Lemon Coriander Chicken (p. 116), and *tandoori* dishes. It is rich and filling.

3 cups plain low-fat or nonfat yogurt
2 tablespoons minced fresh coriander
1 teaspoon ground roasted coriander seeds (p. 466)
1 teaspoon ground roasted cumin seeds (p. 465)
¼ teaspoon black pepper
¼ teaspoon red pepper flakes (optional)
Kosher salt to taste

2 medium-size (¾ pound) cucumbers, peeled, seeded, and diced into ½-inch cubes
1 large (½ pound) tomato, halved, seeded, and diced into ½-inch cubes
1 small avocado, peeled, pitted, diced into ½-inch cubes, and sprinkled with 1 teaspoon lemon juice
Sweet or hot paprika

Place yogurt in a medium-size bowl. Add fresh coriander, coriander spice, cumin, black pepper, and red pepper and mix until smoothly blended. Stir in salt to taste and refrigerate. Just before serving, fold in cucumbers, tomatoes, and avocado, stirring just until blended. Sprinkle with paprika and serve.

NOTE   The avocado *raita* may be made ahead up to a day and kept, covered, in the refrigerator.

PEAR (OR PAPAYA) AND GREEN PEPPERCORN YOGURT RAITA

MOLAHA PACHADI

MICROWAVE

Yield
—*3 cups*
Servings
—*4 to 6*
Preparation time
—*3 minutes*

A scrumptious *raita* of contrasts: sweet ripe pears or papaya and sharp green peppercorns. In south India, freshly picked tender green peppercorns are used, which are crunchy and aromatic with a teasing, hot bite. This *raita*, with its cool heat, is refreshing on hot days served with *tandoori* dishes and kabobs.

1½ *cups plain yogurt*
½ *teaspoon dried ginger powder*
⅛ *teaspoon freshly grated nutmeg*
1 *tablespoon minced fresh, or 1 teaspoon crushed dried, mint or curry leaves (p. 482)*
1 *tablespoon canned green peppercorns, drained, rinsed, and coarsely chopped*
½ *teaspoon ground roasted cumin seeds (p. 465)*
3 *medium-size (1 pound) ripe pears, peeled, cored, quartered, and thinly sliced, or 1 firm, ripe papaya, peeled, seeded, and cubed into ½-inch pieces*

Place yogurt, ginger, nutmeg, mint or curry leaves, peppercorns, and cumin in a medium-size bowl. Mix until smoothly blended. Fold in fruit and either serve or refrigerate.

NOTE The pear or papaya *raita* may be made ahead up to a day and kept, covered, in the refrigerator.

MOGHUL SAFFRON AND MANGO YOGURT RAITA

SHAHI AAM RAITA

MICROWAVE

Yield
—5 cups
Servings
—4 to 6
Preparation time
—5 minutes plus additional time for chilling

This *raita* of royal Moghul heritage is made with ripe mango, raisins, pistachio nuts, and yogurt and flavored with saffron and candied ginger. The flavors are brought together with a pinch of aromatic spices and the essence of pine. For a princely climax, the *raita* is decorated with silver. It is subtle and stunning. Remember to get a mango that has smooth and custardlike nonfibrous flesh as the fibers are prone to catch in the teeth. Serve this lavish salad with *tandoori* dishes and Moghul curries such as Braised Cod in Aromatic Moghul Sauce (p. 87) or Moghul Lamb in Creamed Spinach Sauce (p. 155)

1 large (about 1 pound) firm, ripe mango
2 cups plain low-fat or nonfat yogurt
¼ teaspoon crushed saffron threads or powdered saffron
½ teaspoon Moghul garam masala (p. 477) or garam masala (p. 478)
¼ cup dark raisins

2 tablespoons finely chopped crystallized ginger
2 tablespoons unsalted or salted pistachio nuts, sliced
½ teaspoon pine leaves kewra water (p. 456) or 2 drops almond essence
2 4-inch squares silver leaf vark (p. 476) (optional)

1. Peel mango, cut meat off the pit in large sections, and chop into ½-inch cubes. Reserve three-fourths of the chopped mango (making sure to select attractive-looking pieces). Put the remaining one-quarter por-

tion of chopped mango into the container of a blender or food processor and process until smoothly pureed. Transfer mango puree into a medium-size bowl.

2. Add yogurt, saffron, Moghul *garam masala,* raisins, ginger, pistachios, and pine leaves *kewra* water. Blend thoroughly and chill. Just before serving, fold in chopped mango, transfer into a shallow serving dish, and serve, if desired, decorated with silver leaf.

VARIATION

ROYAL MACADAMIA AND RED RASPBERRIES YOGURT RAITA   Fold in ½ cup chopped roasted macadamia nuts (salted or unsalted) and ½ pint red raspberries in place of the mango.

NOTE   The mango *raita* may be made ahead up to a day and kept, covered, in the refrigerator.

SWEET PEPPER AND YOGURT RAITA

SIMLA MIRCH KA RAITA

MICROWAVE

Yield
—3½ cups
Servings
—6
Preparation time
—2 minutes plus additional time for cooling
Cooking time
—9 minutes
Heat
—100 percent power
MW oven size
—650 to 700 watts
MW cookware
—One 10-inch covered skillet

This *raita* combines sweet peppers and tart yogurt with sharp garlic and hot chilies. These contrasting flavors could create havoc on the palate, but together they taste harmoniously balanced. The microwave is fantastic for cooking peppers. They keep their crunch and retain their bright shiny appeal.

1 tablespoon light sesame oil or light vegetable oil
1 teaspoon mustard seeds
½ teaspoon minced garlic or ¼ teaspoon ground asafetida (p. 481)
2 fresh hot green chilies, stemmed, seeded, and thinly sliced

1 scallion stalk, trimmed and thinly sliced
1 pound medium-hot or sweet peppers (or a combination), cored and cut into 1-inch pieces
2 cups plain low-fat or nonfat yogurt
Kosher salt to taste

1. Heat the oil in a 10-inch microwave-safe covered skillet at 100 percent power in a 650- to 700-watt carousel oven for 3 minutes. Uncover, add mustard seeds, and replace the lid. Cook at 100 percent power for 3 minutes (or until seeds pop). Uncover and stir in garlic or asafetida, chilies, and scallions. Add peppers, stir to mix, and cover with the lid.

2. Cook at 100 percent power for 3 minutes (or until vegetables are cooked but still crisp). Remove from oven, uncover, and completely cool peppers.

3. Place yogurt and salt in a medium-size bowl and beat with a fork or whisk until smooth and creamy. Add peppers, together with their seasoned oil, and mix just until blended. Serve immediately.

SPINACH AND YOGURT RAITA

PALAK RAITA

This is a simple coolly satisfying *raita* in which cooked spinach is combined with yogurt and fragrant smoky roasted cumin and coriander. Sometimes a few roasted walnuts or pine nuts are folded in to provide a textural contrast. The *raita* goes well with spicy tomato-based curries, such as Garlic-braised Eggplant, Chickpeas, and Tomato Casserole (p. 165), *tandoori* dishes, kabobs, and steamed-fish preparations, such as Steamed Fish in Ginger-Thyme Essence (p. 81).

1 pound fresh spinach greens or Swiss chard	½ teaspoon ground roasted coriander seeds (p. 466)
2 cups plain low-fat or nonfat yogurt	¼ teaspoon cayenne or black pepper (or a combination) (optional)
1 teaspoon ground roasted cumin seeds (p. 465)	1 teaspoon sugar
	Kosher salt to taste

FOR THE GARNISH:

4 tablespoons chopped roasted walnuts (p. 463) or toasted pine nuts (p. 464) (optional)

1. Trim stems off the greens and wash thoroughly in several changes of water. Drain and place in a 3-quart microwave-safe casserole and cover with the lid.

2. Cook at 100 percent power in a 650- to 700-watt carousel oven for 4 minutes (or until greens wilt). Remove from oven. Uncover and transfer greens into

MICROWAVE

Yield
—1½ cups

Servings
—4

Preparation time
—8 minutes plus additional time for chilling

Cooking time
—4 minutes

Heat
—100 percent power

MW oven size
—650 to 700 watts

MW cookware
—One 3-quart covered casserole

a bowl of cold water. Drain, squeezing lightly to remove excess water. Place greens on work board and finely chop.

3. Place greens in a bowl. Add yogurt, cumin, coriander, pepper, sugar, and salt. Mix well and serve chilled, garnished, if desired, with walnuts or pine nuts.

NOTE   The spinach *raita* may be made ahead up to a day and kept, covered, in the refrigerator.

SPICY POTATO AND YOGURT RAITA

ALOO RAITA

A specialty of north India, this *raita* is traditionally featured at wedding banquets. It is made with cooked potatoes and yogurt and flavored with smoky roasted cumin and coriander. The addition of a hefty dose of cayenne and black pepper—its trademark—makes it the hottest *raita* in the Indian repertoire. The potatoes absorb the highly seasoned yogurt and render it spicily delicious. You can reduce the heat of the dish by cutting down the pepper, but don't eliminate it entirely as the potatoes will taste starchy and insipid. Serve the *raita* with mild entrées such as Ooty-style Sole in Fragrant Tomato Sauce (p. 83) or Butter Cornish Hen (p. 126).

MICROWAVE

Yield
—*3½ cups*
Servings
—*4*
Preparation time
—*6 minutes plus additional time for cooling*
Cooking time
—*6 minutes*
Heat
—*100 percent power*
MW oven size
—*650 to 700 watts*
MW cookware
—*One 10-inch covered skillet*

=============== ROOM TEMPERATURE ===============

4 medium-size (1 pound) new red wax potatoes
¼ cup low-fat or whole milk
2 cups plain low-fat or nonfat yogurt
¾ teaspoon ground roasted cumin seeds (p. 465)

¾ teaspoon ground roasted coriander seeds (p. 466)
½ teaspoon cayenne pepper, or to taste
½ teaspoon black pepper, or to taste
Kosher salt to taste
Paprika to taste

1. Peel potatoes and dice into ¼-inch cubes. Place potatoes in a 10-inch microwave-safe skillet and cover with the lid. Cook at 100 percent power in a 650- to 700-watt carousel oven for 6 minutes (or until potatoes are fully cooked and soft). Remove from oven. Uncover and pour milk over potatoes, and replace cover. Set aside to cool completely.

2. Place yogurt, cumin, coriander, cayenne, black pepper, and salt in a medium-size bowl and beat with a fork or whisk until smooth and creamy. Fold in potatoes and serve sprinkled with paprika.

NOTE   The potato *raita* may be made ahead up to 2 days and kept, covered, in the refrigerator.

ZUCCHINI AND WALNUT YOGURT RAITA

LAUKI RAITA

MICROWAVE

Yield
—3 cups
Servings
—4 to 6
Preparation time
—2 minutes plus addi-
tional time for
cooling
Cooking time
—7 minutes
Heat
—100 percent power
MW oven size
—650 to 700 watts
MW cookware
—One 10-inch cov-
ered skillet

Make this *raita* with young, tender garden-fresh zucchini for a truly delightful experience. The microwave is great for roasting walnuts. They come out very crunchy and fragrant. This mildly spiced, meaty-tasting *raita* goes well with assertively aromatized vegetarian main courses and fish preparations such as Braised Okra with Spices and Tomatoes (p. 167), Whole Cauliflower with Vendaloo Sauce (p. 175), or Scallops in Garlicky Mustard Oil (p. 101).

=== ROOM TEMPERATURE ===

3 medium-size (1 pound) zucchini, cubed into ½-inch pieces
1½ cups plain nonfat yogurt
½ cup chopped roasted walnuts (p. 463)
1 teaspoon ground roasted cumin seeds (p. 465)

½ teaspoon celery seeds
¼ teaspoon freshly ground black pepper
1 tablespoon sugar
½ teaspoon kosher salt
1 tablespoon minced fresh, or 1 teaspoon crushed dried, mint

FOR THE GARNISH:
Walnut halves (optional)

Place zucchini in a 10-inch microwave-safe skillet and cover with the lid. Cook at 100 percent power in a 650- to 700-watt oven for 7 minutes (or until zucchini is cooked but not mushy). Remove from oven and uncover. When completely cool, fold in all other ingredients and serve at room temperature or chilled, if desired, garnished with walnut halves.

NOTE   The zucchini *raita* may be made ahead up to 2 days and kept, covered, in the refrigerator.

RAITA OF CRISP FRIED OKRA AND COOL YOGURT

VENDAKAI PACHADI

MICROWAVE

Yield
    —3 cups
Servings
    —4 to 6
Preparation time
    —3 minutes
Cooking time
    —20 minutes
Heat
    —100 percent power
MW oven size
    —650 to 700 watts
MW cookware
    —One 10-inch skillet

The contrast of crisp, crunchy, chili-spiked okra against cool and creamy yogurt is sensational in this *raita* from Madras. Remember to add the okra to the yogurt just before serving as it quickly turns soggy and discolors the yogurt. Serve this with all southern specialties, such as Madras Fish in Red Gravy (p. 91) or Duck Vendaloo (p. 130). I particularly like it with seafood and chicken dishes. You can also make this *raita* using precooked Crisp Fried Okra (p. 222).

2 cups plain yogurt
Kosher salt to taste, if
    desired
3 tablespoons light ses-
    ame oil or light vege-
    table oil
½ teaspoon mustard
    seeds
¼ teaspoon ground
    asafetida (p. 481) or
    ½ teaspoon minced
    garlic

2 fresh hot green chilies,
    stemmed, seeded, and
    thinly sliced
1 pound tender okra,
    trimmed and cut into
    ⅜-inch-thick rings
1½ teaspoons lemon
    juice

FOR THE GARNISH:
2 tablespoons Candied Pistachios (p. 419) or roasted
    pistachio nuts (p. 463) (optional)

1. Beat yogurt and salt in a medium-size bowl until smooth and pour into a shallow serving dish. Cover and refrigerate until needed.

2. Heat the oil in a 10-inch microwave-safe covered skillet at 100 percent power in a 650- to 700-watt carousel oven for 3 minutes. Uncover, add mustard seeds, and replace the lid. Cook at 100 percent power for 3 minutes (or until seeds pop). Remove from oven, uncover, add asafetida or garlic, chilies, and okra, and mix well.

3. Cook, uncovered, at 100 percent power in a 650- to 700-watt carousel oven for 8 minutes, stirring twice. Sprinkle lemon juice, mix lightly, and continue cooking, uncovered, at 100 percent power for an additional 6 minutes (or until okra is fully cooked and browned), stirring twice. Remove from oven.

4. Take out the yogurt mixture from the refrigerator. Mound okra mixture on top. Serve immediately, if desired, garnished with pistachio nuts.

DAL AND
LEGUME DISHES

L egumes, which include all lentils, peas, and beans, are an important protein food source and have been universally popular with vegetarians. For centuries Indian cooks have used legumes not just for their health benefits or religious taboos but because they find them downright irresistible. In Indian cooking both dried uncooked legumes as well as cooked legume preparations are referred to as *dal*.

There are many varieties of *dal* used in Indian cooking (see page 460), some hulled, others with skin. The selection of a particular legume in a dish often depends on the specific flavor you seek and the cooking time you have. For example, beans in general take more time to cook than lentils but less time than peas, which take the longest. Then there is the issue of "whole" and "hulled." The whole *dal*—with the tough, leathery skin still on—take longer to cook than the hulled—without the skin and split—because the skin creates a barrier that prevents the moisture from penetrating. Therefore, the perception that *dal* dishes take so long that they must be begun a day in advance is not that far wrong.

But the microwave has changed all that. You can decide to cook many of the dishes here an hour before serving, and in doing so add beautiful colors and wonderful flavors to any meal. Lovely red lentils, for example, not only cook fast but take on the character of cumin, garlic, or fresh coriander magnificently. The recipes I have selected reflect the range of flavors found throughout India, from mustard and cayenne (south) to garlic and cumin (north) and fennel (east).

With most *dal* preparations, first cook the legume separately (a process that may be done long in advance since legumes freeze well; use the microwave for defrosting). Just before serving, make a spice-infused oil, fold in the cooked legumes, and garnish with fresh herbs. *Dal* not only provides welcome vegetable protein and fiber but is also a saucelike dish, which is especially appreciated if it is served with kabobs, roasts, or other dry dishes. Here, *dal* performs a role similar to *raita*. When served with pilaf, hearty bread, and a salad, *dal* can easily become a main dish. In addition, all *dals,* leftover or freshly made, can be thinned and turned into warming and refreshing soups.

Except for red (pink) lentils, which technically are the only lentils, all other legumes benefit from soaking, a step that turns legumes soft and moist, enabling them to cook more quickly. Whole peas and beans particularly profit from this step because it flexes their skins, allowing them to expand more readily without bursting. For this reason whole beans and peas, as a rule, are soaked before cooking.

You can soak legumes or not, as you choose, before cooking; instructions for both approaches are given in the recipes. Soaking, of course, shortens cooking time, but the results are the same; either way, the microwave makes quick work of these dishes.

COOKED RED (PINK) LENTIL PUREE

MASAR DAL

MICROWAVE

Yield
—2½ cups lentil puree
or 3 cups thin lentil
puree
Preparation time
—5 minutes
Cooking time
—15 minutes
Standing time
—5 minutes
Heat
—100 percent power
MW oven size
—650 to 700 watts
MW cookware
—One 2½-quart cas-
serole or soufflé dish

Of all the legumes, red or pink lentils benefit the most from being cooked in the microwave. No presoaking or stirring is required. You can cook them in just eight minutes if you start with hot water, as seven minutes of the cooking time in the recipe is just to heat the water! They are less gelatinous and starchy-mealy–tasting than either split peas or yellow lentils. Since red lentils fall apart the instant they begin to cook and soften, they are ideal in soupy *dal* recipes. You can further serve the cooked lentil puree, flavored with spice-infused oil (p. 484), as a side-dish *dal* or a first-course soup, and use it in recipes calling for cooked red or pink lentil puree or pureed yellow or green split peas.

=== ROOM TEMPERATURE ===

1 cup dried red (pink)   2½ cups water
lentils (p. 460)   ¼ teaspoon turmeric

1. Pick clean lentils and rinse in several changes of water. Place lentils, water, and turmeric in a 2½-quart microwave-safe dish.

2. Cook, uncovered, at 100 percent power in a 650- to 700-watt carousel oven for 15 minutes (or until the lentils are cooked soft and most of the liquid is absorbed into them), stirring twice.

3. Remove from oven and cover with the lid. Let lentils stand for 5 minutes. Uncover and whisk with a beater until lentils are pureed. Measure puree. There should be about 2½ cups; if not, add enough water to make that quantity. For a thinner puree, stir in more water to yield 3 cups.

RED (PINK) LENTIL BROTH Place one recipe (2½ cups) red (pink) lentil puree in a container of a blender or food processor and process until smoothly pureed. Stir in 1½ cups water, or enough to make 4 cups broth.

NOTE This lentil puree keeps well in the refrigerator, stored in a covered container, for up to 5 days.

COOKED YELLOW LENTILS OR AMERICAN YELLOW SPLIT PEAS

TOOVAR DAL

Yellow lentils and American split peas, rich vegetarian protein sources, are important ingredients in Indian cooking. Because of its gelatinous consistency, lentil or pea puree is ideal as a sauce base in braised and stewed dishes.

Lentils and peas are notorious for taking a long time to cook, but the microwave takes half the time of any conventional method. The grains cook flawlessly and taste more fragrant and meaty. Presoaking lentils and peas cuts down the cooking time considerably, but not the end results, therefore choose the technique that best fits your schedule. During the cooking of lentils and peas, sometimes a little oil is added, which is believed to hasten cooking and produce creamier results.

Serve the cooked lentil puree, flavored with spice-infused oil (p. 484), as a side-dish *dal* or first-course soup, and use it in recipes calling for cooked yellow lentils or split peas.

METHOD I (NONSOAKING)

MICROWAVE

Yield
—2 cups
Preparation time
—6 minutes
Cooking time
—40 minutes
Standing time
—10 minutes
Heat
—100 percent power
MW oven size
—650 to 700 watts
MW cookware
—One 3-quart covered casserole

1 cup dried yellow lentils (p. 461) or American yellow split peas (p. 461)

3 cups water

1/3 teaspoon turmeric

1 teaspoon kosher salt (optional)

1 teaspoon light vegetable oil (optional)

1. Pick clean lentils or peas, rinse thoroughly, and place in a 3-quart microwave-safe casserole. Add 2 cups water, turmeric, and, if desired, salt and oil, and cover with the lid.

2. Cook at 100 percent power in a 650- to 700-watt carousel oven for 20 minutes (or until lentils or peas absorb water and are cooked but crunchy). Uncover, add the remaining 1 cup water, and replace cover. Continue cooking at 100 percent power for another 20 minutes (or until lentils and peas are fully cooked and soft but still hold their shape), stirring once. Remove from oven. Let lentils or peas stand, covered, for 10 minutes before using.

NOTE   The cooked lentils or peas keep well in the refrigerator, stored in a covered container, for up to 5 days.

METHOD II (SOAKING)

MICROWAVE

Yield
—2 cups
Preparation time
—5 minutes plus 4
hours for soaking
Cooking time
—25 minutes
Standing time
—10 minutes
Heat
—100 percent power
MW oven size
—650 to 700 watts
MW cookware
—One 3-quart covered
casserole

ROOM TEMPERATURE

1 cup dried yellow lentils
(p. 461) or American
yellow split peas
(p. 461)
2 cups water

⅓ teaspoon turmeric
1 teaspoon kosher salt
(optional)
1 teaspoon light vegeta-
ble oil (optional)

1. Pick clean lentils or peas, rinse thoroughly, and place in a medium-size bowl. Add enough water to cover the lentils or peas by at least an inch and a half. Soak them for 4 hours. Drain, rinse, and drain again.

2. Transfer lentils or peas into a 3- to 4-quart micro-wave-safe casserole. Add 2 cups water, turmeric, and, if desired, salt and oil. Cook, uncovered, at 100 per-cent power in a 650- to 700-watt carousel oven for 25 minutes (or until lentils or peas are cooked), stir-ring twice. Remove from oven and cover with the lid. Let lentils or peas stand for 10 minutes before using.

NOTE The cooked lentils or peas keep well in the refrig-erator, stored in a covered container, for up to 5 days.

PUREED YELLOW LENTILS OR AMERICAN YELLOW SPLIT PEAS

TOOVAR DAL

MICROWAVE

Yield
  —3 cups
Cooking time
  —10 minutes
Standing time
  —5 minutes
Heat
  —100 percent power
MW oven size
  —650 to 700 watts
MW cookware
  —One 3-quart covered casserole

Pureed yellow lentils or split peas have innumerable uses in Indian cooking, including enriching vegetable stews, creating velvety sauce-bases for poultry, and as fragrant soups. The simplest and most popular way to serve lentil puree is as a side-dish *dal,* flavored with spice-infused oil (p. 484). Use this puree in recipes calling for pureed yellow lentils or American yellow split peas.

Pureed lentils or peas are made by making Cooked Yellow Lentils or American Yellow Split Peas (p. 269), covered, at 100 percent power for an additional 10 minutes (or until all the liquid is absorbed and peas are very soft and burst open). Remove from oven. Uncover, add 1½ cups hot water, and replace cover. Let peas stand, covered, for 5 minutes. Uncover and process in a blender or beat with a whisk until peas are creamy-pureed.

NOTE   The pureed peas keep well in the refrigerator, stored in a covered container, for up to 5 days.

FRAGRANT SPICED LENTILS WITH HERBS

MASALA DAL

MICROWAVE

Yield
—2½ *cups*
Servings
—4 *to* 6
Cooking time
—9 *minutes*
Heat
—100 *percent power*
MW oven size
—650 *to* 700 *watts*
MW cookware
—*One 8-inch skillet*

This mild and very herbal *dal* is a specialty of New Delhi in north India, where creamy pureed lentils are flavored with sweet cumin, onion-infused oil, and fresh coriander. If you already have the cooked lentils, then all you do is cook the spices and fold them into the *dal*. Watch when you are frying the cumin seeds as they turn dark almost instantly. This *dal* may be served warm or chilled as a first-course soup. It is a traditional side dish with north Indian meals. For a light meal, serve with Crisp Okra and Spiced Basmati Pilaf (p. 306), Garlic-braised Tomatoes (p. 232), and Green Beans in Peppered-Mustard Dressing (p. 220).

=== *ROOM TEMPERATURE* ===

2½ *cups Cooked Yellow Lentils or American Yellow Split Peas (p. 269) or Cooked Red (Pink) Lentil Puree (p. 267), heated*
Kosher salt to taste
3 *tablespoons light vegetable oil*
1 *teaspoon cumin seeds*
¼ *cup chopped onion*

1–2 *fresh hot green chilies, stemmed, seeded, and thinly sliced*
½ *teaspoon garam masala (p. 478) or fragrant spice powder (p. 481)*
½ *teaspoon cayenne pepper or paprika*
2 *tablespoons finely chopped fresh coriander*

1. Heat the oil in an 8-inch microwave-safe skillet, uncovered, at 100 percent power for 3 minutes. Add cumin seeds. Cook, uncovered, at 100 percent power for 1 minute 30 seconds (or until cumin turns a few shades darker), then add onion and green chilies.

2. Cook, uncovered, at 100 percent power for 4 minutes (or until onions look cooked and light golden), stirring once. Remove from oven. Stir in *garam masala* and cayenne and immediately pour the entire contents of the skillet, distributing them evenly, over the lentils or peas. Do not stir. Sprinkle with coriander and serve.

NOTE   The *dal* may be made ahead and set aside for several hours, covered, at room temperature, and served reheated. It may also be refrigerated for 3 days, but the fragrance of the spices will weaken. To invigorate the *dal,* add a new batch of spice-infused oil and some fresh herbs.

BOMBAY SWEETISH-SOUR GARLIC LENTILS

MARATHI DAL

This sweetish-sour *dal*, complexly flavored with garlic, chilies, tamarind, jaggery, and mustard-infused oil, is great tasting and satisfying. It can be made very quickly in the microwave if you already have a batch of cooked lentils; otherwise allow an additional fifteen minutes' cooking time. It makes a lovely side-dish *dal* as well as a first-course soup. Fish, seafood, and chicken main courses such as Madras Fish in Red Gravy (p. 91), Mangalore Cayenne Shrimp (p. 97), and Chicken Frazer (p. 120) are particularly good choices to serve it with. For a light meal, serve with Moghul-scented Basmati Pilaf (p. 302), Cauliflower and Fennel in Aromatic Oil (p. 209), and Spicy Potato and Yogurt Raita (p. 260).

MICROWAVE

Yield
  —*3 cups*
Servings
  —*4 to 6*
Cooking time
  —*11 minutes*
Heat
  —*100 percent power*
MW oven size
  —*650 to 700 watts*
MW cookware
  —*One 1½-quart covered casserole or souffle dish and one 8-inch skillet*

=== ROOM TEMPERATURE ===

3 cups Pureed Yellow Lentils or American Yellow Split Peas (p. 272) or 2½ cups Cooked Red (Pink) Lentil Puree (p. 267)

2 teaspoons jaggery (p. 460), unsulfured molasses, or dark brown sugar

2 tablespoons, or 1 frozen cube, tamarind juice, or 1 teaspoon tamarind concentrate (p. 491), or 2 teaspoons lemon juice

Kosher salt to taste

3 tablespoons usli ghee (p. 492) or light vegetable oil

1½ teaspoons minced garlic

1–2 fresh hot green chilies, stemmed, seeded, and thinly sliced

1 small tomato, finely chopped with skin

1 teaspoon fragrant spice powder (p. 481) or 1 teaspoon ground cumin

---

½ teaspoon cayenne
   pepper or paprika

2 tablespoons finely
   chopped fresh
   coriander

1. Place lentil or split pea puree in a 1½-quart microwave-safe dish. Add jaggery, tamarind, and salt and cover with the lid. Cook at 100 percent power in a 650- to 700-watt carousel oven for 5 minutes (or until steaming hot). Remove from oven and set aside, covered.

2. Heat *usli ghee* or oil in an 8-inch microwave-safe skillet, uncovered, at 100 percent power for 2 minutes. Add garlic and chilies. Cook, uncovered, at 100 percent power for 30 seconds (or until garlic looks lightly fried and cooked). Remove from oven. Add tomatoes along with spice powder and cayenne.

3. Cook, uncovered, at 100 percent power for 3 minutes (or until tomatoes lose their raw aroma and turn soft). Remove from oven.

4. Uncover lentil puree and pour the entire contents of the browning skillet over it. Mix well and serve sprinkled with coriander.

NOTE The *dal* may be made ahead and set aside for several hours, covered, at room temperature, and served reheated. It may also be refrigerated for 3 days, but the fragrance of the spices will numb. To invigorate the *dal*, add a new batch of spice-infused oil and some fresh herbs.

MUSTARD- AND GARLIC-FLAVORED AMERICAN YELLOW SPLIT PEAS

PAHADI DAL

MICROWAVE

Yield
  —*3 cups*
Servings
  —*4 to 6*
Cooking time
  —*9 minutes*
Heat
  —*100 percent power*
MW oven size
  —*650 to 700 watts*
MW cookware
  —*One 1½-quart cov-
  ered casserole or
  soufflé dish and one
  8-inch skillet*

This *dal*, cooked by the people of Manali in the Himalayan province, is similar to the other north Indian specialty—Fragrant Spiced Lentils with Herbs (p. 273)—except that this is a more rustic and assertively flavored dish. The garlic in this *dal* should be cooked slowly until it turns dark brown in order to lend the desired smoky-spicy flavor. Dark fried garlic is not burned garlic, which is bitter, unpalatable, and usually unacceptable in any cooking. This is a nice *dal* dish to serve with all north Indian–style meals, especially those including kabobs and roasts such as Ginger Chicken Kabob (p. 109), Indian Beef Sausage Kabob (p. 138), or Goanese Roast Pork with Cinnamon-Ginger Gravy (p. 157). For a complete meal, include Tomato Basmati Pilaf (p. 308), New Delhi Spicy Potatoes (p. 226), and Sweet Pepper and Yogurt Raita (p. 256).

=== *ROOM TEMPERATURE* ===

3 cups Pureed Yellow
  Lentils or American
  Yellow Split Peas
  (p. 272) or 2½ cups
  Cooked Red (Pink)
  Lentil Puree (p. 267)
Kosher salt to taste
3 tablespoons mustard oil
  or olive oil
2 tablespoons thinly
  sliced garlic

1 teaspoon ground cumin
½ teaspoon cayenne
  pepper or paprika
1 teaspoon dry mustard
  (omit if using
  mustard oil)
2 tablespoons finely
  chopped fresh
  coriander

1. Place lentil or split pea puree in a 1½-quart microwave-safe dish, add salt, and cover with the lid. Cook at 100 percent power in a 650- to 700-watt carousel oven for 5 minutes (or until steaming hot). Remove from oven and set aside, covered, while you make the spice-infused oil.

2. Heat the oil, garlic, and cumin in an 8-inch microwave-safe skillet at 100 percent power for 3 minutes 30 seconds (or until cumin turns darker and garlic is lightly browned). Stir in cayenne and mustard powder during the last 30 seconds of cooking. Remove from oven, pour the entire contents of the skillet onto the pea or lentil puree. Mix well and serve sprinkled with coriander.

NOTE The *dal* may be made ahead and set aside for several hours, covered, at room temperature, and served reheated. It may also be refrigerated for 3 days, but the fragrance of the spices will numb. To invigorate the *dal,* add a new batch of spice-infused oil and some fresh herbs.

COOKED BROWN
LENTILS

CHOTI MA DAL

MICROWAVE

Yield
—*3 cups*
Preparation time
—*5 minutes plus 4
hours for soaking*
Cooking time
—*14 minutes*
Standing time
—*5 minutes*
Heat
—*70 percent power*
MW oven size
—*650 to 700 watts*
MW cookware
—*One 2½-quart cov-
ered casserole*

What I like most about cooking lentils in the microwave is that it combines the concept of pressure
cooking, with its speed, with stove top, where there
is texture control. In the microwave these lentils cook
in half the time (meaning minutes instead of hours),
and, in addition, each grain remains swelled, moist,
and separate. Serve cooked lentils, flavored with spice-
infused oil (p. 484), as a warm Lentil Salad in Cumin-
Citrus Dressing (p. 29) or side-dish *dal,* and use them
in stuffings. You can substitute cooked brown lentils
in recipes calling for whole mung beans such as Spicy
Whole Mung Bean Stew (p. 290).

================ *ROOM TEMPERATURE* ================

1½ cups dried brown   ½ cup water
  lentils (p. 461)

1. Pick clean lentils, rinse, and place in a bowl. Add
enough water to cover lentils by at least an inch. Soak
for 4 hours. Drain, rinse, and drain again. Place lentils and ½ cup water in a 2½-quart microwave-safe
casserole and cover with the lid.

2. Cook at 70 percent (medium) power for 14 minutes (or until lentils are cooked soft but still hold their
shape). Remove from oven. Let lentils stand, covered,
for 5 minutes. Uncover and use, laced with spice-
infused oil dressing, in salads and dry *dal* recipes, or
fold into pilaf.

NOTE The cooked lentils keep well in the refrigerator,
stored in a covered container, for up to 6 days.

BROWN LENTILS IN SPICY TOMATO DRESSING

SOOKHI DAL

MICROWAVE

Yield
—3 cups
Servings
—6
Cooking time
—14 minutes
Standing time
—5 minutes
Heat
—100 percent power
MW oven size
—650 to 700 watts
MW cookware
—One 10-inch covered skillet

Whole lentils dressed in sprightly lemon-cumin oil is very popular in Gujarat in western India. The *dal* is meaty tasting and filling; therefore, serve it with any light main entrée such as Steamed Fish in Ginger-Thyme Essence (p. 81) or Chicken Frazer (p. 120). Spoon *dal* over endive leaves to make a stunning appetizer.

═══════ ROOM TEMPERATURE ═══════

2 tablespoons light vegetable oil	1 teaspoon kosher salt
1 teaspoon cumin seeds	1 teaspoon lemon juice
1 teaspoon mustard seeds, crushed	½ teaspoon garam masala (p. 478) or ground roasted cumin seeds (p. 465)
1 teaspoon fennel seeds	
1 cup chopped onion	2 fresh hot green chilies, stemmed, seeded, and thinly sliced
2 teaspoons finely chopped garlic	
¾ cup tomato puree (fresh or canned)	1 tablespoon minced fresh or 1½ teaspoons dried thyme or dill
3 cups Cooked Brown Lentils (p. 279)	2 tablespoons chopped fresh coriander

1. Heat the oil in a 10-inch microwave-safe skillet, uncovered, at 100 percent power in a 650- to 700-watt carousel oven for 3 minutes 30 seconds. Add cumin, mustard, and fennel. Cook, uncovered, at 100 percent power for 2 minutes (or until spices turn a

little darker). Add onion and garlic. Cook, uncovered, at 100 percent power for 2 minutes (or until onions just begin to wilt). Remove from oven.

2. Add tomato puree, cooked brown lentils, and salt. Mix well and cover with the lid. Cook at 100 percent power for 6 minutes (or until lentils are heated through). Remove from oven and let lentils stand, covered, for 5 minutes. Uncover, stir in lemon juice, *garam masala,* chilies, thyme or dill, and coriander, and serve.

NOTE The *dal* may be made ahead and set aside, covered, for several hours at room temperature or refrigerated for 3 days, and served reheated.

COOKED YELLOW MUNG BEANS

DHOLI MOONG

MICROWAVE

Yield
—2½ cups
Preparation time
—5 minutes plus, 4
hours for soaking
Cooking time
—10 minutes
Standing time
—5 minutes
Heat
—100 percent power
MW oven size
—650 to 700 watts
MW cookware
—One 10-inch cov-
ered skillet

The microwave is great for yellow mung beans. They cook unattended, without any stirring, and the grains turn plump and juicy. No need for constant vigilance. Serve these cooked beans, flavored with spice-infused oil (p. 484), as a side-dish *dal* to accompany dry dishes such as Creamed Chicken Kabob (p. 111), Savory Keema Cake (p. 147), warm salad, or use in stuffings and recipes calling for cooked yellow mung beans. Or turn it into pureed beans (p. 483) for additional uses, for example, laced with herbs as a lovely soup.

=========== ROOM TEMPERATURE ===========

1 cup dried yellow mung beans (p. 461)	1 teaspoon kosher salt, if desired
⅓ teaspoon turmeric	½ cup water

1. Pick clean beans, rinse in several changes of water, and place in a medium-size bowl. Add enough water to cover the beans by at least 2 inches. Soak for 4 hours. Drain, rinse, and drain again.

2. Place beans in a 10-inch microwave-safe skillet. Add turmeric, salt, and ½ cup water and cover with the lid. Cook at 100 percent power in a 650- to 700-watt carousel oven for 10 minutes (or until beans are soft and most of the water has evaporated). Remove from oven and let beans stand, covered, for 5 minutes. Uncover and fluff beans. Serve laced with spice-infused oil as a warm bean salad or *dal*.

NOTE The cooked beans keep well in the refrigerator, stored in a covered container, for up to 2 days.

PUREED YELLOW MUNG BEANS

MOONG DAL

MICROWAVE

Yield
  —3 cups
Cooking time
  —5 minutes
Standing time
  —5 minutes
Heat
  —100 percent power
MW oven size
  —650 to 700 watts
MW cookware
  *—One 10-inch cov-
    ered skillet*

Pureed yellow mung beans are subtle and light-tasting, hence make a delectable soup. For traditional serving, flavor the puree with spice-infused oil (p. 484) for a side-dish *dal*. Use pureed yellow mung beans in place of pureed lentils or split peas in dishes such as Lentil Stew with Broccoli, Carrots, and Pearl Onions (p. 189) or Vishal's Cauliflower Sambar Stew (p. 194).

For creamy puree of mung beans, cook beans for 10 minutes, as for soft Cooked Yellow Mung Beans (p. 282). But instead of removing from oven, add ½ cup water, cover with the lid, and continue cooking at 100 percent power for an additional 5 minutes (or until beans are very soft and begin to burst open). Remove from oven and let beans stand, covered, for 5 minutes. Uncover and beat vigorously with a whisk, crushing beans into a puree. Measure and add enough water to make 3 cups puree. Use immediately, flavored with spice-infused oil, as a creamy *dal* side dish.

NOTE The pureed beans keep well in the refrigerator, stored in a covered container, for up to 2 days.

NEW DELHI FRAGRANT CREAMY MUNG BEANS

MOONG DAL

MICROWAVE

Yield
—3½ cups
Servings
—4 to 6
Cooking time
—16 minutes
Heat
—100 percent power
MW oven size
—650 to 700 watts
MW cookware
—One 2½-quart cov-
ered casserole

I love mung beans, particularly cooked in this familiar New Delhi style. Simply fry the spices and seasonings in oil and stir them into the beans. If you don't
already have a batch of cooked mung beans, then allow additional time for soaking and cooking beans.
This cumin-and-herb-scented *dal* is marvelous as either
a side dish or a first-course soup. Chicken, seafood,
and vegetarian main courses are particularly good
choices to serve it with. For a light meal, serve with
Moghul-scented Basmati Pilaf (p. 302), Eggplant Slices
Smothered with Coconut-Spice Paste (p. 215), and
Zucchini and Walnut Yogurt Raita (p. 262).

═══════════════ ROOM TEMPERATURE ═══════════════

3 cups Pureed Yellow
　Mung Beans (p. 283)
　or Pureed Whole
　Mung Beans (p. 290)
1 teaspoon or more
　lemon juice
Kosher salt to taste
3 tablespoons mustard oil
　or olive oil
1 teaspoon cumin seeds,
　lightly crushed
½ teaspoon cayenne
　pepper or paprika

1 tablespoon minced
　fresh ginger
1 cup finely chopped
　onion
4 tablespoons chopped
　fresh coriander
1 teaspoon ground
　roasted cumin seeds
　(p. 465) or ½ tea-
　spoon garam masala
　(p. 478)

1. Place bean puree in a bowl and season to taste
with lemon juice and salt.

2. Place the oil in a 2½-quart microwave-safe casserole. Heat, uncovered, at 100 percent power in a 650- to 700-watt carousel oven for 2 minutes. Add cumin, cayenne, ginger, and onion and stir to mix. Cook, uncovered, at 100 percent power for 8 minutes (or until onions look shriveled up), stirring twice. Remove from oven.

3. Fold in bean puree and cover with the lid. Cook at 100 percent power for 6 minutes (or until contents are steaming hot). Remove from oven. Uncover and fold in half the coriander. Serve sprinkled with remaining coriander and cumin.

NOTE   The *dal* may be made ahead and set aside for several hours, covered, at room temperature, and served reheated. It may also be refrigerated for 3 days, but the fragrance of the spices will numb. To invigorate the *dal*, add a new batch of spice-infused oil and some fresh herbs.

WARM MUNG BEAN SALAD IN CUMIN-TOMATO DRESSING

SOOKHI DAL

MICROWAVE

Yield
  —3 cups
Servings
  —4 to 6
Preparation time
  —2 minutes plus additional time for soaking
Cooking time
  —17 minutes
Standing time
  —5 minutes
Heat
  —100 percent power
MW oven size
  —650 to 700 watts
MW cookware
  —One 10-inch covered skillet

The microwave is wonderful for cooking whole yellow mung beans. Not only do they cook in half the time, but they turn plump and moist and do not fall apart and turn mushy. This lovely preparation is from the Sikh community of western India, who dress beans in a sweet fennel-and-tomato-laced oil. This fragrant and addictive salad *dal* may be served hot, at room temperature, or straight out of the refrigerator as a side dish or first course. You can also use it as a filling for vegetables.

=== ROOM TEMPERATURE ===

1 cup dried yellow mung beans (p. 461)
2 tablespoons light vegetable oil
1 teaspoon cumin seeds
½ teaspoon fennel seeds
1 cup chopped onion
1 cup chopped tomatoes
½ teaspoon turmeric
1 teaspoon kosher salt
⅓ cup water
1 teaspoon lemon juice

½ teaspoon garam masala (p. 478) or ground roasted cumin seeds (p. 465)
2 fresh hot green chilies, stemmed, seeded, and thinly sliced
2 tablespoons chopped fresh coriander or mint

1. Pick clean mung beans, put in a bowl, and rinse in several changes of water. Add enough water to cover beans by at least two inches and soak for 8 hours or overnight. Drain, rinse, and drain again.

2. Heat the oil in a 10-inch microwave-safe skillet, uncovered, at 100 percent power in a 650-to 700-watt carousel oven for 3 minutes 30 seconds. Add cumin and fennel. Cook, uncovered, at 100 percent power for 2 minutes (or until spices exude aroma and turn darker), then add onions.

3. Cook, uncovered, at 100 percent power for 2 minutes (or until onions just begin to wilt). Add tomatoes and continue cooking, uncovered, at 100 percent power for an additional 2 minutes (or until tomatoes begin to soften). Remove from oven.

4. Add beans, turmeric, salt, and water, mix well, and cover with the lid. Cook at 100 percent power for 7 minutes 30 seconds (or until beans are cooked soft but are not mushy and excess moisture has evaporated). Remove from oven and let beans stand, covered, for 5 minutes. Uncover, stir in lemon juice, *garam masala,* chilies, and coriander or mint, and refrigerate or serve.

NOTE The *dal* may be made ahead and set aside for several hours, covered, at room temperature, and served reheated. It may also be refrigerated for 3 days, but the fragrance of the spices will numb. To invigorate the *dal,* add a new batch of spice-infused oil and some fresh herbs.

COOKED WHOLE MUNG BEANS

SABAT MOONG

MICROWAVE

Yield
— 2½ cups
Preparation time
— 3 minutes plus 4
hours for soaking
Cooking time
— 15 minutes
Standing time
— 5 minutes
Heat
— 100 percent power
MW oven size
— 650 to 700 watts
MW cookware
— One 10-inch cov-
ered skillet

NOTE   The cooked beans keep well in the refrigerator, stored in a covered container, for up to 3 days.

Whole mung beans cook to perfection in the micro-wave without splitting, cracking, or bursting open. The cooking times are given for cooking these beans is approximate because much depends upon moisture content (i.e., the freshness of the beans). Serve cooked beans, flavored with spice-infused oil (p. 484), as a warm salad, side-dish *dal,* and over pilafs, and use in stuffings and recipes calling for cooked green mung beans. Or turn it into pureed beans (p. 289) for ad-ditional uses.

=========== ROOM TEMPERATURE ===========

1 cup dried whole mung
  beans (p. 462)
¼ teaspoon turmeric
2 teaspoons light
  vegetable oil

1 teaspoon kosher salt,
  if desired
2 cups water

1. Pick clean beans and place in a medium-size bowl. Add enough water to cover the beans by at least 2 inches and soak for 4 hours. Drain, rinse, and drain again.

2. Place beans in a 10-inch microwave-safe skillet. Add turmeric, oil, salt, and 1⅓ cups water and cover with the lid. Cook at 100 percent power in a 650- to 700-watt carousel oven for 8 minutes (or until most of the water is absorbed into the beans). Uncover, add the remaining ⅔ cup water, and replace cover. Continue cooking at 100 percent power for 7 minutes (or until beans are cooked soft but still hold their shape), stir-ring once. Remove from oven and let beans stand, covered, for 5 minutes before using.

PUREED WHOLE MUNG BEANS

SABAT MOONG

MICROWAVE

Yield
—3 cups

Preparation time
—3 minutes

Cooking time
—4 minutes

Standing time
—5 minutes

Heat
—100 percent power

MW oven size
—650 to 700 watts

MW cookware
—One 10-inch cov-
ered skillet

Serve pureed whole mung beans, flavored with spice-infused oil (p. 484), as a creamy side-dish *dal*, hearty soup, or use in recipes calling for pureed yellow mung beans such as New Delhi Fragrant Creamy Mung Beans (p. 284) or Warm Mung Bean Salad in Cumin-Tomato Dressing (p. 286).

For creamy pureed whole mung beans, cook exactly as for Cooked Whole Mung Beans (p. 288), except continue cooking beans at 100 percent power for an additional 4 minutes (or until beans are very soft and begin to burst open). Remove from oven and let beans stand, covered, for 5 minutes. Uncover and beat vigorously with a whisk, crushing beans into a puree. Measure and add enough water to make 3 cups puree.

NOTE   The pureed whole mung beans keep well in the refrigerator, stored in a covered container, for up to 2 days.

SPICY WHOLE MUNG BEAN STEW

MASALA DAL

MICROWAVE

Yield
—4 cups
Servings
—6
Preparation time
—2 minutes
Cooking time
—16 minutes
Standing time
—5 minutes
Heat
—100 percent power
MW oven size
—650 to 700 watts
MW cookware
—One 10-inch cov-
ered skillet

This mouth-watering stew is from Kanpur in the Northern Province. The cooked whole mung beans are flavored with spicy cumin-ginger oil.

This light preparation goes well with *tandoori* dishes, roasts, kabobs, and vegetarian main courses that do not contain legumes in any form. For a simple meal, serve Plain Basmati Rice (p. 299), Broccoli in Spicy-Garlic Oil (p. 205), and Crushed Cucumber Salsa (p. 239).

=== ROOM TEMPERATURE ===

2 teaspoons ground
cumin
2 teaspoons ground
coriander
½ teaspoon ground
cardamom
½ teaspoon cayenne
pepper
¼ teaspoon freshly
ground black pepper
3 tablespoons light vege-
table oil
¾ cup (1 medium-size)
finely chopped onion

1 tablespoon chopped
fresh ginger
3 cups Pureed Whole
Mung Beans (p. 289)
or Pureed Yellow
Mung Beans (p. 283)
Kosher salt to taste
2 medium-size (12
ounces) red ripe toma-
toes, cut into ½-inch-
thick wedges
4 tablespoons chopped
fresh coriander or 2
tablespoons finely
chopped dill

1. Combine cumin, coriander, cardamom, cayenne, and black pepper in a bowl and set aside.

2. Pour oil into a 10-inch microwave-safe skillet. Heat, uncovered, at 100 percent power in a 650- to 700-watt carousel oven for 2 minutes. Remove from oven, add spice mixture, onion, and ginger, and mix well. Cook, uncovered, at 100 percent power for 6 minutes (or until onions just begin to brown), stirring twice during the last 2 minutes of cooking. Remove from oven.

3. Stir in beans and salt to taste and replace cover. Cook at 100 percent power for 5 minutes (or until stew is steaming hot). Uncover, fold in tomatoes, and replace cover. Cook at 100 percent power for 3 minutes (or until tomatoes are cooked but still hold their shape). Remove from oven. Let stew stand, covered, for 5 minutes. Uncover, sprinkle with coriander, and serve.

NOTE   The *dal* may be made ahead and set aside for several hours, covered, at room temperature, and served reheated. It may also be refrigerated for 3 days, but the fragrance of the spices will numb. To invigorate the *dal,* add a new batch of spice-infused oil and some fresh herbs.

COOKED BLACK-EYED PEAS

LOBHIA DAL

Black-eyed peas have one wonderful quality: When cooked they lose their starchy-mealy flavor and taste like a vegetable, therefore they become much lighter and easier on the palate. Dried peas need to be soaked before cooking. While cooking peas, remember to keep them moist in order for them to soften and puff up properly. If you want your peas extremely soft, cook them for an additional five minutes. Do not worry about overcooking peas as they will not fall apart and become mushy. Use cooked black-eyed peas in salads (pp. 31 or 249) and stews (p. 294).

MICROWAVE

Yield
—*3 cups*

Preparation time
—*3 minutes plus 4 hours for soaking*

Cooking time
—*18 to 28 minutes*

Standing time
—*30 minutes*

MW oven size
—*650 to 700 watts*

MW cookware
—*One 3-quart covered casserole*

================ *ROOM TEMPERATURE* ================

1 cup dried, 2½ cups fresh, or 1 10-ounce package frozen black-eyed peas (p. 462)	2 teaspoons minced garlic
2 tablespoons mustard oil or light vegetable oil	½ teaspoon turmeric
	2 teaspoons kosher salt
	2⅓ cups water

1. Pick clean peas and rinse thoroughly. If you are using dried peas, place them in a medium-size bowl and add enough water to cover by at least an inch. Soak for 4 hours and drain.

2. Place peas, along with all other ingredients, in a 3-quart microwave-safe casserole and cover with the lid. Cook at 100 percent power in a 650- to 700-watt carousel oven for 10 to 28 minutes, depending upon the peas (or until most of the water is absorbed and peas are tender and cooked), stirring twice. Remove from oven. Let peas stand, covered, for 30 minutes to

absorb more moisture and become soft. Drain, if necessary, and use.

Cooking times (approximate):

Type of Peas	Quantity of Peas	Quantity of Water	Time	Yield
Fresh	2½ cups	1½ cups	10 minutes	3 cups
Frozen	2 cups	1¼ cups	18 minutes	3 cups
Dried Peas	1 cup	2⅓ cups	28 minutes	3 cups

BLACK-EYED PEA STEW
LOBHIA

MICROWAVE

Yield
  —3½ cups
Servings
  —6
Cooking time
  —13 minutes
Standing time
  —5 minutes
Heat
  —100 percent power
MW oven size
  —650 to 700 watts
MW cookware
  —One 3-quart covered
   casserole

In Indian cooking both fresh and dried black-eyed peas are used and are both treated as a vegetable because, unlike other dried peas and beans, when cooked they are very light and herbal on the palate and gentle on the digestive system. Stewed with tomatoes, ginger, and spices is one popular way Indians enjoy these peas. The mustard oil, although not essential, is added to lend a sweet, smoky flavor.

Both dried and fresh peas work well in this recipe, but remember to make allowance for the additional cooking time for dried peas.

This delicately spiced black-eyed pea stew is very filling, and therefore best served with a simple cooked Plain Basmati Rice (p. 299) and Crushed Cucumber Salsa (p. 239). Peach Chutney with Raisins and Walnuts (p. 349) and Broccoli in Spicy-Garlic Oil (p. 205) are nice additions. To elaborate the meal, precede with Cream of Vegetable Soup (p. 51).

================= *ROOM TEMPERATURE* =================

4 tablespoons mustard oil or olive oil

1 tablespoon curry powder, homemade (p. 479) or store-bought

1 cup chopped onion

3 cups Cooked Black-eyed Peas (p. 292) or use 3 cups canned, drained blackeyed peas

1½ cups finely chopped red ripe tomatoes

1 tablespoon finely chopped fresh ginger

2 or more fresh hot green chilies, stemmed, seeded, and thinly sliced (optional)

1½ teaspoons ground roasted cumin seeds (p. 465) or 1 teaspoon garam masala, homemade (p. 478) or store-bought

FOR THE GARNISH: *6 lemon wedges*

3 tablespoons chopped
* fresh coriander*

1. Pour oil into a 3-quart microwave-safe casserole. Heat, uncovered, at 100 percent power in a 650- to 700-watt carousel oven for 2 minutes. Add curry powder and onion and cook, uncovered, at 100 percent power for an additional 5 minutes (or until onions look lightly fried but are still white), stirring once. Remove from oven.

2. Uncover, add cooked peas, tomatoes, ginger, and chilies, and replace cover. Cook at 100 percent power for 6 minutes (or until tomatoes lose their uncooked aroma and stew is bubbling).

3. Remove from oven. Let stew stand, covered, for 5 minutes. Uncover and stir in cumin. Serve garnished with coriander and lemon wedges.

NOTE   For a thinner consistency of sauce, stir in ½ cup water before adding tomatoes, mash some of the beans with the back of the spoon, and proceed as recommended in the recipe.

NOTE   The *dal* may be made ahead and set aside for several hours, covered, at room temperature, and served reheated. It may also be refrigerated for 3 days, but the fragrance of the spices will weaken. To invigorate the *dal,* add a new batch of spice-infused oil and some fresh herbs.

PILAFS
AND STEAMED CAKES

L ike traditional American meals, those of India are almost unthinkable without an accompanying starchy staple. But since Indian food contains more spices, often leaving a soothing glow at the back of the mouth, Indian staples must balance the spicy flavor. For this reason, Indian pilafs and steamed cakes, the staples, tend to be bland, mellow, gentle, or sweet. The selection of a rice dish, therefore, is critically important; the ultimate in Indian cooking is not provided by a single dish, but in how a total meal is enjoyed.

The recipes here call for *basmati* rice (see page 448). In conventional cooking, this nutty, heavenly scented long-grained rice of India entails prolonged soaking and gentle cooking. In the microwave, it cooks in just twelve to fourteen minutes and requires no soaking. Thanks to the rice's own chemistry as it reacts to the microwaves, the grains cook long and without cracking.

The process of cooking plain *basmati* is very straightforward. The rice is combined with the liquid in a dish and cooked, first uncovered, until most of the moisture is absorbed into the rice and its surface is dotted with steamy holes (eight to ten minutes), then covered with the lid until the rice is soft (four minutes). The range of time at the first stage is simple to explain. Like any staple, *basmati,* as it sits, has a tendency to become dry, changing in its moisture content. It may need a bit more water and a slightly longer cooking time. I have developed recipes keeping this in mind. You will know the rice is done when steam holes appear on top, generally in eight minutes. If there is a puddle of water on top and the rice is still hard and uncooked, extend the cooking time (usually two minutes for each cup of uncooked rice) until you reach the steamy-hole stage, then proceed to the next stage as described for each recipe.

Many of the pilafs in this section contain fruit—mango, peach, tomato—or a wonderful combination of many vegetables. There are also recipes for pilafs made with cream of wheat; these are light, almost like soft polenta, and are wonderful at breakfast, used as a stuffing for poultry and game, or just as a mellow side dish. The steamed cakes from Bombay are made with a lentil base; rice cakes come from Madras, Ceylon (now Sri Lanka), and Malabar, along the coastal southern regions such as Kerala, Tamil Nadu, and are flavored accordingly with seafood, herbs, or coconut.

Worth noting is the recipe for the Steamed Rice and Bean Dumplings, which traditionally requires assembling a steaming apparatus in which to boil water and steam the dumplings, all of which can take well over thirty minutes. In a microwave the recipe can be cooked in two minutes. Not only are the dumplings superbly moist and fluffy, they can be frozen for up to a year and reheated at a moment's notice.

PLAIN BASMATI RICE

SADA CHAWAL

MICROWAVE

Yield
  —3 cups
Servings
  —4 to 6
Preparation time
  —4 minutes
Cooking time
  —12 to 14 minutes
Standing time
  —5 minutes
Heat
  —100 percent power
MW oven size
  —650 to 700 watts
MW cookware
  —One 2½-quart cov-
   ered casserole or
   soufflé dish

NOTE Plain *basmati* keeps well, stored in a microwave-safe covered container, in the refrigerator for 5 days.

I don't think I fully appreciated the microwave until I saw how it cooked *basmati*. *Basmati* rice generally takes 25 minutes to cook after having soaked 30 minutes—55 minutes in all. In the microwave *basmati* rice cooks in 12 minutes and eliminates the soaking step. This is a fast and trouble-free technique that produces fluffy, springy, and nonsticky grains of *basmati*.

As in the conventional technique, the *basmati* is cooked uncovered during the first half of cooking. This speeds evaporation. During the second half it is covered. The *basmati* is then allowed to stand for a few minutes before serving so that the grains firm up.

The following timing is only for the new fresh stock of rice. Old rice that has been sitting in the kitchen cupboard for a year or more will take an additional 4½ minutes of cooking time to absorb the water, increasing the cooking time to 16 minutes.

═══════ *ROOM TEMPERATURE* ═══════

1 cup raw basmati *rice*   *2¼ cups water*

1. Pick clean rice and wash in several changes of water. Drain the rice thoroughly and place in a 2½-quart microwave-safe dish. Add water and mix well. Cook, uncovered, at 100 percent power in a 650- to 700-watt carousel oven for 8 to 10 minutes (or until most of the water is absorbed into the rice and its surface is covered with steamy holes), stirring twice.

2. Cover with the lid and continue cooking at 100 percent power for 4 minutes (or until rice is fully cooked and soft). Remove from oven and let the rice rest, covered, for 5 minutes. Uncover, lightly fluff with fork, and serve.

COCONUT RICE

NARIAL CHAWAL

MICROWAVE

Yield
—3 cups
Servings
—6
Preparation time
—4 minutes
Cooking time
—12 to 14 minutes
Standing time
—5 minutes
Heat
—100 percent power
MW oven size
—650 to 700 watts
MW cookware
—One 2½-quart cov-
ered casserole or
soufflé dish

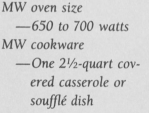

Bengal, Tamil Nadu, Kerala, Maharashtra, and Goa, the regions along the Indian coastline, are speckled with groves of coconut palm trees and famous for their spicy-hot fish curries with coconut. Local cooks serve these dishes with a delicately sweet coconut rice in order to temper the heat and accentuate the coconut flavor on the palate. Coconut rice is made exactly like Plain Basmati Rice (p. 299), except that coconut milk is substituted for cooking water. Remember to use only the freshest and sweetest coconut milk in this recipe, or else the rice will not be as fragrant.

ROOM TEMPERATURE

1 cup raw basmati rice
2¼ cups coconut milk
  (p. 250)

¼ cup sweetened coconut
  flakes (optional)

1. Pick clean rice and wash in several changes of water. Drain the rice thoroughly and place in a 2½-quart microwave-safe dish. Add coconut milk and mix well. Cook, uncovered, at 100 percent power in a 650- to 700-watt carousel oven, for 8 to 10 minutes (or until most of the coconut milk is absorbed into the rice and its surface is covered with steamy holes), stirring twice.

2. Cover with the lid and continue cooking, at 100 percent power, for 4 minutes (or until rice is fully cooked and soft). Remove from oven and let the rice rest, covered, for 5 minutes. Uncover, lightly fluff rice with fork. Fold in coconut flakes, if you are using, and serve.

NOTE The coconut rice keeps well, stored in a micro-wave-safe covered container, in the refrigerator for 2 days.

PARSI CARAMELIZED ONION PILAF

BHONA CHAWAL

MICROWAVE

Yield
—*3 cups*
Servings
—*4 to 6*
Preparation time
—*4 minutes*
Cooking time
—*12 to 14 minutes*
Standing time
—*5 minutes*
Heat
—*100 percent power*
MW oven size
—*650 to 700 watts*
MW cookware
—*One 2½-quart covered casserole or soufflé dish*

This is a simple yet delicious technique of the Parsis for making pilaf where the rice is cooked in a broth of caramelized onions. It is mild, sweet and fragrant, and traditionally accompanies Parsi Chicken Braised in Spiced Pumpkin-Lentil Puree (p. 124). The pilaf is equally good served with eggs at breakfast, or accompanied with grilled lamb, chicken, or fish, in a western-style menu.

=============== *ROOM TEMPERATURE* ===============

1 cup raw basmati *rice*	*2 teaspoons tomato paste*
¼ cup (1 recipe) fried onion shreds (p. 475) or onion, garlic, and ginger Roux I (p. 474)	*⅓ teaspoon kosher salt, if desired*
	2¼ cups water

1. Pick clean rice and wash in several changes of water. Drain the rice thoroughly and place in a 2½-quart microwave-safe dish. Add onion mixture, tomato paste, salt, and water and mix well. Cook, uncovered, at 100 percent power, in a 650- to 700-watt carousel oven, for 8 to 10 minutes (or until most of the water is absorbed into the rice and its surface is covered with steamy holes), stirring twice.

2. Cover with the lid and continue cooking at 100 percent power for 4 minutes (or until rice is fully cooked and soft). Remove from oven and let the rice rest, covered, for 5 minutes. Uncover, lightly fluff with fork, and serve.

NOTE The Parsi onion pilaf keeps well, stored in a microwave-safe covered container, in the refrigerator for 3 days.

MOGHUL-SCENTED BASMATI PILAF

PULLAO CHAWAL

MICROWAVE

Yield
—*3 cups*
Servings
—*4 to 6*
Cooking time
—*19 to 21 minutes*
Standing time
—*5 minutes*
Heat
—*100 percent power*
MW oven size
—*650 to 700 watts*
MW cookware
—*One 2½-quart cov-
ered casserole or
soufflé dish*

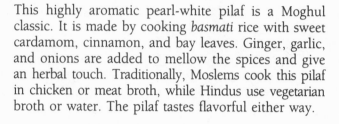

This highly aromatic pearl-white pilaf is a Moghul classic. It is made by cooking *basmati* rice with sweet cardamom, cinnamon, and bay leaves. Ginger, garlic, and onions are added to mellow the spices and give an herbal touch. Traditionally, Moslems cook this pilaf in chicken or meat broth, while Hindus use vegetarian broth or water. The pilaf tastes flavorful either way.

=== ROOM TEMPERATURE ===

2 tablespoons light vege-table oil	*1 teaspoon crushed or grated fresh ginger*
4 green or white carda-mom pods, lightly crushed	*¾ cup chopped onion*
	1 cup raw basmati rice, picked clean and rinsed
1 3-inch piece cinnamon stick	
6 whole cloves	*2½ cups chicken or meat stock (p. 488), vege-tarian stock (p. 489), or water*
2 bay leaves	
½ teaspoon minced garlic	*1 teaspoon kosher salt*

FOR THE GARNISH:

¼ cup fried onion shreds (p. 475)	*2 tablespoons roasted slivered almonds (p. 463) (optional)*

1. Pour the oil into a 2½-quart microwave-safe dish. Cook, uncovered, at 100 percent power in a 650- to 700-watt carousel oven for 1 minute. Add cardamom, cinnamon, cloves, and bay leaves. Cook, uncovered, at 100 percent power for 2 minutes (or until spices exude a sweet aroma). Add garlic, ginger, and onion

and continue cooking, uncovered, at 100 percent power for 4 minutes (or until the onions look limp and glazed), stirring once. Remove from oven.

2. Add rice, stock or water, and salt, and stir to mix. Cook, uncovered, at 100 percent power for 8 to 10 minutes (or until most of the water is absorbed into the rice and its surface is covered with steamy holes), stirring twice. Cover with the lid and continue cooking at 100 percent power for 4 minutes (or until rice is fully cooked and soft). Remove from oven.

3. Let pilaf rest, covered, for 5 minutes. Uncover, lightly fluff pilaf with a fork, and transfer to a heated platter. Spread fried onion shreds or almonds on top and serve.

NOTE This pilaf keeps well, stored in a microwave-safe covered container, in the refrigerator for 3 days.

SAFFRON PILAF
ZAFRANI PULLAO

Steeped in the essence of sweet saffron, this pilaf is another great Moghul classic. Apricot puree is added for balance and also to impart a sweet, piny taste. To get the most color and aroma from the saffron, crush the threads finely before adding them. This is a simple task if the saffron threads, which are normally moist and soft, can be dried. The microwave not only toasts and dries these fragile threads without burning them, it also intensifies their aroma in the process. Serve this subtle and elegant pilaf with all *tandoori* dishes and Moghul curries.

MICROWAVE

Yield
 —*3 cups*
Servings
 —*4 to 6*
Cooking time
 —*16 to 18 minutes*
Standing time
 —*5 minutes*
Heat
 —*100 percent power*
MW oven size
 —*650 to 700 watts*
MW cookware
 —*One 2½-quart covered casserole or soufflé dish*

=========== *ROOM TEMPERATURE* ===========

½ teaspoon crushed saffron threads or powdered saffron

2 tablespoons usli ghee (p. 492) or light vegetable oil

1 tablespoon sugar

2 tablespoons minced onion

1 cup raw basmati rice, picked clean and rinsed

2¼ cups water

¼ cup, or 2 frozen cubes, apricot puree (p. 473) or water

¼ cup dark raisins

1 teaspoon kosher salt, if desired

FOR THE GARNISH:

2 tablespoons roasted slivered almonds (p. 463) (optional)

2 3-inch-square pieces silver leaf vark (p. 476) (optional)

1. Spread saffron threads in an 8-inch microwave-safe skillet. Toast, uncovered, at 100 percent power in a 650- to 700-watt carousel oven for 30 seconds (or until saffron begins to exude an aroma). Remove from

oven. When cool, crush saffron and reserve. Omit this step if you are using powdered saffron.

2. Pour the *usli ghee* into a 2½-quart microwave-safe dish. Cook, uncovered, at 100 percent power for 1 minute. Add sugar and onion and cook, uncovered, at 100 percent power for 2 minutes (or until onions look limp and glazed). Remove from oven.

3. Stir in saffron, rice, water, apricot puree (or more water), raisins, and salt. Cook, uncovered, at 100 percent power for 8 to 10 minutes (or until most of the water is absorbed into the rice and its surface is covered with steamy holes), stirring twice. Cover with the lid and continue cooking at 100 percent power for 4 minutes (or until the rice is fully cooked and soft). Remove from oven.

4. Let pilaf rest, covered, for 5 minutes. Uncover, lightly fluff with a fork, and transfer to a heated platter. Serve garnished with nuts and silver foil.

NOTE The saffron pilaf keeps well, stored in a microwave-safe covered container, in the refrigerator for 4 days.

CRISP OKRA AND SPICED BASMATI PILAF

BHINDI PULLAO

MICROWAVE

Yield
—3½ cups
Servings
—4 to 6
Cooking time
—15 to 17 minutes
Standing time
—5 minutes
Heat
—100 percent power
MW oven size
—650 to 700 watts
MW cookware
—One 2½-quart cov-
ered casserole or
soufflé dish

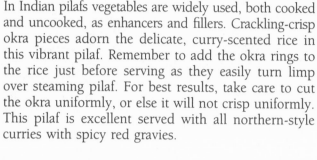

In Indian pilafs vegetables are widely used, both cooked and uncooked, as enhancers and fillers. Crackling-crisp okra pieces adorn the delicate, curry-scented rice in this vibrant pilaf. Remember to add the okra rings to the rice just before serving as they easily turn limp over steaming pilaf. For best results, take care to cut the okra uniformly, or else it will not crisp uniformly. This pilaf is excellent served with all northern-style curries with spicy red gravies.

=============== ROOM TEMPERATURE ===============

2 tablespoons light vege-
   table oil
2 tablespoons minced
   onion
½ teaspoon minced
   garlic
1 teaspoon fragrant spice
   powder (p. 481) or
   Moghul garam masala
   (p. 477)

1 cup raw basmati rice,
   picked clean and
   rinsed
2½ cups water
1 teaspoon kosher salt
1 cup (1 recipe) Crisp
   Fried Okra (p. 222)

FOR THE GARNISH:
¼ cup (1 recipe) fried onion shreds (p. 475)

1. Pour the oil into a 2½-quart microwave-safe dish. Cook, uncovered, at 100 percent power in a 650- to 700-watt carousel oven for 1 minute. Add onion, garlic, and spice powder and cook, uncovered, at 100 percent power for 2 minutes (or until onions look limp and glazed). Remove from oven.

2. Add rice, water, and salt and mix well. Cook, uncovered, at 100 percent power for 8 to 10 minutes (or until most of the water is absorbed into the rice and its surface is covered with steamy holes), stirring twice. Cover with the lid and continue cooking at 100 percent power for 4 minutes (or until rice is fully cooked and soft). Remove from oven.

3. Let pilaf rest, covered, for 5 minutes. Uncover, lightly fluff pilaf with a fork, and transfer to a heated platter. Spread Crisp Fried Okra on top and serve garnished with fried onion shreds.

TOMATO BASMATI PILAF
TAMATAR PULLAO

MICROWAVE

Yield
 —3 cups
Servings
 —4 to 16
Preparation time
 —3 minutes
Cooking time
 —15 to 17 minutes
Standing time
 —5 minutes
Heat
 —100 percent power
MW oven size
 —650 to 700 watts
MW cookware
 —One 2½-quart cov-
   ered casserole or
   soufflé dish

Cooks in south India have a way with rice. They create complex-flavored pilafs by combining rice with juicy fruits (or vegetables) and hot, assertive spices. This slightly gingery, rose-red tomato-flavored pilaf is beautiful in both flavor and appeal. The more rich and luscious the tomato is, the more glorious the pilaf will be. Use, therefore, only vine-ripened tomatoes. This pilaf is particularly good with fish and light chicken main courses.

=========== ROOM TEMPERATURE ===========

1 large tomato (½ pound), roughly chopped with the skin	½ teaspoon minced garlic
¼ cup water	1½ teaspoons grated or crushed fresh ginger
3 tablespoons light vegetable oil	1 cup raw basmati rice, picked clean and rinsed
1 teaspoon cumin seeds, crushed	1½ teaspoons kosher salt
¾ cup finely chopped onion	¼ teaspoon or more freshly ground black pepper

FOR THE GARNISH:

¼ cup (1 recipe) fried onion shreds (p. 475), or ½ cup thinly sliced scallions, or 3 tablespoons roasted slivered almonds (p. 463)

1. Place tomato and water in the container of a food processor or blender and process until completely liquefied. Transfer tomato puree into a measuring cup, add enough water to make 2¼ cups tomato juice, and reserve.

2. Pour the oil into a 2½-quart microwave-safe casserole. Cook, uncovered, at 100 percent power in a 650- to 700-watt carousel oven for 1 minute. Add cumin, onion, garlic, and ginger and continue cooking at 100 percent power for 2 minutes (or until onions look soft and glazed). Remove from oven.

3. Add rice, tomato juice, salt, and pepper and mix well. Cook, uncovered, at 100 percent power for 8 to 10 minutes (or until most of the water is absorbed into the rice and its surface is covered with steamy holes), stirring twice. Cover with the lid and continue cooking at 100 percent power for 4 minutes (or until rice is fully cooked and soft). Remove from oven.

4. Let pilaf stand, covered, for 5 minutes. Uncover, lightly fluff with a fork, transfer to a heated platter, and serve, if desired, garnished with fried onion shreds and accompanied with Minted Red Onion Salad (p. 241) or Crushed Cucumber Salsa (p. 239).

NOTE The tomato pilaf keeps well, stored in a microwave-safe covered container, in the refrigerator for 5 days.

MANGO AND BASMATI PILAF

AAM PULLAO

A lovely pilaf to make when ripe, juicy mangoes are in season. Mango pilaf is made by first cooking the rice in mango puree and then serving it with additional mango slices. It is very fragrant, very tropical, and very sensuous. Serve this pilaf with *tandoori* dishes, kabobs, and grilled foods.

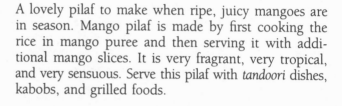

MICROWAVE

Yield
  —*4 cups*
Servings
  —*6 to 8*
Preparation time
  —*5 minutes*
Cooking time
  —*15 to 17 minutes*
Standing time
  —*5 minutes*
MW oven size
  —*650 to 700 watts*
MW cookware
  —*One 2½-quart covered casserole or soufflé dish*

=================== ROOM TEMPERATURE ===================

1 medium-size (½ pound) ripe mango	¼ teaspoon dried ginger powder
2 tablespoons usli ghee (p. 492), unsalted butter, or light vegetable oil	⅛ teaspoon freshly grated nutmeg
2 tablespoons minced onion	1 cup raw basmati rice, picked clean and rinsed
¼ teaspoon ground cardamom	½ teaspoon kosher salt, if desired

FOR THE GARNISH:
2 tablespoons roasted slivered almonds (p. 463)

1. Peel mango, separate the meat from the pit in large chunks, and discard pit. Cut the meat into 1-inch cubes. Place 1 cup odd-shaped mango pieces (set aside remaining nicer pieces for folding into the pilaf at the end) into the container of a food processor or blender and process until pureed. Add 1 cup water and continue processing until the mango is completely liquefied. Transfer mango juice into a measuring cup, add enough water to make 2¼ cups mango juice, and reserve.

2. Pour *usli ghee* into a 2½-quart microwave-safe dish. Cook, uncovered, at 100 percent power in a 650- to 700-watt carousel oven for 1 minute. Add onion and cardamom and cook, uncovered, at 100 percent power for 2 minutes (or until onions look limp and glazed). Remove from oven.

3. Stir in ginger, nutmeg, rice, mango juice, and salt. Cook, uncovered, at 100 percent power for 8 to 10 minutes (or until most of the water is absorbed into the rice and its surface is covered with steamy holes), stirring twice. Cover with the lid and continue cooking at 100 percent power for 4 minutes (or until rice is fully cooked and soft). Remove from oven.

4. Let pilaf rest, covered, for 5 minutes. Uncover, lightly fluff with a fork, and transfer to a heated platter. Distribute reserved mango pieces and almonds on the pilaf and serve.

VARIATION

To make peach, pear, nectarine, apricot, pineapple, plum, orange, or tangerine pilaf, substitute 2½ cups prepared fruit in place of mango and proceed with the recipe the same way.

NOTE The mango pilaf keeps well, stored in a microwave-safe covered container, in the refrigerator for 2 days. Assemble pilaf just before serving.

MOGHUL GLAZED PEACH PILAF

KHOOBANI PULLAO

MICROWAVE

Yield
  —5 cups
Servings
  —6 to 8
Cooking time
  —17 to 19 minutes
Heat
  —100 percent power
MW oven size
  —650 to 700 watts
MW cookware
  —One 2½-quart covered casserole or soufflé dish and one 10-inch skillet

Delicately perfumed with ginger and cinnamon and studded with shimmering glazed peaches and toasted almonds, this royal Moghul pilaf is stunningly beautiful. Do not substitute canned peaches if ripe, juicy peaches are not available; instead use fresh nectarines, oranges, or pineapple. Serve this pilaf with Moghul curries that have delicate cream sauces such as Moghul Lamb in Creamed Spinach Sauce (p. 155) or Moghul Vegetables in Cream Sauce (p. 173), *tandoori* dishes, and kabobs.

=============== ROOM TEMPERATURE ===============

1 cup raw basmati rice, picked clean and rinsed

½ cup, or 4 frozen cubes, apricot puree (p. 473) or ½ cup unsweetened apricot or peach butter

1 teaspoon grated or crushed fresh ginger

¼ teaspoon ground cinnamon

1¾ cups water

½ teaspoon kosher salt, or to taste

2 tablespoons usli ghee (p. 492) or unsalted butter

2 medium-size ripe peaches, peeled, pitted, sliced into thin wedges, and dressed with 1 teaspoon lemon juice

⅛ teaspoon freshly grated nutmeg

FOR THE GARNISH:

2 tablespoons roasted slivered almonds (p. 463) or sliced unsalted pistachio nuts

1. Place rice in a 2½-quart microwave-safe dish. Add apricot puree, ginger, cinnamon, and water. Add salt to taste and mix well. Cook, uncovered, at 100 percent power in a 650- to 700-watt carousel oven for 8 to 10 minutes (or until most of the water is absorbed into the rice and its surface is covered with steamy holes), stirring twice.

2. Cover with the lid and continue cooking at 100 percent power for 4 minutes (or until rice is fully cooked and soft). Remove from oven and set aside, covered, while you make the glazed peaches.

3. Heat *usli ghee* or butter in a 10-inch microwave-safe skillet at 100 percent power for 3 minutes. Remove from oven, add peaches, and toss to coat with *ghee*. Sauté peaches at 100 percent power for 2 minutes (or until peaches are just cooked). Remove from oven. Sprinkle with nutmeg.

4. To assemble pilaf, uncover rice, lightly fluff with a fork, and transfer to a heated platter. Arrange peach slices on top. Garnish with almonds or pistachio nuts and serve.

NOTE The rice keeps well, stored in a microwave-safe covered container, in the refrigerator for 2 days. Assemble pilaf just before serving.

SPLIT PEA AND BASMATI PILAF

CHANNA PULLAO

Combining rice and split peas in a pilaf is popular in the region of Assam along the eastern border of India. This particular version, accented with peas and fragrant with cumin, is sweet, subtle, and meaty-tasting. The secret is in cooking the rice and peas until both are tender but not mushy. The microwave is ideal for this dish, as the rice and peas swell to juicy plumpness and yet remain whole because there is little stirring or agitation during cooking. This filling pilaf is good paired with any light main course. You can serve it as a light meal accompanied with Minted Red Onion Salad (p. 241) or Crushed Cucumber Salsa (p. 239) and a yogurt *raita* (pp. 251–263).

MICROWAVE

Yield
  —*6 cups*
Servings
  —*8 to 12*
Preparation time
  —*3 minutes plus 8 hours for soaking*
Cooking time
  —*19 to 21 minutes*
Standing time
  —*5 minutes*
Heat
  —*100 percent power*
MW oven size
  —*650 to 700 watts*
MW cookware
  —*One 2½-quart covered casserole or soufflé dish*

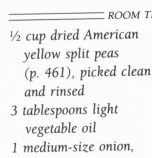

=========== ROOM TEMPERATURE ===========

½ *cup dried American yellow split peas (p. 461), picked clean and rinsed*

3 *tablespoons light vegetable oil*

1 *medium-size onion, peeled and chopped*

1 *teaspoon cumin seeds, crushed*

1 *cup raw* basmati *rice, picked clean and rinsed*

2½ *cups chicken or meat stock (p. 488), vegetarian stock (p. 489), mung broth (p. 490), or water*

1½ *teaspoons kosher salt*

FOR THE GARNISH:
¼ *cup fried onion shreds (p. 475) or roasted slivered almonds (p. 463)*

1. Place split peas in a medium-size bowl and add enough water to cover them by at least an inch and a half. Soak peas for 8 hours or overnight (maximum 18 hours). Drain, rinse, and drain again.

2. Pour the oil into a 2½-quart microwave-safe dish. Cook, uncovered, at 100 percent power in a 650- to 700-watt carousel oven for 1 minute. Add onion and cumin and continue cooking at 100 percent power for 2 minutes (or until onions look soft and glazed). Remove from oven.

3. Add rice, drained peas, stock, and salt and stir to mix. Cook, uncovered, at 100 percent power for 12 to 14 minutes (or until most of the water is absorbed into the rice and its surface is covered with steamy holes), stirring twice. Cover dish with the lid and continue cooking at 100 percent power for 4 minutes (or until the rice is fully cooked and expanded). Remove from oven.

4. Let pilaf rest, covered, for 5 minutes. Uncover, lightly fluff pilaf with a fork, and transfer to a heated platter. Spread fried onion shreds or almonds on top and serve.

NOTE The rice keeps well, stored in a microwave-safe covered container, in the refrigerator for 2 days. Garnish pilaf before serving.

WHOLE MUNG BEAN AND BASMATI PILAF

MOONG DAL BHAT

MICROWAVE

Yield
—5 cups
Servings
—8 to 12
Preparation time
—3 minutes plus 8
    hours for soaking
Cooking time
—23 to 25 minutes
Standing time
—5 minutes
Heat
—100 percent power
MW oven size
—650 to 700 watts
MW cookware
—One 2½-quart cov-
    ered casserole or
    soufflé dish

I love meaty, plump mung beans, particularly in a pilaf, because they do not fall apart even after repeated heating—something you could do with this pilaf, which keeps well in the refrigerator for two weeks! Flavored with ginger and cumin, this pilaf has an earthy appeal and is popular in southwestern India. The microwave does wonders with the beans, expanding them to uncommonly large, moist nuggets. This robust, slightly mealy pilaf is perfect with light main courses that have assertive sauces.

ROOM TEMPERATURE

½ cup dried whole mung
  beans (p. 461)
2 tablespoons usli ghee
  (p. 492) or light vege-
  table oil
2 teaspoons canned green
  peppercorns, drained
  and rinsed, or 1 tea-
  spoon whole black
  peppercorns, crushed
1 teaspoon ground cumin

½ teaspoon turmeric
1 medium-size onion,
  peeled and chopped
2 teaspoons finely
  chopped fresh ginger
2¾ cups water
1½ teaspoons kosher
  salt, or to taste
1 cup raw basmati rice,
  picked clean and
  rinsed

FOR THE GARNISH:
2 medium-size tomatoes,
  sliced thinly

4 tablespoons melted
  usli ghee (p. 492)
  (optional)

1. Pick clean mung beans, rinse, and place in a medium-size bowl. Add enough water to cover them by at least an inch and a half. Soak for 8 hours or over-

night (maximum 18 hours). Drain, rinse, and drain again.

2. Place *usli ghee* or oil in a 2½-quart microwave-safe dish. Cook, uncovered, at 100 percent power in a 650- to 700-watt carousel oven for 1 minute. Stir in peppercorns, cumin, turmeric, and onion and continue cooking at 100 percent power for 2 minutes (or until onions look soft and glazed). Remove from oven.

3. Add beans, ginger, water, and salt to taste and mix well. Cook, covered, at 100 percent power for 10 minutes (or until water is boiling and beans are slightly cooked). Stir in rice. Cook, uncovered, at 100 percent power for 6 to 8 minutes (or until most of the water is absorbed into the rice and its surface is covered with steamy holes), stirring once.

4. Cover with the lid and continue cooking at 100 percent power for 4 minutes (or until rice and beans are fully cooked and expanded). Remove from oven.

5. Let pilaf rest, covered, for 5 minutes. Uncover, lightly fluff with a fork. Transfer onto a heated platter and serve garnished with tomato slices. Pass melted *usli ghee* in a bowl.

NOTE This pilaf keeps well in the refrigerator, stored in a covered container, for up to 2 weeks.

CREAM OF WHEAT PILAF WITH SHALLOTS AND CHILIES

UPMA

MICROWAVE

Yield
—2½ cups
Servings
—4 to 6
Cooking time
—13 minutes
Standing time
—5 minutes
Heat
—100 percent power
MW oven size
—650 to 700 watts
MW cookware
—One 10-inch cov-
ered skillet

Upma is the southern version of pilaf, made with wheat, rice, or millet cereal. Its texture ranges from the delicate Moroccan couscous to our grainy American grits. It is made by cooking toasted cereal with water and seasonings until the grains absorb the moisture and swell into soft, plump granules. The moist heat of the microwave is ideally suited for making this dish, as the cereal expands even more than on top of direct heat, yielding lighter, fluffy-textured *upma*. Cream of wheat *upmas,* by far, are the most popular because they taste like pasta—meaty and chewy. This *upma,* flavored with shallots and chilies, is traditionally served at breakfast or at afternoon tiffin, in south India. It also makes a nice light lunch accompanied with a yogurt *raita* and a salad. *Upma* is good accompanied with all spicy southern main courses such as Malabar Salmon in Delicate Coconut Sauce (p. 89), Duck Vendaloo (p. 130), and Eggplant-Lentil Stew with Tamarind and Garlic (p. 191).

═══════════ ROOM TEMPERATURE ═══════════

3 tablespoons light sesame oil or light vegetable oil

1 teaspoon mustard seeds

½ cup chopped shallots or red onions

3 fresh hot green chilies, stemmed, seeded, and thinly sliced

2 teaspoons chopped fresh ginger

1 cup quick-cooking cream of wheat

2¼ cups water

12 fresh, or 2 tablespoons crushed dried, curry leaves (p. 482)

| 4 tablespoons chopped roasted cashew nuts or almonds (p. 463) | 1 teaspoon kosher salt 1 teaspoon lemon juice |

1. Heat the oil in a 10-inch microwave-safe covered skillet at 100 percent power in a 650- to 700-watt carousel oven for 3 minutes. Uncover, add mustard seeds, and replace the lid. Cook at 100 percent power for 3 minutes (or until seeds pop). Uncover and stir in shallots, green chilies, and ginger. Cook, uncovered, at 100 percent power for 3 minutes (or until shallots look soft and glazed). Remove from oven.

2. Add cream of wheat and blend well to coat with oil. Add water, curry leaves, cashew nuts, and salt. Mix well and cover with the lid. Cook at 100 percent power for 4 minutes (or until cream of wheat is cooked, puffed, and resembles slightly dry grits). Remove from oven.

3. Let *upma* rest, covered, for 5 minutes (or until cream-of-wheat grains absorb excess moisture and turn plump and chewy). Uncover, fluff *upma* with a fork, and serve sprinkled with lemon juice, warm, at room temperature, or cold.

NOTE The *upma* may be made ahead and set aside, in a microwave-safe covered container, for up to 3 days in the refrigerator. To serve warm, reheat in its container, partially covered, at 100 percent power for 2 minutes (or until heated through).

CREAM OF WHEAT PILAF WITH TOMATOES AND GREEN PEAS

DAMATO UPMA

MICROWAVE

Yield
—2½ cups
Servings
—4 to 6
Cooking time
—10 minutes
Standing time
—5 minutes
Heat
—100 percent power
MW oven size
—650 to 700 watts
MW cookware
—One 10-inch cov-
ered skillet

This cream-of-wheat pilaf, flavored with tomatoes and sweet green peas, is cooked the same way as the Cream of Wheat Pilaf with Shallots and Chilies (p. 318). This *upma,* however, is milder and moister because of the tomatoes and the absence of chili peppers. It is lovely served at breakfast, as a first course on endive leaves, or at tiffin in the afternoon. For a light meal, serve this *upma* with a yogurt *raita* and a salad. You can also use the *upma* as a stuffing for vegetables, such as sweet green peppers, zucchini, eggplant, acorn squash, and cabbage. In fact you can substitute *upma* mixtures in place of ground meat stuffing in the Stuffed Cabbage Rolls with Fragrant Tomato Sauce (p. 161) recipe.

=============== ROOM TEMPERATURE ===============

3 tablespoons light vege-
table oil
1 teaspoon cumin seeds
1 teaspoon minced garlic
½ cup chopped onions
1 cup quick-cooking
cream of wheat
2¼ cups tomato juice or
1 cup chopped tomato
mixed with 1⅓ cups
water

1 cup green peas (fresh
or frozen)
½ teaspoon coarsely
ground black or white
pepper
½ teaspoon kosher salt,
or to taste
3 tablespoons chopped
fresh coriander

1. Heat the oil in a 10-inch microwave-safe skillet, uncovered, at 100 percent power in a 650- to 700-

watt carousel oven for 3 minutes. Add cumin and garlic. Cook, uncovered, at 100 percent power for 1 minute (or until garlic is just cooked). Add onion. Cook, uncovered, at 100 percent power for 2 minutes (or until onions look soft and glazed). Remove from oven.

2. Add cream of wheat and blend well to coat with oil. Add tomato juice, peas, pepper, and salt, mix well, and cover with the lid. Cook at 100 percent power for 4 minutes (or until cream of wheat is cooked, puffed, and resembles slightly dry grits). Remove from oven.

3. Let *upma* rest, covered, for 5 minutes (or until cream-of-wheat grains absorb excess moisture and turn plump and chewy). Uncover, fluff *upma* with a fork, and sprinkle with coriander. Serve hot, at room temperature, or cold.

NOTE The *upma* may be made ahead and set aside, in a microwave-safe covered container, for up to 3 days in the refrigerator. To serve hot, reheat in its container, partially covered, at 100 percent power for 2 minutes (or until heated through).

BASIC CREAMED RICE

SADA DALIA

MICROWAVE

Yield
—3 cups
Cooking time
—13 minutes
Heat
—100 percent power
MW oven size
—650 to 700 watts
MW cookware
—One 8-cup glass
measure or one 2½-
quart casserole or
soufflé dish

Making this creamed rice in the microwave is pure pleasure. It displays one of the strongest points of the oven, its ability to cook the cereal to a creamy smoothness without any lumps. Creamed rice is an important ingredient in Indian cooking. It is used for thickening puddings, sauces, and as a custard base. I love it by itself as a mild and subtle cereal hot, at room temperature, or straight out of the refrigerator, sometimes with additional milk and sugar, and thinned as a light soup.

═══════ ROOM TEMPERATURE ═══════

3 cups water   ⅓ cup cream of rice
                                      (p. 463)

1. Place water in an 8-cup glass measure or a 2½-quart microwave-safe dish. Cook, uncovered, at 100 percent power in a 650- to 700-watt carousel oven for 8 minutes (or until water comes to a rolling boil). Remove from oven.

2. Wait until the water stops boiling, then carefully stir in cream of rice. Cook, uncovered, at 100 percent power for 5 minutes (or until cream of rice is cooked and thickens like custard). Remove from oven and serve.

NOTE   The creamed rice keeps well, stored in a microwave-safe covered container, in the refrigerator for 6 days.

CREAMED RICE WITH SLICED FRUITS AND NUTS

DALIA

MICROWAVE

Yield

—6 cups

Servings

—6

Cooking time

—13 minutes

Heat

—100 percent power

MW oven size

—650 to 700 watts

MW cookware

—One 8-cup glass measure or one 2½-quart casserole or soufflé dish

I remember eating this cereal as a child and thinking I was being served a dessert for good behavior! This north Indian Jain specialty from Rajasthan is similar to Basic Creamed Rice (p. 322) except that milk is used in place of water, which lends the cereal a fragrant puddinglike sweetness. It is traditionally served with juicy, sweet sliced fruits. It is subtly soothing on the palate, particularly first thing in the early morning. I like it warm, at room temperature, or straight out of the refrigerator. Remember to use a deep dish for cooking cereal as milk has a tendency to boil over. Otherwise, cooking this cereal in the microwave is pure delight as there is no worry of milk sticking and burning.

===================== ROOM TEMPERATURE =====================

3 cups whole or low-fat milk

⅓ cup cream of rice (p. 463)

1½ cups whole or low-fat milk, or creamy milk (p. 254)

¼ cup dark raisins

3 cups prepared chopped fruits (such as blueberries, red raspberries, strawberries, bananas, mangoes, and cantaloupe)

¼ cup roasted slivered almonds (p. 463)

1. Place milk in an 8-cup glass measure or a 2½-quart microwave-safe dish. Cook, uncovered, at 100 percent power in a 650- to 700-watt carousel oven for 8 minutes (or until milk or water comes to a rolling boil). Remove from oven.

2. Wait until the liquid stops boiling, then carefully stir in cream of rice. Cook, uncovered, at 100 percent power for 5 minutes (or until cream of rice is cooked and thickens like custard). Remove from oven.

3. Stir milk and raisins into the cereal and spoon into 6 bowls. Distribute fruits and nuts on top and serve.

MADRAS STEAMED RICE CAKES

IDLEE

MICROWAVE

Yield
—12 idlees

Servings
—4 to 6

Preparation time
—10 minutes plus 4
hours 35 minutes
for soaking and fer-
menting

Cooking time
—3 minutes

Heat
—100 percent power

MW oven size
—650 to 700 watts

MW cookware
—One egg poacher/
muffin tray

Steamed cakes (muffins or breads) are the specialty of south India, and each region has its own version to tout. *Idlee,* popular in Tamil Nadu, is made by first making a batter of rice and white gram beans called *urad dal.* The batter is poured into muffin or egg-poacher trays and steamed until it puffs into spongy cakes. In the microwave these cakes are a pleasure to make as no steamers or steaming racks are needed. In just a few minutes they are cooked to an uncommon lightness! *Idlees* are traditionally accompanied with a coconut chutney (pp. 339–343) and a lentil vegetable stew (pp. 189–193) and served at breakfast, tiffin, a light lunch, or as a first course. Accompanied with Savory Coconut Sauce (p. 471), *idlee* is also served with Goanese and Mangalorean main courses.

=========== *ROOM TEMPERATURE* ===========

½ cup dried white gram
  beans (Urad dal)
1⅓ cups buttermilk
1 cup rice flour (p. 463)

½ teaspoon kosher salt
1⅓ teaspoons baking
  soda
Light vegetable oil for
  greasing

1. Place beans in a medium-size bowl and wash in several changes of water. Add enough water to cover the beans by at least 2 inches and soak for at least 4 hours or overnight. Drain, rinse, and drain again.

2. Pour ½ cup buttermilk into the container of a blender or food processor. Add beans and process until the contents are finely pureed into a smooth batter (3–4 minutes), adding more buttermilk as needed. Return batter to the bowl and blend in the remaining buttermilk and rice flour. Let batter rest for 30 min-

utes. The batter should be of pouring consistency; if not, stir in a little (1–2 tablespoons) buttermilk or water.

3. Stir in salt and baking soda and allow batter to foam, undisturbed, for 2 minutes. Pour batter by heaping tablespoonful into the 6 depressions of a lightly greased egg poacher/muffin tray, filling it halfway.

4. Cook, uncovered, at 100 percent power in a 650- to 700-watt carousel oven for 1 minute 30 seconds (or until *idlees* have risen and a toothpick inserted in the center comes out clean). Remove from oven, loosen *idlees* by running a paring knife along the edges, and unmold into a microwave-safe covered dish. Repeat with the remaining batter the same way.

NOTE *Idlee* may be made ahead and set aside for 6 hours at room temperature, for 3 days in the refrigerator, or frozen. When ready to serve, heat in a covered dish at 100 percent power until piping hot (2 minutes if at room temperature, 3 minutes if refrigerated, or 5 minutes if frozen).

BOMBAY SPICY LENTIL CAKES

DHOKLA

MICROWAVE

Yield
—16 dhokla
Servings
—6 to 8 as a main-
course bread; 8 to
16 as an appetizer
Preparation time
—5 minutes plus 4
hours 15 minutes
for soaking
Cooking time
—13 minutes
MW oven size
—650 to 700 watts
MW cookware
—One egg poacher/
muffin tray and
one 8-inch covered
skillet

Dhokla is the ingenious creation of the Gujarati cooks of western India. It is a steamed bread similar to *idlee* (p. 325), except in this recipe lentil batter is used. The batter, consisting of lentil puree, ginger, lemon juice, cayenne, and baking soda, is first steamed into a 9-inch cake. It is then cut into diamonds and served coated with mustard-, cumin-, and sesame-oil-perfumed dressing. It looks and feels like corn bread, except that the garnish of coriander, coconut, and chilies on top give the bread a tropical appeal.

Dhokla, called lentil cakes, are made with either lentils or mung beans. I prefer making them in muffin tins, thus eliminating the cutting step, which can be messy. *Dhokla* is good served at afternoon tea or tiffin. It also makes a lovely first course or appetizer. *Dhokla* goes well as a starch with all vegetable main courses.

══════════ ROOM TEMPERATURE ══════════

FOR THE BATTER:
1 cup dried yellow mung
    beans (p. 461)
1 cup plain yogurt
1 tablespoon lemon juice
½-inch piece fresh
    ginger, peeled
¼ teaspoon turmeric

¼ teaspoon cayenne
    pepper
2 tablespoons cream of
    rice (p. 463)
½ teaspoon kosher salt
1 teaspoon baking soda
Oil for greasing

FOR THE SPICE-INFUSED
    OIL:
3 tablespoons light vege-
    table oil

½ teaspoon mustard
    seeds
¼ teaspoon cumin seeds
1 teaspoon sesame seeds

Tiny pinch asafetida
(p. 481) (optional)

2 fresh hot green chilies,
stemmed, seeded, and
thinly sliced

FOR THE GARNISH:
¼ teaspoon paprika
2 tablespoons grated
or flaked coconut
(p. 449)
2 tablespoons chopped
fresh coriander

A combination of ¾
pound trimmed bean
sprouts, 1 cup finely
shredded radicchio,
and 1 finely shredded
endive (optional)

1. Put mung beans in a medium-size bowl and wash in several changes of water. Add enough water to cover by at least 2 inches. Soak beans for 4 hours or overnight. Drain, rinse, and drain again.

2. Put the beans, along with all the other ingredients for the batter except baking soda, into the container of a blender or food processor and process for several minutes until the contents are finely pureed into a smooth batter. Return batter to the bowl. Stir in baking soda. Let batter rest for 5 minutes.

3. Pour a heaping tablespoonful of batter into the 6 depressions of a lightly greased egg poacher/muffin tray, filling it halfway. Cook, uncovered, at 100 percent power in a 650- to 700-watt carousel oven for 2 minutes 30 seconds (or until batter is set and does not stick when touched with a finger). Remove from oven.

4. Loosen *dhokla* by running a sharp, thin knife along the edges and unmold. Arrange *dhokla* in a shallow microwave-safe covered dish and continue with the remaining batter the same way.

5. Heat the oil in an 8-inch microwave-safe covered skillet at 100 percent power for 3 minutes. Add mustard seeds and replace the lid. Cook at 100 percent power for 3 minutes (or until seeds pop). Uncover and add cumin and sesame. Cook at 100 percent for

45 seconds (or until sesame begins to color). Remove from oven and stir in asafetida and chilies.

6. To assemble *dhokla,* spread salad greens on a serving platter and arrange *dhokla* cakes on top. Pour the spice-infused oil over the *dhokla,* scraping all the spices with a rubber spatula. Sprinkle with paprika, coconut, and coriander and serve.

NOTE Dhokla may be made up to this stage and set aside at room temperature for 6 hours, refrigerated for 6 days, or frozen. When ready to serve, heat in a covered microwave-safe dish at 100 percent power until piping hot (2 minutes if at room temperature, 4 minutes if refrigerated, or 6 minutes if frozen). Remove from oven.

VARIATIONS

BOMBAY SPICY SPLIT PEA CAKES   Use American yellow split peas in place of mung beans.
BOMBAY SPICY SPLIT PEA CAKES WITH CRABMEAT   Fold ½ cup cooked flaked crabmeat into the batter. In this case you will have 18 muffins, to serve 9 to 18.

CEYLONESE STEAMED RICE CAKES
POTTOO

Sri Lanka (or Ceylon, as it used to be called) has its own version of steamed bread. Ceylonese rice cakes, called *pottoo,* are made with cream of rice and coconut milk, thus are sweeter and more aromatic. In addition, the Ceylonese fold beaten egg whites into the batter, rendering the cakes airy-light. *Pottoo* are generally served with spicy southern fish curries Madras Fish in Red Gravy (p. 91) or Mangalore Cayenne Shrimp (p. 97), sometimes accompanied with Savory Coconut Sauce (p. 471) or Fragrant Coconut Sauce (p. 403).

=============== ROOM TEMPERATURE ===============

1 cup cream of rice (p. 463)	1 cup coconut milk (p. 450)
⅛ teaspoon kosher salt	2 large egg whites
1 teaspoon baking powder	Oil for greasing

1. Combine cream of rice, salt, and baking powder in a medium-size bowl. Add coconut milk and mix with a beater. Set aside, covered, for 10 minutes.

2. Beat egg whites in a small bowl until stiff and fold into cream-of-rice batter. Pour a heaping tablespoon of batter into the 6 depressions of a lightly greased egg poacher/muffin tray, filling it halfway.

3. Cook, uncovered, at 100 percent power in a 650- to 700-watt carousel oven for 2 minutes (or until *pottoo* have risen and a toothpick inserted in the center comes out clean). Remove from oven, loosen *pottoo* by running a paring knife along the edges, and un-

MICROWAVE

Yield
—12 pottoo
Servings
—4 to 6
Preparation time
—15 minutes
Cooking time
—4 minutes
Heat
—100 percent power
MW oven size
—650 to 700 watts
MW cookware
—One egg poacher/ muffin tray

mold into a microwave-safe covered dish. Repeat with the remaining batter the same way.

NOTE   *Pottoo* may be made ahead and set aside for 2 hours at room temperature, for a day in the refrigerator, or frozen. When ready to serve, heat in a covered microwave-safe dish at 100 percent power until piping hot (2 minutes if at room temperature, 3 minutes if refrigerated, or 5 minutes if frozen).

STEAMED RICE CAKES
WITH HERBS
TAMIL POTTOO

MICROWAVE

Yield
— *12 pottoo*
Servings
— *4 to 6*
Preparation time
— *15 minutes*
Cooking time
— *4 minutes*
Heat
— *100 percent power*
MW oven size
— *650 to 700 watts*
MW cookware
— *One egg poacher/*
muffin tray

These rice cakes are similar to Ceylonese Steamed Rice Cakes (p. 330), except that in this recipe a few tablespoons of chopped coriander, fresh ginger, and green chilies are folded into the batter. During steaming in the microwave the rice cakes are infused with the fragrance of the herbs and become uncommonly flavorful. This very herbal and light-tasting *pottoo,* popular with the Tamilians of Sri Lanka, is good served with all hot and spicy southern curries such as Madras Fish in Red Gravy (p. 91), Mangalore Cayenne Shrimp (p. 97), or Fiery Mangalorian Eggplant (p. 213). For a sweet accent, accompany them with Fragrant Coconut Sauce (p. 403).

=========== ROOM TEMPERATURE ===========

1 cup cream of rice (p. 463)	2 fresh hot green chilies, stemmed, seeded, and thinly sliced
⅛ teaspoon kosher salt	1 cup coconut milk (p. 450)
1 teaspoon baking powder	2 egg whites
2 teaspoons finely chopped fresh ginger	Light vegetable oil for greasing
2 tablespoons finely chopped fresh coriander	

1. Combine cream of rice, salt, baking powder, ginger, coriander, and chilies in a medium-size bowl. Add coconut milk and mix with a beater. Set aside, covered, for 10 minutes.

2. Beat egg whites in a small bowl until hard peaks form and fold into cream-of-rice batter. Pour a heap-

ing tablespoon of batter into the 6 depressions of a lightly greased egg poacher/muffin tray, filling it halfway.

3. Cook, uncovered, at 100 percent power in a 650- to 700-watt carousel oven for 2 minutes (or until *pottoos* have risen and a toothpick inserted in the center comes out clean). Remove from oven, loosen *pottoo* by running a paring knife along the edges, and unmold into a microwave-safe covered dish. Repeat with the remaining batter.

NOTE *Pottoo* may be made ahead and set aside for 2 hours at room temperature, for a day in the refrigerator, or frozen. When ready to serve, heat in a covered microwave-safe dish at 100 percent power until piping hot (2 minutes if at room temperature, 3 minutes if refrigerated, or 5 minutes if frozen).

MALABAR SHRIMP AND RICE CAKES

MALABAR MEEN POTTOO

MICROWAVE

Yield
  —18 pottoo
Servings
  —6 to 8
Preparation time
  —5 minutes
Cooking time
  —10 minutes
Heat
  —100 percent power
MW oven size
  —650 to 700 watts
MW cookware
  —One egg poacher/
    muffin tray and one
    8-inch skillet

Residents of Malabar, along the western coast of India, also make *pottoo,* which they flavor with any number of ingredients, such as fresh coconut, herbs, sweet bananas, and fish and shellfish. The *pottoo* flavored with fish or shrimps are, without question, the most popular. Shrimp *pottoo* cook up in just a few minutes in the microwave. The shrimps remain tender and moist without overcooking. Serve *pottoo* with Savory Coconut Sauce (p. 471) or any of the lentil-vegetable stews such as Eggplant-Lentil Stew with Tamarind and Garlic (p. 191), Vishal's Cauliflower Sambar Stew (p. 194), or Malabar Vegetable Stew with Coconut (p. 187).

ROOM TEMPERATURE

1 cup cream of rice (p. 463)

1¾ cups buttermilk

2 tablespoons light sesame oil or light vegetable oil

1 small onion, peeled and finely chopped

2 tablespoons finely chopped fresh ginger

2 tablespoons finely chopped fresh coriander

2 fresh hot green chilies, stemmed and minced with seeds

1 cup (8 ounces) peeled, cleaned, and finely chopped uncooked shrimps

⅓ teaspoon kosher salt

1 teaspoon baking powder

Light vegetable oil for greasing

1. Place cream of rice in a medium-size bowl. Add buttermilk and mix with a beater. Set aside, covered, for 15 minutes.

2. Heat the oil in a 8-inch microwave-safe skillet at 100 percent power in a 650- to 700-watt carousel oven for 2 minutes. Add onion and cook, uncovered, at 100 percent power for 2 minutes (or until onions are soft). Remove from oven.

3. Add oil-onion mixture to the batter along with ginger, coriander, chilies, and shrimps and mix well. Stir in salt and baking powder. Pour batter by heaping tablespoonful into the 6 depressions of a lightly greased egg poacher/muffin tray, filling it halfway.

4. Cook, uncovered, at 100 percent power in a 650- to 700-watt carousel oven for 2 minutes (or until *pottoos* have risen and a toothpick inserted in the center comes out clean). Remove from oven, loosen *potto* by running a paring knife along the edges, and unmold into a microwave-safe covered dish. Repeat with the remaining batter the same way.

NOTE   *Meen pottoo* may be made ahead and set aside in the refrigerator for a day or frozen. When ready to serve, heat in a microwave-safe covered dish at 100 percent power until piping hot (3 minutes if refrigerated or 5 minutes if frozen).

CHUTNEYS
AND DIPPING SAUCES

The word *chutney* is the anglicized spelling and pronunciation of *chatni,* a noun derived from the ancient Indian language Sanskrit. *Chatni* comes from the verb *chatna,* meaning "to taste" or "to lick." Appropriately, all chutneys are flavored assertively to bring taste buds alive.

Chutneys, in general, can be grouped into two categories—soupy like a dip or chunky like a relish. In the Moghul tradition chutneys are used two ways: as a sauce with dry food, such as cool yogurt sauce with *tandoori* Cornish hen or fragrant mint sauce with ginger chicken. Fruity relishlike chutneys, on the other hand, are paired carefully with main dishes—to enhance and intensify the complex experience of the meal. Green mango chutney, for example, with braised cod in aromatic Moghul sauce, peach chutney with raisins and walnuts with duck vendaloo.

When most people see a nice piece of fruit they think of eating it; I think of the chutneys and dipping sauces that can be made from it. These Indian condiments—which combine fruits, spices, herbs, sweeteners, and vegetables—range in flavor from sweet and mellow to fiery hot. And although they are obviously Indian in origin, they make great accompaniments to traditional American roasted and grilled foods. Try pairing Sweet Cranberry Pistachio Chutney with California Black Figs with a Thanksgiving turkey or Christmas goose; Peach Chutney with Raisins and Walnuts or Fragrant Mint Sauce with grilled lamb; or Pineapple Apricot Chutney with glazed ham.

When an American friend of mine first looked at a chutney recipe she became intimidated because the ingredients list comprised a combination of fruits, nuts, sugar, vinegar, and a number of spices. (Given that the only chutney she'd ever had was a commercial variety, she also questioned whether the work would be worth the effort). But, in the microwave, preparing chutney means combining the ingredients and cooking them until the fruit just "gives," or softens. It is a one-step process and could not be easier.

All of these chutneys are made with fresh fruits or vegetables and are best made when the fresh ingredients are in season and at their peak of flavor. Since there is no season without some fruit, it is always possible to make chutney. And all of these chutneys keep for several months in the refrigerator without any seal. This is due to the preserving abilities of the spices, which also allow for the reduction of sugar.

These chutneys and dipping sauces are so visually appealing and appetite stimulating that it would be lovely to present several of them, as done in the Indian tradition, on a lazy Susan or carousel to accompany various dishes.

INSTANT COCONUT CHUTNEY

TENGA CHATNI

Tiny shimmering mustard seeds bathed in oil dot the juicy minced coconut puree in this classic south Indian coconut chutney. South Indian delicacies such as *idlee* (p. 325) and *pottoo* (pp. 330–335) are never served without this chutney. There are many variations to it, the most popular featuring hot green chilies and fresh ginger. I make this chutney in just a few minutes in the microwave, using supermarket sweetened coconut flakes. The result is unbelievably good. I prefer using sweetened coconut flakes because fresh coconut available in America lacks natural sweetness. Besides, it gives me the chance to use more hot chilies, which produce an incredible palate-tingling sensation. If, however, you desire a less sweet chutney, rinse the coconut flakes to remove clinging sugar before using. This coconut chutney is delicious with fish and shellfish curries, especially salmon, shrimps, and scallops.

MICROWAVE

Yield
 —1⅓ cups
Preparation time
 —3 minutes
Cooking time
 —6 minutes
Heat
 —100 percent power
MW oven size
 —650 to 700 watts
MW cookware
 —One 8-inch covered skillet

1 cup plain yogurt
1 cup packed sweetened
 coconut flakes (p. 449)
1 fresh hot green chili,
 stemmed and cut into
 1-inch pieces

½-inch piece fresh ginger, peeled
1 tablespoon light sesame oil or light vegetable oil
½ teaspoon mustard seeds

1. Put yogurt, coconut, chili, and ginger into the container of a blender or food processor and process until the contents are finely pureed. Transfer into a bowl.

2. Heat the oil in an 8-inch microwave-safe covered skillet at 100 percent power in a 650- to 700-watt carousel oven for 3 minutes. Uncover, add mustard seeds, and replace the lid. Cook at 100 percent power for 3 minutes (or until seeds pop). Remove from oven, uncover, and pour the spice-infused oil on the coconut chutney, scraping the skillet with a rubber spatula. Mix well and serve.

NOTE   The chutney keeps well stored in a covered container for up to 10 days in the refrigerator or a year in the freezer.

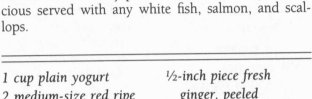

INSTANT TOMATO-FLAVORED COCONUT CHUTNEY

TENGA TAKKALIPAYAM CHATNI

MICROWAVE

Yield
  —*1⅓ cups*
Preparation time
  —*2 minutes*
Cooking time
  —*6 minutes*
Heat
  —*100 percent power*
MW oven size
  —*650 to 700 watts*
MW cookware
  —*One 8-inch covered skillet*

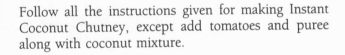

This coconut chutney is prepared exactly like Instant Coconut Chutney (p. 339), except that in this recipe pureed tomatoes are added to lend a piquant flavor and a beautiful rosy-pink hue. This chutney is delicious served with any white fish, salmon, and scallops.

1 cup plain yogurt
2 medium-size red ripe
  tomatoes, quartered
1 cup packed sweetened
  coconut flakes (p. 449)
1 fresh hot green chili,
  stemmed and cut into
  1-inch pieces

½-inch piece fresh
  ginger, peeled
1 tablespoon light sesame
  oil or light vegetable
  oil
½ teaspoon mustard
  seeds

Follow all the instructions given for making Instant Coconut Chutney, except add tomatoes and puree along with coconut mixture.

HYDERABAD COCONUT
MINT CHUTNEY

NARIAL CHATNI

MICROWAVE

Yield
  —1⅓ cups
Preparation time
  —2 minutes
Cooking time
  —4 minutes
MW oven size
  —650 to 700 watts
MW cookware
  —One 8-inch covered
    skillet

Coconut chutney is a southern specialty while mint is a north Indian or, more precisely, Moghul ingredient. How have these gotten into the same pot? Hyderabad, a city (a pocket) in Hindu south India, is predominantly Moslem because it was under Moghul rule for centuries. Its cuisine, therefore, reflects cross-cultural influences. This chutney from Hyderabad combines not only mint and coconut but also spices from both regions. It is very fragrant, very delicious, and very Hyderabadish. It is perfect served with kabobs, *tandoori* dishes, rice pilafs, and Moghul specialties.

1 cup plain yogurt	1 large clove garlic, peeled
2 teaspoons lemon juice	½-inch piece fresh ginger, peeled
1 cup packed sweetened coconut flakes (p. 449)	1 tablespoon light sesame oil or light vegetable oil
¼ cup lightly packed fresh, or 1 tablespoon crushed dried, mint	½ teaspoon dry mustard
4 fresh hot green chilies, stemmed	½ teaspoon ground cumin
	Kosher salt to taste, if desired

1. Put yogurt, lemon juice, coconut, mint, chilies, garlic, and ginger into the container of a blender or food processor and process until the contents are finely pureed. Transfer the mixture into a bowl.

2. Heat the oil in an 8-inch microwave-safe skillet at 100 percent power in a 650- to 700-watt carousel

oven for 3 minutes. Remove from oven. Add mustard, and cumin. Mix rapidly for 10 seconds, then pour the entire spice-infused oil on the coconut mixture, scraping the skillet with a rubber spatula to get all the spices. Add salt, mix well, and serve.

NOTE   The chutney keeps well, stored in a covered container, for up to 10 days in the refrigerator or a year in the freezer.

SWEET CRANBERRY PISTACHIO CHUTNEY WITH CALIFORNIA BLACK FIGS

KARONDA CHATNI

MICROWAVE

Yield
  —3 cups
Preparation time
  —5 minutes
Cooking time
  —9 minutes
Heat
  —100 percent power
MW oven size
  —650 to 700 watts
MW cookware
  —One 2½ quart cov-
   ered casserole or
   soufflé dish

This fruit-filled chutney is one of my very favorites because not only is it wonderfully flavored and amazingly easy to prepare—it is extremely versatile. Try it with *tandoori* dishes, kabobs, roast pork, or your Thanksgiving turkey. It's great on breakfast toast too.

=== ROOM TEMPERATURE ===

1 12-ounce package cranberries
1 medium-size orange
2 tablespoons lemon juice
2 tablespoons finely chopped shallots
1 teaspoon dried ginger powder
1 cup sugar
¾ teaspoon kosher salt
½ teaspoon cinnamon
1 teaspoon ground cumin
⅓ teaspoon cayenne pepper
1 teaspoon mustard seeds, lightly crushed
⅓ cup shelled raw unsalted pistachio nuts
⅔ cup black California figs, or any other fig, or dark raisins

1. Pick through cranberries and remove all stems and rotting berries. Dice orange into ¼-inch pieces with the skin and white pith. Pick out seeds and discard.

2. Combine all the ingredients, except pistachios and figs, in a 2½-quart microwave-safe casserole and cover with the lid. Cook at 100 percent power in a 650- to 700-watt carousel oven for 4 minutes. Uncover and continue cooking at 100 percent power for 5 minutes

(or until chutney is boiling and cranberries begin to burst open), stirring once. Remove from oven.

3. Uncover, stir in pistachios and figs, and replace cover. When completely cool, spoon chutney into sterilized jars. Seal or refrigerate. Let chutney ripen for a day before serving.

NOTE   The chutney keeps well, stored in a covered container, in the refrigerator for several months.

SPICY-SWEET CRANBERRY WALNUT CHUTNEY

KARONDA CHATNI

MICROWAVE

Yield
—*3 cups*
Preparation time
—*5 minutes*
Cooking time
—*9 minutes*
Heat
—*100 percent power*
MW oven size
—*650 to 700 watts*
MW cookware
—*One 2½-quart covered casserole or soufflé dish*

Karonda are sour-tasting berries that resemble our American cranberries in shape and taste. Their high acidity makes them ideally suited for chutneys. Once again, the microwave is magical for this recipe. The chutney is a simple process—combine all the ingredients and cook. Serve this spicy-chunky cinnamon-scented chutney with pork, duck, or Cornish hens.

=========== ROOM TEMPERATURE ===========

1 12-ounce package cranberries (about 3 cups)	1 teaspoon cayenne pepper
1 medium-size orange	1 teaspoon mustard seeds, lightly crushed
¼ cup chopped red onion	½ teaspoon celery seeds
3 tablespoons julienned fresh ginger	¾ teaspoon kosher salt
1½ cups sugar	¼ cup dark raisins
¾ teaspoon ground cinnamon	¾ cup chopped walnuts

1. Pick through cranberries and remove all stems and rotting berries. Dice orange into ¼-inch pieces with the skin and white pith. Pick out seeds and discard.

2. Combine all the ingredients except raisins and walnuts in a 2½-quart microwave-safe casserole and cover with the lid. Cook at 100 percent power in a 650- to 700-watt carousel oven for 4 minutes. Uncover and continue cooking at 100 percent power for 5 minutes (or until chutney is boiling and cranberries begin to burst open), stirring once. Remove from oven.

3. Uncover, stir in raisins and walnuts, and replace cover. When completely cool, spoon chutney into sterilized jars. Seal or refrigerate. Let chutney ripen for a day before serving.

NOTE   The chutney keeps well, stored in a covered container, in the refrigerator for several months.

GREEN MANGO CHUTNEY

AAM CHATNI

MICROWAVE

Yield
—2 cups
Cooking time
—15 minutes
Heat
—100 percent power
MW oven size
—650 to 700 watts
MW cookware
—One 10-inch skillet

Around March is the time to make this classic mango chutney when hard, unripe green mangoes start to appear at vegetable stores. It is sweetish-hot and very fragrant—a great accompaniment with all lamb preparations.

ROOM TEMPERATURE

1½ cups sugar
½ cup wine vinegar
¾ teaspoon minced garlic
1 tablespoon dried ginger powder
2½ teaspoons dry mustard
½ teaspoon allspice
½ teaspoon cayenne pepper

1 large (¾ to 1 pound) firm, unripe or medium-ripe mango, peeled, pitted, and sliced into ¼-inch-thick wedges
¼ cup sliced almonds
¼ cup dark raisins

Combine sugar, vinegar, garlic, ginger, mustard, allspice, and cayenne in a 10-inch microwave-safe skillet. Cook, uncovered, at 100 percent power in a 650- to 700-watt carousel oven for 10 minutes (or until sauce turns thick and syrupy), stirring twice. Add mango slices, mix, and continue cooking, uncovered, at 100 percent power for 5 minutes (or until mangoes look translucent). Remove from oven, stir in almonds and raisins, and serve or spoon into sterilized jars. When completely cool, cover and store.

NOTE   The chutney keeps well, stored in a covered container, in the refrigerator for up to 4 weeks.

PEACH CHUTNEY WITH RAISINS AND WALNUTS

KHOOBANI CHATNI

MICROWAVE

Yield
　—4 cups
Preparation time
　—3 minutes
Cooking time
　—15 minutes
Heat
　—100 percent power
MW oven size
　—650 to 700 watts
MW cookware
　*—One 2½-quart cov-
　　ered casserole or
　　soufflé dish*

I still remember the time I made this chutney and took it to some friends for dinner, where it was instantly devoured upon arrival by spoonfuls—like a dessert! This very addictive fruity chutney studded with mustard, fennel, and cumin is meant to be served with all traditional Indian meals. I like it with chicken, duck, and pork. It's a snap in the microwave. All you need to do is make syrup and cook the fruits in it. Remember not to overcook the peaches as they will turn mushy. The flavor will not be altered but the chutney will not look as pretty. Make this only with fresh tree-ripened juicy peaches available in season at green markets or roadside farmers' stands—supermarket cold-storage peaches will not yield flavorful results.

=========== *ROOM TEMPERATURE* ===========

1½ cups sugar

¼ cup white vinegar

1 teaspoon ground cumin

1 teaspoon red pepper flakes

½ teaspoon whole black peppercorns

¼ teaspoon ajowan seeds (p. 481) or ½ teaspoon dried oregano

1 teaspoon fennel seeds

1 teaspoon coriander seeds

½ teaspoon kosher salt

½ teaspoon mustard seeds

4 cups (2 pounds) peeled, pitted, and sliced peaches dressed in 2 tablespoons lemon juice

1 cup roughly chopped walnuts

1 cup dark raisins

1. Combine all the ingredients except peaches, walnuts, and raisins in a 2½-quart microwave-safe cas-

serole and cover with the lid. Cook at 100 percent power in a 650- to 700-watt carousel oven for 10 minutes (or until syrup is thick and sticks to the bottom of the spoon). Remove from oven.

2. Uncover and fold in peaches. Cook, uncovered, at 100 percent power for 5 minutes (or until peaches are cooked but not mushy). Remove from oven and set aside, covered with the lid. When cool, carefully fold in walnuts and raisins. Spoon chutney into sterilized jars. Seal or refrigerate. Let chutney ripen for a day before serving.

NOTE   The chutney keeps well, stored in a covered container, in the refrigerator for several months.

PINEAPPLE APRICOT CHUTNEY

ANNANAAS KHOOBANI CHATNI

MICROWAVE

Yield
  —2 cups
Cooking time
  —23 minutes
Heat
  —100 percent power
MW oven size
  —650 to 700 watts
MW cookware
  —One 2½-quart cas-
  serole or soufflé dish

I was delightfully pleased to discover that this classic pineapple chutney can be made using canned pineapple and still taste straight from heaven! Pineapple, with its strong, aromatic flesh, has a unique ability to blend with the most assertive of spices, such as cumin, mustard, fennel, and ginger in this chutney. The red pepper is added to balance sweetness and round off flavors. Apricots and walnuts absorb excess juices, lending the chutney a chunky texture. This too is simple to make in a microwave. All you do is combine all ingredients and cook until done. Serve this fragrant chutney with pork, chicken, and seafood main courses.

=== ROOM TEMPERATURE ===

1 20-ounce can pineapple chunks in unsweetened pineapple juice

⅓ cup lemon juice

1½ cups sugar

1 teaspoon cumin seeds

1 teaspoon fennel seeds

1 teaspoon mustard seeds

1 teaspoon whole black peppercorns

½ teaspoon red pepper flakes

1 tablespoon julienne of fresh ginger or 1 teaspoon dried ginger powder

1 cup coarsely chopped walnuts

1 cup sliced dried apricots

⅓ cup dried fruits (black or red currants, cranberries, or raisins)

1. Combine pineapple, lemon juice, and sugar in a 2½-quart microwave-safe dish. Cook, uncovered, at 100 percent power in a 650- to 700-watt carousel oven for 13 minutes (or until chutney is boiling and

pineapple is cooked), stirring 3 times. Remove from oven.

2. Add cumin, fennel, mustard, peppercorns, red pepper, and ginger and mix well. Cook, uncovered, at 100 percent power for 10 minutes (or until syrup thickens and chutney develops a sheen). Remove from oven. Fold in walnuts, apricots, and dried fruits and spoon into sterilized jars. When completely cool, cover with lids. Let chutney ripen for a day before serving.

NOTE   The chutney keeps well, stored in a covered container, for 2 weeks at room temperature and 6 months in the refrigerator.

SWEET PERSIMMON AND PLUM CHUTNEY WITH CINNAMON

PERSIMMON KI CHATNI

MICROWAVE

Yield
—4 cups
Preparation time
—3 minutes
Cooking time
—30 minutes
Heat
—100 percent power
MW oven size
—650 to 700 watts
MW cookware
—One 5-quart covered casserole

This pulpy scarlet chutney of tart plums, sweet, gingery persimmon and cashews is vivid and sensuous. Interestingly, the microwave affects the two fruits quite differently. While the plums soften and almost disintegrate when cooked, the persimmons firm up. As a result, the chutney has a delightful thick and chunky texture. It is great with chicken, duck, fish, and seafood curries.

=== ROOM TEMPERATURE ===

8 medium-size garlic cloves, peeled

2-inch piece (2 ounces) fresh ginger, peeled

1 cup wine vinegar

2 cups sugar

1½ pounds (9 medium-size) red plums, pitted and sliced into ¾-inch wedges

1⅓ pounds (4 medium-size) persimmons, peeled and quartered

2 teaspoons dried ginger powder

2 teaspoons dry mustard

½ teaspoon ground cloves

2 teaspoons kosher salt

1 teaspoon cayenne pepper

2 teaspoons paprika

⅔ cup raw whole unsalted cashew nuts or slivered almonds

1. Process garlic and ginger with ½ cup vinegar in a blender or food processor until the contents are finely pureed. Pour the mixture into a 5-quart microwave-safe casserole. Add remaining vinegar and sugar and mix well.

2. Cook, uncovered, at 100 percent power in a 650- to 700-watt carousel oven for 15 minutes (or until liquid turns syrupy), stirring 2 times. Remove from oven.

3. Add all other ingredients except cashew nuts and cover with the lid. Cook at 100 percent power for 15 minutes (or until contents look thick and glazed like jam), stirring twice. Remove from oven. Uncover, fold in cashew nuts, spoon into sterilized jars, and seal or refrigerate. Let chutney ripen for a day before serving.

NOTE   The chutney keeps well, stored in a covered container, in the refrigerator for up to 4 months.

SWEET DATE AND PLUM CHUTNEY

KHAJOOR CHATNI

MICROWAVE

Yield
   —6 cups
Cooking time
   —25 minutes
Heat
   —100 percent power
MW oven size
   —650 to 700 watts
MW cookware
   —One 5-quart covered casserole

This classic Moghul chutney from Kashmir is made with tart mountain plums from Kashmir in the Himalayan mountains of northern India and the much-adored sugar-sweet dates from Afghanistan (the native land of the Moghuls). It is laced with a delicate Moghul spice blend: cardamom, pungent coriander, mustard, and fiery cayenne. The walnuts and raisins absorb the excess juices, lending it a chunky texture. This sweet, hot, and very fragrant chutney is wonderful served with all Moghul and north Indian braised and stewed curries, *kaftas, kormas, kabas,* and *tandoori* dishes.

========== ROOM TEMPERATURE ==========

¾ cup wine vinegar

1 cup sugar

1 cup chopped onions

2 tablespoons finely chopped garlic

1 tablespoon grated or crushed fresh ginger

2 medium-size lemons, sliced, pitted, and finely chopped with the skin

1 tablespoon ground coriander

1 tablespoon dry mustard

1 teaspoon ground cardamom

1 teaspoon cayenne pepper

2 pounds (12 medium-size) red plums, pitted and sliced into ¾-inch wedges

10 ounces Afghanistan or California pitted dates, chopped

1 cup chopped walnuts

1 cup dark raisins

1. Combine vinegar, sugar, onion, garlic, ginger, lemon, coriander, mustard, cardamom, and cayenne

in a 5-quart microwave-safe casserole and cover with the lid. Cook at 100 percent power in 650- to 700-watt carousel oven for 15 minutes (or until liquid is thick and syrupy), stirring twice. Remove from oven.

2. Uncover, stir in plums and dates, and replace cover. Cook, covered, at 100 percent power for 10 minutes (or until plums are cooked through), stirring once. Remove from oven. Uncover, stir in walnuts and raisins, spoon into sterilized jars, and seal or refrigerate. Let chutney ripen for a day before serving.

NOTE   The chutney keeps well, stored in a covered container, in the refrigerator for several months.

SPICY TOMATO GINGER CHUTNEY

GARAM TAMATAR CHATNI

MICROWAVE

Yield
—*2 cups*
Cooking time
—*25 minutes*
Heat
—*100 percent power*
MW oven size
—*650 to 700 watts*
MW cookware
—*One 2½-quart cas-
serole or soufflé dish*

Make this chutney in summer, when red vine-ripened tomatoes are abundant. It is astonishingly easy to pre-pare—all one needs to do is combine half the ingre-dients and cook, add the remaining ingredients, and continue cooking until done. Unlike other chutneys which are sweet, this one is hot and spicy. It is good served with steamed or baked fish and chicken. You can also stir the chutney into any of the sauces for enhancing flavor. Combined with an equal portion of apricot puree (p. 473) or *vendaloo* sauce (p. 470), it makes an irresistible barbecue sauce.

ROOM TEMPERATURE

2 pounds red ripe toma-
toes, peeled, seeded,
and sliced into wedges
½ cup chopped onion
1 teaspoon minced garlic
¼ cup julienned fresh
ginger
¼ cup fresh lemon juice
or cider vinegar

1 teaspoon dried ginger
powder
1 teaspoon dry mustard
¼ teaspoon ground
cloves
2 teaspoons cayenne
pepper
1 teaspoon paprika
2 tablespoons sugar
2 teaspoons kosher salt

1. Combine tomatoes, onion, and garlic in a 2½-quart microwave-safe dish. Cook, uncovered, at 100 per-cent power in a 650- to 700-watt carousel oven for 10 minutes (or until tomatoes are cooked), stirring twice. Remove from oven.

2. Add all other ingredients and mix well. Cook, un-covered, for 15 minutes (or until sauce looks thick and glossy), stirring 3 times. Remove from oven and

pour into sterilized jars. When completely cool, refrigerate.

NOTE The jam will keep well, stored in a covered container, for several weeks in the refrigerator or up to 4 months in the freezer.

SPICY CRANBERRY SPREAD

TOKKOO

A very hot and spicy spread fragrant with mustard oil. This is a perfect accompaniment to subtle Moghul dishes that need an additional punch.

=============== *ROOM TEMPERATURE* ===============

1 12-ounce bag cran-
  berries
2 teaspoons mustard
  seeds
1 teaspoon fenugreek
  seeds (p.483)
1½ tablespoons cayenne
  pepper
½ teaspoon turmeric

¼ teaspoon ground asa-
  fetida (p. 481) or ¾
  teaspoon minced garlic
⅔ cup mustard oil, light
  sesame oil, or olive oil
2 tablespoons lemon juice
2 teaspoons kosher salt

1. Pick through cranberries and remove all stems and rotting berries. Mince berries in a food processor or by using a knife and reserve.

2. Grind mustard and fenugreek seeds in a coffee grinder until finely powdered and transfer into a small bowl. Add cayenne, turmeric, and asafetida or garlic and set aside.

3. Heat 4 tablespoons oil in a 10-inch microwave-safe skillet at 100 percent power in a 650- to 700-watt oven for 3 minutes. Remove from oven. Stir in spice mixture, then add the remaining oil. Cook at 100 percent power for 2 minutes or until the oil is hot. Remove from oven.

4. Add cranberries, lemon juice, and salt and stir to mix. Cook for 15 minutes (or until oil separates from cranberries), stirring twice. Remove from oven and

spoon into sterilized jars. When completely cool, refrigerate or freeze.

NOTE The cranberry spread keeps well, stored in a covered container, for up to 12 weeks in the refrigerator or a year frozen.

LEMONS IN PEPPERED SYRUP

MEETHA NIMBOO ACHAAR

MICROWAVE

Yield
  —6 cups
Preparation time
  —5 minutes
Cooking time
  —28 minutes
Heat
  —100 percent power
MW oven size
  —650 to 700 watts
MW cookware
  *—One 3-quart covered
    casserole*

In the past I was reluctant to make this sweet lemon pickle because it called for an unusual cooking step. The lemon slices had to be placed in the sun to soften (which generally took anywhere from three to seven days) before they could be combined with cumin-and-black-pepper-flavored syrup and pickled. In the microwave I can soften the lemons in four minutes. In fact, the entire pickle is ready within thirty minutes! Serve these sweet peppery lemon slices with all north Indian main curries, particularly fish, shellfish, chicken, and vegetarian entrees. You can also serve it with meat or tomatoes in pita pockets. Packed in attractive jars it makes a beautiful Christmas gift.

=== *ROOM TEMPERATURE* ===

*6 large (2 pounds)
  lemons*
½ cup kosher salt
*2 tablespoons cumin
  seeds, crushed*
*2 tablespoons black
  peppercorns, crushed*
*1 teaspoon ajowan seeds
  (p. 481) or 1 teaspoon
  dried thyme*

*1 cup lemon juice (from
  4 to 5 juicy lemons)*
3½ cups sugar
*20 dried whole hot red
  chili pods*
*¾ cup (4 ounces)
  California pitted dates,
  sliced into julienne
  strips*

1. Cut lemons into eighths or ⅛-inch-thick slices. Carefully remove seeds and discard. Put lemons into a 3-quart microwave-safe casserole. Add salt, cumin, pepper, and ajowan, toss well, and cover with the lid.

2. Cook at 100 percent power in a 650- to 700-watt carousel oven for 4 minutes (or until lemon looks slightly limp and turns dull yellow).

3. Remove from oven, transfer lemon slices with a slotted spoon into a bowl, and reserve. Add lemon juice and sugar to the casserole and mix well. Cook, uncovered, at 100 percent power for 20 minutes (or until solution turns thick and syrupy). Remove from oven.

4. Add lemon slices and their accumulated juices, pepper pods, and dates and mix well. Cook, uncovered, at 100 percent power for 4 minutes (or until contents are bubbling hot). Remove from oven. Spoon lemon slices and syrup into sterilized jars. When completely cool, cover with the lid.

NOTE   The pickle will keep well, stored in a covered container, for a year at room temperature.

SWEET AND SPICY PUNJAB VEGETABLE PICKLE

PAHADI ACHAAR

MICROWAVE

Yield
—5 cups
Preparation time
—11 minutes
Cooking time
—30 minutes
Heat
—100 percent power
MW oven size
—650 to 700 watts
MW cookware
—One 5-quart covered
casserole

Julienne pieces of carrot and turnip and florets of cauliflower are coated with a garlicky spice paste and steeped in hot mustard oil in this rustic sweetish-hot pickle from Amritsar, the home of the sacred Golden Temple of the Sikhs in Punjab province in northern India. The microwave not only cooks the vegetables in this pickle to perfect crunchy crispness but also cuts short many cooking steps. Since the vegetables are blanched without any water, there is no added moisture. As a result, the steps to evaporate moisture—sun-drying for two days and frying in oil—are eliminated. Besides, the vegetables taste more flavorful. I love this pickle with robust north Indian curries, *tandoori* dishes, and kabobs. For a light meal you can also serve this pickle as a highly seasoned vegetable with a rice pilaf and yogurt *raita*.

ROOM TEMPERATURE

5 small (¾ pound) carrots

4 medium-size (1 pound) white turnips

1 small head (1¼ pounds) cauliflower

1 medium-size (¼ pound) onion

6 large cloves garlic

4-inch piece fresh ginger, peeled

1¼ cups mustard oil, olive oil, or light vegetable oil

¾ teaspoon ground cloves

1¼ teaspoons ground cardamom

1 teaspoon turmeric

1 tablespoon cayenne pepper

2 teaspoons kosher salt   *¼ cup unsulfured*
¼ cup light brown sugar   *molasses*

1. Peel carrots and turnips and cut them into ½ × ½ × 2-inch pieces. Cut the stem off the cauliflower and separate or cut florets into 1-inch pieces.

2. Pile vegetables in a 5-quart microwave-safe casserole and cover with the lid. Cook at 100 percent power in a 650- to 700-watt carousel oven for 9 minutes (or until vegetables are cooked but still very crisp). Remove from oven. Transfer vegetables to a baking sheet lined with paper towels and drain.

3. Peel onion, garlic, and ginger, cut all three into large pieces, and place in the container of a blender or food processor. Add ¾ cup oil and process until finely pureed. Transfer the puree into the casserole and stir in the remaining oil. Cook, uncovered, at 100 percent power for 13 minutes (or until seasonings are cooked and lightly browned), stirring twice. Remove from oven.

4. Add clove, cardamom, turmeric, and cayenne pepper, mixing well. When spices stop sizzling (about 30 seconds), add salt, brown sugar, and molasses and stir to mix. Cook, uncovered, at 100 percent power for 8 minutes (or until sauce is bubbling and thick).

5. Remove from oven. Add blanched vegetables and mix thoroughly. Cook, uncovered, at 100 percent power for 7 minutes (or until oil begins to separate and float on top of the sauce). Remove from oven, spoon into sterilized jars, and seal. Or, alternatively, when completely cool, refrigerate.

NOTE   The pickle will keep well, stored in a covered container, for several months in the refrigerator.

COOL YOGURT SAUCE
DAHI CHATNI

MICROWAVE

Yield
 —1¼ cups
Preparation time
 —2 minutes

A refreshing dipping sauce to serve with *tandoori* dishes or kabobs to provide additional moisture and a cool herbal touch. You can also thin out the yogurt sauce with water, adjust seasonings, and serve as a delicious chilled soup for two people.

1 cup plain yogurt
2 teaspoons sugar
Kosher salt to taste, if
  desired
¼ teaspoon ground
  roasted cumin seeds
  (p. 465), garam mas-
  ala (p. 478), or curry
  powder (p. 479)

1 tablespoon chopped
  fresh, or 1 teaspoon
  crushed dried, mint
1 small cucumber,
  peeled, seeded, and
  finely grated
1 tablespoon dried fruit
  (currants, blueberries,
  cranberries, or raisins)
  (optional)

Combine all the ingredients in a bowl until thoroughly blended. Refrigerate and chill before serving. Yogurt sauce is at its best when made fresh just before serving.

FRAGRANT MINT SAUCE

PODINA CHATNI

MICROWAVE

Yield
  —2 cups
Preparation time
  —3 minutes

Mint sauce (or chutney) is one of the two most popular chutneys served in Indian restaurants in America today (tamarind being the other). A Moghul meal is almost unthinkable without this chutney because it adds a characteristic herbal fragrance to the palate. This version of mint chutney is thin and saucelike, hence great served as a dipping condiment with finger foods such as Sesame Shrimp (p. 13), Bombay Coconut Shrimp (p. 11), Ginger Chicken Kabob (p. 109), or Indian Beef Sausage Kabob (p. 138). It is also good with *tandoori* dishes.

⅔ cup white vinegar
¼ cup sugar
1 teaspoon kosher salt
2–6 fresh hot green chilies, stemmed and cut into 1-inch pieces
1-inch cube fresh ginger, peeled and cut into large pieces
¼ teaspoon ground roasted cumin seeds (p. 465)
1 cup tightly packed, coarsely chopped fresh coriander leaves and stems

1 small (⅓ pound) green, unripe mango, peeled, pitted, and chopped, or use ½ cup canned salted mango, drained, rinsed, and chopped into large chunks, or substitute 1 small sweet green pepper, cored, chopped, and combined with 2 teaspoons lemon juice
1 cup tightly packed fresh mint leaves and tender stems

1. Pour vinegar into a blender. Add sugar, salt, chilies, ginger, and cumin. Process for 1 minute (or until sugar

is dissolved into the liquid and seasonings have minced).

2. Add mango, coriander, and mint in small quantities and process until the contents are finely pureed. Transfer sauce into a covered jar.

NOTE   The sauce will keep well, stored in a covered container, for up to 8 hours at room temperature, 10 days in the refrigerator, and a year in the freezer.

SPICY INDIAN TOMATO SAUCE

KACCHA TAMATAR CHATNI

MICROWAVE

Yield
  —1 cup
Preparation time
  —3 minutes
Cooking time
  —10 minutes
Heat
  —100 percent power
MW oven size
  —650 to 700 watts
MW cookware
  —One 2½-quart cas-
    serole or soufflé dish

Red ripe tomatoes are crushed and accented with sharp ginger and hot chilies and perfumed with cumin and fresh coriander in this saucelike chutney from Punjab in north India. It is particularly good made in the microwave, as the tomatoes retain their fresh spring-like flavor. It is marvelous as a dipping sauce with chicken, such as Creamed Chicken Kabob (p. 111), and fish and seafood, such as Steamed Fish in Ginger-Thyme Essence (p. 81) and Sesame Shrimp (p. 13). Accompany the sauce with meals featuring north Indian curries and kabobs.

4 medium-size (1 pound) red ripe tomatoes, chopped	1–3 fresh hot green chilies, stemmed
½-inch piece fresh ginger, peeled	½ teaspoon ground cumin
1 large shallot, peeled	¼ teaspoon kosher salt
	2 tablespoons fresh coriander leaves

1. Put tomatoes, ginger, shallot, chilies, cumin, and salt into the container of a blender or food processor and process until the contents are pureed. Transfer sauce into a 2½-quart microwave-safe dish.

2. Cook, uncovered, at 100 percent power in a 650- to 700-watt carousel oven for 10 minutes (or until sauce is boiling and loses its raw fragrance). Remove from oven and stir in coriander. Return sauce to the blender or food processor and process until the herb is thoroughly blended in. When completely cool, pour sauce into sterilized jars and refrigerate.

NOTE The sauce keeps well, stored in a covered container, for a week in the refrigerator.

INSTANT PRUNE DIP

ALOO BOKHARA CHATNI

MICROWAVE

Yield
—*1⅓ cups*
Preparation time
—*3 minutes*

On days when you get the urge for tamarind chutney, make this instant prune dip instead, as all you do is combine all ingredients and serve. It looks, tastes, and smells exactly like tamarind chutney, except it is fruitier and lighter on the palate. It is this prune dip most Indian restaurants in America are serving as tamarind chutney. It takes only a minute to make if you already have roasted spices, or else you will need to set aside additional time. Serve as you would tamarind chutney with kabobs, roasts, and fried foods.

½ cup prune butter
   (p. 462)
1 cup cold water
4 tablespoons lemon juice
   or cider vinegar
1 tablespoon sugar
½ teaspoon kosher salt
½ teaspoon cayenne
   pepper
1 teaspoon dried ginger
   powder
1 teaspoon finely
   chopped fresh or
   crystallized ginger

1 teaspoon finely minced
   fresh, or ½ teaspoon
   crushed dried, mint
   leaves
1 teaspoon garam masala
   (p. 478) or fragrant
   spice powder (p. 481)
1 teaspoon ground
   roasted cumin seeds
   (p. 465)

Combine all the ingredients in a mixing bowl or a 4-cup bowl and beat with a whisk until thoroughly blended. Serve immediately or pour into sterilized jars and refrigerate.

NOTE   The dip keeps well, stored in a covered container, for 6 weeks in the refrigerator and up to a year in the freezer.

CHUTNEYS AND DIPPING SAUCES

369

SWEET AND SPICY TOMATO SAUCE

TAMATAR CHATNI

MICROWAVE

Yield
—*2¼ cups*
Preparation time
—*3 minutes*
Cooking time
—*31 minutes*
Heat
—*100 percent power*
MW oven size
—*650 to 700 watts*
MW cookware
—*One 2½-quart cas-
serole or soufflé dish*

This garlicky-sweet tomato chutney is just hot enough to leave a gentle glow in your mouth and simple and quick to make. It is the miracle of the microwave that the sauce does not stick or burn. Serve this chutney as a dipping sauce for dry foods such as Sesame Shrimp (p. 13), Ginger Chicken Kabob (p. 109), or Indian Beef Sausage Kabob (p. 138).

=========== *ROOM TEMPERATURE* ===========

2 pounds red ripe
   tomatoes, chopped
1 medium-size (¼
   pound) onion, peeled
   and chopped
3 medium-size garlic
   cloves, peeled and
   chopped

⅓ cup vinegar
⅓ teaspoon ground
   allspice
2 teaspoons dried ginger
   powder
½ teaspoon cayenne
   pepper
½ teaspoon paprika
⅔ cup sugar
2 teaspoons kosher salt

1. Combine tomatoes, onion, and garlic in a 2½-quart microwave-safe dish. Cook, uncovered, at 100 percent power, in a 650- to 700-watt carousel oven for 15 minutes (or until tomatoes are cooked soft), stirring twice. Remove from oven.

2. Transfer the contents into the container of a food processor. Process until the ingredients are completely pureed. Strain the sauce through a sieve back into the dish, squeezing as much sauce out of the pulp as possible. Discard the residue with seeds. Add all other ingredients and mix well.

3. Cook, uncovered, at 100 percent power for 16 minutes (or until sauce looks thick and glossy), stirring 3 times. Remove from oven, pour sauce into sterilized jars, and seal. Or, alternatively, when completely cool, refrigerate.

NOTE   This chutney keeps well, stored in a covered container, for several months in the refrigerator or up to a year in the freezer.

SWEET AND SPICY TAMARIND SAUCE I

IMLI CHATNI

MICROWAVE

Yield
  —3 cups
Preparation time
  —6 minutes plus 1
    hour for soaking
Cooking time
  —9 minutes
MW oven size
  —650 to 700 watts
MW cookware
  —One 1½-quart cov-
    ered casserole or
    soufflé dish

This is the classic tamarind chutney of Punjab in north India—piquant, sweet, and hot. Its consistency can range anywhere from watery-thin to creamy. For this reason, tamarind chutney (or sauce) is classically served as a dipping sauce with all Indian savories. It can be made very quickly if you already have a batch of tamarind juice (p. 492), as all you do is combine all the ingredients and cook for four minutes. Serve this chutney as a dipping sauce for dry foods such as Bombay Coconut Shrimp (p. 11), Creamed Chicken Kabob (p. 111), or Savory Keema Cake (p. 147).

=========================== ROOM TEMPERATURE ===========================

4 ounces (half an 8.75-ounce slab) tamarind pulp (p. 491)

2 cups water

1 teaspoon kosher salt

¼ cup sugar

2 tablespoons paprika

2 teaspoons cayenne pepper

2 teaspoons dried ginger powder

2 teaspoons ground cumin

1 teaspoon garam masala, homemade (p. 478) or store-bought

1. Tear tamarind into 3 to 4 pieces and place in a 1½-quart microwave-safe casserole. Add 2 cups water and cover with the lid. Cook at 100 percent power in a 650- to 700-watt carousel oven for 5 minutes (or until water is boiling).

2. Remove from oven and let tamarind stand, covered, for 1 hour. Uncover and mash the pulp with your fingers or use a spoon. Strain the juices through a sieve into another bowl, squeezing as much juice

out of the pulp as possible. Return the residue to the casserole and add ½ cup water. Mash pulp and strain again. Repeat the process until you have 2¾ cups tamarind liquid. Discard the fibrous residue.

3. Return tamarind juice to the casserole. Add the remaining ingredients, mix well, and cover with the lid. Cook at 100 percent power for 4 minutes (or until spices lose their uncooked aroma). Remove from oven. Uncover and pour sauce into sterilized jars. When cool, serve, cover and refrigerate, or freeze.

NOTE   The tamarind sauce will keep, stored in a covered container, for up to 12 weeks in the refrigerator and a year in the freezer.

SWEET AND SPICY TAMARIND SAUCE II

IMLI CHATNI

MICROWAVE

Yield
—3½ cups
Cooking time
—4 minutes
Heat
—100 percent power
MW oven size
—650 to 700 watts
MW cookware
—One 2½-quart cov-
ered casserole or
soufflé dish

This is another version of tamarind chutney. It is sweeter and mellow-tasting. The addition of black salt lends it a delicate smokiness. This chutney can be made very quickly if you already have a batch of tamarind juice (p. 492); otherwise allow an additional hour and a quarter for soaking and extracting juice from tamarind pulp.

=== ROOM TEMPERATURE ===

3 cups, or 24 frozen
 cubes, defrosted, tam-
 arind juice (p. 492)
⅔ cup dark brown sugar
2 teaspoons kosher salt
2 teaspoons ground
 roasted cumin seeds
 (p. 465)

2 teaspoons dried ginger
 powder
1 teaspoon cayenne
 pepper
2 teaspoons paprika
¼ teaspoon black salt
 (p. 482) (optional)
¼ cup raisins, dark or
 light

Combine all the ingredients in a 2½-quart micro-wave-safe dish and cover with the lid. Cook at 100 percent power for 4 minutes or until the chutney is boiling. Remove from oven and pour into sterilized jars. When cool, cover and refrigerate or freeze.

NOTE The sauce keeps well, stored in a covered container, for up to 3 weeks in the refrigerator and a year in the freezer.

SWEET AND SPICY TAMARIND SAUCE WITH FIGS AND ALMONDS

IMLI CHATNI

MICROWAVE

Yield
  —4 cups
Preparation time
  —4 hours for ripening
Cooking time
  —4 minutes
Heat
  —100 percent power
MW oven size
  —650 to 700 watts
MW cookware
  —One 2½-quart cov-
    ered casserole or
    soufflé dish

NOTE The sauce keeps well, stored in a covered container, for up to 12 weeks in the refrigerator and a year in the freezer.

Very fragrant with cardamom and slightly hot, this tamarind sauce, studded with juicy California figs and buttery almonds, is fabulous served with all Moghul and north Indian main courses.

=== ROOM TEMPERATURE ===

3 cups, or 24 frozen cubes, defrosted, tamarind juice (p. 492)
1 teaspoon kosher salt
¼ cup light brown sugar
2 tablespoons paprika
2 teaspoons cayenne pepper
2 teaspoons dried ginger powder
2 teaspoons ground cumin

½ teaspoon ground cardamom
1 cup chopped dried figs, preferably black California figs
⅓ cup sliced almonds
1 teaspoon ground roasted cumin seeds (p. 465)

1. Combine all the ingredients, except figs, almonds, and cumin, in a 2½-quart microwave-safe casserole and cover with the lid. Cook at 100 percent power in a 650- to 700-watt carousel oven for 4 minutes (or until spices lose their uncooked aroma). Remove from oven.

2. Uncover, add all other ingredients, stir well, and replace cover. When cool, pour sauce into sterilized jars and refrigerate. Let sauce ripen for 4 hours before serving.

SWEET AND SPICY FRUIT SAUCE

MEETHI CHATNI

MICROWAVE

Yield
  —*2 cups*
Preparation time
  —*3 minutes*
Cooking time
  —*9 minutes*
Heat
  —*100 percent power*
MW oven size
  —*650 to 700 watts*
MW cookware
  —*One 1½ quart cov-
    ered casserole or
    soufflé dish*

Slightly piquant, delicate, and fragrant with fennel, this fruit sauce will amaze you because it tastes of neither apricot nor tomato. The combined experience, however, is wonderful. The onion is essential in the chutney to mellow and bind the flavors in delicate harmony. Serve the sauce warm, at room temperature, or chilled with Creamed Chicken Kabob (p. 111) or Ginger Chicken Kabob (p. 109) and Ceylonese Steamed Rice Cakes (p. 330).

═══════════ ROOM TEMPERATURE ═══════════

1 cup (4 ounces) chopped dried apricots	1 tablespoon grated or crushed fresh ginger
1 large (½ pound) peeled, seeded, and chopped red ripe tomato	1 teaspoon ground cumin
	¾ teaspoon ground fennel
1 medium-size (¼ pound) onion, finely chopped	2 fresh hot green chilies, stemmed and coarsely chopped
	1 tablespoon sugar
	⅔ cup water

1. Place all the ingredients in a 1½-quart microwave-safe casserole and cover with the lid. Cook at 100 percent power in a 650- to 700-watt carousel oven for 9 minutes (or until contents reduce to a thick sauce). Remove from oven.

2. Transfer contents into the container of a food processor or blender and process until just pureed but *not* liquefied. Serve immediately or pour into sterilized jars and refrigerate.

NOTE The sauce keeps well, stored in a covered container, in the refrigerator for up to a week.

DESSERTS

Many Indian desserts are milk-based, and, as experienced home cooks know, they have an annoying tendency to form lumps. In conventional cooking, thickening is also unreliable. But the microwave never produces lumpy sauces, and it always thickens these cornstarch-based puddings perfectly.

These are light fruit-and-milk-based desserts that deliver just a hint of sweetness to the palate at the end of a meal. Even the dessert sauces, such as Warm Mango Sauce with Almonds, are delicate and fruity rather than intensely sweet. These sauces make wonderful toppings for ice cream or crêpes, and are splendid on pancakes or waffles.

The fact that the microwave heightens and preserves the flavor of fruits and vegetables is beautifully demonstrated in Glazed Carrot Fudge, an unlikely dessert in which carrots are cooked in a light cardamom-scented cream. The carrots retain their flavor and crunch even after prolonged cooking, and provide a lovely contrast with the caramelized milk and perfumed slivers of green pistachio nuts.

When it comes to sorbets, the microwave is a dream. Dried-fruit sorbets are a particular fascination of mine because of the unique and appealing flavors of the fruit, which are more intense on the senses. The microwave turns these fruits buttery soft without any loss or change in their delicate tastes or aromas. The velvety puree forms the basis of sorbets such as Tamarind (p. 379).

TAMARIND SORBET

IMLI SHARBAT

MICROWAVE

Yield
  —5½ cups
Servings
  —6 to 8
Preparation time
  —10 minutes plus ad-
    ditional time for
    freezing

Surprisingly, I never get a craving for frozen ices in summer. It is when I see snow covering the cold earth and barren branches shivering in the winter breeze that I am drawn to icy concoctions, as if I were in a celestial union with nature. Just consider this one of my idiosyncrasies and serve the sorbet, if you will please, when the mercury hits the nineties.

This sorbet is fragrant. Its low-sweet, tart taste also makes it a refreshing interlude between courses.

=============== *ROOM TEMPERATURE* ===============

2½ cups tomato juice
½ cup, or 4 frozen
  cubes, tamarind juice
  or 4 teaspoons tama-
  rind concentrate
  (p. 491)
12 fresh, or 1 teaspoon
  powdered dried, mint
  leaves

½ teaspoon dried ginger
  powder
¼ teaspoon freshly
  ground black pepper
2–3 tablespoons sugar
½ teaspoon kosher salt
2½ cups water or a com-
  bination of water and
  red wine

1. Combine 1 cup tomato juice, tamarind juice, mint leaves, ginger, black pepper, sugar, and salt in the container of a blender or food processor and process until liquefied. Strain the mixture through a fine-mesh sieve into a tall pitcher. Add the remaining tomato juice and water and stir to blend. Pour the juice into standard (16 cubes per tray) ice trays and freeze. When frozen (about 4 hours), transfer to plastic bags and store. The frozen cubes will keep for up to a year in the freezer.

2. To serve, place 12 cubes in the container of a food processor and process until the contents resemble snow, adding a little cold water, if necessary. Spoon sorbet into 4 parfait glasses or wineglasses and serve. Do the same with the remaining cubes.

CARAMELIZED RICE PUDDING

BANARASI KHEER

MICROWAVE

Yield
—3 cups
Servings
—6
Preparation time
—3 minutes
Cooking time
—30 minutes
Heat
—100 percent power
MW oven size
—650 to 700 watts
MW cookware
—One 5-quart casserole

Some of the best memories of my childhood are of those afternoons spent in my grandmother's kitchen eating her rice pudding. Today, on those days when I feel drained to my roots, remembering those times—the fun and care that went into the pudding's preparation—lifts me right up from my darkest of moods!

I remember accompanying my grandmother to our milkman's quarters at the back of our house. His barn, shaded by tamarind trees, smelled sweetly of hay, moist earth, and fresh milk. Under one of the trees stood Gulabkali (Rosebud), his cow, painted in vivid colors and adorned with bells that tinkled with her every movement. The milkman stroked Rosebud tenderly, whispering flattering words, coaxing her to part with her milk! When at last she yielded, warm, frothy milk began to fill the bucket in rhythmic streams.

Grandmother brought the milk home, filled her shiny brass pot, and placed it on her wood-burning clay stove. As the milk cooked down slowly, for over an hour, the fudgelike aroma filled the room. She then added some rice and palm jaggery and cooked it, stirring slowly. I sat by her side on the floor, inhaling the hypnotic fragrance hungrily. Finally, when the rice pudding turned thick, smooth, and creamy with a light caramel color, as grandmother preferred it, she served it to me—still hot—in a hollowed-out coconut shell. It tasted as if it were food from heaven!

The following recipe, created for the microwave, enlivens this memory. The pudding is equally good hot, at room temperature, or chilled.

½ cup long-grain rice,
  preferably basmati
2 cups creamy milk
  (p. 454), light cream,
  or half-and-half
1 cup whole milk
2 cups heavy cream

¾ cup dark brown sugar
1 teaspoon ground
  cardamom
¼ cup blanched sliced
  almonds
¼ cup raisins

1. Rinse rice in several changes of water. Drain and put in a 5-quart microwave-safe dish. Stir in creamy milk and whole milk. Cook, uncovered at 100 percent power in a 650- to 700-watt carousel oven for 20 minutes (or until milk begins to thicken and its surface gets covered with bubbles), stirring 4 to 5 times, especially during the last 2 to 3 minutes, to break the skin as it forms on the surface.

2. Add heavy cream and sugar and stir to mix. Continue cooking, uncovered, at 100 percent power for an additional 10 minutes (or until pudding thickens and develops a light caramel color and fragrance). Remove from oven and stir in cardamom, almonds, and raisins. Serve the pudding spooned into dessert bowls.

NOTE   The pudding keeps well, stored in a covered container in the refrigerator, for up to 4 weeks.

ALMOND RICE PUDDING

FIRNI

Firni, the classic dessert of the Moghuls, has many interpretations. In its purest form, it is a light rose-scented rice-flour pudding dotted with almond slivers and raisins. It is cool and comforting. The microwave cooks *firni* to perfection, to a silky-smooth consistency without lumping, sticking, or burning.

MICROWAVE

Yield
—*5 cups*
Servings
—*8 to 10*
Preparation time
—*3 minutes plus additional time for chilling*
Cooking time
—*14 minutes*
Heat
—*100 percent power*
MW oven size
—*650 to 700 watts*
MW cookware
—*One 3-quart casserole*

=========== ROOM TEMPERATURE ============

½ cup rice flour (p. 463)
4 cups whole milk or
  light cream
⅔ cup sugar
⅓ teaspoon rose flower
  water (p. 456)

½ cup blanched sliced
  almonds
⅔ cup heavy cream,
  whipped

FOR THE GARNISH:
¼ cup chopped raw un-
  salted pistachio nuts

¼ cup dark raisins

1. Dissolve rice flour in ½ cup milk in a small bowl and reserve.

2. Combine the remaining 3½ cups milk and sugar in a 3-quart microwave-safe casserole. Cook, uncovered, at 100 percent power in a 650- to 700-watt carousel oven for 8 minutes (or until milk comes to a boil), stirring twice.

3. Remove from oven and stir in rice-flour solution. Cook, uncovered, at 100 percent power for 5 minutes 30 seconds (or until pudding boils and thickens), stirring twice. Remove from oven.

4. Add rose flower water and almonds, mix thoroughly, cover, and chill thoroughly. Remove from refrigerator, beat with a whisk until the pudding is smooth, and fold in the whipped cream. Spoon pudding into dessert bowls, distribute the pistachios and raisins on top, and serve.

BANANA BAVARIAN CREAM WITH CASHEW NUTS

PRASADAM

MICROWAVE

Yield
—3 cups
Servings
—6 to 8
Preparation time
—10 minutes plus 4
    hours for soaking
Cooking time
—10 minutes
Heat
—100 percent power
MW oven size
—650 to 700 watts
MW cookware
—One 8-cup glass
    measure

Split peas are a favorite ingredient in dessert-making in southern India. They lend puddings a nutty flavor and a creamy texture. This light and fluffy cardamom-scented banana version has the consistency of Bavarian cream. For best results use only unblemished ripe bananas with lovely white flesh.

=========== ROOM TEMPERATURE ===========

½ cup dried American
    yellow split peas (p.
    461)
2 cups creamy milk
    (p. 454), coconut milk
    (p. 450), light cream,
    or half-and-half
⅓ cup sugar
1 medium-size banana,
    peeled and chopped
¼ teaspoon dried ginger
    powder

¼ teaspoon ground
    cardamom
¼ cup dark raisins
½ cup chopped roasted
    cashew nuts or ⅓ cup
    roasted slivered al-
    monds (p. 463)
1½ cups heavy cream,
    whipped, plus addi-
    tional for garnish
    (optional)

1. Pick clean split peas, rinse, and place in a medium-size bowl. Add enough water to cover the peas by at least 2 inches. Soak for 4 hours or overnight. Drain, rinse, and drain again.

2. Place peas in the container of a blender or food processor. Add enough creamy milk to barely cover them and process until the contents are smoothly pureed. Transfer puree into an 8-cup glass measure.

Rinse the container with the remaining creamy milk and pour into the pea puree. Stir to mix.

3. Cook, uncovered, at 100 percent power in a 650- to 700-watt carousel oven for 8 minutes (or until peas are cooked and pudding begins to thicken), stirring twice and breaking the skin that forms on the surface. Stir in sugar and bananas and continue cooking at 100 percent power for an additional 2 minutes (or until bananas are cooked). Remove from oven.

4. Beat the pudding vigorously, using a wooden spoon, to lend the pudding a creamier texture. Or, alternatively, process the mixture in the blender or food processor until smooth. Stir in ginger, cardamom, raisins, and half the cashew nuts and refrigerate. When thoroughly chilled, fold in whipped cream and spoon into dessert bowls. Distribute the remaining cashew nuts on top and serve, if desired, accompanied with whipped cream.

BOMBAY CHEESE PUDDING

CHENNA KA SRIKHAND

MICROWAVE

Yield
  —¾ cup
Servings
  —2
Preparation time
  —8 minutes

I love to make this cheese pudding, a specialty of the Maharashtrians in Bombay, as the cheese cooked in the microwave develops a unique mellow tenderness. Laced with crystallized ginger and saffron, the pudding is herbal and refreshing, particularly after a spicy Indian meal.

=== *ROOM TEMPERATURE* ===

1 recipe Indian chenna cheese (p. 456)
3 tablespoons confectioners' sugar
Small pinch of crushed saffron threads or powdered saffron
Pinch of freshly grated nutmeg

1 tablespoon finely chopped crystallized ginger
½ cup chopped fresh pineapple, mangoes, peaches, apricots, red raspberries, or strawberries
1 tablespoon sliced raw unsalted pistachio nuts

Place cheese, sugar, saffron, and nutmeg in a mixing bowl and beat vigorously, using a wooden spoon, until cheese is smooth and creamy. Fold in crystallized ginger, prepared fruit, and half the nuts and refrigerate. When thoroughly chilled, spoon mixture into dessert glasses and distribute the remaining nuts on top.

COCONUT CHEESE CAKE

CHENNA KI BARFI

Webbed with coconut shreds and perfumed with cardamom, this elegant tropical cheese cake, *paneer ki barfi*, is a Bengal specialty. It is traditionally made with fresh homemade cheese but I have developed this recipe using commercially available ricotta cheese. The results are moister and fluffier. The microwave works particularly well in this recipe as the cake remains ivory white—as required—during baking. Remember to use a deep baking dish for this cake as the batter has a tendency to froth and boil over during cooking. The freshly baked cake is very moist and fragile. It should rest at room temperature for about an hour, for all the juices to absorb before serving.

MICROWAVE

Yield
—*One 10-inch round cake, about 1 inch thick*

Servings
—*8 to 10*

Preparation time
—*5 minutes*

Cooking time
—*14 minutes*

Heat
—*100 percent power*

MW oven size
—*650 to 700 watts*

MW cookware
—*One 10-inch tart or quiche plate or one 10-inch skillet*

=== ROOM TEMPERATURE ===

3½ cups whole-milk ricotta cheese	½ cup sugar
1⅓ cups packed fresh bread crumbs	1 teaspoon ground cardamom
⅔ cup packed sweetened coconut flakes (p. 449)	2 tablespoons dark or light raisins
1 medium-size egg	6 tablespoons unsalted butter

FOR THE GARNISH:
1 quart ripe red strawberries, hulled (large ones halved)

2½ cups (½ recipe) Saffron Sauce (p. 402)

1. Combine ricotta, bread crumbs, coconut, egg, sugar, cardamom, and raisins in a medium-size bowl until thoroughly blended.

2. Place butter in a 10-inch microwave-safe pie plate, or round or square skillet. Cook, uncovered, at 100 percent power in a 650- to 700-watt carousel oven for 1 minute 30 seconds (or until it melts). Remove from oven. Pour butter on the cheese mixture and fold in evenly. Transfer cheese mixture into the plate and press lightly to even off the surface.

3. Cook at 100 percent power for 12 minutes (or until cake is cooked and set—a thin skewer pierced in the center of the cake comes out clean). Remove from oven. When cool, cover and refrigerate. Serve cake cut into 2-inch wedges, accompanied with strawberries and Saffron Sauce.

NOTE The cheese cake may be made ahead and stored, in a covered microwave-safe container, in the refrigerator for up to 4 weeks or frozen. Defrost cake in the container, partially opened, at 100 percent power for 3 minutes.

MADRAS BRIDAL PUDDING WITH CASHEW NUTS

SOJJEE

MICROWAVE

Yield
—2½ cups
Servings
—4 to 6
Preparation time
—5 minutes
Cooking time
—17 minutes
Heat
—100 percent power
MW oven size
—650 to 700 watts
MW cookware
—One 8-cup glass
measure and one
2½-quart covered
casserole or soufflé
dish

Sojjee, a saffron-flavored cream-of-wheat pudding, is part of a delicious ritual that takes place during the matchmaking ceremony in south India. It is prepared by the prospective bride's mother to welcome the visiting prospective groom and his family and to display her family's affluence and talent. The more rich and fragrant with *usli ghee* and saffron the pudding is and the more delicately balanced the flavors are, the higher the score for the bride and her family. This comes, of course, after more important considerations, such as the girl's astrological signs, her length of hair, largeness of eyes, lightness of complexion, and so on. With or without the ritual, *sojjee* is absolutely heavenly. I love it hot, at room temperature, or straight out of the refrigerator as a snack, for breakfast, or for dessert. The microwave is ideally suited for making *sojjee* as the moist heat enables the cereal to expand more, thus yielding lighter, fluffy-textured *sojjee.* This pudding is traditionally scented with an edible natural raw camphor *paccha kalpuram,* but I have discovered that rosemary, which has camphorous overtones, makes an excellent substitute.

=== ROOM TEMPERATURE ===

2⅓ cups water
¾ cup sugar
½–1 teaspoon crushed
    saffron threads or
    powdered saffron

Small pinch edible
    natural raw camphor,
    or 1 3-inch sprig
    fresh rosemary, or
    ½ teaspoon ground
    rosemary

1 teaspoon ground
cardamom
6 tablespoons usli ghee
(p. 492) or unsalted
butter

½ cup quick-cooking
cream of wheat
¼ cup dark raisins
⅓ cup chopped roasted
unsalted cashew nuts
(p. 463)

1. Combine water and sugar in an 8-cup glass measure. Cook, uncovered, at 100 percent power in a 650- to 700-watt carousel oven for 5 minutes 30 seconds (or until syrup is boiling). Remove from oven, stir in saffron, rosemary sprig or powder (if you are using camphor, do not add it here), and cardamom, and reserve.

2. Place *usli ghee* or butter in a 2½-quart microwave-safe dish. Cook, uncovered, at 100 percent power for 3 minutes (or until *usli ghee* melts and begins to cook). Stir in cream of wheat and continue cooking, uncovered, at 100 percent power for an additional 2 minutes (or until cream of wheat begins to foam and color), stirring once. Remove from oven.

3. Add syrup and raisins, mix well, and cover with the lid. Cook at 100 percent power for 4 minutes. Uncover, stir the pudding, and continue cooking, uncovered, for an additional 2 minutes (or until excess moisture evaporates and the consistency is that of American Indian corn pudding). Remove from oven.

4. Fluff and remove rosemary sprig and discard. Fold in cashew nuts and camphor (if you are using it). Spoon pudding into 6 custard cups and pack it down. Invert pudding onto serving plates and serve.

NOTE The pudding may be made ahead and set aside, stored in a covered microwave-safe container, in the refrigerator for up to 3 weeks or frozen for 6 months. Defrost pudding in the container, partially opened, at 100 percent power for 4 minutes.

KASHMIR SEMOLINA PUDDING

SOJJEE HALWA

MICROWAVE

Yield
—2½ cups
Servings
—4 to 6
Cooking time
—17 minutes
Heat
—100 percent power
MW oven size
—650 to 700 watts
MW cookware
—One 8-cup glass
measure and one
2½-quart covered
casserole or
soufflé dish

This is prepared similarly to the Madras *sojjee,* the difference being that this pudding is cooked in milk and flavored with buttery, powdered saffron, thus lending it a peachy hue. Serve this semolina pudding as either a traditional breakfast cereal, accompanied with sliced apples and cream crackers, or a dessert, accompanied with ripe, juicy berries and sweetened whipped sour cream.

=== ROOM TEMPERATURE ===

2⅓ cups low-fat milk, whole milk, or water	6 tablespoons unsalted butter
½ cup sugar	½ cup quick-cooking cream of wheat
1 teaspoon ground cardamom	¼ cup dark raisins
½ teaspoon crushed saffron threads or powdered saffron	2 tablespoons blanched sliced almonds

1. Combine milk and sugar in a 8-cup glass measure. Cook, uncovered, at 100 percent power in a 650- to 700-watt carousel oven for 5 minutes 30 seconds (or until syrup is boiling). Remove from oven, stir in cardamom and saffron, and reserve.

2. Place butter in a 2½-quart microwave-safe dish and cover with the lid. Cook, at 100 percent power for 3 minutes (or until butter melts and begins to cook). Stir in cream of wheat and cook for an additional 2 minutes (or until cream of wheat begins to foam and color), stirring once. Remove from oven.

3. Add syrup and raisins, mix well, and cover with the lid. Cook at 100 percent power for 4 minutes. Uncover, stir the pudding, and continue cooking, uncovered, for an additional 2 minutes (or until excess moisture evaporates and the consistency is that of American Indian corn pudding). Remove from oven. Fluff the pudding and serve garnished with almonds, hot, at room temperature, or cold.

NOTE The pudding may be made ahead and set aside, stored in a covered microwave-safe container, in the refrigerator for up to 3 weeks or frozen for 6 months. Reheat pudding in the container, partially opened, at 100 percent power for 2 minutes if refrigerated, and for 5 minutes if frozen.

PARSI SEMOLINA PUDDING

SOJJEE

If I had to choose my favorite from among the dozens of semolina puddings made throughout India, I probably would pick this Parsi version because I love its subtle flavor of sweet cinnamon and its ginger undertones. It is refreshingly light and very addictive. Serve the pudding warm with sliced peaches and nectarines and accompanied with a pitcher of heavy cream. Fresh raspberries, blueberries, red currants, and strawberries are also good with it.

=========== ROOM TEMPERATURE ===========

2⅓ cups water	¼ teaspoon dried ginger
10 tablespoons sugar	powder
1 teaspoon ground	¼ cup light raisins
cardamom	6 tablespoons unsalted
½ teaspoon ground	butter
cinnamon	½ cup quick-cooking
	cream of wheat

FOR THE GARNISH:
2 tablespoons chopped raw unsalted pistachio nuts

1. Combine water and sugar in an 8-cup glass measure. Cook, uncovered, at 100 percent power in a 650- to 700-watt carousel oven for 5 minutes 30 seconds (or until syrup is boiling). Remove from oven, stir in cardamom, cinnamon, ginger, and raisins, and reserve.

2. Place butter in a 2½-quart microwave-safe dish. Cook, uncovered, at 100 percent power for 2 minutes 30 seconds (or until butter melts). Stir in cream of

wheat and cook for an additional 2 minutes (or until cream of wheat begins to foam and color), stirring once. Remove from oven.

3. Add syrup, mix well, and cover with the lid. Cook at 100 percent power for 4 minutes. Uncover, stir the pudding, and continue cooking, uncovered, for an additional 2 minutes (or until excess moisture evaporates and the consistency is that of Indian corn pudding). Remove from oven.

4. Fluff, scoop pudding onto 6 dessert plates, garnish with sliced pistachio nuts, and serve.

NOTE The pudding may be made ahead and set aside, stored in a covered microwave-safe container, in the refrigerator for up to 3 weeks or frozen for 6 months. Reheat pudding in the container, partially opened, at 100 percent power for 2 minutes if refrigerated, and for 5 minutes if frozen.

GLAZED CARROT FUDGE

GAJAR HALWA

MICROWAVE

Yield
—1½ cups
Servings
—6
Preparation time
—5 minutes
Cooking time
—30 minutes
Heat
—100 percent power
MW oven size
—650 to 700 watts
MW cookware
—One 2½-quart cas-
serole or soufflé dish

Carrot *halwa,* a soft, glistening pudding scented with cardamom and studded with pistachio nuts and almonds, is the specialty of the Sikh community in Punjab. Purely for aesthetic reasons, the *halwa* is made with a special variety of red carrots that bleed during cooking and dye it a deep crimson color. You may either disregard color or use a little red food coloring, since we do not grow red carrots in America. The microwave is particularly suited for cooking this milk-rich *halwa,* as there is no worry of sticking and burning. In addition, the carrot shreds cook to a buttery softness while retaining their delightfully chewy texture. Carrot *halwa* is best enjoyed piping hot or warm by itself, or for an elegant dessert, with Saffron Sauce (p. 402) or sweetened whipped cream.

=== ROOM TEMPERATURE ===

3 cups lightly packed
   grated carrots (about
   1 pound)
2 cups creamy milk
   (p. 454), light cream,
   or half-and-half
½ teaspoon red food
   coloring (optional)
2 tablespoons usli ghee
   (p. 492) or unsalted
   butter

¼ cup sugar
1 teaspoon ground
   cardamom
½ cup dark raisins
2 tablespoons chopped
   raw unsalted pista-
   chio nuts
½ cup blanched slivered
   almonds
Butter for greasing

1. Combine carrots, creamy milk, and optional coloring in a 2½-quart microwave-safe dish. Cook, uncovered, at 100 percent power in a 650- to 700-watt carousel oven for 25 minutes (or until milk reduces

to a thick sauce and coats the carrot shreds), stirring 3 times.

2. Remove from oven, add *usli ghee,* sugar, cardamom, raisins, pistachios, and half the almonds, and mix well. Cook, uncovered, at 100 percent power for 5 minutes (or until mixture looks very thick—like fudge), stirring once. Remove from oven.

3. Transfer fudge into a greased shallow (1½ cups) glass bowl and pack it in evenly. Place a serving plate upside down over the bowl. Holding both securely, invert the bowl over the plate to let the fudge slide onto the plate. Decorate fudge with the remaining almonds and serve.

NOTE   The carrot *halwa* keeps well, stored in a covered microwave-safe container, in the refrigerator for up to 2 weeks. Reheat *halwa* in the container, partially opened, at 100 percent power for 1 minute 30 seconds. Stir well before serving.

INDIAN SPICED PEACH CAKE

ALOO BOKHARA HALWA

MICROWAVE

Yield
—12 individual 3-inch
cakes
Servings
—6 to 12
Preparation time
—8 minutes
Cooking time
—9 minutes
Heat
—100 percent power
MW oven size
—650 to 700 watts
MW cookware
—One egg poacher/
muffin tray or six
6-ounce custard
bowls

Visions of fruity, buttery cakes and crumbly pies are farthest from one's mind when one thinks of Indian food, but they are very much a part of India's culinary heritage due to its colonization under the English, French, Portuguese, and Dutch. This nutmeg-and-cardamom-infused cake is soft, moist, and delicate—like Christmas pudding—and amazingly easy to prepare. All one needs to do is combine all the ingredients and cook until done. The natural sweetish-tart flavor of the peach against the buttery sweet cake and pistachio is a delightful experience on the palate. It is good warm or at room temperature, served by itself or accompanied with sweetened whipped cream, Saffron Sauce (p. 402), or Fragrant Coconut Sauce (p. 403).

=========== ROOM TEMPERATURE ===========

4 cups lightly packed
    fresh bread crumbs
1½ teaspoons baking
    powder
¼ teaspoon freshly
    grated nutmeg
2⅔ cups (1 recipe)
    Warm Peach Sauce
    with Pistachios
    (p. 404)

¼ cup dark raisins
¼ cup crumbled Indian
    khoya milk (p. 459)
    (optional)
4 tablespoons unsalted
    butter plus additional
    for greasing

1. Combine bread crumbs, baking powder, and nutmeg in a bowl and reserve.

2. Pour peach sauce in a bowl. Add raisins and *khoya*, if you are using it, and reserve.

3. Place butter in a small glass bowl or cup measure. Cook at 100 percent power in a 650- to 700-watt carousel oven for 1 minute (or until melted). Remove from oven.

4. Add melted butter to the peach mixture and stir to mix. Carefully fold bread-crumb mixture into the peach sauce. Spoon half the batter into the 6 depressions of a lightly greased egg poacher/muffin tray. Cook, uncovered, at 100 percent power for 4 minutes 30 seconds (or until cakes have risen and the surfaces of cakes look glazed and feel firm to the touch. Remove from oven and cool cakes briefly before unmolding. Cook the remaining cakes the same way.

NOTE The peach cake keeps well, stored in a covered microwave-safe container, in the refrigerator for up to 1 week. Reheat cake in the container, partially opened, at 100 percent power for 1 minute 30 seconds.

INDIAN SPICED MANGO CAKE

AAM HALWA

MICROWAVE

Yield
—*12 individual 3-inch cakes*

Servings
—*6 to 12*

Preparation time
—*8 minutes*

Cooking time
—*9 minutes*

Heat
—*100 percent power*

MW oven size
—*650 to 700 watts*

MW cookware
—*One egg poacher/ muffin tray or six 6-ounce custard bowls*

This fragile and moist sweet mango cake is delightful hot, or at room temperature, served by itself or accompanied with lightly sweetened whipped sour cream (made by beating 1 cup sour cream with 2 tablespoons confectioners' sugar and 4 drops vanilla, or 2 drops almond extract).

=============== ROOM TEMPERATURE ===============

4 cups lightly packed fresh bread crumbs

1½ teaspoons baking powder

¼ teaspoon ground cardamom or dried ginger powder

2⅔ cups (1 recipe) Warm Mango Sauce with Almonds (p. 406)

¼ teaspoon rose flower water (p. 456) or vanilla extract

¼ cup dark raisins

¼ cup crumbled Indian khoya milk (p. 459) (optional)

4 tablespoons unsalted butter plus additional for greasing

1. Combine bread crumbs, baking powder, and cardamom in a bowl and reserve.

2. Pour mango and almond sauce in a bowl. Add rose flower water, raisins, and *khoya,* if you are using it, and reserve.

3. Place butter in a small glass bowl or cup measure. Cook at 100 percent power in a 650- to 700-watt carousel oven for 1 minute (or until melted). Remove from oven.

4. Add melted butter to the mango mixture and stir to mix. Carefully fold bread crumb mixture into the sauce. Spoon half the batter into the 6 depressions of

a lightly greased egg poacher/muffin tray, filling it halfway. Cook, uncovered, at 100 percent power for 4 minutes 30 seconds (or until surfaces of cakes look glazed and feel firm to the touch). Remove from oven and cool cakes briefly before unmolding. Cook the remaining cakes the same way.

NOTE   The cakes may be baked ahead and set aside, in a covered microwave-safe container, in the refrigerator for a week. Reheat cakes in the container, partially opened, at 100 percent power for 1 minute 30 seconds.

SAFFRON SAUCE

SAS ZAFFRAN

MICROWAVE

Yield

—*4½ cups*

Servings

—*18 to 36*

Preparation time

—*5 minutes*

Cooking time

—*14 minutes*

Heat

—*100 percent power*

MW oven size

—*650 to 700 watts*

MW cookware

—*One 8-cup glass
measure*

NOTE The sauce may be kept stored in a covered container in the refrigerator for up to 6 weeks or frozen for 6 months.

I love this sublime sauce hot, at room temperature, or straight out of the refrigerator over Glazed Carrot Fudge (p. 396), Coconut Cheese Cake (p. 388), Indian Spiced Mango Cake (p. 400), and with berries such as raspberries, blueberries, or strawberries.

=========== ROOM TEMPERATURE ===========

3 tablespoons cornstarch	2 tablespoons sugar
2¼ cups light cream	1 teaspoon crushed saffron threads or powdered saffron
7-ounce packet Odense almond paste	
2 cups whole milk	¼ teaspoon almond extract

1. Dissolve cornstarch in ¼ cup cream in a small bowl and reserve.

2. Cut almond paste roughly into 6 to 8 pieces and put in an 8-cup glass measure together with the remaining cream, milk, sugar, and saffron. Cook, uncovered, at 100 percent power in a 650- to 700-watt carousel oven for 11 minutes (or until milk is boiling and almond paste is fully dissolved into the milk), stirring twice.

3. Remove from oven and stir in cornstarch solution. Cook, uncovered, at 100 percent power for 3 minutes (or until sauce thickens), stirring twice.

4. Remove from oven, uncover, and stir in almond extract. When cool, transfer into a covered container and chill. Before serving, beat sauce with a whisk or fork until completely smooth.

FRAGRANT COCONUT SAUCE

SAS NARIAL

NOTE   The sauce keeps well, stored in a covered container, for 6 weeks in the refrigerator or 6 months in the freezer.

You can make this sweet, fragrant, and very tropical sauce quickly and effortlessly in the microwave. Make sure to use a deep dish for cooking it as the milk has a tendency to boil over. Serve the sauce over fresh sliced fruits, Coconut Cheese Cake (p. 388), Bombay Cheese Pudding (p. 387), Parsi Semolina Pudding (p. 394), or Glazed Carrot Fudge (p. 396).

ROOM TEMPERATURE

1½ tablespoons corn-
starch
¼ cup whole milk, low-
fat milk, or water
2½ cups coconut milk
(p. 450)

3 tablespoons sugar
2 tablespoons Frangelico,
coconut liqueur, or
light rum (optional)

1. Dissolve cornstarch in ¼ cup milk in a small bowl and reserve.

2. Pour coconut milk into an 8-cup glass measure and stir in sugar. Cook, uncovered, at 100 percent power in a 650- to 700-watt carousel oven for 4 minutes (or until milk comes to a boil). Remove from oven.

3. Add cornstarch solution, stirring the milk rapidly. Cook, uncovered, at 100 percent power for 3 minutes (or until sauce comes to a boil and thickens), stirring once.

4. Remove from oven and stir in liqueur or rum (if you are using it). Cool thoroughly and chill. Beat sauce with a whisk or fork to smoothen it and serve.

WARM PEACH SAUCE WITH PISTACHIOS

ALOO BOKHARA SAS

MICROWAVE

Yield
—2¾ *cups*
Servings
—12
Cooking time
—11 *minutes*
Heat
—70 *percent and 100 percent power*
MW oven size
—650 *to 700 watts*
MW cookware
—*One 8-cup glass measure*

This peach sauce is delectable yet quick to prepare in the microwave. All you do is make syrup with coconut milk, jaggery, and butter, add spices and peaches, and cook. The distinct burnt-sugar–like aroma in the sauce is imparted by jaggery, Indian raw sugar. Although a substitute is suggested, try using jaggery whenever possible. For best results use only juicy, fragrant peaches and remember not to overcook them as they turn mushy easily. Spoon warm sauce over Ceylonese Steamed Rice Muffins (p. 330) or Bombay Cheese Pudding (p. 387). It is also delicious over vanilla ice cream, waffles, pancakes, and crêpes.

=== ROOM TEMPERATURE ===

½ *cup coconut milk* (*p. 450*)

¼ *cup jaggery* (*p. 460*) *or light brown sugar*

2 *tablespoons unsalted butter*

¼ *teaspoon ground cardamom*

¼ *teaspoon ground cinnamon*

¼ *cup sliced raw unsalted pistachio nuts*

2 *tablespoons cornstarch dissolved in 4 tablespoons coconut milk or water*

1½ *pounds ripe peaches, peeled, pitted, thinly sliced or finely chopped* (*see Note*) (*about 3 cups*), *and tossed with 1 tablespoon lemon juice*

1. Place coconut milk, jaggery, and butter in an 8-cup glass measure. Cook, uncovered, at 70 percent (medium) power in a 650- to 700-watt carousel oven for 2 minutes 30 seconds (or until butter melts and jaggery softens). Remove from oven and stir until jag-

gery melts completely in the coconut milk. Cook un-covered at 100 percent power for 4 minutes (or until sauce begins to turn syrupy). Remove from oven.

2. Stir in cardamom, cinnamon, pistachios, and the cornstarch solution. Immediately fold in the peaches. Cook, uncovered, at 100 percent power for 4 minutes 30 seconds (or until sauce thickens and peaches look cooked but still hold their shape). Remove from oven and serve.

NOTE For visual and textural enhancement, use sliced peaches in the sauce; however, if the sauce is to be used for making Indian Spiced Peach Cake (p. 398), chop finely into ¼-inch dices—the cake will hold better.

NOTE The sauce keeps well, stored in a tightly covered microwave-safe jar, for up to 6 weeks in the refrigerator. Reheat sauce in the container, uncovered, at 100 percent power for 2 minutes 30 seconds. Stir well before serving.

WARM MANGO SAUCE WITH ALMONDS

AAM SAS

MICROWAVE

Yield
  —2¾ cups
Servings
  —12 to 16
Cooking time
  —11 minutes
Heat
  —70 percent and 100
    percent power
MW oven size
  —650 to 700 watts
MW cookware
  —One 8-cup glass
    measure

A luscious sauce to make when soft, overripe mangoes are on hand. Serve it warm over Coconut Cheese Cake (p. 388), Indian Spiced Mango Cake (p. 400), and sliced fruits such as pineapple, kiwi, bananas, and papaya. It is also delicious spooned over vanilla ice cream and garnished with macademia nuts and as a topping on waffles, pancakes, and crêpes.

Make Warm Mango Sauce with Almonds following all the directions given for making Warm Peach Sauce with Pistachios (p. 404), except substitute 3 cups chopped ripe mangoes for peaches.

WARM FIVE-NECTAR SAUCE

PANCHAMRITAM

Combining the five divine foods of the Vedic Aryans, namely coconut milk, jaggery, clarified butter, fruits, and nuts, this delicious sauce was created to appease the ancient gods in temples in southern India, but I like it just as much warm, spooned over vanilla ice cream and garnished with pomegranate fruit, or Ceylonese Steamed Rice Cakes (p. 330) or Coconut Cheese Cake (p. 388). It is also comforting over waffles, pancakes, and crêpes.

MICROWAVE

Yield
 —2 cups
Servings
 —8
Cooking time
 —7 minutes
Heat
 —100 percent power
MW oven size
 —650 to 700 watts
MW cookware
 —One 4-cup glass measure

=== ROOM TEMPERATURE ===

1 cup coconut milk (p. 450)

¼ cup jaggery (p. 460) or light brown sugar

2 tablespoons usli ghee (p. 492) or unsalted butter

1 tablespoon cornstarch dissolved in 2 tablespoons coconut milk, whole milk, or water

¼ teaspoon ground cardamom

¼ teaspoon dried ginger powder

¼ cup chopped raw unsalted cashew nuts or blanched slivered almonds

1 medium-size ripe banana, peeled and thinly sliced

1. Place coconut milk, jaggery, and *ghee* into a 4-cup glass measure. Cook, uncovered, at 100 percent power in a 650- to 700-watt carousel oven for 5 minutes (or until jaggery dissolves and coconut milk reduces a little), stirring twice.

2. Remove from oven and stir in the cornstarch solution. Add all other ingredients and stir to mix. Cook, uncovered, at 100 percent power for 2 minutes (or

until sauce thickens and bananas look cooked). Remove from oven and serve.

NOTE The sauce keeps well, stored in a tightly covered microwave-safe jar, for up to 6 weeks in the refrigerator. Reheat sauce in the container, uncovered, at 100 percent power for 2 minutes 30 seconds. Stir well before serving.

SWEET
SOMETHINGS

I ndian sweets are in a class by themselves. They are not part of a meal but are eaten like American candies—as gifts, for a sweet taste, or as a quick snack with a beverage. For this reason, Indian sweets are small in size and loaded with flavor.

Nutty Coconut Candy, for example, combines a variety of nuts with coconut, brown sugar, and cardamom. Although the candy is made almost like a peanut brittle, the texture is more like halvah—soft, chewy, and firm like fudge. In the microwave it takes just eleven minutes to cook.

In fact, all of these sweets require little of the effort to which veteran candy-makers are accustomed; nothing sticks and nothing burns. You can, of course, overcook a candy by leaving it in the microwave, but usually this will just lend a little caramel flavor to the finished product, a flavor that is hardly objectionable.

Also included in this section are candied nuts—almonds, walnuts, and pistachios— and candied fennel with pine nuts. These are the after-dinner mints of India. Some are laced with black pepper, and all contain fennel; both of these are considered excellent after-dinner digestive spices.

Finally nowhere is the potential of the microwave more evident than in milk reduction, where milk is cooked and evaporated to produce a concentrate, a process basic to Indian desserts and candy-making. Conventional methods required hours plus constant vigilance due to fears of milk sticking and burning. The microwave has revolutionized all that. In the microwave milk evaporates and reduces quickly without constant watching because milk won't stick or burn. Best of all, the reduction develops a more intense aroma and flavor.

PISTACHIO FUDGE

PISTA BURFI

MICROWAVE

Yield
—64 1-inch squares
Preparation time
—5 minutes
Cooking time
—12 minutes
Heat
—100 percent power
MW oven size
—650 to 700 watts
MW cookware
—One 10-inch skillet

Made with ground pistachio nuts and perfumed with the essence of rose petals and aromatic cardamom, jade-colored *pista burfi* was beloved to the Moghuls, who regarded pistachios as one of the most sensuous gifts from heaven. *Pista burfi* is made by first cooking ground pistachio nuts with milk, sugar, and butter to a fudgelike consistency and then setting the mixture into marble and adorning it with sheets of pounded sterling silver. Cut into diamonds they look precious and regal. I find it pure pleasure to make this classic sweet in the microwave, as the fudge cooks quickly, with ease, and evenly without stirring and the flavor of the delicate pistachio is distinct and pronounced. For variation, almonds, cashew nuts, or pine nuts may be substituted for the pistachio nuts.

=== ROOM TEMPERATURE ===

1 cup whole milk

1¾ sticks (7 ounces) unsalted butter

1¼ cups light brown or white sugar

4 ounces plain cream cheese, cut into ½-inch cubes

½ teaspoon ground cardamom

3½ cups dry nonfat milk powder

½ cup finely ground raw unsalted pistachio nuts

½ teaspoon rose flower water (p. 456) (optional)

¼ cup thinly sliced un-salted raw pista-chio nuts

4 tablespoons heavy cream, or as needed

4 4-inch-square silver leaf vark (p. 476) (optional)

1. Place milk, butter, and sugar in a 10-inch micro-wave-safe skillet. Cook, uncovered, at 100 percent

power in a 650- to 700-watt carousel oven for 8 minutes (or until milk is reduced to a creamy consistency), stirring twice. Remove from oven.

2. Add cream cheese and cardamom and mix until the cheese is fully incorporated into the milk. Fold in dry milk powder and ground pistachio nuts. Cook, uncovered, at 100 percent power for 3½ minutes (or until mixture thickens to fudge consistency), stirring once. Remove from oven.

3. Stir in rose flower water and sliced pistachio nuts. If the *burfi* mixture looks too dry and crumbly, add a little cream to bring it to soft fudge consistency. Pour the mixture, while still warm, into a greased 8-inch-square baking pan and, using a greased flat spatula, pat it down into an even thickness. Decorate with silver leaf (if you are using it) by covering the top surface of the fudge with it in a single layer. When cool, cut the *burfi* into 1-inch squares and store in a tightly sealed container.

NOTE   The pistachio *burfi* will keep stored in a covered container for a week at room temperature, 3 months in the refrigerator, or a year in the freezer.

BANARAS MILK SWEET

BURFI

MICROWAVE

Yield
 —*64 1-inch squares*
Preparation time
 —*5 minutes*
Cooking time
 —*12 minutes*
Heat
 —*100 percent power*
MW oven size
 —*650 to 700 watts*
MW cookware
 —*One 10-inch skillet*

Banaras, the holy city of the Hindus and the home of Lord Shiva, the supreme god of destruction (also known as "dancing Nataraja"), is renowned for its milk sweets, one flavored with pine leaves *kewra* water (p. 456) in particular. This *burfi*, popularly known as *Banarasi burfi*, is traditionally made during the Indian festival of light, Diwali. The classic technique takes close to four hours to produce it, but I have developed a recipe, using the microwave and a few shortcuts, that takes less than twelve minutes. The flavor is as classical as ever.

=========== *ROOM TEMPERATURE* ===========

1 cup whole milk
1¾ sticks (7 ounces) unsalted butter
1¼ cups light brown or white sugar
4 ounces plain cream cheese, cut into ½-inch cubes

½ teaspoon ground cardamom
4 cups dry nonfat milk powder
½ teaspoon pine leaves kewra water (p. 456) or vanilla extract
4 tablespoons heavy cream, or as needed

1. Place milk, butter, and sugar in a 10-inch microwave-safe skillet. Cook, uncovered, at 100 percent power in a 650- to 700-watt carousel oven for 8 minutes, sitrring once. Remove from oven.

2. Add cream cheese and cardamom and mix until the cheese is fully incorporated into the milk. Fold in dry milk powder. Cook, uncovered, at 100 percent power for 3½ minutes (or until mixture thickens to fudge consistency), stirring once. Remove from oven.

3. Stir in pine leaves water. If the *burfi* mixture looks

too dry and crumbly, add a little cream to bring it to soft fudge consistency. Pour the mixture, while still warm, into a greased 8-inch-square baking pan and, using a greased flat spatula, pat it down into an even thickness. When cool, cut the *burfi* into 1-inch squares. Store *burfi* in a tightly sealed container.

NOTE The *burfi* keeps well, stored in a covered container, for a week at room temperature, up to a month in the refrigerator, or 4 months in the freezer.

NUTTY COCONUT CANDY

KADALAI ORANDAI

MICROWAVE

Yield
—48 1½-inch squares
Preparation time
—5 minutes
Cooking time
—10 minutes
Heat
—100 percent power
MW oven size
—650 to 700 watts
MW cookware
—One pie or dinner
plate and one 10-
inch skillet

You must make this candy to experience how easy it is to work with sugar syrup in the microwave, particularly since the results are so uncommonly good and it takes hardly any time. All you do is combine all the ingredients and cook. After adding the soda, remember to let the syrup bubble and foam or else the candy will not be light-textured. This mixed-nuts-and-coconut candy, with its firm, chewy texture—like fruitcake—is an all-occasion pleaser. It makes a lovely Christmas gift too.

========= ROOM TEMPERATURE =========

½ cup raw unsalted
cashew nuts
½ cup shelled raw
unsalted pecans
or walnuts
½ cup slivered almonds
½ cup shelled raw un-
salted pistachio nuts
½ cup toasted melon,
pumpkin, or sunflower
seeds, homemade
(p. 464) or store-
bought, or roasted un-
salted peanuts

½ cup toasted sesame
seeds, homemade
(p. 464) or store-
bought
1 cup (3½ ounces)
packed sweetened
coconut flakes (p. 449)
1 cup (½ pound) packed
dark brown sugar
¼ cup light corn syrup
2 tablespoons water
1 tablespoon unsalted
butter
½ teaspooon ground
cardamom
½ teaspoon baking soda

1. Spread cashew nuts, pecans or walnuts, almonds, and pistachios on a microwave-safe flat plate in a single layer. Roast, uncovered, at 100 percent power in a 650- to 700-watt carousel oven for 3 minutes (or

until nuts are lightly colored, puffed, and exude a nutty aroma), stirring once. Remove from oven.

2. Combine nuts and all other ingredients except baking soda in a 10-inch microwave-safe skillet. Cook, uncovered, at 100 percent power for 4 minutes (or until sugar melts and turns dark and syrupy and the contents thicken). Stir in baking soda and continue cooking, uncovered, at 100 percent power for 2 minutes 30 seconds (or until mixture bubbles and foams), stirring once.

3. Remove from oven and pour the mixture onto a cookie sheet lined with wax paper or a greased marble slab. Spread the mixture into a neat 9-inch square. When slightly cool, cut into 1½-inch squares. Wrap candy in attractive paper and store in an airtight container.

NOTE   The candy keeps well, stored in a covered container, for 3 weeks at room temperature, 6 months in the refrigerator, or a year in the freezer.

PEANUT CANDY

PATTI

Roasted peanuts, jaggery, and cardamom are combined in this glorious candy that is popularly sold by sidewalk vendors in India. I love its slightly chewy-crumbly texture and intense smoky-sweet aroma. Candy-making normally requires several hours of stirring and watchful cooking. In this technique, the candy is cooked in less than six minutes without being stirred. If you don't already have a batch of roasted peanuts, then allow an additional five minutes for roasting them. For variation, almonds, cashew nuts, or pistachios may be substituted for the peanuts.

=================== *ROOM TEMPERATURE* ===================

1 cup (½ pound) packed jaggery (p. 460) or dark brown sugar
¼ cup light corn syrup
2 tablespoons water
1 tablespoon unsalted butter

½ teaspoon ground cardamom
¼ teaspoon dried ginger powder
4 cups unsalted whole roasted peanuts
½ teaspoon baking soda

1. Combine all the ingredients except baking soda in a 10-inch microwave-safe skillet. Cook, uncovered, at 100 percent power for 4 minutes (or until sugar melts and turns dark and syrupy and the contents thicken). Stir in baking soda and continue cooking, uncovered, at 100 percent power for 1 minute 30 seconds (or until mixture bubbles and foams), stirring once.

2. Remove from oven and pour the mixture onto a greased cookie sheet or a greased marble slab. Spread the mixture into a neat 10-inch square. When slightly cool, cut into 2-inch squares and store in an airtight container.

MICROWAVE

Yield
—*24 2½-inch squares*
Preparation time
—*5 minutes*
Cooking time
—*6 minutes*
Heat
—*100 percent power*
MW oven size
—*650 to 700 watts*
MW cookware
—*One pie or dinner plate and one 10-inch skillet*

NOTE The peanut candy keeps well, stored in a covered container, for 3 weeks at room temperature, 6 months in the refrigerator, or a year in the freezer.

CANDIED NUTS
KHAJA

These candied, fennel-coated frosted nuts are traditionally served as after-dinner sweets at Indian meals
because they are a wonderful digestive. They are also
delicious to munch with a cup of tea or coffee and
fabulous sprinkled over sliced fruits, desserts, and ice
creams. The technique for making candied nuts is
slightly different from that for the spiced nuts described in the appetizer section (pp. 3–9). Spiced nuts
are made by *cooking* the nuts in the syrup, which makes
them chewy and shiny. Candied nuts, on the other
hand, are made by *coating* toasted nuts in a baking-
soda–frothed syrup, which makes them frosty while
retaining their crispness. You can make these goodies
with pistachios, almonds, walnuts, or pecans. The addition in some recipes of black pepper (also a digestive), which cuts down the sweetness, is traditional.
You can, if desired, eliminate it, but the nuts will taste
sweeter and less interesting.

CANDIED PISTACHIOS

PATTI PISTA

ROOM TEMPERATURE

MICROWAVE

Yield
—*3 cups*
Preparation time
—*5 minutes*
Cooking time
—*4 minutes*
Heat
—*100 percent power*
MW oven size
—*650 to 700 watts*
MW cookware
—*One 1½-quart cas-serole or soufflé dish*

½ cup sugar
¼ cup water
1 tablespoon unsalted butter
¼ teaspoon baking soda

1 tablespoon ground fennel
1½ teaspoons white pepper
3 cups shelled raw unsalted pistachio nuts

1. Place sugar, water, and butter in a 1½-quart microwave-safe dish. Cook, uncovered, at 100 percent power in a 650- to 700-watt carousel oven for 3 minutes 45 seconds (or until liquid is thick and syrupy), stirring twice.

2. Remove from oven. Add baking soda, fennel, pepper, and pistachio nuts. Mix rapidly to coat nuts evenly with syrup. Immediately transfer nuts to a cookie sheet, spreading them into a single layer. When cool, separate pistachio nuts if they cling together in a bunch. Store in airtight containers.

NOTE The nuts keep well, stored in a covered container, for several weeks at room temperature and several months in the refrigerator.

CANDIED ALMONDS

MEETHA BADAM

=== ROOM TEMPERATURE ===

½ cup sugar
¼ cup water
1 tablespoon unsalted
  butter
1 tablespoon ground
  fennel

½ teaspoon dried ginger
  powder
¼ teaspoon baking soda
3 cups roasted raw
  whole almonds
  (p. 463)

MICROWAVE

Yield
  —3 cups
Preparation time
  —5 minutes
Cooking time
  — 4 minutes
Heat
  —100 percent power
MW oven size
  —650 to 700 watts
MW cookware
  —One 1½-quart cas-
    serole or soufflé dish

1. Place sugar, water, and butter in a 1½-quart microwave-safe dish. Cook, uncovered, at 100 percent power in a 650- to 700-watt carousel oven for 4 minutes (or until liquid is thick and syrupy), stirring twice.

2. Remove from oven. Add fennel, ginger, baking soda, and almonds. Mix rapidly to coat nuts evenly with syrup. Immediately transfer nuts to a cookie sheet, spreading them into a single layer. When cool, separate nuts if they cling together in a bunch and store in airtight containers.

NOTE   The nuts keep well, stored in a covered container, for several weeks at room temperature and several months in the refrigerator.

CANDIED WALNUTS AND CANDIED PECANS

MEETHA AKHROT

MICROWAVE

Yield
—3 cups
Preparation time
—5 minutes
Cooking time
—4 minutes
Heat
—100 percent power
MW oven size
—650 to 700 watts
MW cookware
—One 1½-quart cas-
serole or soufflé dish

=========== ROOM TEMPERATURE ===========

½ cup sugar
¼ cup water
1 tablespoon unsalted butter
1 tablespoon ground fennel

1 teaspoon ground long pepper (p. 483) or freshly ground black pepper
¼ teaspoon baking soda
3 cups roasted unsalted walnuts (p. 463)

1. Place sugar, water, and butter in a 1½-quart microwave-safe dish. Cook, uncovered, at 100 percent power in a 650- to 700-watt carousel oven for 4 minutes (or until liquid is thick and syrupy), stirring twice.

2. Remove from oven. Add fennel, long pepper, baking soda, and walnuts. Mix rapidly to coat nuts evenly with syrup. Immediately transfer nuts to a cookie sheet lined with wax paper, spreading them into a single layer. When cool, separate nuts if they are stuck together and store in airtight containers. The nuts keep well for several weeks at room temperature and several months in the refrigerator.

NOTE   This recipe works equally well with pecans. You might even want to combine them.

CANDIED FENNEL WITH PINE NUTS

MEETHA SAUF AUR NIOJA

MICROWAVE

Yield
  —3 cups
Preparation time
  —5 minutes
Cooking time
  — 4 minutes
Heat
  —100 percent power
MW oven size
  —650 to 700 watts
MW cookware
  *—One 1½-quart cas-
  serole or soufflé dish*

Candied fennel is classic, but together with pine nuts it is sublime!

ROOM TEMPERATURE

1½ cups fennel seeds
1½ cups pine nuts
½ cup sugar
¼ cup water
1 tablespoon unsalted
  butter

¼ teaspoon baking soda
1 tablespoon ground
  fennel
2 teaspoons black pepper

1. Spread fennel seeds and pine nuts on an unseasoned microwave-safe pie or dinner plate. Toast, uncovered, at 100 percent power for 4 minutes (or until fennel and pine nuts look slightly puffed but not colored and exude a sweet fragrance), stirring once. Remove from oven.

2. Place sugar, water, and butter in a 1½-quart microwave-safe dish. Cook, uncovered, at 100 percent power in a 650- to 700-watt carousel oven for 3 minutes 30 seconds (or until liquid is thick and syrupy), stirring twice.

3. Remove from oven. Add baking soda, ground fennel, pepper, and toasted nuts. Mix rapidly to coat nuts evenly with syrup. Immediately transfer nuts to a cookie sheet, spreading them into a single layer. When cool, separate nuts if they cling together in a bunch. Serve warm or cold.

NOTE The candied fennel and pine nuts keep well, stored in a covered container, for several weeks at room temperature and several months in the refrigerator.

BEVERAGES

There is no better way to end a spicy Indian meal than with a warm lightly spiced tea, which can be made in the microwave in a couple of minutes. In conventional Indian cooking, spiced tea is made by soaking the spices for rather a long while, and this tends to turn the beverage bitter as well as distort their flavor. The quick cooking in the microwave makes for a tea that is more fragrant and at the same time delicate.

The microwave is also useful in making the fruit sauces used in Indian punches, fruit coolers, and fruit shakes. When fruit is in season, it can be turned into sauce and frozen indefinitely. Then, on those days when you are running short of time, the *lassis,* coolers, and punches are ready to be made in seconds.

Many of these drinks make wonderful nonalcoholic beverages for an Indian meal. *Lassis,* especially, are also great for breakfast. The punches are perfect for packing for picnics and trips to the beach.

GURKHA REGIMENT TEA OR INDIAN G.I.'S TEA

GURKHA CHAH

Some Indians believe that if it weren't for this tea, India would have lost the fight with the Japanese near the Burmese border in World War II. Also known as "the Frontier Brew," this milky tea is what sustained the Gurkha regiments during battle. It is rich, filling, and potent. Serve as a dessert in demitasse cups.

MICROWAVE

Yield
  —1 cup
Servings
  —1 to 2
Cooking time
  —3 minutes
Standing time
  —1 minute
Heat
  —100 percent power
MW oven size
  —650 to 700 watts
MW cookware
  —One 2-cup glass
    measure

=== ROOM TEMPERATURE ===

1 cup creamy milk
  (p. 454) or whole milk
2 heaping teaspoons leaf
  or 2 bags Assam or
  Darjeeling tea

4 teaspoons dark or light
  brown sugar, molas-
  ses, or honey

Combine milk, tea leaves or tea bags, and sugar in a 2-cup glass measure. Cook, uncovered, at 100 percent power in a 650- to 700-watt carousel oven for 2 minutes 30 seconds (or until milk comes to a vigorous boil). Remove from oven. Let tea stand, preferably covered with a saucer or a small plate, for 1 minute, then strain into a mug or cup and serve.

NEW DELHI TEA

PUNJABI CHAH

MICROWAVE

Yield
— 1 cup
Servings
— 1 to 2
Cooking time
— 4 minutes
Standing time
— 1 minute
Heat
— 100 percent power
MW oven size
— 650 to 700 watts
MW cookware
— One 2-cup glass
measure

This is the spiced tea most often served in Indian restaurants. Imbued with the fragrance of cinnamon and cardamom, its delicate flavor provides an appropriate ending to a spicy meal. I love making this tea in the microwave, as not only is the process fast, neat, and simple but the tea is more aromatic.

=================== *ROOM TEMPERATURE* ===================

1 cup low-fat milk, skim
  milk, or water
1⅛-inch-thick slice fresh
  ginger
1-inch piece cinnamon
  stick, broken into 2
  pieces

2 green or white carda-
  mom pods, lightly
  crushed
1 heaping teaspoon leaf
  or 1 bag Assam or
  orange pekoe tea

Combine milk or water and ginger in a 2-cup glass measure. Cook, uncovered, at 100 percent power in a 650- to 700-watt carousel oven for 3 minutes (or until milk or water is boiling vigorously). Add cinnamon, cardamom, and tea leaves or tea bags. Cook, uncovered, at 100 percent power for 1 minute (or until tea is brewed and milk or water turns light brown). Remove from oven. Let tea steep, preferably covered with a saucer or a small plate, for 1 minute, then strain into a mug or cup. Pass sugar, or any sweetener, and milk (if you are brewing tea in water) on the side.

VARIATION

To make 4 servings, use 4 cups milk or water, 2 slices ginger, 3-inch piece cinnamon stick, 6 cardamom pods, and 3 heaping teaspoons leaf tea or 4 tea bags. Cook milk, uncovered, at 100 percent power for 7 minutes. Follow all other steps given above. Remove from oven and serve strained into teacups or a warmed teapot.

SPICED TEA
MASALA CHAH

MICROWAVE

Yield
  —3½ cups
Servings
  —4
Cooking time
  —9 minutes
Heat
  —100 percent power
MW oven size
  —650 to 700 watts
MW cookware
  —One 8-cup glass
  measure

This is the herbal-tea infusion that refreshed and re-energized me through my long grueling hours at the drawing board during my final years of architecture school. It is a snap to make in the microwave: Add all the ingredients to the boiling water and cook. Since the brewing is so rapid in the microwave, only the essence of herbs and spices is released, leaving no bitter aftertaste. This tea is very refreshing served either hot or chilled over ice at afternoon tea or after a spicy Indian meal.

===== ROOM TEMPERATURE =====

3½ cups water	½ × 3-inch strip fresh or
1 3-inch piece cinnamon,	dried orange peel
broken into pieces	5 fresh basil leaves
8 green or white	2 heaping teaspoons leaf
cardamom pods,	or 3 bags orange
lightly crushed	pekoe or Darjeeling
3 whole cloves	tea

Pour water into an 8-cup glass measure. Heat, uncovered, at 100 percent power in a 650- to 700-watt carousel oven for 7 minutes (or until water comes to a boil). Add all other ingredients. Cook, uncovered, at 100 percent power for 2 minutes (or until the color of the tea comes out). Remove from oven and pour into a warmed teapot. Serve tea strained into cups and pass milk and sweetener as desired.

VARIATION

To make 1 cup classic spiced tea, combine 1 cup water with 1-inch piece cinnamon, 2 whole cardamom pods, 1 whole clove, ½ × 1-inch piece orange peel, 1 basil leaf, and 1 heaping teaspoon leaf tea or 1 tea bag in a 2-cup glass measure. Cook, uncovered, at 100 percent power for 2 minutes 30 seconds (or until water comes to a boil). Serve as suggested above.

BLUSHED PEACH COOLER

SHARBAT

MICROWAVE

Yield
—*2½ cups*
Servings
—*2*
Preparation time
—*2 minutes*

A most refreshing cooler, with a crisp-tart flavor and a fruity fragrance. Make it only when you have fully ripe peaches or nectarines, or the cooler will not be as fragrant. Just a touch of dried apricot puree and ginger give the cooler that special tropical flavor.

½ cup finely chopped fresh ripe peaches or nectarine with their juice
1 tablespoon sugar
1 teaspoon fresh ginger juice (see Note) or ½ teaspoon dried ginger powder

¼ cup, or 2 frozen cubes, apricot puree (p. 473)
1 cup fresh pomegranate or cranberry juice
4 standard-size ice cubes
Peach or nectarine slices for garnish

Place peaches or nectarines, sugar, and ginger in the container of a blender or food processor and process until the contents are smoothly pureed. Add apricot puree, pomegranate or cranberry juice, and ice cubes and continue processing until ice cubes are crushed. Transfer into a pitcher and chill. To serve, pour cooler into 2 10- to 12-ounce glasses filled with ice cubes and serve garnished with peach or nectarine slices.

NOTE   To make fresh ginger juice, crush or grate a 1-inch cube fresh ginger and strain through cheesecloth.

MONSOON COOLER

MOWSAMI

MICROWAVE

Yield
—5 cups
Servings
—4 to 6
Preparation time
—2 minutes

I created this nonalcoholic beverage a few years ago for a Festival of India banquet. I called the drink "Monsoon" because it reminded me of green mango and tamarind leaves warmed under the tropical sun after a monsoon shower. The cooler can be made for one person or in volume. The secret ingredient is the tea. The more herbal a brew you make, the more fragrant your cooler will be.

28 ounces strongly
   brewed Spiced Tea
   (p. 428), orange-spice
   tea, or plain Darjeel-
   ing tea, chilled
1 cup fresh cranberry or
   red raspberry juice
¼ cup apple juice

¼ cup grape juice
1 teaspoon fresh ginger
   juice (see Note) or ½
   teaspoon dried ginger
   powder
Sugar to taste
1 teaspoon anise seed or
   anisette liqueur
Mint sprigs for garnish

1. If you are using anise seeds, add them with the tea leaves and spices to the boiling water to brew the spiced tea.

2. Pour tea, cranberry juice, apple juice, grape juice, and ginger juice into a tall pitcher. Add sugar to taste and mix until fully dissolved. Stir in anisette (if you are using it) and chill. To serve, pour into 4 10- to 12-ounce glasses filled with ice cubes and garnish with mint sprigs.

NOTE   To make fresh ginger juice, crush or grate a 1-inch cube ginger and strain through cheesecloth.

CHOWPATI BEACH PUNCH

MUMBAI SHARBAT

MICROWAVE

Yield
—1¼ cups
Servings
—2
Preparation time
—1 minute

I guarantee that even if you hate coconut you will love this punch! Combined with banana to form a delicately herbal-tasting sauce, the coconut is only barely discernible. Traditionally one would use the juice of *mowsambi*, a mildly sweet Indian grapefruit, and *phalsa*, a sweetish-sour, crimson-colored berry, but our American grapefruit and cranberry juices make excellent substitutes.

½ cup, or 4 frozen cubes, banana-coconut sauce (p. 472)

⅓ cup pineapple, orange, or mango juice

⅓ cup Indian grapefruit (mowsambi) juice (or use regular grapefruit juice)

⅓ cup Indian cranberry (phalsa) juice (or use regular cranberry juice)

2 slices grapefruit

Put all the ingredients except the grapefruit slices into the container of a blender and process until thoroughly blended and liquefied. Pour into 2 10- to 12-ounce glasses filled with ice cubes. Serve immediately garnished with grapefruit slices.

TROPICAL BEACH PUNCH

ANNANAAS SHARBAT

MICROWAVE

Yield
*   —3½ cups*
Servings
*   —3 to 4*
Preparation time
*   —1 minute*

A wonderfully refreshing punch made with pineapple and pomegranate juice. The apricot puree is essential to mellow and bind the flavors in delicate harmony. Ginger is the added tropical touch. To make fresh pomegranate juice, cut a red ripe pomegranate in half and extract its juice using a citrus juicer.

½ cup chopped fresh ripe pineapple (or use canned unsweetened crushed pineapple with the juice)

1 tablespoon sugar

1 teaspoon fresh ginger juice (see Note) or ½ teaspoon dried ginger powder

¼ cup, or 2 frozen cubes, apricot puree (p. 473)

1 cup fresh pomegranate or cranberry juice

14 ounces club soda

Mint sprigs for garnish

Place all the ingredients except club soda and mint into the container of a blender or food processor and process until the contents are smoothly pureed. Serve immediately or transfer into a pitcher and chill. To serve, distribute punch into 3 to 4 tall glasses half-filled with ice cubes, fill with club soda, and garnish with mint sprigs.

NOTE   To make fresh ginger juice, crush or grate a 1-inch cube ginger and strain through cheesecloth.

INDIAN SUMMER COOLER

AAM SHARBAT

MICROWAVE

Yield
  —2½ cups
Servings
  —2
Preparation time
  —1 minute

Sweet ripe mango bursting with fragrance is essential for making this cooler. Do not worry if the mango is fibrous, as the blender will take care of that. This cooler, combining mango, grapefruit juice, apricot puree, and a touch of ginger, is very tropical and very refreshing. It is lovely served at cocktails as a nonalcoholic drink.

ROOM TEMPERATURE

½ cup chopped fresh ripe mango (or use canned mango slices or mango puree)

2 teaspoons sugar

1 teaspoon fresh ginger juice (see Note) or ½ teaspoon dried ginger powder

¼ cup, or 2 frozen cubes, apricot puree (p. 473)

1 cup orange or grapefruit juice

4 standard-size ice cubes

Mint sprigs for garnish

Place mango, sugar, and ginger into the container of a blender or food processor and process until the contents are smoothly pureed. Add apricot puree, orange juice, and ice cubes and continue processing until ice cubes are crushed. Serve immediately or transfer into a pitcher and chill. To serve, pour into 2 10- to 12-ounce glasses filled with ice cubes and garnish with mint sprigs.

NOTE   To make fresh ginger juice, crush or grate a 1-inch cube ginger and strain through cheesecloth.

INDIAN SUMMER PUNCH

AAM SHARBAT

MICROWAVE

Yield
—*2½ cups*
Servings
—*3 to 4*
Preparation time
—*2 minutes*

This is similar to Indian Summer Cooler (p. 434), except that sparkling water is used in place of ice cubes. In this form I find it's a fabulous thirst quencher, particularly after a workout, a tennis game, or a day at the beach.

½ cup chopped fresh ripe mango (or use canned mango slices or mango puree)

2 teaspoons sugar

1 teaspoon fresh ginger juice (see Note) or ½ teaspoon dried ginger powder

¼ cup, or 2 frozen cubes, apricot puree (p. 473)

1 cup orange or grapefruit juice

14 ounces club soda

Mint sprigs for garnish

Place all the ingredients except club soda and mint into the container of a blender or food processor and process until the contents are smoothly pureed. Transfer into a pitcher and chill. To serve, distribute punch into 3 to 4 tall glasses half-filled with ice cubes. Fill with club soda and garnish with mint sprigs.

NOTE   To make fresh ginger juice, crush or grate a 1-inch cube ginger and strain through cheesecloth.

INDIAN SUMMER COCKTAIL

AAM SHARBAT

MICROWAVE

Yield
  —3 cups
Servings
  —2
Preparation time
  —1 minute

This is the Indian Summer Cooler (p. 434), except with a kick!

4 ounces light rum　　　　*6 lime slices for garnish*
1 recipe (2½ cups) In-
  dian Summer Cooler
  (p. 434)

Distribute light rum into 2 10- to 12-ounce glasses filled with ice cubes. Fill with Indian Summer Cooler and serve garnished with lime slices.

MANGO
SHAKE

AAM LASSI

MICROWAVE

Yield
  —2 cups
Servings
  —2
Preparation time
  —2 minutes

I love this light and refreshing shake made with mangoes and low-fat buttermilk. It is low in calories yet flavorful. The apricot puree is a necessary addition to diffuse the mango flavor and give the shake a more interesting, rounded-off taste. It is wonderful served with Indian meals.

*1 cup chopped ripe
  mango*
⅔ cup plain yogurt
*2 tablespoons, or 1
  frozen cube, apricot
  puree (p. 473)*

*2 tablespoons sugar or
  honey (optional)*
⅓ cup water
4 standard-size ice cubes

Put mango, yogurt, apricot puree, and sugar or honey into the container of a blender and process until the sugar melts. Add water and ice cubes and continue processing until some of the ice gets crushed and the contents are frothy. Pour into 2 tall 10-ounce glasses and serve or chill.

MOGHUL SHAKE

BADSHAHI LASSI

MICROWAVE

Yield
—1¼ cups
Servings
—1
Preparation time
—1 minute

This royal *lassi,* gloriously fruity and spicy, is made with yogurt and a special banana-coconut sauce that tastes of neither banana nor coconut. The combined experience, however, is heavenly, which is probably why the holy Moghul cooks decided to save it for special banquets. If you already have a batch of banana-coconut sauce, than the *lassi* is made in a minute. If not, allow for an additional five minutes to make the sauce.

½ cup, or 4 frozen
  cubes, banana-coconut
  sauce (p. 472)

⅔ cup low-fat or fat-free
  plain yogurt
⅓ cup water
Pinch of ground saffron
Fresh orange or lime
  slices for garnish

Put all the ingredients into the container of a blender and process until thoroughly blended and liquefied. Serve in a 10- or 12-ounce glass, if desired, over crushed ice and with a slice of fresh orange or lime.

ROSE MILK

GULAB DOODH

MICROWAVE

Yield
  —2 cups
Servings
  —2
Preparation time
  —1 minute

Milk drinks are very popular in India. Flavored with fragrant flower essences, nuts, and aromatic tropical fruits, these icy-cold drinks are almost a must in summer when the mercury rises above 100. This rose drink made with creamy milk has a fudgelike flavor and the fragrance of rose petals. In India a few drops of red coloring are usually added to give the drink a pink color, but I prefer using strawberries because they are healthier. Besides, they temper the strong scent of the rose flower water.

1 cup cold creamy milk (p. 454) or half-and-half
4 large red ripe strawberries

4 tablespoons sugar or honey (optional)
4 standard-size ice cubes
¼ teaspoon rose flower water (p. 456)

Put milk, strawberries, and sugar into the container of a blender and process until the sugar dissolves. Add ice cubes and essence and continue processing until some of the ice gets crushed and the contents are frothy. Pour into 2 10-ounce glasses and serve or chill.

MANGO MILK

AAM DOODH

MICROWAVE

Yield
  —2 cups
Servings
  —2
Preparation time
  —2 minutes

This is the drink to make when ripe, juicy mangoes are in season. It doesn't matter if they are fibrous, since they will be liquefied, as long as they are sweet and fragrant. The creamy milk adds a lovely, delicate milk-fudge flavor to the shake without making it rich or heavy.

*1 cup chopped ripe
  mango*
*1 cup cold creamy
  milk (p. 454) or
  half-and-half*

*2 tablespoons sugar or
  honey (optional)*
4 standard-size ice cubes
*2 drops pine leaves
  kewra water (p. 456)*

Put mango, milk, and sugar into the container of a blender and process until the sugar dissolves. Add ice cubes and essence and continue processing until some of the ice gets crushed and the contents are frothy. Pour into 2 10-ounce glasses and serve right away or chill.

BANANA COCONUT MILK

KELA DOODH

MICROWAVE

Yield
—1¼ cups
Servings
—2
Preparation time
—1 minute

This milk drink is made with cardamom and a ginger-fragrant banana-coconut sauce. It is light yet rich-tasting, therefore lovely to serve as a thirst quencher on hot, sultry days.

½ cup, or 4 frozen cubes, banana-coconut sauce (p. 472)

1¾ cups low-fat or whole milk, chilled

Small pinch ground cardamom or nutmeg

Put all the ingredients into the container of a blender and process until thoroughly blended and liquefied. Distribute the cooler into 2 old-fashioned 10- to 12-ounce glasses filled with ice cubes and serve.

SAFFRON MILK

KESARI DOODH

MICROWAVE

Yield
  —9 cups
Servings
  —8
Preparation time
  —3 minutes
Cooking time
  —9 minutes
Heat
  —100 percent power
MW oven size
  —650 to 700 watts
MW cookware
  —One 8-cup glass
  measure

Of all the milk drinks, Indians love saffron milk most. It is made by combining milk with almonds, sugar, and fragrant saffron. Normally it takes a long time to make as one first has to make the almond milk, but I use a marvelous shortcut: Odense almond paste, which works beautifully. In addition, in the microwave the almond, milk, and cornstarch mixture cooks lump-free. The milk is lightly sweetened, as I prefer it, and has a lovely almond-saffron taste. In south India this is served as a first-course soup and called sweet almond soup.

3 tablespoons cornstarch	*½ cup sugar*
9 cups whole or low-fat milk	*1 teaspoon crushed saffron threads or powdered saffron*
7-ounce packet Odense almond paste	*¼ teaspoon almond extract*

1. In a small bowl dissolve cornstarch in ¼ cup milk and reserve.

2. Cut almond paste roughly into 6 to 8 pieces and put in an 8-cup glass measure. Add 3 cups milk, sugar, and saffron. Cook, uncovered, at 100 percent power in a 650- to 700-watt carousel oven for 9 minutes (or until almond paste and sugar are fully dissolved and milk is boiling), stirring twice.

3. Remove from oven and stir in the remaining milk and almond extract. Cool and chill. Serve in 10-ounce old-fashioned glasses, if desired, over crushed ice.

HOLY GURU

PRASADI DOODH

MICROWAVE

Yield
  —6½ cups
Servings
  —6
Preparation time
  —2 minutes

A cocktail for a blissful experience. Saffron, the sacred spice of the holy gurus in India, is enlivened with tropical rum.

½ recipe (4½ cups) Saffron Milk (p. 442)	*2 trays standard-size ice cubes*
2 cups light rum	*6 lime wedges or slices for garnish*

Combine saffron milk and rum in a pitcher. Distribute punch into 6 10-ounce glasses filled with ice cubes. Add a lime wedge or slice and serve.

NOTE To make one drink, pour 2 ounces light rum into a tall glass filled with ice cubes. Add about 6 ounces saffron milk and serve garnished with a lime wedge or slice.

HOLY COW
KHWABI THANDAI

MICROWAVE

Yield
  —6 cups
Servings
  —6
Preparation time
  —2 minutes

Laced with bourbon and combined with saffron and anise, two of the greatest gifts of the sun-drenched earth, the Holy Cow is sensuously smooth. For variation, and a less potent cocktail, use sake in place of bourbon.

½ recipe (4½ cups) Saffron Milk (p. 442)
1½ cups bourbon
3 tablespoons Pernod or any other anise-flavored brandy

3 trays standard-size ice cubes
6 mint sprigs for garnish

Combine saffron milk, bourbon, and Pernod in a pitcher. Distribute punch into 6 10-ounce glasses filled with ice cubes. Add a sprig of mint and serve.

NOTE To make one drink, pour about 2 ounces bourbon and 1 teaspoon Pernod into a 10-ounce glass filled with ice cubes. Add 6 ounces saffron milk and serve garnished with a mint sprig.

MOGHUL DREAM

KHWABI MAHAL DOODH

MICROWAVE

Yield
  —6 cups
Servings
  —6
Preparation time
  —2 minutes

This is a spectacular cocktail, made by combining the delicate fragrances of saffron and apricots and a touch of pure twenty-four-carat gold, that brings visions of crystal lakes and ivory palaces! For a less potent cocktail, reduce the amount of brandy.

¼ recipe (2¼ cups)
  Saffron Milk (p. 442)
2½ cups apricot brandy
6 heaping tablespoons
  crushed ice

Saffron threads
4 2-inch-square gold or
  silver leaf vark
  (p. 476) (optional)

Combine saffron milk, brandy, and crushed ice in a mixer or pitcher and shake or mix well. Distribute punch into 6 martini glasses with sugar-lined rims, sprinkle each with a few saffron threads and a few tiny ½-inch pieces of *vark*. Serve immediately.

NOTE   To make one drink, combine 3 ounces saffron milk with 3 ounces brandy and a heaping tablespoon of crushed ice in a mixer, shake well, and serve as suggested above.

MOGHUL
MICROWAVE PANTRY

The cuisine of India, like those of other countries, uses certain preparations in many different recipes. These include tamarind juice, prepared spice blends such as *garam masala,* fresh cheese, and stocks. Since one of the prime benefits of microwave cooking is speed, it pays to have those preparations that store well made in some quantity in advance, ready to play its role in a given dish without added hassle. It is not, of course, essential to have any of these items made in advance in order to succeed in Indian cooking. But logic suggests that cooking is more efficient when those components that store well are made ahead of time, as long as flavor is not compromised.

This section also describes those unique or unusual spices, herbs, and other ingredients that are frequently used in Indian recipes but are not readily found in most supermarkets and usually must be purchased in Indian groceries, such as ajowan seeds, curry leaves, and asafetida. (These are also available by mail order; see list, pp. 495–496. And do not fear if you cannot find these spices; I have recommended substitutes in all of the recipes.)

BASMATI *RICE*

This long-grain rice from India has a distinctive nutty-pine fragrance (its name means queen of fragrance), delicate buttery flavor, and firm texture. The most unique characteristic of the *basmati* is its cooking quality. While most rice expand in all directions when cooked, *basmati* lengthens, forming a long, thin strand much like vermicelli. In addition, it cooks without getting mushy and holds its shape. *Basmati* is widely available in Indian, Middle Eastern, health food, and specialty grocery stores and several supermarkets. Stored in a covered container in a cool place, *basmati* keeps indefinitely.

BULGUR

Bulgur, a processed cracked-wheat cereal, is used in Middle Eastern salads such as tabbouleh. Bulgur, like other grains, adapts exquisitely to microwave cooking, becoming more fluffy. Bulgur is available in Middle Eastern and health-food stores.

CHICK-PEA FLOUR

Chick-pea flour is made by finely grinding dried chick-peas, or garbanzo. Its spicy-rich flavor is much in demand in Indian cooking for making batter for fritters, dumplings, steamed bread, sauces, and sweet meats. Chick-pea flour, available in Indian grocery stores, stores well, kept in airtight containers in a cool place.

COCONUT

Coconut, the sweet, creamy fruit of the coconut palm tree, is an important ingredient in Indian cooking. Grated, shredded into flakes, or in milk form, coconut has many uses, ranging from lending texture and enriching sauces to being used as a substitute for regular milk or cream.

GRATED OR FLAKED COCONUT

Fresh grated coconut or frozen flaked coconut can be used interchangeably in recipes calling for grated coconut. Baker's sweetened coconut flakes is delicious but sweet, therefore use it only when a recipe specifically calls for it. In an emergency, when fresh grated coconut is not available, then dry unsweetened coconut flakes or sweetened coconut flakes with the clinging sugar rinsed off may be substituted.

Cracking coconut in the microwave is not recommended as the prolonged exposure to heat not only dries the coconut but alters its flavor from herbal to an unpleasant burnt-oily one.

1 medium-size (1¼–1½ pounds) coconut

Pierce the "eyes" (the three dark-brown spots at one end of the coconut) using a sharp pointed object such as an ice pick, a skewer, or a nail and drain off the liquid. Wrap coconut in a kitchen towel and give it a whack with a hammer or a kitchen mallet until it cracks into a few pieces. Using a sharp paring knife, release the meat from the shell and peel off the brown skin. Cut the meat into 1-inch pieces and, using a food processor or blender, finely grate it.

COCONUT MILK

Coconut milk is made by extracting juices from crushed or ground coconut pulp. Fresh, frozen unsweetened, canned unsweetened (imported from Thailand), and coconut milk made from a block of creamed coconut are all acceptable and can therefore be used interchangeably in recipes calling for coconut milk. Making fresh coconut milk is, in fact, very simple.

FRESH COCONUT MILK

MICROWAVE

Yield
—2 cups
Preparation time
—5 minutes
Cooking time
—4 minutes
Heat
—100 percent power
MW oven size
—650 to 700 watts
MW cookware
—One 1½-quart cov-
ered casserole or
soufflé dish

2½ cups grated or flaked
coconut (meat from 1
coconut)

2 cups low-fat milk, or 1
cup whole milk plus 1
cup water, or 2 cups
water

1. Combine grated coconut and milk in a 1½-quart microwave-safe dish and cover with the lid. Cook at 100 percent power in a 650- to 700-watt carousel oven for 4 minutes (or until liquid is steaming hot). Remove from oven.

2. Transfer contents into the container of a food processor or blender and process for 2 minutes. Pour the coconut puree into a fine mesh sieve held over a bowl. Gently squeeze the pulp to extract as much liquid as possible. Discard the residue or use for making Thin Coconut Milk (recipe follows). Use immediately or refrigerate. The cream that will separate at the top can either be scooped up and used separately to lend a richer, more velvety texture to the sauce or stirred back into the liquid.

THIN FRESH COCONUT MILK

MICROWAVE

Yield
—1 cup
Preparation time
—3 minutes
Cooking time
—2 minutes
Heat
—100 percent power
MW oven size
—650 to 700 watts
MW cookware
—One 1-cup glass
measure

The coconut residue left over from making coconut milk still has some flavor that can be extracted. This light coconut broth may be used in recipes in place of water.

Heat 1 cup low-fat milk or water in a 1-cup glass measure at 100 percent power for 2 minutes (or until very hot). Add the water and coconut residue (remaining after extracting coconut milk) to the food processor, process until thoroughly blended, and strain this diluted coconut milk through double layers of cheesecloth. Use in sauces, gravies, and soups in place of water or stock.

INSTANT COCONUT MILK

MICROWAVE

Yield
—2½ cups
Preparation time
—5 minutes
Cooking time
—4 minutes
Heat
—100 percent power
MW oven size
—650 to 700 watts
MW cookware
—One 4-cup glass
measure

In an emergency, when unsweetened coconut milk is not available, you can make this coconut milk using sweetened coconut flakes. To reduce or eliminate sweetness, rinse coconut flakes under running water and drain before proceeding with the recipe.

1 7-ounce package (2½ cups lightly packed) sweetened coconut (Baker's style)	2½ cups whole or low-fat milk or water

Place coconut flakes and milk in a 4-cup glass measure. Cook, uncovered, at 100 percent power in a 650- to 700-watt carousel oven for 4 minutes (or until milk is very hot). Remove from oven, transfer contents into the container of a blender or food processor, and process for 2 minutes or until finely pureed. Strain coconut juice through a fine mesh sieve into a reserved bowl—pressing the pulp to extract as much liquid as possible. Use immediately as recommended in the recipe or refrigerate.

MICROWAVE

Yield
   —1 cup
Cooking time
   —3 minutes
Heat
   —100 percent power
MW oven size
   —650 to 700 watts
MW cookware
   —One 2-cup glass
   measure

LIGHT COCONUT CREAM

Here is a quick and delicious substitute for coconut cream—with lots of flavor, not calories—made with coconut milk.

1 cup coconut milk,   *2–3 teaspoons cornstarch*
   fresh, frozen (de-
   frosted), or canned

Place coconut milk in a 2-cup glass measure. Add 2 teaspoons cornstarch and stir well until thoroughly dissolved. Cook, uncovered, at 100 percent power in a 650- to 700-watt carousel oven for 3 minutes (or until milk boils and thickens to light-cream consistency). Remove from oven. For a thicker consistency, increase cornstarch to 3 teaspoons.

CREAMY MILK

RABADI DOODH

Rabadi doodh is made by cooking milk until it reduces to half its original volume. It is thinner and lower in butterfat than light cream but has more flavor. It is amusing to watch how easily this classic preparation is made in the microwave. Since nothing sticks stubbornly, there is no messy dish to clean. Remember, however, to use a deep dish to prevent the boiling milk from spilling over. *Rabadi doodh* is used in milk punches (pp. 439–440) and puddings and for enriching dessert sauces.

MICROWAVE

Yield
  —1 or 2 cups
Cooking time
  —20 or 34 minutes
Heat
  —100 percent power
MW oven size
  —650 to 700 watts
MW cookware
  —One 5-quart casserole

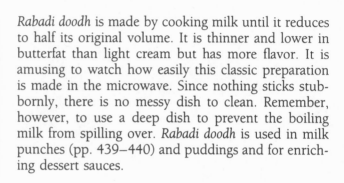

2 cups whole milk (if making 1 cup), or 4 cups (if making 2 cups) rabadi doodh

Pour milk into a 5-quart microwave-safe dish. Cook, uncovered, at 100 percent power in a 650- to 700-watt carousel oven for 20 to 34 minutes (or until milk is reduced to half its original volume and resembles light cream), stirring 2 to 3 times to break the skin as it forms on the surface. Remove from oven. Use as recommended in the recipe or cool and transfer into a covered container.

NOTE The creamy milk keeps in the refrigerator for up to 5 days.

CREAMY MILK SAUCE
RABADI

MICROWAVE

Yield
—*½ cup*
Cooking time
—*25 minutes*
Heat
—*100 percent power*
MW oven size
—*650 to 700 watts*
MW cookware
—*One 5-quart casse-role*

Rabadi is the next by-product of the milk if, after making *rabadi doodh,* the cooking is continued and the milk is allowed to further reduce to half the quantity (or one quarter of its original volume). The sauce, with its distinct characteristic *khoya* aroma and delectable sweetness, is used in countless desserts and sweets throughout India. *Rabadi* is delicious served by itself warm, at room temperature, or chilled, garnished with nuts as a dessert, or accompanied with sliced fruits as a dessert sauce.

2 cups whole milk

Pour milk into a 5-quart microwave-safe dish. Cook, uncovered, at 100 percent power in a 650- to 700-watt carousel oven for 25 minutes (or until milk is reduced to one quarter of its original volume and resembles cream soup), stirring often to break the skin as it forms on the surface. Remove from oven and whip to incorporate the lumped skin into the sauce. Use as recommended in the recipe or cool and transfer into a covered container.

NOTE   The creamy milk sauce keeps in the refrigerator for up to 2 weeks.

FLOWER WATERS
RUH

As vanilla and almond essences are used in Western cooking, extracts of highly fragrant flowers and leaves such as rose (*gulab*) flower and pine leaves *kewra* are used in Indian cooking. Favored by the Moghuls, these essences are used to aromatize desserts, sweets, pilafs, and beverages. Flower extracts are available in Middle Eastern, specialty, and Indian grocery stores as waters as well as concentrates called essences. If using an essence, then use only half as much.

INDIAN CHENNA CHEESE

There are few things that delight my palate as much as fresh homemade cheese—soft, moist, and crumbly and still warm and fragrant with the delicate citrus aroma of whey. Nourishing and flavorful, fresh milk cheese is a nearly perfect food. It is low in fat, calories, and cholesterol, and rich in protein, vitamin A, and minerals. Compressed into a block, just a few moments in the food processor can alter its texture from dense and firm, in which form it can be sliced, to smooth and creamy, making it suitable for use in sauces. Since fresh cheese is essentially an altered state of milk, the quality of the milk itself is of obvious importance. The fresher the milk, the sweeter, more flavorful the cheese will be. Fresh cheese keeps in the refrigerator, if tightly wrapped in plastic wrap, for up to two days, although much of its delicate flavor is lost after a day.

INDIAN CHENNA CHEESE

Making fresh cheese in the microwave is extremely simple. In fact, the cheese curd becomes softer and more flavorful. Bring milk to the boil, add an acid agent such as lemon juice, and cook again until the milky-white cheese separates into large curds from the greenish-yellow whey. Drain the curds and you will have the sweetest-smelling and freshest-tasting cheese imaginable, to be eaten—while still warm—spread over toasts, pastries, and muffins. Fresh cheese is lovely served by itself, plain or seasoned, or contrasted with sweetish-sour fruits such as kiwi, apricot, grapefruit, and berries (raspberries, strawberries, and blueberries in particular). Fresh cheese makes delicious spreads (p. 19) and dips (p. 17), puddings and cakes (pp. 387–388), appetizers, and hearty main dishes.

4 cups whole or low-fat milk	2 tablespoons lemon juice

MICROWAVE

Yield
  —5 ounces (½ cup)
Preparation time
  —8 minutes
Cooking time
  —11 minutes
Heat
  —100 percent power
MW oven size
  —650 to 700 watts
MW cookware
  —One 8-cup glass measure

1. Place a medium-size strainer or colander with a layer of cheesecloth over a large bowl.

2. Pour milk into an 8-cup glass measure or 4-quart microwave-safe casserole. Cook, uncovered, at 100 percent power in a 650- to 700-watt carousel oven for 10 minutes (or until milk comes to a boil).

3. Add lemon juice and stir lightly. Almost immediately, milk will curdle and milky-white curd will float to the surface, and liquid whey will turn greenish-yellow. If the curd does not form, cook the milk, uncovered, at 100 percent power for an additional 30 to 45 seconds. Remove from oven.

4. Turn mixture into the strainer or colander and drain. When whey has drained, press cheese lightly with the back of a spoon for 30 seconds (or until most of the excess whey has drained). Do not squeeze or apply excess pressure to drain the cheese completely, as this will cause it to taste dry, tough, and flavorless. Remove cheese from cheesecloth and serve or transfer into a covered container and refrigerate.

INDIAN PANEER CHEESE

Paneer, beloved to vegetarians, is made by molding fresh drained cheese, which is then cut into neat pieces. Fresh cheese is lovely served by itself, plain or seasoned, in salads, pilafs, soups, or with fresh fruits. *Paneer* is used in the classic Moghul dish *Matar Paneer* (p. 179).

MICROWAVE

Yield
—16 ½ × ½ × 2-inch
paneer *pieces*
(¾ cup)
Servings
—2 to 4
Preparation time
—5 minutes plus 30
minutes for draining
Cooking time
—1 minute
Heat
—70 percent power
MW oven size
—650 to 700 watts
MW cookware
—One 10-inch pie or
dinner plate

4 cups whole or low-fat milk	2 tablespoons lemon juice
	⅓ cup all-purpose flour

1. Make the cheese following all the directions given for making Indian *Chenna* Cheese (p. 456), except do not remove the cheese from the cheesecloth. Instead, wrap tightly in the cloth, forming the cheese into a 4-inch patty, and set aside to cool (about 30 minutes).

2. Uncover cheese and place on a work board dusted with about 2 tablespoons of flour. Using a knife with a sharp, thin blade, cut cheese into 16 wedges. Separate the cheese pieces and lay them on their sides. Sprinkle the remaining flour on the cheese pieces to coat them evenly. Arrange cheese pieces on a microwave-safe pie or dinner plate in petal fashion.

3. Cook, uncovered, at 70 percent (medium) power for 1 minute (or until flour on the cheese pieces cooks and bonds the surface). Remove from oven. Use as recommended in the recipe or transfer into a covered container and refrigerate.

FIRM TOFU SLICES

MICROWAVE

Yield
—36 ½ × ½ × 2-inch
    tofu slices (¾ cup)
Preparation time
—5 minutes
Cooking time
—10 minutes
Heat
—100 percent power
MW oven size
—650 to 700 watts
MW cookware
—One 3-quart casse-
    role

Although not as flavorful, tofu makes an acceptable substitute for *paneer*, especially considering all its nutritional benefits. I love the texture and flavor of tofu and often use it in recipes in place of *paneer*. To ensure tofu does not disintegrate during cooking, I have devised the following technique using the microwave. The tofu slices are heated immersed in a vinegar-water solution in the microwave, where they develop a firm texture. The vinegar does not affect the flavor of the tofu.

ROOM TEMPERATURE

2 pieces Chinese-style tofu	¼ cup white vinegar
	3 cups water

Cut each piece of tofu in half. Slice each half into six ½-inch-thick slices. Pour water and vinegar into a 3-quart microwave-safe casserole and add tofu slices. Cook, uncovered, at 100 percent power in a 650- to 700-watt carousel oven for 10 minutes (or until water is boiling and tofu pieces feel firm to the touch). Remove from oven and let tofu cool in the vinegar water. Drain and use as needed.

INDIAN KHOYA MILK

INDIAN KHOYA MILK

When milk is cooked for a long period of time—until most (85 percent) of the moisture present evaporates—it reduces to a fudgelike moist dough. This butter-rich milk fudge with a nutty aroma, called *khoya,* is one of the primary ingredients in Indian sweet-making.

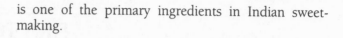

MICROWAVE

Yield
—*2½ ounces or ¼ cup (a ball about the size of a lime)*
Cooking time
—*29 minutes*
Heat
—*100 and 70 percent power*
MW oven size
—*650 to 700 watts*
MW cookware
—*One 5-quart casserole*

2 cups whole milk

1. Pour milk into a 5-quart microwave-safe dish. Cook, uncovered, at 100 percent power in a 650- to 700-watt carousel oven for 25 minutes (or until milk is reduced to ½ cup and resembles cream soup), stirring 4 times to break the skin as it forms on the surface.

2. Cook at 70 percent (medium) power for 4 minutes (or until contents reduce to a thick doughlike mass and turn light caramel), stirring twice. Remove from oven. Use immediately or cool and transfer into a covered container.

NOTE The milk fudge keeps for up to 6 weeks in the refrigerator and 6 months in the freezer.

JAGGERY
GUDH

Jaggery is the unrefined natural raw sugar made from the pressed juices of the sugar cane. It is a moist, soft light- to dark-brown-colored sugar with a distinct flavor and fragrance reminiscent of maple sugar. Jaggery is available in Indian grocery stores, although dark or light brown sugar make acceptable substitutes.

LEGUMES DAL

RED (PINK) LENTILS
MASAR DAL

These thin, small lens-shaped hulled red or pink seeds cook quickly and essentially disintegrate into a sauce. Hence they are very popular in side- and main-dish *dals*. Stored in airtight containers, these lentils keep indefinitely. Red (pink) lentils are available in Middle Eastern, specialty, and Indian stores.

YELLOW LENTILS
TOOVAR DAL

Yellow lentils, technically a variety of Indian peas, are similar to American yellow split peas but they are much thinner. Lens-shaped, hulled, and split yellow lentils take longer to cook than red lentils, but they produce a more velvety puree. They are used in vegetarian curries, soups, sauces, sweets, and as stuffings for vegetables, dumplings, and breads. Dried yellow lentils, available in Indian grocery stores, keep indefinitely in a covered container.

**AMERICAN YELLOW
SPLIT PEAS**
VILAYATI CHANA DAL

American split peas, available at your supermarket in both yellow and green varieties, are not the same as Indian split peas. American yellow split peas are like a cross between Indian yellow split peas and yellow lentils. They possess the same meaty, spicy flavor of the Indian split peas and yet are lighter and easier to digest, in addition to cooking faster. American split peas have many uses in Indian cooking—in *dal*, vegetarian *dal* stews, desserts, etc. Both dried yellow and green American split peas are available at supermarkets.

BROWN LENTILS
SABAT MASAR DAL

Brown lentils are similar to red (pink) lentils except they have greenish-yellow skins. Brown lentils are generally soaked before cooking in order to relax their skins. The sweet-tasting brown lentils are used in salads, soups, rice pilafs, sweets, and as a stuffing for poultry, game, and vegetables. Dried brown lentils are available at supermarkets.

YELLOW MUNG BEANS
MOONG DAL

These are tiny, hulled and split lemon-yellow-colored rectangular seeds of whole green mung beans. In this form they are easy to digest and quick-cooking. Yellow mung beans are used in making *dal*, puddings, dumplings, sweets, and as stuffing for vegetables and dumplings. The beans are also ground in flour for use in making broth and candies. Dried yellow mung beans and mung bean flour, available in Indian grocery stores, can be stored in covered containers and kept indefinitely.

WHOLE MUNG BEANS
SABAT MOONG DAL

Also known as green mung beans, these oval-shaped beans still have their green skins covering the beans. For this reason they generally are soaked before cooking. Whole mung beans are earthy tasting and lovely cooked in pilafs, soups, salads, puddings, and *dals*. Dried whole mung beans are available in Oriental and Indian grocery stores.

BLACK-EYED PEAS
LOBHIA

The American southern staple black-eyed peas are also popular in Indian cooking. These small, kidney-shaped, grayish seeds are generally cooked whole in combination with vegetables, meat, and seafood in casseroles, pilafs, salads, and *dal* stews. Dried, frozen, and fresh black-eyed peas are available at supermarkets.

LENTIL WAFERS
PUPPADUM
OR PAPAD

Lentil wafers are made by grinding soaked beans (white *gram urad dal* or yellow mung *moong dal*) into a pliable dough, rolling it into disks, and then air drying. Pre-rolled paper-thin 8-inch-round wafers, ready for toasting, are available in Indian grocery stores in many flavors: plain, cumin, garlic, black pepper, red pepper, and green chilies. Stored in tightly covered containers, lentil wafers keep for a year, but they are most fragrant when used within four months.

PRUNE BUTTER

Natural prune butter, similar to apple butter, is available at supermarkets in the preserves section, next to the peanut butter. You can also make prune butter at home by combining 1 cup pitted prunes with ⅓ cup boiling water and processing it in a food processor until smoothly pureed.

RICE FLOUR AND CREAM OF RICE

The *rice flour,* also called rice powder, is finely ground long-grain rice. In India, rice flour is primarily used in confections and savories, and to make creamy puddings, dumplings, and crêpes. Rice flour can also be used as we do cornstarch—as a thickener for sauces. Rice flour is available in health-food, specialty, Oriental, and Indian grocery stores.

Cream of rice, also known as rice cereal, is similar to rice flour except that it is coarsely ground and hence grainier. Regular rice cereal available at supermarkets is what you want for more flavor and texture in recipes calling for cream of rice.

ROASTED NUTS: ALMONDS, CASHEW NUTS, PISTACHIOS, WALNUTS, PECANS

Roasted nuts are indispensable to Moghul cooking. They are used as a garnish on innumerable rice pilafs, braised meats, nut fudges, and candies. Coated with hot spices they are served with drinks, and frosted with digestive spices and eaten after dinner.

Spread shelled raw nuts on a microwave-safe pie or dinner plate in a single layer. You could even use the carousel of the oven, directly. Roast, uncovered, at 100 percent power in a 650- to 700-watt carousel oven until the nuts look puffed and get traces of brown on their edges. Remove from oven. Cool completely and use or store in an airtight container in a cool place.

MICROWAVE

Heat
—100 percent power
MW oven size
—650 to 700 watts
MW cookware
—One 10-inch pie or dinner plate

AMOUNT	COOKING TIME	NUMBER OF STIRRINGS
2 tablespoons	1 minute 15 seconds to 1 minute 30 seconds	–
¼ cup	1 minute 45 seconds to 2 minutes	1
½ cup	2 minutes	1
1 cup	2 minutes 15 seconds	1
1½ cups	2 minutes 30 seconds	1
2 cups	3 minutes 30 seconds to 4 minutes	2
3 cups	4 minutes 30 seconds	2

TOASTED PINE NUTS

Pine nuts are best toasted separately, as they take a little longer to brown than walnuts, almonds, or cashew nuts. Toast only the amount needed in the recipe because the nuts contain a high proportion of natural oil and turn rancid after a few days at room temperature, while refrigerating totally destroys their fragrance.

========= ROOM TEMPERATURE =========

¼ cup raw pine nuts

Spread nuts on an unseasoned microwave-safe pie or dinner plate. Toast, uncovered, at 100 percent power in a 650- to 700-watt carousel oven for 2 minutes (or until barely colored and aromatic), stirring once. Remove from oven and cool. Use immediately or transfer into an airtight container and store in a cool place for up to a couple of days.

MICROWAVE

Yield
  —¼ cup
Cooking time
  —2 minutes
Heat
  —100 percent power
MW oven size
  —650 to 700 watts
MW cookware
  *—One 10-inch pie or
    dinner plate*

TOASTED SEEDS

Toasted seeds are needed to make that wonderful candy with coconut and mixed nuts (pp. 411–422). Toasted sesame seeds are available at stores selling Middle Eastern groceries, but toasting them as well as other seeds in the microwave is quick and easy. Remember to stir them while toasting, as recommended in the recipe, or else the browning will be uneven.

========= ROOM TEMPERATURE =========

¾ cup raw seeds (sesame, melon, pumpkin, or sunflower)

MICROWAVE

Yield
  —¾ cup
Cooking time
  —6 minutes
Heat
  —100 percent power
MW oven size
  —650 to 700 watts
MW cookware
  *—One 10-inch pie or
    dinner plate*

Spread seeds on an unseasoned microwave-safe pie or dinner plate. Toast, uncovered, at 100 percent power in a 650- to 700-watt carousel oven for 6 minutes (or until lightly colored and puffed), stirring twice. Remove from oven and cool completely before using. Transfer into an airtight container and store in a cool place.

ROASTED SPICES

To lend a distinct smoky fragrance, spices are often roasted (also called toasted) and ground before being added to a dish in Indian cooking. Roasting spices in the microwave is simple. All you do is spread them in a single layer on a plate, or directly on the carousel, and cook. The only thing you need to know is that during the last minute of cooking, when the spices suddenly begin to brown, stirring is essential to prevent burned spots and ensure even browning.

MICROWAVE

Yield
  —2 tablespoons
Cooking time
  —4 minutes
Heat
  —100 percent power
MW oven size
  —650 to 700 watts
MW cookware
  —One 10-inch pie or dinner plate

ROASTED CUMIN SEEDS

Roasted cumin is used extensively in north India to heighten the flavor of the finished dish such as lentils, yogurt *raita,* salad, chutney, and yogurt or buttermilk drinks. Roasted ground cumin is most aromatic if used within a day, although you can keep it for up to two weeks.

=== *ROOM TEMPERATURE* ===

2 tablespoons cumin seeds

Spread cumin seeds on an unseasoned microwave-safe pie or dinner plate. Roast, uncovered, at 100 percent power in a 650- to 700-watt carousel oven for 4 minutes (or until seeds get several shades darker), stirring once. Remove from oven. When completely cool, grind to a fine powder. Store in an airtight container in a cool place.

ROASTED CORIANDER SEEDS

You will need ground roasted coriander to flavor yogurt *raitas* and salads. Make only a small amount, as suggested below, as they lose much of their pungency after a week.

=== ROOM TEMPERATURE ===

2 tablespoons coriander seeds

Spread coriander seeds on an unseasoned microwave-safe pie or dinner plate. Roast, uncovered, at 100 percent power in a 650- to 700-watt carousel oven for 4 minutes 30 seconds (or until seeds get several shades darker), stirring once. Remove from oven. When completely cool, grind to a fine powder. Store in an airtight container in a cool place.

TOASTED CURRY POWDER AND OTHER GROUND SPICES

This technique is recommended for toasting raw ground spices such as store-bought curry powder, turmeric, cayenne pepper, dry mustard, ground cumin, ground coriander, etc. Make only the amount needed in the recipe as the spices lose their fragrance with keeping.

=== ROOM TEMPERATURE ===

1–2 tablespoons ground spice

Place ground spice in an 8-inch microwave-safe skillet in a 650- to 700-watt carousel oven. Heat at 100 percent power for 2 to 3 minutes (or until it turns darker and exudes an aroma), stirring once. Remove from oven and scrape spice onto a plate and cool. Use immediately or store in an airtight container in a cool place.

NOTE To toast 1 to 2 teaspoons ground spice, reduce toasting time to 1½ to 2½ minutes.

SAUCES

Many Indian dishes contain sauces in one form or another. Savory or sweet, complex or subtle, these sauces lend the dishes distinctive flavors, enticing aromas, and appealing textures. In Indian cooking the sauces are often used as a braising liquid. For example, to make Duck Vendaloo (p. 130), you first have to prepare the *vendaloo* sauce before the duck can be cooked in it. All these sauces, which traditionally take a long time to cook, can be made in the microwave effortlessly in a matter of minutes! They also keep well in the refrigerator and freeze without any loss of flavor or texture. Keep a supply of these sauces handy for days when you are running short of time.

FRAGRANT TOMATO SAUCE

I make a large supply of this palate-soothing tomato sauce when red ripe tomatoes flood the market in summer and freeze it to use in the winter. I love its mild, aromatic flavor and use it to make tomato-based curries with meat, chicken, and fish. You will need this sauce in Chicken Frazer (p. 120) and Kafta Kabob in Creamed Tomato Sauce (p. 140). The sauce is also good by itself served with grilled or poached fish or chicken.

MICROWAVE

Yield
—2½ cups sauce or
20 (2 tablespoons
each) frozen cubes

Preparation time
—3 minutes

Cooking time
—20 minutes

Heat
—100 percent power

MW oven size
—650 to 700 watts

MW cookware
—One 2½-quart cas-
serole or soufflé dish

2 pounds red ripe toma-
toes (or substitute 3
cups canned drained
tomatoes)

3 large cloves garlic,
peeled

1-inch cube fresh ginger,
peeled

1 tablespoon dry mustard

½ teaspoon cayenne
pepper

1 tablespoon paprika

½ teaspoon ground
fennel

Kosher salt to taste

1. Combine all ingredients in the container of a blender or food processor and process until the contents are finely pureed. Transfer puree into a 2½-quart microwave-safe dish.

2. Cook, uncovered, at 100 percent power in a 650- to 700-watt carousel oven for 20 minutes (or until tomatoes and spices lose their raw aroma and sauce is slightly thickened), stirring twice. Remove from oven. Use immediately or transfer into a tightly covered container and store.

NOTE   The sauce keeps well, stored in a covered container, for up to 8 hours at room temperature, 5 days in the refrigerator, or up to a year in the freezer. To freeze, pour sauce into standard (16 cubes per tray) ice trays and place in freezer for about 4 hours. Transfer cubes into plastic bags and store.

BUTTER SAUCE

This is the classic creamy-rich tomato sauce that combines with *tandoori* Cornish hen in the famous preparation Butter Cornish Hen (p. 126). It is very fragrant and aromatic. Traditionally the sauce contains a large amount of cream and butter, but I have eliminated the butter without any loss to its flavor or silky glaze. The butter sauce is also good served by itself with fish, chicken, or vegetables.

=============== ROOM TEMPERATURE ===============

1¾ pounds red ripe tomatoes, quartered	1¼ teaspoons cayenne pepper
2½-inch piece fresh ginger, peeled	1¾ teaspoons kosher salt
1 cup heavy cream	1⅓ teaspoons garam masala (p. 478)
1½ tablespoons tomato paste	¾ teaspoon ground roasted cumin seeds
1½ tablespoons paprika	(p. 465)

1. Place tomatoes, ginger, heavy cream, tomato paste, paprika, cayenne, and salt in the container of a blender or food processor and process until smoothly pureed. Transfer the mixture into a 2½-quart microwave-safe casserole and cover with the lid.

2. Cook at 100 percent power in a 650- to 700-watt carousel oven for 10 minutes (or until tomatoes and spices are cooked). Remove from oven. Uncover, stir in *garam masala,* and cumin. Use sauce immediately or transfer into a microwave-safe covered container and refrigerate or freeze.

NOTE   The sauce keeps well for 5 days in the refrigerator or 6 months in the freezer. Reheat in the container, partially opened, at 100 percent power for 4 minutes (9 minutes if frozen), stirring once.

MICROWAVE

Yield
  —2½ *cups sauce or*
    20 (2 tablespoons
    each) frozen cubes
Preparation time
  —2 *minutes*
Cooking time
  —13 *minutes*
Heat
  —100 *percent power*
MW oven size
  —650 *to 700 watts*
MW cookware
  —One 10-inch cov-
    ered skillet

VENDALOO SAUCE

This very hot and spicy sauce flavored with cayenne and tempered with sweet seasoning is primarily used for making *vendaloo* dishes such as Duck Vendaloo (p. 130), Kafta Kabob in Hot Vendaloo Sauce (p. 142), Potatoes and Peas Vendaloo (p. 177), and Whole Cauliflower with Vendaloo Sauce (p. 175). It may be used over hot dogs, hamburgers, grilled fish, or meat. Combined with an equal portion of Sweet and Spicy Tomato Sauce (p. 370), it makes a delightful barbecue sauce.

═══════ ROOM TEMPERATURE ═══════

2 tablespoons coriander seeds	1 tablespoon minced garlic
2 teaspoons cumin seeds	1 tablespoon crushed or grated fresh ginger
1½ teaspoons mustard seeds	1 cup water
1 teaspoon ground cinnamon	¼ cup, or 4 frozen cubes, tamarind juice or 4 teaspoons tamarind concentrate (p. 491)
½ teaspoon ground cloves	
1 teaspoon turmeric	
2 teaspoons cayenne pepper	½ cup tomato puree (canned or fresh)
5 tablespoons mustard oil or olive oil	1 tablespoon paprika
	1 teaspoon sugar
1 cup minced onions	1½ teaspoons kosher salt

1. Combine coriander seeds, cumin seeds, and mustard seeds and grind into a fine powder using a spice mill or coffee grinder. Remove into a bowl, add cinnamon, clove, turmeric, and cayenne, and set aside.

2. Place oil, onion, garlic, and ginger in a 10-inch microwave-safe covered skillet in a 650- to 700-watt carousel oven. Cook at 100 percent power for 6 min-

utes (or until onions are cooked soft). Remove cover, stir in spice mixture, and continue cooking, uncovered, at 100 percent power for an additional 2 minutes (or until spices are lightly fried). Remove from oven.

3. Add water, tamarind, tomato puree, paprika, sugar, and salt, mix well, and cover with the lid. Cook at 100 percent power for 5 minutes (or until sauce has thickened). Remove from oven. Use immediately or transfer into a tightly covered container and store.

NOTE   The sauce keeps for up to 8 hours at room temperature, 5 days in the refrigerator, or up to a year in the freezer. To freeze, pour sauce into standard (16 cubes per tray) ice trays and place in freezer for about 4 hours. Transfer cubes into plastic bags and store.

MICROWAVE

Yield
  —1 cup
Cooking time
  —1 minute
Heat
  —100 percent power
MW oven size
  —650 to 700 watts
MW cookware
  —One 1-cup glass
  measure

SAVORY COCONUT SAUCE

A subtle and mellow coconut sauce that traditionally accompanies Ceylonese Steamed Rice Cakes (p. 330).

ROOM TEMPERATURE

⅔ cup coconut milk   *⅓ cup milk*
  (p. 450)   *1 teaspoon sugar*
                         Pinch of salt

Combine all the ingredients in a 1-cup glass measure and heat, uncovered, at 100 percent power in a 650- to 700-watt carousel oven for 1 minute (or until hot).

MICROWAVE

Yield
—2 cups sauce or 16
  (2 tablespoons each)
  frozen cubes
Cooking time
—5 minutes
MW oven size
—650 to 700 watts
MW cookware
—One 4-cup glass
  measure or one 1½-
  quart casserole or
  soufflé dish

NOTE The banana-coconut sauce keeps for up to 6 weeks in the refrigerator or 6 months in the freezer. To freeze, pour sauce into a standard (16 cubes per tray) ice tray and place in freezer for about 4 hours. Transfer cubes into plastic bags and store.

BANANA-COCONUT SAUCE

This sensuous banana-coconut sauce will amaze you because it tastes of neither banana nor coconut! The combined experience, however, is extraordinary. It is also a breeze to make in the microwave. But it seems that every time I want a ripe banana I have to plan at least two days in advance! Finding a banana is not a problem, but finding a fully ripe one is. Like every-one else, I buy bananas as they come—underripe. When my stock of bananas gets fully ripe but is still firm and unblemished, I make this wonderful sauce and store it for making Chowpati Beach Punch (p. 432), Banana Coconut Milk (p. 441) or Moghul Shake (p. 438).

======= ROOM TEMPERATURE =======

1 cup coconut milk
  (p. 450)
⅓ cup light jaggery
  (p. 460) or light
  brown sugar
2 medium-size ripe
  bananas, peeled and
  finely chopped

Pinch of ground
  cardamom
½ teaspoon dried ginger
  powder

1. Place coconut milk, jaggery, and bananas in a 4-cup glass measure or 1½-quart microwave-safe dish. Cook, uncovered, at 100 percent power in a 650- to 700-watt carousel oven for 5 minutes (or until ba-nanas become very soft and disintegrate into the sauce), stirring once.

2. Remove from oven. Add cardamom and dry gin-ger and beat with a whisk to smoothen sauce. When completely cool, use or immediately transfer into a tightly covered container and store.

Yield

—½ cup puree or 4
(2 tablespoons each)
frozen cubes

Cooking time

—1 minute 15 seconds

Heat

—100 percent power

MW oven size

—650 to 700 watts

MW cookware

—One 1-cup glass
measure

APRICOT PUREE

Anyone will tell you that dried apricots take a good eight hours' or overnight soaking and at least an hour of cooking before they are considered ready for use. Not when you have a microwave. You can make this apricot puree in less than two minutes! Not only is it quick and easy but the apricots retain their springlike fragrance, which almost always gets subdued or lost in the overnight bath. This apricot puree has many uses in sauces, dips, fruit coolers, and yogurt *lassis*.

=========== *ROOM TEMPERATURE* ===========

12 dried apricots   ½ cup water
(⅓ cup)

1. Place apricots and water in 1-cup glass measure. Cook, uncovered, at 100 percent power in a 650- to 700-watt carousel oven for 1 minute 15 seconds (or until water is rapidly boiling). Remove from oven.

2. Pour the water and apricots into the container of a blender or food processor and process until smoothly pureed. Use immediately or transfer into a tightly sealed jar and store.

NOTE   The apricot puree keeps for up to 4 weeks in the refrigerator or 6 months in the freezer. To freeze, pour sauce into a standard (16 cubes per tray) ice tray and place in freezer for about 4 hours. Transfer cubes into plastic bags and store. To make double the quantity, simply double the ingredients and increase the cooking time to 2 minutes.

SEASONINGS

Onion, garlic, and ginger roux, a classic north Indian preparation, is an important ingredient of north Indian curries. It is this roux that lends the sauce its characteristic brownish-red color and caramel-sweet flavor. It is made by cooking the seasonings in oil until the flavor and fragrance of the caramelizing onion saturates. Meat, chicken, vegetables, etc, are then added and cooked in the roux. Generally it is made as one of the steps for cooking the dish you are using it in, but it can also be made ahead separately and added. The roux keeps in the refrigerator for four weeks or frozen for three months.

MICROWAVE

Yield
  —¼ cup
Cooking time
  —7 minutes
Heat
  —100 percent power
MW oven size
  —650 to 700 watts
MW cookware
  —One 8-inch skillet

ONION, GARLIC, AND GINGER ROUX I

=== *ROOM TEMPERATURE* ===

¼ cup finely chopped onion

1 tablespoon minced garlic

1 tablespoon crushed or grated fresh ginger

1½ teaspoons light vegetable oil

Combine all ingredients in an 8-inch microwave-safe skillet. Cook at 100 percent power in a 650- to 700-watt carousel oven for 7 minutes (or until onions turn light brown), stirring twice. The browning will be uneven, which is fine as it will lend a more complex flavor to the dish it is incorporated in. Remove from oven and use immediately or cool and transfer into a covered container and store.

ONION, GARLIC, AND GINGER ROUX II

=== *ROOM TEMPERATURE* ===

¼ cup light vegetable oil
¾ cup finely chopped
  onion

1 tablespoon minced
  garlic
2 tablespoons crushed or
  grated fresh ginger

Heat the oil in a 10-inch microwave-safe skillet at 100 percent power in a 650- to 700-watt carousel oven for 2 minutes. Add onions and stir to coat them with oil. Cook at 100 percent power for 5 minutes (or until onions are browned), stirring twice. Stir in garlic and ginger and continue cooking at 100 percent power for an additional 2 minutes. Remove from oven and use immediately or cool and transfer into a covered container and store.

FRIED ONION SHREDS

These crunchy fine shreds of onion are primarily used in Moghul cooking to garnish or flavor their delicate pilafs. In addition to lending a sweet flavor, they provide a textural contrast and visual appeal to the dish. Save the onion-infused oil after cooking the onion shreds and use it to flavor *dal* dishes, salads, or in cooking fish and seafood. The fried onion shreds may be made and kept at room temperature for up to two days.

=== *ROOM TEMPERATURE* ===

¼ cup light vegetable oil

1 medium-size (¼
  pound) onion, peeled
  and thinly sliced

Heat the oil in an 8-inch microwave-safe skillet at 100 percent power in a 650- to 700-watt carousel oven for 2 minutes. Add onion slices and stir to coat them with oil. Cook at 100 percent power for 7 minutes (or until onions turn caramel brown), stirring twice. Watch carefully during the last 2 minutes of cooking as the onions, after losing their moisture, fry rapidly and can overbrown and burn. Remove from oven. Transfer onion shreds with tongs or a fork to a paper towel and drain. Use immediately or transfer into a covered container.

SILVER AND GOLD LEAF

It is the Moghuls, known for their exquisite and extravagant garnishes, who introduced *vark,* the edible tissue-thin pure silver and gold, as an adornment on foods. It is visually stunning and its opulence is unmatched in the world. *Vark* is flavorless and odorless and perfectly safe to consume. Silver leaf is available in Indian grocery stores in 2-inch-square pieces at a very moderate cost.

SPICE BLENDS

There are many recipes in Indian cooking that call for certain spice blends to give the dish their distinctive characteristic flavors. It would be a good idea, therefore, to make these blends and have them ready.

Yield
—2 tablespoons
Preparation time
—3 minutes
Cooking time
—30 seconds
Heat
—100 percent power
MW oven size
—650 to 700 watts
MW cookware
—One 8-inch skillet
or small plate

MOGHUL GARAM MASALA

This Moghul classic is the most exquisitely flavored and aromatic of all spice blends. It is used primarily in Moghul cooking to flavor meat and poultry dishes, particularly those containing yogurt and cream sauces. This Moghul *garam masala* keeps for up to two weeks, although for best results it should be used almost immediately while its fragrance is at its peak.

=== ROOM TEMPERATURE ===

1 teaspoon crushed saffron threads or powdered saffron

4 teaspoons ground cardamom

¾ teaspoon ground cinnamon

½ teaspoon ground cloves

½ teaspoon freshly ground black pepper

¼ teaspoon freshly grated nutmeg

Spread saffron threads in an 8-inch microwave-safe skillet. Toast, uncovered, at 100 percent power in a 650- to 700-watt carousel oven for 30 seconds (or until saffron begins to exude its aroma). Remove from oven. When cool, combine with all other ground spices. Store Moghul *garam masala* in an airtight container in a cool place.

MICROWAVE

Yield
  —¼ *cup*
Cooking time
  —*5 minutes*
Heat
  —*100 percent power*
MW oven size
  —*650 to 700 watts*
MW cookware
  —*One 10-inch pie or*
    dinner plate

GARAM MASALA

This is a spicy blend of highly aromatic spices from north India. It is used in all north Indian main-course preparations, *dal* dishes, and vegetables. *Garam masala* keeps for up to six weeks, although its pungent fragrance subdues after a few days.

======================= *ROOM TEMPERATURE* =======================

1 tablespoon cumin seeds
1 tablespoon coriander
  seeds
2 teaspoons green or
  white whole cardamom
  pods, crushed
2 teaspoons black
  peppercorns

2-inch stick cinnamon,
  crushed into bits
1 teaspoon whole cloves
2 bay leaves, crumbled
¼ teaspoon freshly
  grated nutmeg

Combine all the spices except nutmeg on an unseasoned microwave-safe pie or dinner plate. Roast, uncovered, at 100 percent power in a 650- to 700-watt carousel oven for 5 minutes (or until spices look a few shades darker and exude a smoky aroma), stirring twice. Remove from oven. When completely cool, grind to a fine powder. Stir in nutmeg, transfer into an airtight container, and store in a cool place.

MICROWAVE

Yield
  —½ cup
Cooking time
  —7 minutes
Heat
  —100 percent power
MW oven size
  —650 to 700 watts
MW cookware
  —One 10-inch pie or
    dinner plate

CURRY POWDER

Curry powder, the most popular spice blend in south Indian cooking, is widely used in lentil and vegetable soups, spicy fish curries, and turn-fried vegetables. Although curry powder is readily available in supermarkets, I recommend making this blend as none of them are as fresh, fragrant, or flavorful. Curry powder may be kept for up to three months, although for best results it should be used within a month.

══════════════ ROOM TEMPERATURE ══════════════

3 tablespoons coriander
  seeds
2 tablespoons cumin
  seeds
2 tablespoons mustard
  seeds

1 tablespoon fenugreek
  seeds (p. 483)
1 tablespoon turmeric
1 tablespoon cayenne
  pepper
1 tablespoon freshly
  ground black pepper

Combine coriander, cumin, mustard, and fenugreek seeds and spread them on an unseasoned microwave-safe pie or dinner plate. Roast, uncovered, at 100 percent power in a 650- to 700-watt carousel oven for 7 minutes (or until spices turn several shades darker and exude a smoky aroma), stirring once. Remove from oven. When completely cool, grind to a fine powder. Stir in turmeric, cayenne, and black pepper, transfer into an airtight container, and store in a cool place.

SAMBAAR POWDER

A spicily aromatic blend from south India, *sambaar* powder is used for flavoring rich and robust lentil and vegetable stews and spicy broths. This special version of *sambaar* powder from the Blue Mountains is very aromatic and mild. It contains no turmeric (the spice that turns food yellow) and a much smaller amount of cayenne pepper than is generally used in *sambaar* powder. This spice blend keeps for up to three months.

ROOM TEMPERATURE

1½ tablespoons
 coriander seeds
1 tablespoon cumin seeds
2 teaspoons black
 peppercorns

¾ teaspoon fenugreek
 seeds (p. 483)
¾ teaspoon cayenne
 pepper

Combine all the spices except cayenne pepper and spread them on an unseasoned microwave-safe pie or dinner plate. Roast, uncovered, at 100 percent power in a 650- to 700-watt carousel oven for 5 minutes (or until spices are dried and begin to brown), stirring once. Remove from oven. When completely cool, grind to a fine powder. Stir in cayenne pepper and store in an airtight container in a cool place.

MICROWAVE

Yield
  —¼ cup
Cooking time
  —5 minutes
Heat
  —100 percent power
MW oven size
  —650 to 700 watts
MW cookware
  —One 10-inch pie or
    dinner plate

FRAGRANT SPICE POWDER

This five-spice powder, an eastern Indian classic from Calcutta, is used for flavoring soups and *dal* dishes. Its high accent on fennel and thyme makes it particularly good with vegetables, fish, and poultry. Fragrant spice powder may be kept for up to two months, although for best results it should be used within three weeks.

=============== ROOM TEMPERATURE ===============

1 tablespoon coriander seeds	1 tablespoon mustard seeds
1 tablespoon cumin seeds	½ teaspoon ajowan seeds
1 tablespoon fennel seeds	(p. 481) or 1 teaspoon thyme

Combine all the spices (if you are using thyme, do not add it here) and spread them on an unseasoned microwave-safe pie or dinner plate. Roast, uncovered, at 100 percent power in a 650- to 700-watt carousel oven for 5 minutes (or until spices get several shades darker and exude a smoky aroma), stirring once. Remove from oven. When completely cool, add thyme (if you are using it) and grind to a fine powder. Store in an airtight container in a cool place.

SPECIAL SPICES

AJOWAN OR CAROM SEEDS
AJWAIN

Also known as omum or Bishop's weed, ajowan or carom seeds resemble celery seeds. They are often called thyme seeds as they contain thymol oil and exude a thymelike aroma. Logically, thyme makes a good substitute for Ajowan or carom.

ASAFETIDA
HING

This strong-smelling spice, known to lend an onion-garlic—like flavor to food, is used by certain Indian communities that abstain from using such seasonings in their food. Logically, a little chopped onion or shallot makes a fine substitute for asafetida.

BLACK SALT
KALA NAMAK

Do not confuse black salt with the table or seasoned salts, as it has little or no salinity. Black salt is a naturally found sulfur compound that is used as a flavoring spice in north Indian cooking. Because of its pleasant tangy taste, smoky aroma, and inherent appetite-stimulating properties, black salt is used in appetizers, beverages, chutneys, and salads. It is available in Indian grocery stores.

CUBEB BERRIES
KABABCHINI

These ginger-nutmeg smelling berries, resembling black peppercorns in shape except smaller, are used both in herbal medicine and cooking. Because of their appealing aroma, cubeb berries are added to create intrigue in subtle dishes. A Moghul spice, cubeb berries are used in kabobs (hence the Indian name *kababchini), kaftas,* soups, salads, and curries. Cubeb berries are available in specialty stores (such as Aphrodisia, see p. 496), but a little black pepper makes a fine substitute.

CURRY LEAVES
KARI PATTA

Curry leaves are an herb, not a spice. These balmy, fragrant leaves are the favorite seasoning of southern Indians, who use them in their lentil and vegetable stews, fish curries, chutneys, salads, beverages, and rice preparations. Fresh and dried curry leaves are available in Indian grocery stores. Fresh leaves keep in the refrigerator for up to three weeks, while dried keep for a year. Curry leaves also freeze well.

FENUGREEK LEAVES
KASOORI METHI

These are the highly fragrant, slightly bitter dried leaves of a special variety of fenugreek plant called *kasoori methi*. The leaves are used as an herb throughout India primarily to enhance the flavor of sauces and gravies. A little *kasoori methi* added to spinach intensifies the flavor of the green. It is available in Indian grocery stores.

FENUGREEK SEEDS
METHI

These burnt-caramel–tasting seeds are an important spice in Indian cooking. Known for their digestive properties in counteracting flatulence, these seeds are generally added to beans, peas, and root vegetables. Fenugreek is available in stores selling Indian and north African groceries.

GREEN PEPPERCORNS
HARA GOLMIRCH

Green peppercorns are the unripe berries of peppercorns that are picked and pickled in brine. They are milder than black peppercorns and very herbal, so are wonderful in salads, *raitas*, appetizers, soups, and pilafs. A little black pepper makes a fine substitute.

LONG PEPPER
PIPAL

A spicier black pepper with gingerlike aroma, long pepper looks like a 1-inch spike. It is used ground in chutneys, pickling, breads, and sauces. Long pepper is available in Indian grocery stores, but a little black pepper makes a fine substitute.

MANGO POWDER, DRY
AMCHOOR

The flesh of an unripe tart green mango is sun-dried and ground to yield this tan-colored sour-tasting powder. Mango powder is used primarily in northern-style vegetarian curries, vegetables, salads, *dals*, and chutneys. Dry mango powder is available in Indian grocery stores, but a little lemon juice makes a fine substitute.

NIGELLA OR BLACK ONION SEEDS
KALAUNJI

These tiny, teardrop-shaped, satiny black seeds are also known as black onion seeds because of their visual resemblance. Nigella seeds have a celerylike taste and are generally used whole with fish, shellfish, *dal*, pickles, vegetables, and breads.

POMEGRANATE SEEDS
ANARDANA

These seeds are from a special variety of pomegranate grown along the northern hills in India and priced for their piquant taste and delicately spicy fragrance.

Pomegranate is available in Indian grocery stores, but a little lemon juice makes a fine substitute.

SPICE-INFUSED OILS
TARKA

Making spice-infused oils is one of the most important and basic techniques of Indian cooking. In this process the oil (or *usli ghee*) is first heated until it reaches the desired hotness, then the spices are added and cooked until they infuse their fragrance into the oil. This fragrant oil is used as a dressing in salads, in yogurt *raitas,* and to flavor soups, *dal* dishes, and fresh chutneys. It can also be used as a medium for cooking various foods such as fish, vegetables, poultry, etc., to enhance and intensify their flavors. Making the spice-infused oil is effortless in the microwave using a regular skillet or browning skillet. All you do is heat the oil in the skillet, add the spices, and cook until the spices pop or brown as required. While cooking mustard seeds, remember that they must splutter fully in order for the spice to release their fragrance into the oil. Besides, unspluttered mustard seeds taste bitter. Spice-infused oil may be made ahead and kept in a tightly covered container in a cool place for four days and in the refrigerator for three weeks. It is good to have in emergencies, when a recipe calls for it.

MUSTARD-INFUSED OIL
USING REGULAR SKILLET

=== ROOM TEMPERATURE ===

1–2 tablespoons light   1–4 teaspoons mustard
vegetable oil   seeds

Heat the oil in a covered skillet or casserole at 100 percent power in a 650- to 700-watt carousel oven for 3 minutes. Uncover, add mustard seeds, and replace the lid. Cook at 100 percent power for 3 minutes (or until mustard seeds pop). Remove from oven. Uncover and immediately pour oil on the dish as recommended in the recipe, scraping the skillet to get all the mustard seeds and oil.

NOTE   To make a larger batch (⅓ cup), use ⅓ cup oil and 5 to 10 teaspoons mustard seeds. Heat the oil for the same 3 minutes, but after adding mustard seeds, cook for 6 minutes (or until mustard seeds pop).

MUSTARD-INFUSED OIL
USING BROWNING SKILLET

=== ROOM TEMPERATURE ===

2 tablespoons light vege-   1 teaspoon mustard seeds
table oil

Heat an 8-inch browning skillet, uncovered, at 100 percent power in a 650- to 700-watt carousel oven for 3 minutes. Remove from oven. Add oil and mustard seeds and at once cover with the lid. When the seeds stop spluttering (about 10 seconds), uncover and immediately pour the oil on the dish as recommended in the recipe, scraping the skillet to get all the mustard seeds and oil.

MICROWAVE

Yield
  —1 to 2 tablespoons
Cooking time
  —6 minutes
Heat
  —100 percent power
MW oven size
  —650 to 700 watts
MW cookware
  —One small, medium,
   or large skillet or
   casserole

CUMIN-INFUSED OIL
USING REGULAR SKILLET

=== ROOM TEMPERATURE ===

1–2 tablespoons light   1–4 teaspoons cumin
  vegetable oil   seeds

Heat the oil in a skillet or a casserole at 100 percent power in a 650- to 700-watt carousel oven for 3 minutes. Add cumin seeds. Cook at 100 percent power for 1 minute 30 seconds (or until cumin seeds turn a few shades darker). Remove from oven. Immediately pour the oil on the dish as recommended in the recipe, scraping the skillet to get all the cumin seeds and oil.

NOTE   To make a larger batch (1/3 cup), use 1/3 cup oil and 5 to 10 teaspoons cumin seeds. Heat the oil for the same 3 minutes, but after adding cumin seeds, cook for 6 minutes (or until the cumin seeds turn several shades darker).

MICROWAVE

Yield
  —2 tablespoons
Preparation time
  —3 minutes
Cooking time
  —10 seconds
Heat
  —100 percent power
MW oven size
  —650 to 700 watts
MW cookware
  —One 8-inch brown-
   ing skillet

CUMIN-INFUSED OIL
USING BROWNING SKILLET

=== ROOM TEMPERATURE ===

2 tablespoons light vege-   1 teaspoon cumin seeds
  table oil

Heat an 8-inch browning skillet at 100 percent power in a 650- to 700-watt carousel oven for 3 minutes. Remove from oven. Add oil and cumin seeds and stir rapidly for 10 seconds (or until cumin turns a few shades darker). Immediately pour this spice-infused oil on the dish as recommended in the recipe, scraping the skillet to get all the cumin seeds and oil.

SPICY CROUTONS

MICROWAVE

Yield
  —1 cup
Servings
  —4 to 8
Cooking time
  —4 minutes 30
    seconds
Heat
  —100 percent power
MW oven size
  —650 to 700 watts
MW cookware
  —One pie or dinner
    plate

These cayenne-spiked, fennel-fragrant croutons provide the needed counterpoint to many delicate soups and vegetables such as Autumn Tomato Soup with Spicy Croutons (p. 43), Chilled Essence of Shallot Soup (p. 57), Cold Butternut Squash Soup (p. 59), and Mustard-braised Endive (p. 218). The microwave is excellent for making croutons as they come out light and extra crunchy and the flavor of fennel is more pronounced. Spicy croutons may be kept for up to a week at room temperature, six weeks in the refrigerator, or four months in the freezer.

ROOM TEMPERATURE

4 slices white bread,
  trimmed and cut into
  ¼-inch cubes
3 tablespoons olive oil
¼ teaspoon cayenne
  pepper

¼ teaspoon ground
  cumin
¼ teaspoon ground
  fennel
¼ teaspoon kosher salt

Spread bread cubes on a microwave-safe pie or dinner plate. Dribble oil over the bread and stir to coat. Cook, uncovered, at 100 percent power in a 650- to 700-watt carousel oven for 3 minutes 30 seconds (or until cubes look light brown), stirring once. Remove from oven, combine all the spices and salt, sprinkle over the cubes, and stir thoroughly. Cook, uncovered, at 100 percent power for an additional 1 minute (or until spices lose their raw aroma). Remove from oven. Use as recommended in the recipe or cool and transfer into airtight containers.

CHICKEN OR MEAT STOCK

MICROWAVE

Yield
—5½ cups stock or 44
(2 tablespoons each)
frozen cubes

Servings
—6 to 8

Cooking time
—20 minutes

Heat
—100 percent power

MW oven size
—650 to 700 watts

MW cookware
—One 3-quart covered
casserole

Indian stocks, in general, are highly aromatic—laced with spices such as fennel, cumin, cardamom, and cinnamon. They are lovely in soups, pilafs, and dishes of Moghul origin. Making stock in the microwave is extremely easy. All you do is boil bones and aromatic spices in water until their flavors are released into the liquid. It is quick, efficient, and the stock tastes cleaner. You do not have to make stock whenever you have bones handy. They can be kept frozen until you are ready to use them. Simply proceed with the recipe using frozen bones, except allow additional time for them to defrost.

ROOM TEMPERATURE

4 cups chicken/duck/hen/ turkey bones, lightly cracked with kitchen mallet, or 3 cups meaty beef/lamb/pork bones	*2 green or white cardamom pods, crushed*
	1 thin 1-inch piece cinnamon stick
6 cups water	*¼ teaspoon cumin seeds*
1 bay leaf, crumbled	*¼ teaspoon coriander seeds*
1 whole clove	*¼ teaspoon fennel seeds*

Combine all the ingredients for the stock in a 3-quart microwave-safe casserole. Cook, covered, at 100 percent power in a 650- to 700-watt carousel oven for 20 minutes. Remove from oven. When cool, strain stock and use or transfer into a covered container.

NOTE The stock keeps for 2 days in the refrigerator or up to a year in the freezer. To freeze, pour stock into standard (16 cubes per tray) ice trays and place in freezer for about 4 hours. Transfer cubes into plastic bags and store.

VEGETARIAN STOCKS

A flavorful stock made with the essence of vegetables and herbs. It is used in soups calling for vegetarian stock, pilafs, and vegetarian main dishes. It contains the same spices as the meat stock, except a little fresh ginger is added to lend an herbal touch.

=== ROOM TEMPERATURE ===

2 cups chopped vegeta-
  bles (carrots with
  greens, onions, tur-
  nips, beans, cauli-
  flower with celery,
  radish greens)
6 cups water
2 slices fresh ginger
1 bay leaf, crumbled

4 whole cloves
3 green or white carda-
  mom pods, crushed
1 thin 1-inch piece cin-
  namon stick
¼ teaspoon cumin seeds
¼ teaspoon coriander
  seeds
¼ teaspoon fennel seeds

Combine all the ingredients for the stock in a 3-quart microwave-safe covered casserole. Cook, covered, at 100 percent power in a 650- to 700-watt carousel oven for 20 minutes. Remove from oven. When cool, strain stock and use as suggested in the recipe or transfer into a covered container.

NOTE   The stock keeps for a day in the refrigerator or up to 4 months in the freezer. To freeze, pour stock into standard (16 cubes per tray) ice trays and place in freezer for about 4 hours. Transfer cubes into plastic bags and store.

MICROWAVE

Yield
 —*4 cups stock or 32*
  (2 tablespoons each)
  frozen cubes
Servings
 —*6 to 8*
Preparation time
 —*5 minutes*
Cooking time
 —*13 minutes*
Standing time
 —*10 minutes*
Heat
 —*100 percent power*
MW oven size
 —*650 to 700 watts*
MW cookware
 —*One 3-quart covered*
  casserole

MUNG BROTH

This protein-rich mung broth, with a light fermented aroma, is almost essential if you are a vegetarian. It is used in soups calling for vegetarian stock, pilafs, gravies in vegetarian dishes, and for enriching sauces. You can also serve it as a beverage, lightly seasoned.

1 cup dried yellow mung beans (p. 461)

1. Put beans in a 3-quart microwave-safe casserole and wash in several changes of water. Drain thoroughly. Add 2½ cups water and soak beans for a half hour. Cover casserole with the lid and place in a 650- to 700-watt carousel oven. Cook at 100 percent power for 13 minutes (or until beans are cooked and soft).

2. Remove from oven. Let beans stand, covered, for 10 minutes. Transfer beans into the container of a food processor or blender and process until smoothly pureed, using water as needed. Remove into a bowl and stir in enough water to make 4 cups mung bean broth. Alternatively, place cooked beans in a deep pot and whisk in enough water to make 4 cups broth.

MICROWAVE	
Yield	
—4 cups	
Cooking time	
—2 minutes 30 seconds	
Heat	
—100 percent power	
MW oven size	
—650 to 700 watts	
MW cookware	
—One 8-cup glass measure	

Instant mung broth, made with mung flour, is not as flavorful as the one made with whole beans, but you can't beat the speed—it is made in the microwave in less than three minutes! All you do is combine flour and water and cook until the contents thicken to a sauce. Instant mung broth is thicker and slightly viscous, hence use discreetly in soups and sauces. You can substitute instant mung broth in recipes calling for mung broth.

===== *ROOM TEMPERATURE* =====

⅓ cup yellow mung bean   3⅔ cups water
   flour (p. 461)   ¼ teaspoon turmeric

Combine mung bean flour, 1⅔ cups water, and turmeric in an 8-cup glass measure. Cook, uncovered, at 100 percent power in a 650- to 700-watt carousel oven for 2 minutes 30 seconds (or until mixture thickens to a custard consistency). Remove from oven and beat in the remaining 2 cups water using a whisk, or, alternatively, use a food processor or blender.

TAMARIND

The blackish-brown tamarind pulp, with a distinct sweetish-sour taste and an herbal, somewhat smoky flavor, is used as a flavoring in soups, stews, chutneys, and sauces. Tamarind sauces (pp. 372–374) and Tamarind Sorbet (p. 379) are very popular Indian preparations. It is available in compressed one-pound blocks or as a concentrated paste under different trade names such as Tamcon at stores selling Indian groceries. Tamarind juice is simple to make in the microwave. The pulp softens quickly without losing its delicate flavor. The juice can either be used immediately, refrigerated for up to a week, or frozen indefinitely in convenient 2-tablespoon cubes.

TAMARIND JUICE

=========== *ROOM TEMPERATURE* ===========

4 ounces (half of an　　　　*About 3¼ cups water*
　8.75-ounce slab)
　tamarind pulp

1. Tear tamarind into 3 to 4 pieces and place in a 1½-quart microwave-safe casserole. Add 2 cups water and cover with the lid. Cook at 100 percent power in a 650- to 700-watt carousel oven for 5 minutes (or until water is boiling). Remove from oven.

2. Let tamarind stand, covered, for an hour. Uncover and mash the pulp with your fingers or use a spoon. Strain the juices through a sieve into another bowl, squeezing as much juice out of the pulp as possible. Return the residue to the casserole and add ¾ cup water. Mush pulp and strain again. Repeat the process until you have 3 cups tamarind liquid. Discard the fibrous residue.

3. To freeze, pour the tamarind juice into standard (16 cubes per tray) ice trays and freeze. When frozen (about 4 hours), transfer cubes into plastic bags and store.

USLI GHEE

Usli ghee is essentially clarified brown butter used in Indian cooking. It has a light caramel color and a distinct perfume. Since *usli ghee* is pure fat with no trace of moisture, it heats without burning and keeps well for several months at room temperature.

　Most Americans have the notion that Indians use *usli ghee,* Indian clarified butter, in all their cooking. Granted, Indians love *usli ghee*'s wonderful nutty aroma and its rapturous flavor, but they reserve it for flavoring desserts, sweets, and some lentil and pilaf dishes. Most cooking is done in oils, such as peanut, mustard, sesame, and coconut, and this is the way it has been for centuries. Recently, with the increased awareness of the harmful effects of consuming highly saturated fats, many polyunsaturated cholesterol-free oils such as corn, sunflower, and safflower have gained popularity in India. *Usli ghee* and different oils are available at stores selling Indian groceries. Clarified butter makes a good substitute for *usli ghee*.

MICROWAVE

Yield
   —⅓ cup
Cooking time
   —7 minutes
Heat
   —100 percent power
MW oven size
   —650 to 700 watts
MW cookware
   *—One 1½-quart cov-
   ered casserole or
   soufflé dish*

NOTE While making *ghee*, after the butter melts and the process of clarifying begins, the casserole *must not* be opened during the first 4 minutes of cooking as there is considerable spattering. Once the moisture evaporates, the boiling calms down. During the last 2 minutes, the browning of the butter takes place, which lends the distinct aroma associated with *usli ghee*.

USLI GHEE

Usli ghee is extremely simple to make in the microwave. It is almost magical how the butter cooks and turns into *ghee* in less than seven minutes without stirring or constant watching. Remember to stop cooking *usli ghee* when it turns barely light golden, because it will continue to cook for several minutes in its retained heat after it is out of the oven.

ROOM TEMPERATURE

*1 stick (¼ pound) unsalted butter, cut into ½-inch
   pieces*

Place butter in a 1½-quart microwave-safe casserole. Cook, uncovered, at 100 percent power in a 650- to 700-watt carousel oven for 1 minute 30 seconds (or until the butter melts). Cover with the lid and continue cooking at 100 percent power for 5 minutes 30 seconds (or until butter stops spluttering and sizzling—indicating that the moisture trapped in the milk solids has evaporated—and the melted butter has turned clear and golden, separating from the fried brown-milk residue). Remove from oven, uncover, and set aside. When cool enough to handle, pour clear butter *usli ghee* into a tightly covered jar.

Usli ghee keeps well for a month at room temperature, 4 months in the refrigerator, and indefinitely in the freezer.

MAIL-ORDER SOURCES

CALIFORNIA

Bazaar of India
1810 University Avenue
Berkeley, CA 94702
Tel: (415) 548-4110

House of Spices
12223 Centralia Street
Lakewood,CA 96137
Tel: (213) 860-9918

India Gifts and Foods
643 Post Street
San Francisco, CA 94109
Tel: (415) 771-5041

COLORADO

The Indus
111 Broadway
Denver, CO 80014
Tel: (303) 722-4251

Tajmahal Imports
3095 C. South Peoria Street
Aurora, CO 80203
Tel: (303) 751-8571

CONNECTICUT

India Spice and Gift
3295 Fairfield Avenue
Bridgeport, CT 06605
Tel: (203) 384-0666

FLORIDA

Indian Grocery Store
2342 Douglas Road
Coral Gables, FL 33134
Tel: (305) 448-5869

India Spice Center
512 North-East 167th Street
North Miami Boulevard
Miami, FL 33162
Tel: (305) 949-1881

ILLINOIS

India Gifts and Foods
1031 West Belmont Avenue
Chicago, IL 60650
Tel: (312) 348-4392

India Groceries
5010 North Sheridan Road
Chicago, IL 60640
Tel: (312) 334-3351

International Foods
2537 West Devon Avenue
Chicago, IL 60659
Tel: (312) 465-8382

INDIANA

International Foods & Gifts
3059 North High School
   Road
Indianapolis, IN 46224
Tel: (317) 291-5282

MARYLAND

Indian Sub-continental
8107 Fenton Street
Silver Spring, MA 20910
Tel: (301) 589-8417

Sadana International
1524 West Pratt Street
Baltimore, MA 21223
Tel: (301) 947-8312

MASSACHUSETTS

India Tea & Spices
453 Common Street
Belmont, MA 02178
Tel: (617) 484-3737

MICHIGAN

India Food & Boutique
30565 John R. Road
Madison Heights, MI 48071
Tel: (313) 585-5775

International Grocer, Inc.
3545 Cass Avenue
Detroit, MI 48201
Tel: (313) 831-5480

MISSOURI

Seema Enterprises
10612 Page Avenue
St. Louis, MO 63132
Tel: (314) 423-9990

NEW HAMPSHIRE

Country Life Natural Foods
Box 163
Harrisville, NH 03450
Tel: (603) 827-3362

NEW JERSEY

India Bazaar
204 Hudson Street
Hoboken, NJ 07030
Tel: (201) 653-8116

Quality Corner
Rte. 27, Kingston Mall
Princeton, NJ 08540
Tel: (609) 924-0101

NEW YORK

Aphrodisia Products Inc.
282 Bleecker Street
New York, NY 10014
Tel: (212) 986-6440

Dean & Deluca
560 Broadway
New York, NY 10012
Tel: (212) 431-1691

Foods of India
121 Lexington Avenue
New York, NY 10016
Tel: (212) 683-4419

K. Kalustyan
123 Lexington Avenue
New York, NY 10016
Tel: (212) 685-3416

Little India Store Inc.
128 East 28th Street
New York, NY 10016
Tel: (212) 683-1691

Nick's Supermarket
454 South Broadway
Yonkers, NY 10705
Tel: (914) 683-1691

Patel Discount Center
74-17 Woodside Avenue
Elmhurst, NY 11373
Tel: (718) 478-4547

Spice and Sweet Mahal
135 Lexington Avenue
New York, NY 10016
Tel: (212) 683-0900

OHIO

India Imports
Olentangy Plaza Shopping
   Center
Columbus, OH 43214
Tel: (614) 451-8121

OKLAHOMA

Antone's
2606 South Sheridan Road
Tulsa, OK 74129
Tel: (918) 835-5519

B. B. Bazaar
4528 Northwest 16th Street
Oklahoma City, OK 73118
Tel: (405) 942-0108

OREGON

Porter's Food Unlimited
125 West 11th Street
Eugene, OR 97401
Tel: (503) 342-3629

PENNSYLVANIA

Bombay Emporium
294 Craft Avenue
Pittsburgh, PA 15213
Tel: (412) 682-4965

House of Spices
4101 Walnut Street
Philadelphia, PA 19104
Tel: (215) 222-1111

TEXAS

Dana Bazaar
6223 A, S.W. Freeway
Houston, TX 77416
Tel: (713) 774-0180

Tajmahal Imports
66 Richardson Heights
   Village
Richardson, TX 75080
Tel: (214) 644-1329

Tropical Imports
5400 H. Woodway Drive
Fort Worth, TX 77431
Tel: (817) 294-5935

Yoga and Health Center
2912 Oaklawn Avenue
Dallas, TX 75219
Tel: (214) 528-8681

VIRGINIA

Sadana International
3709 Columbia Pike
Arlington, VA 22204
Tel: (703) 979-6262

WASHINGTON

Taj Mahal Emporium
1501 Pike Place Market
Seattle, WA 98115
Tel: (206) 625-0519

WASHINGTON, DC

Bestway Traders, Inc.
1718 Florida Avenue, N.W.
Washington, D.C. 20009
Tel: (202) 265-1909

WISCONSIN

International House of Foods
440 West Gorham Street
Madison, WI 53703
Tel: (608) 225-2554

CANADA

Daya Groceries & Health
   Foods
8236 Yonge Street
Horn Hill, Ontario
L4J 1W6 Canada
Tel: (416) 881-0454

India Food House
408 Dupont Street
Toronto, Ontario
MSR 1V9 Canada
Tel: (416) 924-1141

INDEX

black-eyed pea stew, 294–295

Bombay spicy lentil cakes, 327–329

Bombay spicy split pea cakes, 329

Bombay spicy split pea cakes with crabmeat, 329

Bombay sweetish-sour garlic lentils, 275–276

brown lentils in spicy tomato dressing, 280–281

cooked black-eyed peas, 292–293

cooked brown lentils, 279

cooked red (pink) lentil puree, 267–268

cooked whole mung beans, 288

cooked yellow lentils or American yellow split peas, 269–271

cooked yellow mung beans, 282

cool cream of mint soup, 61–62

crab and lentil salad, 30

duck braised in curried vegetable-lentil puree, 132–133

eggplant-lentil stew with tamarind and garlic, 191–193

fragrant spiced lentils with herbs, 273–274

fresh black-eyed peas in spicy yogurt sauce, 201–202

garlic-braised eggplant, chick-peas, and tomato casserole, 165–166

Grandmother's tomato lentil soup, 39–40

hearty whole mung bean and green pepper soup/stew, 75–76

instant mung broth, 491

kohlrabi, tomato, and chick-pea soup, 73–74

lamb in mint-flavored lentil sauce, 153–154

lentil and minced carrot salad, 30

lentil salad in cumin-citrus dressing, 29–30

lentil stew with broccoli, carrots, and pearl onions, 189–190

mung broth, 490

mustard- and garlic-flavored American yellow split peas, 277–278

New Delhi fragrant creamy mung beans, 284–285

Parsi chicken braised in spiced pumpkin-lentil puree, 124–125

peasant split pea and eggplant soup/stew with dill, 71–72

pureed whole mung beans, 289

pureed yellow lentils or American yellow split peas, 272

pureed yellow mung beans, 283

red (pink) lentil broth, 268

spicy whole mung bean stew, 290–291

split pea and *basmati* pilaf, 314–315

thyme-laced zucchini and black-eyed pea salad, 249–250

toasted lentil wafers (*papad; puppadum*), xv, 2, 10, 462

warm mung bean salad in cumin-tomato dressing, 286–287

whole mung bean and *basmati* pilaf, 316–317

winter warm tomato-lentil broth, 41–42

dalia, 323–324

damato upma, 320–321

date and plum chutney, sweet, 355–356

desserts, 377–408

almond rice pudding, 383–384

banana Bavarian cream with cashew nuts, 385–386

Bombay cheese pudding, 387

caramelized rice pudding, 381–382

coconut cheese cake, 388–389

glazed carrot fudge, 396–397

Gurkha regiment tea (Indian G.I.'s tea), 425

Indian spiced mango cake, 400–401

Indian spiced peach cake, 398–399

Kashmir semolina pudding, 392–393

Madras bridal pudding with cashew nuts, 390–391

Parsi semolina pudding, 394–395

tamarind sorbet, 379–380

see also sweets

dessert sauces:

creamy milk, 455

fragrant coconut, 405

saffron, 402

warm five-nectar, 407–408

warm mango, with almonds, 406

warm peach, with pistachios, 404–405

dhanshak, 124–125

dhokla, 327–329

dholi moong, 282

dill:

peasant split pea and eggplant soup/stew with, 71–72

warm crayfish, fennel, and pine nut salad with, 27–28

dipping sauces, *see* chutneys and dipping sauces

dips:

fresh cheese tuna, 17–18

instant prune, 369

doodh:

aam, 440

gulab, 439

kela, 442

kesari, 442

khwabi mahal, 445

prasadi, 443

rabadi, 454

drinks, *see* beverages

duck, 108

braised in curried vegetable-lentil puree, 132–133

vendaloo, 130–131

dumplings:

mustard green, in fragrant tomato sauce, 196–197

spinach, in yogurt sauce, 198–200

eggplant:

chick-peas, and tomato casserole, garlic-braised, 165–166

cool cream of mint soup, 61–62

fiery Mangalorean, 213–214

lentil stew with tamarind and garlic, 191–193

slices smothered with coconut-spice paste, 215–217

soup with coriander, cream of, 45–46

and split pea soup/stew with dill, peasant, 71–72

endive:

chicken and, braised in coconut, 122–123

mustard-braised, 218–219

warm mustard shrimps on, 15–16

fennel:

candied, with pine nuts, 422

and cauliflower in aromatic oil, 209–210

and cauliflower soup, fragrant, 65–66

crayfish, and pine nut salad with dill, warm, 27–28

fenugreek leaves, 482

fenugreek seeds, 483

fiery Goanese shrimp, 93–94

fiery Mangalorean eggplant, 213–214

figs:

California black, sweet cranberry pistachio chutney with, 344–345

ABOUT THE AUTHOR

Julie Sahni is the author of the most widely used Indian cookbook in America, *Classic Indian Cooking,* which won a commendation from the Andre Simon Award committee, and *Classic Indian Vegetarian and Grain Cooking,* winner of the Glenfiddich Award for the best cookbook of 1987. A teacher and food consultant, Julie Sahni was executive chef of two Indian restaurants and the proprietor of Julie Sahni's Indian Cooking School. She serves on the faculty of Boston University and New York University, is a regular contributor to *The New York Times* and national food magazines, and is featured in *The Book of Bests.*

Julie is a member of many professional food organizations, including Les Dames d'Escoffier and the International Association of Cooking Professionals. She continues to travel extensively throughout India, and is familiar with cuisines from all its regions.

Julie Sahni lives with her eleven-year-old son, Vishal, in Brooklyn Heights and Long Island, New York.